Observing Development of the Young Child

hours:

FOURTH EDITION

WITHDRAWN

Janice J. Beaty

Professor Emerita

Elmira College

Merrill,

an imprint of Prentice Hall

Upper Saddle River, New Jersey   Columbus, Ohio

Library of Congress Cataloging-in-Publication Data

Beaty, Janice J.
    Observing development of the young child / by Janice J. Beaty.—4th ed.
      p.   cm.
    "Designed to be used as a companion volume with the author's text Skills for preschool teachers (Merrill . . . 1996)"—Pref.
    Includes bibliographical references and indexes.
    ISBN 0-13-801986-X
    1. Child development. 2. Observation (Educational method) 3. Education, Preschool. 4. Preschool teachers—Training of. I. Beaty, Janice J. Skills for preschool teachers (5th ed.) II. Title.
    LB1115.B32   1998
    155.4—dc21

                                        97-2909
                                          CIP

Cover photo: The Terry Wild Studios
Editor: Ann C. Davis
Production Editor: Julie Peters
Design Coordinator: Karrie M. Converse
Text Designer: STELLARViSIONs
Cover Designer: Susan Unger
Production Manager: Patricia A. Tonneman
Electronic Text Management: Marilyn Wilson Phelps, Matthew Williams, Karen L. Bretz, Tracey B. Ward
Director of Marketing: Kevin Flanagan
Marketing Manager: Suzanne Stanton
Advertising/Marketing Coordinator: Julie Shough

This book was set in Zapf Humanist by Prentice Hall and was printed and bound by Quebecor Printing/Book Press. The cover was printed by Phoenix Color Corp.

© 1998 by Prentice-Hall, Inc.
Simon & Schuster/A Viacom Company
Upper Saddle River, New Jersey 07458

Photo credits: All photos by Janice J. Beaty

Printed in the United States of America

10 9 8 7 6 5 4 3 2

ISBN: 0-13-801986-X

Prentice-Hall International (UK) Limited, *London*
Prentice-Hall of Australia Pty. Limited, *Sydney*
Prentice-Hall of Canada, Inc., *Toronto*
Prentice-Hall Hispanoamericana, S. A., *Mexico*
Prentice-Hall of India Private Limited, *New Delhi*
Prentice-Hall of Japan, Inc., *Tokyo*
Simon & Schuster Asia Pte. Ltd., *Singapore*
Editora Prentice-Hall do Brasil, Ltda., *Rio de Janeiro*

About the Author

Janice J. Beaty, Professor Emerita, Elmira College, Elmira, New York, is a full-time writer of early childhood college textbooks and a consultant in early childhood education from her new location in Pensacola, Florida. Her textbooks include *Skills for Preschool Teachers,* 5th Edition, and *Building Bridges with Multicultural Picture Books* (both published by Merrill/Prentice Hall), *Preschool Appropriate Practices, Picture Book Storytelling,* and *Converting Conflicts in Preschool.* Dr. Beaty also participates in a distance learning television project, the Early Childhood Professional Development Network, broadcasting to Head Start Programs across the United States, the Caribbean, and the Pacific Islands. This involvement includes development of a new video series on observing child development called *Take a Closer Look.*

*In memory of my
mother and father*

Preface

Observing Development of the Young Child presents a unique system for observing and recording development of children ages two to five in early childhood classroom settings. It is based on a progression of children's skill development in six major areas. The text is designed for use by college students preparing to be teachers in prekindergarten programs, nursery schools, child care centers, Head Start classes, and preschools. The book can also be used in such programs by teachers and assistant teachers who want to learn more about children so they can make individual learning plans. Staff members preparing for Child Development Associate (CDA) assessment will also find this textbook helpful with its suggestions for classroom activities that are developmentally appropriate for young children.

The text focuses on six major aspects of child development: emotional, social, physical, cognitive, language, and creative. It divides each of these aspects further into specific areas: self-identity and emotional development; social play and prosocial behavior; large and small motor development; cognitive development of classification, number, time, and space; spoken language and prewriting/prereading skills; art skills and imagination.

THE *CHILD SKILLS CHECKLIST*—A PRACTICAL TOOL

The areas of child development previously identified are outlined in a *Child Skills Checklist* that includes specific, observable child behaviors in the sequence in which they occur. Each of 11 chapters discusses one of these areas, using the items on the Checklist as subheads for the chapter and giving ideas for classroom activities for children who have not demonstrated the specified behavior. The most recent child development research in each area is presented as background for the Checklist items as they are discussed. Each chapter concludes with a discussion of an actual child observation in the particular area and an interpretation of the data gathered.

The text serves college students as a guide for observing and recording development of young children in their student teaching and coursework. The book is especially well-suited as a supplementary text for child development courses. It also can help in-service teachers and assistants who are upgrading their skills in observing children, as well as those who are learning to plan for individuals based on their developmental needs.

Unique aspects of *Observing Development of the Young Child* include discussions of how to observe, interpret the data recorded, and plan for children based on obsérvations. Important topics include children's emotional development, how young children make friends, how to help children develop empathy toward others as the basis for conflict resolution, how children use exploratory play to learn, and how to develop children's creativity through dramatic play.

NEW FEATURES IN THE FOURTH EDITION

In addition to an expanded discussion of the various observation methods and tools used to assess young children, the fourth edition devotes an entire chapter to using the *Child Skills Checklist* on which this book is based. A revised chapter on spoken language, based on stages of language production in preschool, helps readers support bilingual children and speakers of English as a second language. New information on emergent literacy is presented in Chapter 11, "Prewriting and Prereading Skills," which shows how children teach themselves to write through a natural progression of pictures and scribbles to mock writing and letters.

Using picture books to assist children's development continues to play an important role in this new edition. Under the heading "Read a Book," the chapters suggest 90 new books, 53 of which contain multicultural characters.

The text concludes with Chapter 14, "Sharing Observational Data with Parents," a new approach to involving parents in their children's development through child observations at home and developing collaborative child portfolios with teachers and children in the classroom.

USE AS A COMPANION TEXT

This edition of *Observing Development of the Young Child* is designed to be used as a companion volume with the author's text *Skills for Preschool Teachers* (Merrill/Prentice Hall, 1996). While *Observing Development of the Young Child* is intended as a child development textbook, the companion volume *Skills for Preschool Teachers* is a teacher development book, focusing on 13 areas of teacher competencies.

Like this textbook, *Skills for Preschool Teachers* is also based on an observational checklist, the *Teacher Skills Checklist,* which documents teacher competencies in the 13 CDA functional areas: safe, healthy, learning environment, physical, cognitive, communication, creative, self, social, guidance, families, program management, and professional.

Together, the textbooks form a cohesive, complete training program for preservice teachers, beginning teachers, and in-service teachers preparing for the CDA credential. Both books focus on positive behaviors in children and teachers. Development of children and teacher training look at "areas of strength and confidence" and "areas needing strengthening" to set up individualized training plans.

ACKNOWLEDGMENTS

Once again, my thanks go to my colleague Bonny Helm, a college instructor and CDA Field Supervisor who read the original text and offered valuable suggestions for this new edition; to Sandra Novick, early childhood instructor at Rowan-Cabarrus Community College in Salisbury, NC, for help in revising the *Child Skills Checklist*; to Carolyn Dorrell, Director of the Early Childhood Professional Development Network (ECPDN) in Columbia, SC, for support in developing new ideas in child observation; to Mary Maples, Home Based Head Start specialist, for ideas relating to parent observations of their children at home; to the teachers and parents of children in the Columbia Head Start, Columbia, MO, for allowing me to photograph their children in the classrooms; and to the people in the field who have used the text and offered their constructive criticism for this revised edition.

Finally, I would like to thank the reviewers of this text: Berta Harris, San Diego City College; Adrienne L. Herrell, California State University—Fresno; Patricia Hofbauer, Northwest State Community College; and Joan F. Kuchner, State University of New York—Stony Brook.

Janice J. Beaty

Contents

4 ◻ Emotional Development   88

5 ◻ Social Play   118

6 ☐ Prosocial Behavior   146

7 ☐ Large Motor Development   172

10 Spoken Language 264

11 Prewriting and Prereading Skills 292

12 Art Skills 320

13 Imagination   342

14 Sharing Observational Data with Parents   370

Index of Children's Books   392

Index   394

List of Tables

CHAPTER 1

Assessing Children's Development Through Observation

ASSESSMENT OF YOUNG CHILDREN

Assessment of preschool children is a current issue of great importance and concern to early childhood educators. Programs for young children have always attempted to determine children's needs and to evaluate their accomplishments, sometimes successfully, sometimes not. The number of instruments currently available for assessing the development of preschool children is mind-boggling. Literally hundreds of instruments and procedures have come into use in the past 20 years. Behavior rating scales, tests of visual perception, performance inventories, developmental profiles, portfolios, language batteries, self-concept screening devices, social competence scales, sociometric tests, personality inventories, pictorial intelligence tests, case studies, developmental screening tests, performance-based interviews, and video or audio recording are only a few.

Some of these assessment tools and procedures use the observation of children, some don't. Some need to be administered by professional testers, others do not. Some assessment procedures place children in artificial rather than naturalistic situations. Others ask children to perform contrived activities. Although such tools and tasks may be helpful to researchers and professionals who are evaluating children for developmental problems, most are not appropriate for nonspecialist teachers in ordinary classrooms.

A great deal of the assessment and evaluation of children today focuses on questions such as "What's wrong with the child?" and "How can we intervene to help him or her?" This textbook takes a different point of view. It looks for answers to the question: "What's right with the young child?" and "How can we use his or her strengths to help in the development of the child?" The best method we have found to determine these strengths is to *observe the young child in the regular classroom.*

Early childhood specialist Carolyn Seefeldt agrees when she declares: "Observing is probably the oldest, most frequently used and most rewarding method of assessing children, their growth, development, and learning" (Seefeldt, 1990, p. 313). She and others have found that this is one of the best ways to look at an individual young child. It might not work so well with an older child, but it is eminently suited to a preschooler:

> Young children, who have a limited repertoire of behaviors that can be assessed, may best be studied through observation. In fact, to assess young children, who are unable to express themselves fully with words, with any method other than direct observation may not be possible. Further, young children reveal themselves through their behaviors. Unlike older children and adults, the young are incapable of hiding their feelings, ideas, or emotions with socially approved behaviors, so observing them often yields accurate information. (Seefeldt, 1990, p. 313)

To assist teachers and child caregivers in performing this necessary assessment of their children in the most appropriate manner, the early childhood professional association, the National Association for the Education of Young Children (NAEYC), in conjunction with the National Association of Early Childhood Specialists in State

1

Departments of Education, has published *Guidelines for Appropriate Curriculum Content and Assessment in Programs Serving Children Ages 3 Through 8.*

These guidelines, discussed in a later section of this chapter, define assessment as "the process of observing, recording and otherwise documenting the work children do and how they do it, as a basis for a variety of educational decisions that affect the child" (NAEYC, 1991, p. 32). Their purposes for assessing young children include:

1. to plan instruction for individuals and groups and for communicating with parents.
2. to identify children who may be in need of specialized services or intervention.
3. to evaluate how well the program is meeting its goals. (NAEYC, 1991, p. 32)

This textbook concurs with their definition, purposes, and guidelines, but takes them a step in a somewhat different direction. The focus in this text is on assessing *children's development* through observation. The purpose for such assessment is to plan curriculum activities for children that will promote their growth and success in the classroom. Teachers need to know where each child stands developmentally to plan activities that will speak to his or her needs.

Observing and recording the actions of young children in the classroom are the primary means for gathering such data on the accomplishments of individuals. Observation can also be used to determine the level of children's development. Once these data are collected and interpreted, teachers can identify the strengths of each child as well as areas needing strengthening. Appropriate activities can then be planned that address individual and group needs.

This text gives students of child development and teachers of young children ages three through five a tool for observing and recording this natural development. Chapter 2, "Using the Child Skills Checklist," describes a recording tool that can help observers determine where each child stands in areas of emotional, social, physical, cognitive, language, and creative development. The text then incorporates the items of the checklist as an outline for discussing each area of child development in the chapters to follow.

The purposes of assessing children's development in this manner are twofold: (1) it allows students of child development to gain an in-depth understanding of real children and their sequences of growth and (2) it helps teachers of young children to become aware of each child's growth and to support individual development with appropriate activities and materials.

Systematic observation—using a system to look at and record children's behavior—has thus become an important part of a classroom staff's daily responsibilities. More educators around the country and the world are finally coming to recognize that

Observation is used to chart children's development, to gain insight into children's behavior, and to guide curricular decision making. Observation also plays an important role in assessment, either by replacing or by supplementing standardized evaluation instruments. (Benjamin, 1994, p. 14)

Many teachers using systematic observation for evaluating child development have concluded that it has a number of advantages as an assessment process (see Figure 1–1).

Figure 1–1　Advantages of systematic observation for child assessment

1. Gives observers an in-depth look at a child not available elsewhere

2. Focuses on a child's natural behavior in the classroom setting, the key to assessing development

3. Focuses on what a child can do (not what he/she can*not* do) as a basis for future planning

4. Helps observer to recognize stages of child development and to take responsibility for helping child progress

5. Enables classroom staff to make appropriate plans for individuals based on children's observed strengths and needs

6. Helps classroom staff determine how the program is working to support children's development

7. Gives classroom staff appropriate data on which to base decisions about children, curriculum, and reports to other professionals and parents

TESTS AS TOOLS FOR ASSESSING PRESCHOOL CHILDREN

While observation is important, testing, the traditional means for evaluating children, remains a useful assessment tool. Many testing instruments and procedures have been developed and validated by researchers in the field. When they are applied to young children, however, the results are often mixed. What works with older children does not seem to work as well with preschoolers and kindergartners. Test developers sometimes blame the validation procedures used in developing the tests. Early childhood educators often nod wisely and think to themselves: "It's the kids."

Young children have little interest in tests. Why should they? They don't need to prove to anyone what they can or cannot do. It's true, they can be talked into cooperating with a test-giver. The teacher can administer a test to a child and occasionally get valid results on a particular day. Next week the results may be different with the same child. Honest researchers have had to admit such things as: "The major conclusion of this study is that it is inadvisable to routinely test young children prior to or immediately after their entry into kindergarten" (Wenner, 1988, p. 17). Wenner found that even highly respected and widely used tests predicted little more than a quarter of the actual academic performance of kindergarten children (1988, p. 17).

Nevertheless, assessment procedures routinely include tests of many kinds. While many are reliable and valid instruments, for their results to be used with confidence, teachers and testers alike need to be aware of the "young child factor": Young children do not test well. Thus assessors need to include other more informal but reliable types of assessment, such as observation of children in the regular classroom, to round out the picture when they are evaluating young children.

Table 1–1   Preschool assessment instruments

Title	Publisher/Date	Type	Format
Basic School Skills Inventory-Diagnostic (BSSI-D)	Pro-Ed 1983	Developmental screening	Observing by teacher; questions and response by child; pictures; cards
Brigance Pre-school Screen for 3- & 4-Yr.-Old Children (Preschool Screen)	Curriculum Associates, Inc., 1988	Developmental screening	Observation form; rating scale; parent and teacher; pupil sheet; building blocks
Developmental Indicators for the Assessment of Learning (DIAL-R)	Childcraft Educational Corp., 1983	Developmental screening	Formal testing Rating scale Child score sheets
Developing Skills Checklist	CTB/McGraw-Hill 1990	Developmental screening	Screening test; two observation checklists; manipulatives
Early School Assessment (ESA)	CTB/McGraw-Hill 1990	Readiness/ Achievement	Group administered Pictorial multiple-choice test in six sessions
Early School Inventory— Developmental (ESI-D)	The Psychological Corp., 1986	Developmental screening/ Readiness	80-item observation checklist of child; performance ratings
Early School Inventory— Preliteracy (ESI-P)	The Psychological Corp., 1986	Screening for literacy	Checklist; picture panels; cards; paper and pencil
Early Screening Inventory (ESI)	Teachers College Press, 1988	Developmental screening	Test sheets; paper and pencil; manipulatives
Miller Assessment for Preschools	The Psychological Corp., 1988 (MAP)	Developmental screening	Observation forms test sheets; drawing booklet; manipulatives
Humanics National Child Assessment Form	Humanics Ltd., 1982	Developmental assessment	Developmental checklist

Source: Based on information from Strand, 1989; Martin, 1994.

Among the wide range of assessment instruments on the market today, Table 1–1 lists 10 commonly used tools that teachers can administer themselves (so long as they remember that test results need to be tempered with other assessment procedures). Eight of the tests included are popular developmental screening tools. A screening device is just that; it screens for *possible* developmental problems. If problems show up, then further testing by a professional in the area of concern is necessary. Only screening tests that can be administered by teachers are included here.

Which teachers use tests such as these, you may wonder, and for what reasons? At least four particular groups of teachers need to gather developmental data on children for these specific reasons:

Title	Purpose	Teacher Observation	Child Paper and Pencil Tasks	Child Performance Tasks
Basic School Skills Inventory-Diagnostic (BSSI-D)	Measures readiness for kindergarten	Yes	Yes	Yes
Brigance Pre-school Screen for 3- & 4-Yr.-Old Children (Preschool Screen)	Identify and refer at-risk children for testing, placement and program planning	Yes	Yes	Yes
Developmental Indicators for the Assessment of Learning (DIAL-R)	Identify potentially gifted and problem children	No	Yes	Yes
Developing Skills Checklist	For planning individual instruction	Yes	Yes	Yes
Early School Assessment (ESA)	Measure readiness for kindergarten and first grade	No	Yes	Yes
Early School Inventory—Developmental (ESI-D)	Measure reading for prekindergarten, kindergarten, and first grade; teacher planning	Yes	No	No
Early School Inventory—Preliteracy (ESI-P)	Measures readiness for reading; teacher planning for individuals	No	Yes	Yes
Early Screening Inventory (ESI)	Identify and refer children with potential learning problems or handicapping conditions	No	Yes	Yes
Miller Assessment for Preschools	Identify and refer children at-risk for learning problems	Yes	Yes	Yes
Humanics National Child Assessment Form	Assesses social/emotional, language, cognitive, motor, hygiene	Yes	No	No

1. public school teachers: to screen children for entrance into prekindergarten and kindergarten, and for track placement in kindergarten and first grade

2. special education teachers: to screen children for referral, placement, or special intervention

3. teachers of government-sponsored early intervention programs: as part of the evaluation component of their grants

4. college laboratory school teachers and graduate students: for child development research projects

Tests such as those in Table 1–1 may be helpful in determining that a certain child needs further assessment by a professional or special help of some kind. But again it must be stressed: Tests alone are not the only answer, and may not even be the best answer. Child development specialists remind us:

> Much testing of young children constitutes misassessment because the testing is not developmentally appropriate. Much testing presents young children with a series of demands to answer here and now, although the children may not be inclined to respond immediately. Test questions each have one right answer, although the child may not understand the question or may give a creative answer that is considered incorrect. (Schweinhart, 1993, p. 30)

For classroom teachers who need child assessment data to plan activities that will support individual needs, they must first understand the meaning of developmentally appropriate assessment before choosing such a test or other data-gathering procedure.

GUIDELINES FOR APPROPRIATE ASSESSMENT

The guidelines developed by NAEYC should be considered carefully by all early childhood educators, and followed rigorously whenever young children are to be assessed. These guidelines* can be summarized as follows:

1. Assessment is related to program curriculum, goals, and objectives.
2. Assessment results in benefit to the child such as adjustment of the curriculum or individualized instruction.
3. Children's development in all domains (physical, social, emotional, and cognitive) is routinely assessed by teachers through observing and listening to children.
4. Assessment is used to support children's learning and development, to plan for individuals and groups, and to communicate with parents.
5. Assessment involves regular and periodic observation of the child in a wide variety of circumstances that represent the child's behavior over time.
6. Assessment relies on procedures that reflect typical activities of children and avoids approaches that place children in artificial situations.
7. Assessment relies on demonstrated performance during real not contrived activities.
8. Assessment utilizes an array of tools and a variety of procedures (e.g., collections of representative work by children, records of systematic observations by teachers, records of conversations and interviews with teachers, summaries of children's progress as individuals and in groups.)
9. Assessment recognizes individual diversity of learners and allows for differences in styles and rates of learning, as well as their ability in English or their native language.
10. Assessment supports children's development and learning and does not threaten children's psychological safety or feelings of self-esteem.

---

* Source: Adapted from "Guidelines for Appropriate Curriculum Content and Assessment in Programs Serving Children 3 through 8," *Young Children*, 46, pp. 32–34. Copyright 1991 by NAEYC. Reprinted by permission.

11. Assessment supports parents' relationship with their children and does not undermine parents' confidence in their children's or their own ability, nor devalue the language and culture of the family.
12. Assessment demonstrates children's overall strengths and progress: what children *can* do, not just their wrong answers or what they *cannot* do or do not know.
13. Assessment is an essential component of the teacher's role: the teacher is the *primary* assessor.
14. Assessment is a collaborative process involving children and teachers, teachers and parents, school and community; and information from assessment is shared with parents in language they can understand.
15. Assessment encourages children to participate in self-evaluation.
16. Assessment addresses what children can do independently and what they can demonstrate with assistance.
17. Information about each child's growth, development, and learning is systematically collected and recorded at regular intervals and is used for planning instruction and for communicating with parents.
18. A regular process exists for information sharing between teachers and parents about children's growth and development and performance that provides meaningful descriptive information and not letter or numerical grades.

These guidelines point out that the classroom teacher, rather than an expert from outside the program, should be the primary assessor. In addition, the assessment should be based on activities children typically engage in within the classroom, and

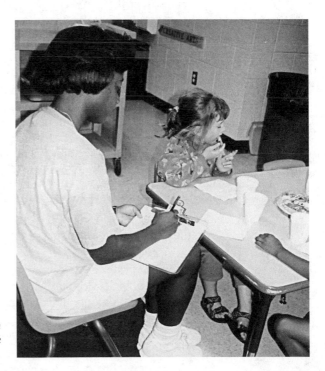

The classroom teacher, rather than an expert from outside, should be the primary assessor.

not contrived activities in artificial situations. Assessment should not threaten children, nor should it focus on wrong answers or what children cannot do.

The 10 assessment instruments in Table 1–1 do not all follow every guideline. They were, of course, developed before the guidelines came out. But several of these instruments include a comprehensive procedure in which the teacher observes children in addition to administering a performance-task-type test. Early childhood assessment has a place for such screening devices, especially those that can identify children with special needs.

WHAT SHOULD CHILD OBSERVERS LOOK FOR?

It is obvious that the *purpose* of the assessment should help determine the kind of assessment instrument used. Teachers who want to find out why a certain child is not getting along with others may spend time observing that child's interpersonal behaviors with peers. Speech correctionists may observe and listen for certain children's spoken language. Psychologists look at the behavior of troubled children to determine what their problems are. Researchers observe particular child behaviors to test hypotheses about child development or to formulate new theories.

This text examines the *sequence of a child's development.* It uses an observation tool, the Child Skills Checklist, to help teachers and child caregivers determine where a child stands in various developmental sequences so that they may plan activities to further the child's growth. Many similar textbooks teach observational skills focusing on children's behavior. These techniques are particularly important for researchers and child psychologists. However, this text goes beyond that level to teach the nonspecialist to understand children by observing their developmental sequence in six major areas of child development: emotional, social, physical, cognitive, language, and creative.

All children go through an observable sequence of development. From large to small motor coordination, from simple ideas to complex thinking, from one-word utterances to lengthy sentences, from scribbles to representational drawings . . . all children everywhere seem to proceed through a step-by-step sequence of development that can be traced by a knowledgeable observer who knows what to look for. The observer records these data and later interprets them to make appropriate plans for individual children.

The Child Skills Checklist, the basis of this text, helps observers focus on 6 major areas divided into 11 important topics of child development. Each chapter then expands on the developmental sequences of one of the 11 topics outlined in the Checklist:

Emotional
    Chapter 3—Self-Identity
    Chapter 4—Emotional Development

Social
    Chapter 5—Social Play
    Chapter 6—Prosocial Behavior

Physical
Chapter 7—Large Motor Development
Chapter 8—Small Motor Development

Cognitive
Chapter 9—Cognitive Development: Classification, Number, Time, and Space

Language
Chapter 10—Spoken Language
Chapter 11—Prewriting and Prereading Skills

Creative
Chapter 12—Art Skills
Chapter 13—Imagination

Each chapter treats one of these topics of development, and each topic focuses on eight observable items of child behavior based on recognized developmental sequences or progressions. Rather than including every detail of development, eight representative items are discussed. This makes the observations inclusive enough to be meaningful, but not so detailed as to be cumbersome. For items the observer does not check as apparent when observing a child, a section of ideas following the item should be useful in planning for individual needs. Chapter 2 discusses in detail how the Child Skills Checklist can be used for observing and recording child development.

Observational assignments at the end of each chapter include not only use of the Child Skills Checklist, but also use of other assessment tools such as anecdotal records, running records, specimen records, time sampling, event sampling, and rating scales to record observations. Chapter 14 discusses the sharing of recorded child observations with parents.

COLLECTING AND RECORDING OBSERVATIONAL DATA

Systematic observation of children (i.e., observation using a particular system) is different from informal observation, which is really little more than watching. In systematic observation there is a specific purpose for gathering the information about the children, as well as a particular method for collecting and recording it. Systematic observation always implies recording. Not only must observers have a particular reason to watch a child and know what to be looking for, but they also need a method for recording the information gathered. A number of useful methods have been developed over the years by observers of young children. The following methods are included for discussion in this chapter:

Narratives
anecdotal records
running records
specimen records

Samples
    time sampling
    event sampling

Rating scales
    graphic scales
    numerical scales
    semantic differential

Checklists
    developmental

Media techniques
    photographs
    audiotapes
    videotapes

Narratives

The most popular method for recording child observations falls under the heading of "narrative recording;" that is, written descriptions of children's actions. Several types of narratives include anecdotal records, running records, and specimen descriptions.

Anecdotal Records

Anecdotal records are brief narrative accounts describing an incident of a child's behavior that is important to the observer. Anecdotes describe what happened in a factual, objective manner, telling how it happened, when and where it happened, and what was said and done. Sometimes they include reasons for the child's behavior, but "why" is better kept in the commentary part of the record. These accounts are most often written *after* the incident has occurred, by someone who witnessed it informally, rather than *while* it was occurring, by someone who was formally observing and recording.

Anecdotal records have long been made by teachers, physicians, psychologists, social workers, and even parents who recorded when their babies first walked and talked. Sometimes these are referred to as "baby biographies."

Although anecdotal records are brief, describing only one incident at a time, they are cumulative. A series of them over a period can be extremely useful in providing rich details about the child being observed. Other advantages of using anecdotal records include

1. The observer needs no special training to record.
2. The observation is open-ended. The recorder writes anything and everything he or she witnesses, and is not restricted to one kind of behavior or recording.

Anecdotal records are brief narrative accounts most often written after the observation by the person who did the observing.

3. The observer can catch an unexpected incident no matter when it occurs, for it is usually recorded afterwards.

4. The observer can look for and record the significant behavior and can ignore the rest.

As in all observational methods, there are disadvantages too. Observers need to decide why they are observing, what they want to find out, and which method will be most useful. Some of the disadvantages of the anecdotal record method are

1. It does not give a complete picture because it records only incidents of interest to the observer.

2. It depends too much on the memory of the observer because it is recorded after the event. Witnesses to events are notoriously poor on details.

3. Incidents may be taken out of context and thus be interpreted incorrectly or used in a biased manner.

4. It is difficult to code or analyze narrative records; thus, the method may not prove useful in a scientific study.

Such records can be more useful if recorded on a vertically divided page with the anecdote on the left side and a space for comments on the right, or the page can be divided horizontally with the anecdote at the top and commentary at the bottom. Figure 1–2 is an example of the latter format.

This anecdote tells what happened in an objective manner. Especially good are the direct quotes. The anecdote could have included more details about the child's facial expression, tone of voice, and gestures. The reader does not get the feeling of whether the boy was enjoying himself as a helper, trying to ingratiate himself with another child who was not paying much attention, or desperately trying to gain the attention of the other boy. Such details are sometimes missing from anecdotes because they have not been written down until the end of the day or even later, and by then are forgotten.

The comments contain several inferences and conclusions based on insufficient evidence. Obviously this observer has spent some time watching Stevie based on her comments, "Stevie is often involved" and "Once engaged in play, he likes to continue, and

---

Anecdotal Record

Child's Name _____Stevie_____   **Age** ___4___   **Date** ___2/23___

Observer _____Anne_____   **Place** _S. Preschool_**Time** _9:00–10:00_

Incident

Stevie went over to the block corner and asked two boys, Ron and Tanner, if he could help them build. They told him it was okay. As they were building he accidentally knocked some blocks down. "I can put it back up," he said, and handed the blocks to Ron. For awhile he watched Ron build and then said,"I found a smoke-stack, Ron," and handed him a cylinder block. Ron told him where to put it, and Stevie then began getting cylinders off of the shelf and handing them to Ron and Tanner to place. Finally, he started placing his own cylinders around the perimeter of the building. The teacher asked him if he wanted to finger-paint but he replied, "I'm not gonna finger-paint unless Ron finger-paints."

Comment

Stevie is often involved in a lot of dramatic play with several other boys. He especially likes to be near or playing with Ron. He seems to look up to him. Whatever rules Ron sets in the play, Stevie follows. Once engaged in play, he likes to continue, and will usually not let another child, or even the teacher, distract him.

Figure 1–2   Anecdotal record of observation

will usually not. . . . " She would need an accumulation of such anecdotes to make valid statements of this nature based on evidence. If this were one page in an accumulation of anecdotes about Stevie, the comments would perhaps be more accurate.

The observer infers that Stevie "likes to be near or playing with Ron," although there is not sufficient evidence here to make that definite an inference. Perhaps she should have said, "whatever rules Ron sets in the play, Stevie follows," if Stevie actually placed a cylinder block where directed. However, this was only hinted at and not stated. Particular words are very important in objective recording. Her conclusion about Stevie's not letting another child or even the teacher distract him is only partially accurate, since the observer recorded no evidence about another child.

If you were writing the comments about this particular anecdotal record, what might you infer from the incident? Can you make any conclusions based on this information alone, or is it too limited? Are there things you might want to look for in the future when observing this boy that you would include in the commentary?

It is also helpful to indicate what the purpose is for the particular observation. Most observation forms do not provide a space for this, but the usefulness of the observation is enhanced if it is included. In this case the observer was looking for evidence of involvement in social play for this child.

Running Records

Another popular observing and recording method is the **running record**. It is a detailed narrative account of behavior recorded in a sequential manner as it happens. The observer sits or stands apart from the children and writes down everything that occurs over a specified period, which may be as short as several minutes or may be recorded from time to time during a full day. The running record is different from the anecdotal record because it includes all behavior and not just selected incidents, and it is written as the behavior occurs instead of later. Sentences are often short and words are abbreviated to keep up with the pace of the action.

As with all factual recording, the observer must be careful not to use descriptive words or phrases that are judgmental. For instance, if the observer records the child as "acting grumpy this morning," he needs to avoid this judgment and instead record the actual details that explain what happened such as: "Jonathan wouldn't respond to teacher's greeting at first, and when he did, muttered 'good morning,' in low voice with head bent down."

The running record has a number of advantages for persons interested in child development:

1. It is a rich, complete, and comprehensive record not limited to particular incidents.
2. It is open-ended, allowing the observer to record everything he or she sees, and not restricting the observations to a particular kind of behavior.
3. It does not require that the observer have special observational skills and therefore is particularly useful to the classroom teacher.

There are also several disadvantages to using this method, once again depending on the purpose for gathering the information:

1. It is time-consuming, which may make it difficult for the observer to find periods of uninterrupted time.
2. It is difficult to record everything for any length of time without missing important details.
3. It works best when observing an individual, but is inefficient and difficult when observing a group.
4. Observers must keep themselves apart from the children, which is sometimes difficult for a teacher.

Running records are more useful if recorded on a form divided into two parts with space for the observer to make comments afterwards, as shown in Figure 1–3.

It is difficult for the observer to record every word of all that is said and every facet of all that occurs when children are busily playing together. This observer has caught the essence. The dialogue is especially well recorded. His inferences and conclusions are carefully kept on the commentary side of the record. Although we cannot make the same conclusion about Katy being more comfortable playing with only one child at a time based on this evidence, the observer had been gathering evidence for several weeks and perhaps felt he could. Such an explanation should then be included here. It also would be helpful to record the time that various incidents occurred to know how much time had elapsed on the gun play, the slide play, and the running back and forth.

Because the running record captures so much important developmental behavior of the preschool child, it has been chosen as the primary recording method for use in conjunction with the Child Skills Checklist in assessing an individual child's development as discussed in this textbook. Its use in combination with the Checklist is discussed in Chapter 2.

Specimen Records

Specimen records or **specimen descriptions**, as they are sometimes called, are similar to running records but more detailed and precise. They are most often used by researchers who want a complete description of behavior, whereas the running record is used especially by teachers in a less formal way. The observer is not a part of the classroom activities and must keep aloof from the children.

Like running records, specimen records are narrative descriptions of behavior or events as they happen, but usually based on predetermined criteria such as the time of day, the person, or the setting. The amount of detail to be recorded depends upon the purpose of observation. Enough detail should be recorded to give the reader of the observation a sense of how things actually happened. The test of a good specimen record is whether it can be visualized or dramatized. Does the description tell how the children moved, what their facial expressions and gestures were, and not only what they said but how they said it? It is better to record too much detail than not enough. Here is an extract from one:

Running Record

Child's Name	Katy	**Age**	4	**Date**	2/9
Observer	Rob	**Place**	S. Nursery School	**Time**	9:00–10:00

Observation	Comments
Katy is playing by herself with plastic blocks, making guns; she walks into other room; "Lisa, would you play with me? I'm tired of playing by myself." They walk into other room to slide & climbing area.	Clips blocks together to make gun; then copies it to make one for Lisa. Cleverly done. Intricate. Shows creativity. (Does teacher allow guns?)
K: "I am Wonder Woman." L: "So am I." K: "No, there is only one Wonder Woman. You are Robin." L: "Robin needs a Batman because Batman & Robin are friends."	Seems to be the leader here as in other activities I have observed. Lisa is the friend she most often plays with.
All this takes place under slide & climber. Lisa shoots block gun which Katy has given to her. Katy falls on floor.	
L: (to teacher) "We're playing Superfriends and Wonder Woman keeps falling down." K: Opens eyes, gets up, and says: "Let's get out our Batmobile and go help the world." She runs to other room and back, making noises like a car.	Katy switches roles here. She shows good concentration and spends much time on one play episode.
L: "Wonder Woman is died. She fell out of the car." She falls down. K: "It's only a game, wake up. Lisa, you be Wonder Woman, I'll be ___ ." L: "Let's play house now."	She can distinguish reality from fantasy.
Katy begins sliding down the slide.	
K: "We have a lot of Superfriends to do." She says this while sliding. "Robin is coming after you!" she shouts to Lisa, running from the slide and into the other room. Lisa has gone into the housekeeping area and says to Katy: "Katy, here is your doll's dress." (Lost yesterday). John joins the girls. L: "I'm Wonder Woman." K: "I'm Robin." J: "I'm Batman. Where is the Batmobile?" K: "It's in here." They run into the other room and Katy points under the slide telling John what the Batmobile can do. Then all run to the other room and back again. Then Katy says: "John we are not playing Superfriends any more."	Shows good large motor coordination. Spends much time every day like this running and skipping around room. Seems to know she is good at this & spends a lot of time doing it. Seems to be more comfortable playing with only one child at a time.

Figure 1–3 Running record of observation

Mark's friend Rob was playing in the play grocery store taking empty food boxes off the shelves, so Mark watches him for a minute and begins to take the boxes off the shelves and places them in a toy shopping cart. Two girls proceed over to where Mark is and they knock his boxes over (which were teetering because there were so many in the cart). Mark then opens his eyes wide, grits his teeth and places his hands on his hips, saying "You guys, why do you knock it down like that?" Meanwhile the girls appear little affected by his question and walk off. Meanwhile his friend Rob is still taking boxes off the shelves and Rob says to Mark, "We are stealing stuff." So Mark joins the act, hiding the boxes in the rear by the playhouse. It appears that no one pays any attention to their act of "stealing" so Mark loses interest.

Can you dramatize this specimen record? That is the test of a good recording. This particular recording does not tell us exactly how the girls took action, nor what Mark does to show his loss of interest, but otherwise it is rich in detail. (The teacher later talked to the children about paying for things in a real store and why people should not "steal.")

Specimen records like this are later coded by researchers to elicit findings regarding kinds of behavior, lengths of incidents, interaction patterns, or other information relevant to the purpose of the observation. Advantages and disadvantages of this particular method are the same as for the running record.

Objective Recording of Narrative Data

Objective recording of the narrative data gained from observing young children—a process required with anecdotal, running, and specimen records—is not a simple task. We are used to observing what happens around us and simultaneously making interpretations about it. In objective recording we must separate these two functions and guard against confusing the observation with its interpretation. What we record must be the objective facts only, not judgments, inferences, nor conclusions. Perhaps if we think of ourselves as witnesses at a trial, we can more easily discern what information is acceptable and what is not.

If we see a child come into the room in the morning, refuse to greet the teacher, walk over to a table and sit down, push away another child who tries to join him, and shake his head in refusal when the teacher suggests an activity, how can we record it? An anecdotal record might read like this:

Jonathan walked into the room this morning as if he were mad at the world. He would not look up at the teacher or respond to her greeting. He sort of slumped as he walked across the room and plunked himself down in a chair at one of the activity tables. Richie tried to join him but was pushed away. The teacher went over and asked him if he wanted to help mix playdough, but he shook his head no.

This record is rich enough in detail for us to visualize it, but is it factually objective? No. The words "as if he were mad at the world," are a conclusion based on insufficient evidence. The recorder might better have described his entrance objectively like this:

Jonathan walked into the room this morning with a frowning kind of look on his face. He lowered his head when the teacher greeted him, and did not respond.

This behavior was unusual for Jonathan. Later the teacher found out that he was not "mad at the world," but sad because his pet cat had been killed by a car the night before. We realize then that frowning looks, lowered head, and refusal to speak or participate may be the result of emotions other than anger. It is up to us to sift out our inferences and judgments, then, and make sure we record only the facts.

The following are judgmental phrases and sentences sometimes found in observation records. Should they ever be used? If not, why not? What could you substitute for them?

He was a good boy today.
Marcie was mad at Patty.
shouted angrily
lost his temper
got upset
made a big mess
acted happy

Other observer errors include (1) omitting some of the facts, (2) recording things that did not happen, and (3) recording things out of order. Here is the "Jonathan incident" again with some of these errors included. Can you find them?

Jonathan walks in the classroom this morning. He doesn't look at the teacher but goes straight to a seat at one of the tables. The teacher wants him to help mix playdough but he refuses. Richie comes over to play with him but he pushes him away.

Facts omitted from the observation:

1. Has frowning look on face.
2. Does not respond to teacher's greeting.
3. Walks across room with shoulders slumped.
4. Drops himself down into seat at activity table.
5. When teacher asks him to help mix playdough, he shakes his head no.

A fact added to the observation:

1. Richie comes over "to play with him."

A fact recorded out of order:

1. Richie tries to join him before teacher asks him to help mix playdough.

Such errors can creep into an observation almost without the recorder being aware. You need to practice with at least two observers recording the same incident, and then compare results. If you find discrepancies between the records, check carefully that you have followed these guidelines:

Guidelines for objective recording
1. Record only the facts.
2. Record every detail without omitting anything.
3. Do not interpret as you observe.
4. Do not record anything you do not see.
5. Use words that describe but do not judge or interpret.
6. Record the facts in the order that they occur.

Samples

A different way of observing children is to look at samples of certain behaviors to discover how often, how long, or when a particular behavior occurs.

Time Sampling

In **time sampling**, the observer records the frequency of a behavior's occurrence over time. The behavior must be overt and frequent (at least once every 15 minutes) to be a candidate for sampling. For example, talking, hitting, or crying are behaviors that a teacher might want to sample for certain children because they can be clearly seen and counted. Problem solving is not a good candidate for time sampling because this behavior is not always clear to the observer, nor can it be counted easily.

Time sampling thus involves observing specified behaviors of an individual or group, and recording the presence or absence of this behavior during short time intervals of uniform length. The observer must prepare ahead of time, determining what specific behavior to look for, what the time interval will be, and how to record the presence or absence of the behavior.

For example, to help an aggressive child named Jamie change his ways, the teacher wants to know how frequently Jamie's inappropriate behavior occurs. First, Jamie's aggressive behavior must be specifically defined. The teacher noted that it included:

hitting
pushing
kicking
holding another against his will
taking another child's toy

These particular behaviors are usually determined by previous observations made to discover exactly what the observer needs to look for in her sampling. Jamie, for instance, did not use words aggressively. Another child might have expressed aggression quite differently, and the observer would sample that.

Next the decision is made about what time intervals to use. In this case the teacher wanted to sample the child's behavior for five-minute intervals during the first half-hour of the morning for a week. She knew that this seemed to be the most difficult time for him.

The teacher then must decide what and how to record on the sheet she has blocked off into time intervals. Often a time sampling observer simply records "1" after the interval if the behavior occurs, and "0" if it does not. This is called **duration recording** and indicates the presence or absence of the behavior.

Check marks or tally marks can also be used if the teacher wants to know how many times the behavior occurred, rather than its presence or absence. Called **event recording**, this shows the frequency of the behavioral event.

Furthermore, the teacher may be more concerned with specific categories of aggression rather than just aggression in general. In that case, each of the categories can be given a code:

h = hitting
p = pushing
k = kicking
hd = holding
t = taking

The teacher will record specific categories of behavior rather than frequency of occurrence. The observation form can be set up like any of the examples in Figure 1–4 or in the teacher's own manner, depending on the information desired. The observation for Jamie's first half-hour of one morning could look like any of the sampling categories in Figure 1–4.

What is your interpretation of the data collected during the first 30 minutes of the first morning? The teacher concluded that Jamie's aggressive actions on this morning occurred mainly during the first 15 minutes and involved mostly hitting and pushing of the other children. If this turned out to be the pattern for the rest of the week, the teacher might want to plan an interesting transition activity for Jamie to do by himself as soon as he arrived. Once he had made the transition from home to school by getting involved in an activity, he might then be able to interact with the other children nonaggressively. Future observations would help the teacher determine whether the intervention strategy had been successful.

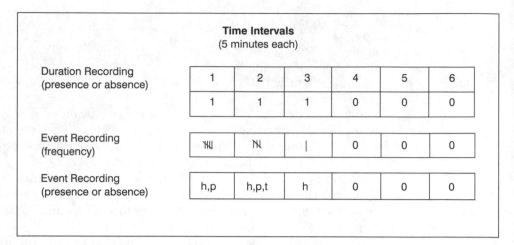

Figure 1–4 Event recording of specific categories

Time sampling is thus a useful method for observing children for some of the following reasons:

1. It takes less time and effort than narrative recording.
2. It is more objective and controlled because the behavior is specified and limited.
3. It allows an observer to collect data on a number of children or a number of behaviors at once.
4. It provides useful information on intervals and frequencies of behavior.
5. It provides quantitative results useful for statistical analysis.

There are, of course, certain disadvantages as well:

1. It is not an open method and therefore may miss much important behavior.
2. It does not describe the behavior, its causes, or results because it is more concerned with time (when or how frequently the behavior occurs).
3. It does not keep units of behavior intact because its principal concern is the time interval, not the behavior.
4. It takes the behavior out of its context and therefore may be biased.
5. It is limited to observable behaviors that occur frequently.
6. It usually focuses on one type of behavior (in this case an inappropriate behavior), and thus may give a biased view of the child.

Event Sampling

Event sampling is another method in which the observer waits for and then records a specific preselected behavior. Event sampling is used to study the conditions under which particular behaviors occur or their frequency. It may be important to learn what triggers a particular kind of behavior—biting, for instance—to find ways to control it. Or, the observer may want to find out how many times a certain behavior occurs. Time sampling could be used if time intervals or time of day were the important factor. If the behavior occurs at odd times or infrequently, then event sampling is more appropriate.

The observer must first define the event or "unit of behavior." Then, the setting in which it is likely to occur must be determined. The observer takes the most advantageous position to observe the behavior, waits for it to occur, and records it.

Recording can be done in several ways, depending on the purpose for the observation. If the observer is studying causes or results for certain behaviors, then the so-called "ABC analysis" is especially useful. It is a narrative description of the entire event, breaking it down into three parts: A = antecedent event, B = behavior, C = consequent event. Each time the event occurs it is recorded (see, for example, the ABC event sampling for Darrell in Figure 1–5).

If subsequent observations of Darrell show the same sort of sequence as in the event sampling, the teacher could interpret this to mean that Darrell does not initiate the kicking, but rather responds to interference with his activities in this inappropriate and harmful manner. Intervention strategies may therefore need to be different with this boy. The teacher may need to help him learn an acceptable way to vent his frustration other than kicking. In addition, he may need help in getting along with other children and in feeling accepted in the classroom. Until these issues are resolved, he may have to keep his shoes off in the classroom to prevent injury. This in itself may reduce his kicking, since his own uncovered toes will soon teach him how it hurts to kick.

If **frequency** of occurrence is the main concern, the observer can record with tally marks rather than narrative description. However, this procedure tends to be more useful for research than for practical classroom applications.

The advantages for using event sampling include:

1. It keeps the event or behavior intact, making analysis easier.
2. It is more objective than some methods because the behavior has been defined ahead of time.
3. It is especially helpful in examining infrequent or rarely occurring behaviors.

There are several disadvantages as well, depending on the purpose of the observation:

1. It takes the event out of context and thus may minimize other phenomena that are important to the interpretation.

Event Sampling

Name	Darrell	**Age**	3 1/2
Center	Head Start	**Date**	10/5
Observer	Sue S.	**Time**	9–12:00

Behavior: Kicking: striking out at other children or teacher with right foot, hard enough to make children cry.

Time	Antecedent Event	Behavior	Consequent Event
9:13	Darrell playing alone in block corner; Rob comes in & puts block on Darrell's building	Darrell looks at Rob with frown; stands; pushes at Rob; Rob pushes back; Darrell kicks Rob on leg	Rob cries & runs to teacher
10:05	On playground; Darrell waiting turn in line with others to go on slide; Sally tries to cut in	Darrell kicks Sally hard on leg Darrell kicks teacher	Sally cries; teacher comes & takes Darrell away by arm to talk to him

Figure 1–5   Event sampling of observation

2. It is a closed method that looks only for specified behavior and ignores other important behavior.
3. It misses the richness of detail that anecdotes, specimen records, or running records provide.

Rating Scales

Rating scales are observation tools that indicate the degree to which a person possesses a certain trait or behavior. Each behavior is rated on a continuum from the lowest to the highest level (or vice versa) and is marked off at certain points along the scale. The observer must make a judgment about where on the scale the child's behavior lies. As an observation tool, rating scales work best where particular degrees of behavior are well-defined or well-understood by the observer, and where there is a distinct difference in the behavior at the various points on the scale.

Figure 1–6 Graphic scale for a single behavior

Graphic Scale
Shares toys: _____ Always   Often   Sometimes   Seldom   Never

These tools are useful in diagnosing a child on a wide range of behaviors all at the same time. The observer watches the child and checks off or circles the point on the scale to indicate the child's current position in regard to behaviors or abilities. Such scales are simple to make: Simply state the behavior, draw a line, then mark off a number of points or intervals along the line. Five intervals are often used so that there is a middle (neutral position), and two intervals on either side of it.

Graphic Scales

The rating scale in Figure 1–6 shows only one item of behavior. Many similar behaviors could be listed on this same scale.

Such scales are called **graphic scales** and can be drawn either horizontally (as shown in Figure 1–6) or vertically. Many traits can be listed on one sheet. Graphic scales may be easier to construct than to use. The observer must know children well, be able to interpret their behavior, and be able to make an objective judgment within a limited time.

Numerical Scales

Other rating scales may be **numerical** in form; that is, they are scored by the number of the behavior that is circled. As an example, the scale in Figure 1–7 shows two items, "attention span" and "curiosity," but altogether this scale has 12 items.

Raters observe children for as long as it takes to circle a number for each item, or they can observe on a daily basis and then average their scores. The numbers on the above scale are also represented by words:

1 = definitely needs help
2 = could use help
3 = adequate
4 = strength

Semantic Differential

A third type of rating scale sometimes used with children is the **semantic differential**, sometimes called the "Osgood scale" because it was developed by Charles Osgood. It uses a seven-point range with adjectives of opposite (bipolar) meanings at either end. Figure 1–8 shows two traits as an example. Obviously a number of traits should be included to develop a comprehensive profile of a child.

Numerical Scale

Attention Span

1. Rarely finishes task, moves rapidly from one to another.
2. Usually needs encouragement to stay with task until complete.
3. Can usually remain with task appropriate to age level until it is finished.
4. Can stay with a chosen activity for very long periods, even returning next day.

Curiosity

1. Shows little or no interest in anything new.
2. Can be intrigued by really exciting things but often uninterested.
3. Actively explores any new things in the room.
4. Interested in new ideas, words, and relationships as well as things.

Figure 1–7   Numerical scale for observation

Note: From Hodgden, 1974, p. 119.

Rating Scale Observer Errors

A different kind of observer error can affect the use of rating scales. Contrary to other types of observation, this tool calls for the observer to make an on-the-spot judgment rather than an objective description. It is extremely difficult for observers to be totally unbiased and objective. They may be influenced by other things they already know about the child or the child's family, or by outside influences completely unrelated to the situation they are observing. For example, one observer persistently gave lower ratings to an overweight child. When asked about it later, the observer admitted a prejudice against overweight children because he had been one himself.

To guard against these tendencies, the observer should rate all of the different children being observed on the same trait before going on to another trait. To check objectivity, a second rater can observe the same children and compare results.

Rating scales may be used on their own, implemented with other observation methods as a part of the procedure, or filled in later after the observation is completed from data gathered from specimen records or running records. As with the other observation methods, rating scales have certain advantages:

Figure 1–8   Semantic differential scale for observation

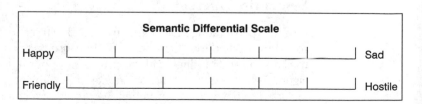

1. They are easy to design and less time-consuming to use.
2. They provide a convenient method to observe a large number of traits at one time, or more than one child at a time.
3. They make it possible to measure difficult-to-quantify traits—shyness, for example.
4. They can be used by nonspecialist observers.
5. They are easier to score and quantify than most other methods.

The disadvantages also need to be considered before the observer decides to use a rating scale:

1. Rating scales use a closed method. They examine specified traits and may overlook other important behavior.
2. They feature the negative as well as the positive side of each trait.
3. Clearly differentiating between each point on the scale is sometimes difficult, both for the designer and the observer.
4. It is difficult to eliminate observer bias when judgments must be made quickly on so many different traits.

Checklists

Checklists are lists of specific traits or behaviors arranged in a logical order. The observer must indicate the presence or absence of the behaviors either as she observes or later when she reflects upon her observation. Checklists are especially useful for types of behaviors or traits that can easily and clearly be specified. We tend to see what we look for. Thus a checklist can prove to be a valuable tool for focusing our attention when many different items need to be observed. A survey or inventory of a situation can be done more efficiently with a checklist than with almost any other observation tool. If the observer needs to know whether a child displays the specified behavior, a checklist is the instrument of choice to use.

Both checklists and rating scales often include large numbers of traits or behaviors. The difference in the two is not necessarily in their appearance but in their use. An observer using a checklist merely checks off the presence of the trait (a blank denotes its absence). The observer using a rating scale must make a snap judgment about the degree to which the trait is present.

Checklists can be used in a number of ways, depending on the purpose for the observation. For instance, a different checklist can be used for each child in the class, if the results are to be used for individual planning. On the other hand, all of the children's names can be included on the same checklist along with the checklist items, if it is the observer's purpose to screen children for certain traits.

The items on a checklist can simply be checked off, or the date or time when they first appear can be entered to make a more complete record. A different checklist can be used for each observation, or a single checklist can serve in a cumulative manner for the same child all year if dates are recorded for each item. A single checklist can be used by one observer or by several observers who will add to the cumulative data over a period of time.

Finally, information gained from anecdotal, specimen, and running records can be transferred to checklists to make their interpretation easier. It is much simpler to scan a list of checked behaviors than to read through long paragraphs of wordy description when attempting to interpret observational evidence. However, it is obvious that checklists need to be prepared carefully.

Whether you plan to make your own checklist or use a prepared list, make sure the items listed are specified very clearly in objective, nonjudgmental terms. The user should be able to understand the items easily; thus, it makes sense to put items through a pretest before actual use in an observation tool. All checklist items should be positive, unlike rating scale items, which include a range of behavior from positive to negative.

Checklist items not observed are left blank, indicating absence of the particular behavior. If the observer does not have the opportunity to witness certain behaviors, these items should not be left blank, but denoted by some symbol (e.g., "N," meaning no opportunity to observe). Some suggestions for developing checklist items include:

1. Items should be short, descriptive, understandable.
2. They should be parallel in construction (i.e., same word order and verb tense for each).
3. They should be objective and nonjudgmental (e.g., not "jumps high" but "jumps over a 1-foot object")
4. They should be positive in nature.
5. They should not be repeated elsewhere in the checklist.
6. They should be representative of children's behavior, but not include every behavior.

Overall, the checklist format should allow the observer to scan the items at a glance. The Child Skills Checklist in Chapter 2 is an example of an observation tool that looks at 11 important areas of child development, breaking down each area into 8 observable items. Each item is brief, represents an important aspect of development, is parallel in construction (beginning with a verb), and is positive. The eight items are listed in either a sequence or a progression of known child development. Together, they form the profile of a whole child as he or she works and plays in the environment of an early childhood classroom.

Advantages for using checklists of this nature include:

1. They are easy, quick, and efficient to use.
2. The nonspecialist observer can use them with ease.
3. They can be used in the presence of the child or later from remembered behaviors or recorded narrative observation.

4. Several observers can gather the same information to check for reliability.
5. These checklists help to focus observation on many behaviors at one time.
6. They are especially useful for curriculum planning for individuals.

Checklists have a number of disadvantages as well. Observers must weigh one against the other, always keeping in mind their purpose for observing. Checklist disadvantages include:

1. They are "closed" in nature, looking at particular behaviors and not everything that occurs; thus they may miss behaviors of importance.
2. They are limited to "presence" or "absence" of behavior.
3. They lack information about quality and duration of behavior and a description.

CHOOSING THE METHOD FOR OBSERVING AND RECORDING

Table 1–2 compares the various methods for observing and recording young children discussed in this chapter. Each has advantages and disadvantages that an observer needs to consider before choosing a particular method. The final choice often depends on the purpose for the observation.

A checklist was chosen as the basis for this book because of checklists' unique ability to give the observer an overview of child development. It is a teaching tool as well as an observational tool. The Child Skills Checklist in Chapter 2 will thus assist the observer not only in gathering information to help plan for specific children, but also in learning the sequences of child growth in the areas of emotional, social, physical, cognitive, language, and creative development.

MEDIA TECHNIQUES

Photographs

You can add another dimension to your observation of children by using cameras, camcorders, and cassette recorders. Instead of writing narrative descriptions, doing behavior sampling, or filling in rating scales or checklists in the presence of children in the classroom, the observer can first capture the moment on film and then, after the photos are developed, write notes about what happened. It involves simply spreading out the photos in the sequence they occurred and then recording the data in the form of a narrative description. Checklists can also be used to interpret photos.

Photos of children are easy to take, so be sure to snap a series of the same child or same incident for later recording. These photos are for your use, not the children's, and should be captioned, dated, and placed in the same file as your recorded notes—perhaps in a child's portfolio (see Chapter 14).

Table 1–2 Comparison of methods for observing and recording

Method	Purpose
Anecdotal Record: A narrative of descriptive paragraphs, recorded *after behavior occurs*	To detail specific behavior for child's record; for case conferences; to plan for individuals
Running Record: A narrative written in sequence over a specified time, recorded *while behavior is occurring*	To discover cause and effects of behavior; for case conferences; to plan for individuals
Specimen Record: A detailed narrative written in sequence over a specified time, recorded *while behavior is occurring*	To discover cause and effects of behavior; for child development research
Time Sampling: Tallies or symbols showing the presence or absence of specified behavior during short time periods, recorded *while behavior is occurring*	For behavior modification baseline data; for child development research
Event Sampling: A brief narrative of conditions preceding and following specified behavior, recorded *while behavior is occurring*	For behavior modification input; for child development research
Rating Scale: A scale of traits or behaviors with check marks, recorded *before, during, and after behavior occurs*	To judge degree to which child behaves or possesses certain traits; to diagnose behavior or traits; to plan for individuals
Checklist: A list of behaviors with check marks, recorded *before, during, and after behavior occurs*	To determine presence or absence of specified behaviors; to plan for individuals; to give observer an overview of child's development or progress

Advantages	Disadvantages
Open-ended; rich in details; no special observer training	Depends on observer's memory; behavior taken out of context; difficult to code or analyze for research
Open-ended; comprehensive; no special observer training	Time-consuming; difficult to use for more than one child at a time; time-consuming to code and analyze for research
Open-ended; comprehensive and complete; rich in details	Time-consuming to record; time-consuming to code or analyze for research; difficult to observe more than one child at a time
Objective and controlled; not time consuming; efficient for observing more than one child at a time; provides quantitative data for research	Closed; limited to observable behaviors that occur frequently; no description of behavior; takes behavior out of context
Objective; helpful for in-depth diagnosis of infrequent behavior	Closed; takes event out of context; limited to specified behaviors
Not time-consuming; easy to design; efficient for observing more than one child at a time for many traits; useful for several observers watching same child	Closed; subjective; limited to specified traits or behaviors
Efficient for observing more than one child at a time for many behaviors; useful for an individual over a period of time; a good survey or inventory tool; useful for several observers at once; no special training needed	Closed; limited to specified behaviors; no information on quality of behavior

Photographs are especially useful for discussion with other staff members who may not have witnessed the behavioral incident you observed. Their opinions should also be recorded in the written data. Do not wait for inappropriate behavior to occur before taking a child's photo. For instance, if you are observing Jessica every morning during arrival time, take your photos of her then, no matter what she is doing.

Videotapes

Videotapes serve the same purpose. Most programs have access to an easy-to-use camcorder these days, making it possible to record live child action for later observation and discussion with staff members. After you have previewed the tape and know what areas of development it documents, ask staff members to check off that section of the Child Skills Checklist when they have seen the video. A group discussion of the tape can be recorded and added to the observational data.

Audiotapes

A cassette tape recorder can also add depth to your written observations by recording a child's spoken language or verbal interactions with other children. Speak the child's name, the date, and the classroom location into the recorder before placing it with the tape running on a table or countertop near the child. After listening to the tape, make notes or check off appropriate items on a checklist to be placed with the tape in the child's portfolio. Some observers speak softly into a cassette recorder instead of writing down their observations. Later a transcription of the tape can be made.

The chapters to follow can serve as guidelines for you in evaluating children's strengths and needs, and planning for activities to help individuals or small groups of children with similar needs. Chapter 2 discusses how to become an observer of children using the Child Skills Checklist, how to interpret recorded results, and how to apply your interpretation in making plans for children. Chapters 3 through 13 discuss each of the 11 developmental areas of the Checklist. Chapter 14 concludes with a discussion of sharing observational data with parents.

Ideas for helping children listed in each chapter under the heading "If You Have Not Checked This Item: Some Helpful Ideas" should not only assist children in their areas of need, but also stimulate your own creativity for developing activities. Once you have learned where one child stands developmentally, then you will know how to make appropriate activity plans for each of the children in your program.

REFERENCES

Benjamin, A. C. (1994). Observations in early childhood classrooms: Advice from the field. *Young Children, 49*(6), 14–20.

Martin, S. (1994). *Take a look: Observation and portfolio assessment in early childhood.* Menlo Park, CA: Addison-Wesley.

NAEYC. (1991). Guidelines for appropriate curriculum content and assessment in programs serving children ages 3 through 8. *Young Children, 46*(3), 21–38.

Schweinhart, L. J. (1993). Observing young children in action: The key to early childhood assessment. *Young Children. 48*(5), 29–33.

Seefeldt, C. (1990). "Assessing Young Children." In C. Seefeldt (Ed.), *Continuing issues in early childhood education* (pp. 311–330). Upper Saddle River, NJ: Merrill/Prentice Hall.

Strand, T. (1989). *Bibliography of tests for early childhood: Chapter 1. Evaluation.* Dept. of Education, Washington, D.C. #ED 331 581, EDRS.

Wenner, G. (1988). *Predictive validity of three preschool developmental assessment instruments for the academic performance of kindergarten students.* State University of New York College at Buffalo. #ED 331 867, EDRS.

SUGGESTED READINGS

Bergan, J. R., & Feld, J. K. (1993). Developmental assessment: New directions. *Young Children, 48*(5), 41–47.

Gullo, D. F. (1994). *Understanding assessment and evaluation in early childhood education.* New York: Teachers College Press.

Hills, T. W. (1993). Assessment in context—Teachers and children at work. *Young Children, 40*(5), 20–28.

Nicolson, S., & Shipstead, S. G. (1994). *Through the looking glass: Observations in the early childhood classroom.* Upper Saddle River, NJ: Merrill/Prentice Hall.

Wortham, S. C. (1995). *Measurement and evaluation in early childhood education.* Upper Saddle River, NJ: Merrill/Prentice Hall.

VIDEOTAPES

Early Childhood Professional Development Network (ECPDN) with J. J. Beaty. (1997). *Take a closer look* (becoming an observer; using observation methods and tools; observing children's development; using observation results). ECPDN, P.O. Box 5574, Columbia, SC 29205-5574.

Magna Systems, Inc. (1993). *The developing child* (observation). Magna Systems, Inc., 95 W. County Line Rd., Barrington, IL 60010.

NAEYC. (1996). *Charting growth—Assessment.* NAEYC, 1509 16th St. NW, Washington, DC 20036–1426.

LEARNING ACTIVITIES

1. Look over the Guidelines for Appropriate Assessment and decide which of the 18 guidelines your program has been following and how you can improve your assessment process; if you are not in a program, describe how you would set up a method for assessing children in a preschool classroom following the guidelines.

2. What is the difference between using systematic observations and paper-and-pencil tests to assess young children? Which would you prefer to use and why?

3. Make an anecdotal record of a child after you have observed him/her for 15 minutes. At the same time, have another observer make an on-the-spot running record. Compare the two. Which showed more detail? Which was more accurate? Which would be more helpful to you in understanding the child or planning for him? Why?

4. Have two different observers make a running record of the same child for 15 minutes. Compare the results. Which, if any, of the problems mentioned under "running records" turned up? How can you overcome these problems in the future?

5. Construct a graphic rating scale on five social behaviors of children and use it to observe children in your class. Discuss your results. Did you have any problems making judgments? How can you use the information gained?

Using the Child Skills Checklist

BECOMING AN OBSERVER

To become a systematic observer of children, you must first step out of the role you normally hold. If you are a teacher or teaching assistant, then you must temporarily give up that role to one of the other staff members. This can be planned ahead of time at a staff meeting. Each staff member should take on an observer's role for brief periods every week. Assignments can be listed on the classroom bulletin board, and the teacher can remind each staff member when it is his or her turn to observe. Student interns can participate, adding another dimension to this important information-gathering task.

As an observer, you should step back unobtrusively and position yourself close to (but not interfering with) the child you are to observe. You may be seated, standing, or walking around—whatever it takes to get close enough to the child without calling attention to yourself. Try to avoid making eye contact with the child you are observing. If he or she looks your way, you can look around at the other children. Children are often much more observant than we give them credit for. In spite of your best efforts, the child you are observing will often pick up the fact that you are watching him or her, if you keep at it long enough. Most children soon forget about the scrutiny they are undergoing and continue their participation in their activity. If you find, however, that a child seems uncomfortable at your presence and even may try to get away, then you should break off your observation. Try again another day, or let another staff member or another student observe that particular child.

Many observers prefer to use a clipboard. Several such boards can be left on countertops or the tops of room dividers in each learning center, to be picked up and used by observers whenever the occasion calls for it.

If children see you writing on a clipboard for any length of time, some will come over to see what you are doing and want to write with your pencil. Tell them that you are busy with your work this morning and that they need to do their own work now. If they persist in wanting to write with your tool, direct them to the classroom writing center, where you can keep a similar clipboard with pencil and paper. If children continue to demand your attention, tell them you are busy at the moment but you will attend to them when you are finished. Redirect them to another staff person or give them a chore to accomplish in one of the learning centers.

Do not announce to the class that you are now doing observations and should be left alone. For youngsters of this age, such an announcement only calls attention to yourself, making everyone stop to look at you. Instead, you should be doing whatever is necessary to make yourself invisible, so that the child you are observing will continue his actions in an undisturbed manner. Once you have started observing on a regular basis, the children will soon understand and respect your need for privacy.

TAKING TIME TO OBSERVE

When is the best time to observe? Any time! You understand how important it is for you to acquire baseline data about each of the children in your program to plan for them. You must therefore *make* time in your busy schedule to gather the necessary

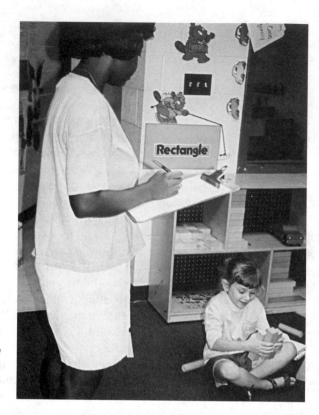

Only five minutes a day, every day, of focused observing produces a great deal of new information about a child.

information about each child through observation. The time of day to do your observing depends on what you want to learn about a child.

Do you want to see how she makes the transition from home to school in the morning? Which learning centers attract her attention? How long she stays with an activity? How she interacts with others in the dramatic play center? How she handles tools such as scissors, paintbrushes, or pencils? Whether she knows how a picture book "works"? Plan to observe her, then, in each of the centers where these activities take place.

It does not take long. Only *five minutes a day* of focused observing on the part of each staff member will produce a surprising amount of new information on children. Make plans to spend your five minutes observing a child you would like to know better. Every day for a week observe the same child for a different five-minute period, and soon you will accumulate enough data for a nearly complete profile of her development.

RECORDING INFORMATION

Start each new observation by recording your name, date, child's name, and the learning center(s) where the action takes place. It is best to start with a **running record** as discussed in Chapter 1. As you may recall, this is an open-ended recording method in which you write down everything you see and hear as it occurs: the child's facial expressions, interactions with materials, interactions with others, body movements, body language, spoken language, attention span. Later this information can be transferred to the Child Skills Checklist.

Children often move from one area to another very rapidly. Even within the same learning center they may not settle down. To catch all the action in your notes you will want to develop your own shorthand by using abbreviations when possible. Use children's initials for their names and abbreviate words: child = ch, teacher = tch, with = w/, different = dif, and so on. Use descriptive verbs whenever you can. Instead of "walks over to sink," can you be more specific by using one of these words?

marches	prances	strolls
stomps	tiptoes	skips
shuffles	toddles	strides

Practice makes perfect, and you will soon be developing your own observational shorthand and vocabulary. Complete sentences are not necessary on a running record. Instead, catch the moment on paper as quickly and completely as you can. Afterwards, you can draw a line under the recording and write any comments or interpretive remarks that may help explain what you saw happening. Your first five-minute running record may be rather short; perhaps not more than a half-page of notes. But as you hone your skills you will soon be filling up more than one page, because the more experienced you become, the more you will see.

Be sure to record as much of the spoken language as possible. Also include how the child sounds as she speaks. Think of the many verbs describing speaking that you can use instead of the word *said*:

whispered	stammered	muttered
shouted	grumbled	announced
declared	told	argued

You may want to keep a card with you with a list of descriptive verbs to substitute for *walked* and *said* and other frequently used but nondescriptive verbs.

Learning Center Logs

Some programs have found that the best way to observe and record on-the-spot actions is to keep a small spiral notebook on the top of the room divider for each learning center. Staff members are asked to record what they see happening in a center whenever they are in the vicinity, and to date their observations. The teacher later gathers these logs to transfer the information onto the Child Skills Checklists being used for each of the children.

This is a way to collect data for several children at once, as well as for child interactions in several learning centers at once. Some programs divide the pages of their logs into the headings of *Child*, *Actions*, and *Language* to help remind observers of what information to record. If the teacher notes that nothing has been recorded in one of the centers by the end of the day, she or he can discuss this with the staff. Did no children play in that particular center, or did none of the staff happen to observe what was going on there?

Using learning center logs like this helps to alert staff members not only to what is occurring throughout the classroom throughout the day, but also as a reminder to record what they see happening. As a result, the teacher can piece together a record for more than one child's entire day of activities as seen by several different observers. In addition, no one feels burdened by stepping out of their role as a teacher to observe. Child observation occurs naturally as a part of the staff's normal checking of learning centers to see how children are doing.

All of the staff including the teacher benefit from this sort of ongoing assessment of children. They learn where each child is developmentally, which centers and which activities seem to attract the most children, and which centers need changing. Learning center log recording like this gives the entire staff a better feel for what is really happening in the program.

Because observing and recording is such an important aspect of a teacher's commitment to children's development, you should explore ways to make it easier for yourself and other staff members to carry out this responsibility. As noted by one observer:

> Making the commitment to observe during the course of a busy day necessarily includes preplanning and organization. Teachers should survey their classrooms to determine how best to approach the task. The focus during this phase should be on identifying ways to use the classroom itself to support your efforts. (Benjamin, 1994, p. 16)

Some child caregivers plan to do their most in-depth recording during free-choice time when children are busily engaged in all of the learning centers. Others preplan by placing an "observation chair" in an unobtrusive spot near children's activities. Having notebooks or clipboards and pencils ready in strategic locations helps. Some programs include a small cassette recorder as a tool so teachers can narrate their observations for transcription later instead of writing them down at the time. You should consider anything that makes your task easier. Share ideas with other staff members and find out what works best for them. Then everyone can get into the act of observing, recording, and planning for children according to their strengths and needs.

USING THE CHILD SKILLS CHECKLIST

The Child Skills Checklist in Figure 2–1, around which this book is written, is as much a learning device for the observer as it is a planning tool for helping the child. With sequences of child development as its focus, it presents the areas of emotional, social, physical, cognitive, language, and creative development by dividing each of these areas into two major categories, then subdividing each category into eight representative items of development.

Emotional development, for example, is divided into "self-identity" and "emotional development," with a chapter devoted to each of these topics. The observer learns from the chapters some representative behavior in the sequence of emotional development that can be seen in the early childhood classroom.

CHILD SKILLS CHECKLIST

Name _____   Observer _____

Program _____   Dates _____

Directions:

Put a ✔ for items you see the child perform regularly. Put *N* for items where there is no opportunity to observe. Leave all other items blank.

Item	Evidence	Date
1. Self-Identity		
___ Separates from parents without difficulty		
___ Does not cling to classroom staff excessively		
___ Makes eye contact with adults		
___ Makes activity choices without teacher's help		
___ Seeks other children to play with		
___ Plays roles confidently in dramatic play		
___ Stands up for own rights		
___ Displays enthusiasm about doing things for self		
2. Emotional Development		
___ Allows self to be comforted during stressful time		
___ Eats, sleeps, toilets without fuss away from home		
___ Handles sudden changes/ startling situations with control		
___ Can express anger in words rather than actions		

Figure 2–1   *Child Skills Checklist*

Item	Evidence	Date
___ Allows aggressive behavior to be redirected		
___ Does not withdraw from others excessively		
___ Shows interest/attention in classroom activities		
___ Smiles, seems happy much of the time		
3. Social Play		
___ Spends time watching others play		
___ Plays by self with own toys/ materials		
___ Plays parallel to others with similar toys/materials		
___ Plays with others in cooperative play		
___ Makes friends with other children		
___ Gains access to play in a positive manner		
___ Maintains role in ongoing play in a positive manner		
___ Resolves play conflicts in a positive manner		
4. Prosocial Behavior		
___ Shows concern for someone in distress		
___ Can tell how another feels during conflict		

Figure 2–1 *continued*

Item	Evidence	Date
___ Shares something with another		
___ Gives something to another		
___ Takes turns without a fuss		
___ Complies with requests without a fuss		
___ Helps another to do a task		
___ Helps (cares for) another in need		
5. Large Motor Development		
___ Walks down steps alternating feet		
___ Runs with control over speed and direction		
___ Jumps up and lands on two feet		
___ Hops on one foot		
___ Throws, catches and kicks balls		
___ Climbs up and down climbing equipment with ease		
___ Moves legs and feet in rhythm to beat		
___ Moves arms and hands in rhythm to beat		

Item	Evidence	Date
6. Small Motor Development		
___ Shows hand preference (which is ___)		
___ Turns with hand easily (knobs, lids, eggbeaters)		
___ Pours liquid into glass without spilling		
___ Unfastens/fastens zippers, buttons, Velcro tabs		
___ Picks up and inserts objects with ease		
___ Uses drawing/writing tools with control		
___ Uses scissors with control		
___ Pounds in nails with control		
7. Cognitive Development: Classification, Number, Time and Space		
___ Identifies objects by shape		
___ Identifies objects by color		
___ Identifies objects by size		
___ Sorts objects by likenesses		
___ Puts events in a sequence; objects in a series		

Figure 2–1 *continued*

Item	Evidence	Date
___ Counts how many are present		
___ Knows what happens today		
___ Can build a block enclosure		

8. Spoken Language

Item	Evidence	Date
___ Listens but does not speak		
___ Gives single word answers		
___ Gives short-phrase responses		
___ Does chanting and singing		
___ Takes part in conversations		
___ Speaks in expanded sentences		
___ Asks questions		
___ Can tell a story		

9. Prewriting and Prereading Skills

Item	Evidence	Date
___ Pretends to write with pictures and scribbles		
___ Makes horizontal lines of writing scribbles		

Item	Evidence	Date
___ Includes letter-like forms in writing		
___ Makes some letters, prints name or initial		
___ Holds book right-side up; turns pages left to right		
___ Pretends to read using pictures to tell story		
___ Retells stories from books with increasing accuracy		
___ Shows awareness that print in books tells the story		
10. Art Skills		
___ Makes random marks on paper		
___ Makes controlled scribbles		
___ Makes basic shapes		
___ Combines circles/squares with crossed lines		
___ Makes "suns"		
___ Draws person as sun-face with arms and legs		
___ Draws animals, trees, flowers		
___ Draws objects together in a picture		

Figure 2–1 *continued*

42

Item	Evidence	Date
11. Imagination		
___ Pretends an action without taking a role		
___ Assigns roles or takes assigned roles		
___ Takes on characteristics and actions of role		
___ Needs particular props to do pretend play		
___ Can pretend with imaginary objects		
___ Uses language for creating and sustaining plot		
___ Uses exciting, danger-packed themes		
___ Uses elaborate themes, ideas, details		

Using One Checklist Section at a Time

As a learning device for the observer, the Checklist is best used one section at a time. To understand the sequence of emotional development as it appears in the early childhood classroom, for instance, the observer should first plan to use the "Self-Identity" section of the Checklist in observing a child *for enough time to see if all eight items are present.* This means coming into the classroom early enough to see how the child enters the room, what she does when her parent leaves, and how she becomes involved in the classroom activities. It also means coming early to the classroom *more than once* to observe how the child behaves on different days, and to record this information. The observer should not only check off the items as they appear, but also record evidence for each item in the space provided.

The observer should then read Chapter 3, "Self-Identity," paying special attention to the items that were not checked, to gain insight into why the child may not have performed certain items. The "Helpful Ideas" section after each item in the chapter gives suggestions that may assist the observer/teacher in planning for the child.

Making a Running Record and Transferring Data to the Checklist

To use the Checklist most effectively, many observers prefer to make a running record of the child they are observing, as noted previously. Afterward they transfer the data they have gathered by marking items on the Checklist that they observed the child performing, and by recording evidence for their check mark in the space provided. This combines the best of both methods of observation: the open-ended and rich descriptive advantages of the running record with the focus on a particular sequence of behaviors of a developmental checklist.

Here is a running record made for three-year-old Sheila on October 22:

Sheila's mother brings her into classroom.
   Sheila holds tightly to her hand. She begins to cry.
   Mother says: "Now, Sheila, you like it here. Be a good girl. See you later."
   Mother leaves. S. stands at entrance to room crying.
   Teacher comes over and S. grabs her hand.
   Tch. takes S. over to girls in doll corner & says something.
   S. shakes her head "no."
   When tch. lvs. S. begins following tch. around.
   Tch. sits S. down at small table with box of crayons in middle & blank sheets of paper in front of 2 chairs.
   S. finally takes 2 crayons & starts coloring on paper.
   Beth comes over & sits down at table.
   Beth takes crayon out of box & starts coloring on her paper.
   No talking at first.
   Then Beth asks S. "May I borrow your orange?" It is on table.
   S. says "No" & covers crayon with hand.
   Beth grabs her hand, takes crayon with other hand & pops it into her mouth!

S. says "That's not fair!" and calls tch.

When tch. comes S. says, "She ate my orange crayon so I can't finish my pumpkin!"

Tch. says to Beth, "People shouldn't eat crayons." Tch. is distracted by other ch. & leaves area.

S. gets up & goes to book corner & takes book.

S. carries book around room, looking carefully at what is going on, but not joining in.

S. whispers to Brian, "Becky painted yesterday & she's going to paint again today. See!" & points to easel.

Brian doesn't respond. S. whines to tch., "I wanna paint!"

Tch. tells her she can paint when Becky is finished.

The observer then takes this running record and fills out the "Self-Identity" section of the Checklist as shown in Figure 2–2.

As the observer reads the chapter on self-identity, she should pay special attention to the items that she did not check. She will learn from her reading that a three-year-old like Sheila may still not be secure enough to let go of her mother easily when she first comes to the preschool. The observer should not be all that concerned when Sheila transfers her clinging to the teacher, for the observer learns that three-year-olds often exhibit such behavior at the beginning of school. The section "Helpful Ideas" after each item in Chapter 3 gives suggestions that may assist this child to make the transition from home to school more easily. Because Sheila has been in school for a month and still has difficulty making this transition, she may need this special help.

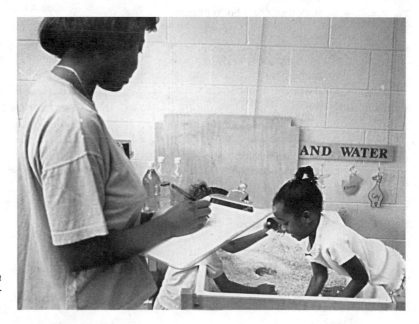

You can start by observing how a certain child plays in a particular learning center.

Child Skills Checklist

Name *Sheila — Age 3*   Observer *Connie R.*

Program *Head Start*   Dates *10-22*

Directions:

Put a ✔ for items you see the child perform regularly. Put *N* for items where there is no opportunity to observe. Leave all other items blank.

Item	Evidence	Date
1. Self-Identity		
_____ Separates from parents without difficulty	*Sheila clings to mother & cries*	10/22
_____ Does not cling to classroom staff excessively	*She grabs teacher's hand & follows teacher.*	10/22
✔ Makes eye contact with adults	*She makes eye contact with teacher*	10/22
_____ Makes activity choices without teacher's help	*Teacher places Sheila at crayon table*	10/22
_____ Seeks other children to play with	*No. She does not.*	10/22
N Plays roles confidently in dramatic play		
✔ Stands up for own rights	*Calls out to teacher: "She ate my orange crayon".*	10/22
_____ Displays enthusiasm about doing things for self	*Watches, but does not get involved.*	10/22

Figure 2–2   Self-identity observations for Sheila

Using the Entire Checklist

Once you are familiar with each of the Checklist areas and items, you can use the entire Checklist for one child to gain a complete overview. How should you begin? You may want to learn something about a particular child in a certain area of development to start. Perhaps she has difficulty getting involved with the others in the pretend play during free choice period. Plan to begin your observation during this period. You will want to look at the items in the Social Play section. Other Checklist areas that can often be seen at the same time as Social Play include: the items under Self-Identity, Emotional Development, Prosocial Behavior, Spoken Language, and Imagination. Either check off the items as you see them, writing in the evidence, or do a running record of everything the child does and convert it to the Checklist afterwards.

Circle the Checklist area you are observing, then place a checkmark for each item you saw the child performing or an "N" for the items you had no opportunity to observe. Leave the item blank if neither of the above conditions apply. A blank means the child had the opportunity to perform the item, but did not do it.

Be sure to make notes after each item, jotting down the evidence that prompted you to check the item (or leave it blank). If you leave the item blank, it is still important to write down your reason—the evidence for leaving the item blank. If you use the same Checklist on more than one day in a cumulative manner, be sure to put the date after each item as well.

The time of your next observation may be determined by the areas you have not had the opportunity to observe. For Self-Identity, for instance, you will want to observe the child when she arrives in the morning, especially at the beginning of the year. Emotional Development items need to be observed during lunch or snack time, toileting, and nap time.

Evidence

It is important to record evidence as brief, nonjudgmental statements of what you actually saw. If you are observing and recording directly onto the Checklist, these statements can be brief descriptions of the child's actions and language that you see and hear. If you are transferring data from a running record, enter that evidence. If you did not have the opportunity to observe the child for a particular item, place N instead of a checkmark beside it. If the child has the opportunity to perform a Checklist item, but does not do it, leave the item blank, but write in an explanation.

For example, in Figure 2–2 the observer leaves the first two items blank but includes under "Evidence" the child's opposite actions that she saw happening. Instead of checking "Separates from parents without difficulty" the observer notes that "Sheila clings to mother & cries." It is important for the teaching staff to have such information in interpreting the Checklist results and making plans for this child.

From the running record previously made about Sheila, the observer can continue to complete the Child Skills Checklist under the 10 other areas, checking off items and filling in "Evidence." Obviously a number of other observations need to be made of Sheila at various time during the day and on different days during arrival, free choice, snack, outdoor play, lunch, nap, and departure, to provide a comprehensive picture of the child.

Because this checklist looks at children's natural development, the observer must record only the child's natural actions and language as she works and plays with materials and other children during the day. Asking the child to write her name, draw a picture, or construct a block building is considered "artificial" and not natural evidence. Be careful not to place children in such contrived situations for observational purposes. As noted in the NAEYC Guidelines for Appropriate Assessment:

> 6. Assessment relies on procedures that reflect typical activities of children and avoids approaches that place children in artificial situations. (NAEYC, 1991, 32)

In other words, the Child Skills Checklist is not a test, but a listing of developmental items that children may or may not perform. If observers leave certain items blank because the child does not perform them, this may mean:

1. She cannot because she has not yet reached that level of development.
2. She does not because she is not interested in what the item describes.
3. The classroom itself is not set up to encourage the child's performance.

You should not ask children questions about whether they recognize certain colors, for instance. The youngsters' performance on the items should become evident as you observe the children in their natural play activities. Set up activities that will engage the children in the areas you wish to observe. Be sure these activities are spontaneous and not forced. If a child does not get involved in Art Skills, even though art activities are available every day, you should leave the items blank. Do not use "N," no opportunity to observe, when in fact the child has the opportunity to participate in art activities, but chooses not to. You may want to make a note, though, after the items that "Easel painting and art activities are available, but B. does not get involved in art."

From the running record previously made, the observer can check off items and fill in evidence for Sheila under Emotional Development such as in Figure 2–3. Under Social Play, items such as those in Figure 2–4 can be checked. Additional items that can be checked based on this running record include those shown in Figure 2–5. Other observations on Sheila can be made, recorded, and dated on the same Checklist until a comprehensive picture of her emerges.

2. Emotional Development ✓ Shows interest/attention in classroom activities	Goes around room trying out everything	10/22

Figure 2–3   Emotional development evidence for Sheila

3. Social Play		
✓ Plays by self with own toys/ materials	Uses crayons on own	10/22
✓ Plays parallel to others with similar toys/materials	Colors on own but next to Beth	10/22

Figure 2–4 Social play evidence for Sheila

6. Small Motor Development		
✓ Uses drawing/writing tools with control	Draws pumpkin with crayon	10/22
9. Spoken Language ✓ Speaks in expanded sentences	"She ate my orange crayon so I can't finish my pumpkin".	10/22
11. Art Skills ✓ Makes pictorial drawings	Draws a pumpkin	10/22

Figure 2–5 Additional developmental evidence for Sheila

INTERPRETING THE DATA

Once you have observed a child and recorded data about her in a running record on the Child Skills Checklist, the next step is to interpret the information. Learning to know and understand a child is a fascinating process. Objective observing and recording like this help enable a deeper understanding than a lifetime of merely being around children can do. We need to step back from children and look at them impartially and objectively. Only then do we truly see who they are and what they are. Only then do we begin to understand how we can help them reach their greatest potential.

Interpreting information your observations have provided takes knowledge and skill. You need to know a great deal about child development both from reading and studying about children and from actual experience with them. Then you can begin to make valid inferences and conclusions about children based on your observations.

This textbook is organized to help you gain such knowledge. Using the Child Skills Checklist will focus your attention on important child behaviors in each area of child development. Reading the chapters that feature these areas will help you to acquire knowledge of that particular area. Interpreting the data you acquire will then be more meaningful to you and helpful to the child as you apply it in your individual planning.

The first step in interpreting the data you have gathered is to read it through carefully, both the running record and especially the Checklist, to see if you can make any inferences about the child. An inference is a statement of interpretation considered to be true, tentatively at least, because it is founded upon objective information believed to be true. In other words, it is a possible explanation derived from the behavior you have witnessed. To make an inference, you must actually have seen and recorded objectively the behavior upon which you are basing the inference.

Looking back at the running record made for Sheila, we might consider making the following inferences:

Incident	*Faulty Inference*	*Valid Inference*
Sheila would not let Beth borrow her orange crayon.	Sheila does not know how to share.	Sheila was not finished using her crayon.
Sheila whispers to Brian that Becky painted yesterday and she's going to paint again today.	Sheila likes to tattle on other children.	Sheila is alert to what Becky did with paint yesterday and today.

After reading carefully the first incident in the running record involving Sheila (which states that she says "no" when Beth asks to borrow her orange crayon, then covers the crayon with her hand), we need to ask ourselves what we can infer, if anything, from this. Do the words tell us that Sheila does not know how to share? They do not seem to indicate this. Then the inference "Sheila does not know how to share" is probably not a valid one. We just do not have enough information to make this particular inference. We may want to observe Sheila further to see if she is able to share materials with others before we can infer that she does not know how to share. Does the running record tell us that Sheila was not finished using the orange crayon? Yes. The words say, "She ate my orange crayon so I can't finish my pumpkin." Thus we can infer that Sheila was not finished using the crayon.

The second incident, in which Sheila whispers to Brian that Becky painted yesterday and she's going to paint again today, should be approached in the same way. What, if anything, can we infer from this incident? Does it mean Sheila likes to tattle on other children? Since we do not have any indication this is true, such an inference is faulty. We can infer that Sheila is alert to what Becky did with paint yesterday and now today. That is about all. We may want to infer that Sheila is using such an approach to gain access to an activity she likes, or that Sheila whispers about others to get attention, or that Sheila just likes to stir up things in the classroom in this manner—but we truly do not have such information about Sheila, and thus cannot make any of these three last inferences.

Try making your own inferences from an anecdotal or running record you have made after observing a child. One thing you will learn from such an exercise is the importance of recording with rich detail in the first place. You need to learn this skill through practice as you observe children. You can always add something more to a running record: facial expressions, gestures, reactions of other children. They may be the keys to the inferences you are trying to draw about a child.

The principal stumbling block in making valid inferences based on recorded observational data is that we try to read more into the data than is actually there. We are used to making judgments continuously about people and situations in our lives. Often they are faulty judgments based on insufficient or misinterpreted information. Do not allow yourself to be misled like this when you have the written observation data before you. Look at the data and ask yourself the question: Is there evidence to support my inference? If there is not, then you cannot make it.

Conclusions

The final step in your interpretation of recorded data about children is to make whatever conclusions you can. A conclusion in this case is a reasoned judgment based on *valid inferences made from accumulated observational evidence*. As with inferences, you cannot make such a judgment unless you can show sufficient evidence. Read through your observational data. Based on what you have recorded, what can you conclude about the child? In Sheila's case, very little can be concluded from one brief running record. We cannot really conclude that she is always so alert to other children and activities in the classroom unless future observations show this to be the case. It may be that she is only concerned with painting. To make valid conclusions an observer needs a great deal of recorded information about a child.

Observing, recording, and interpreting in this careful, objective manner should help you sort out what children are really like. You may be surprised by what you discover.

PLANNING FOR CHILDREN BASED ON OBSERVATIONS

The ultimate reason for observing and recording is not just to learn what children are like, but to help them grow and develop. That is why they have come to your classroom. You can assist them in this goal if your observations have helped you identify their strengths and areas that need strengthening.

After observing Sheila for only one morning and transferring her observational data from a running record to the Child Skills Checklist, you can begin to get a picture of where she is strong and not-so-strong. From this partial picture as shown on the Checklist, you can begin to make plans for Sheila that will help build on her strengths and speak to her needs—always accentuating the positive.

Learning Prescription

Creating a "learning prescription" for Sheila is the next step in the process of planning for an individual child based on interpreted observational data. To create such a prescription, you should look over the Child Skills Checklist to find at least three *areas of strength*. Although her Checklist is far from complete, it is still possible to come up with real strengths for Sheila: for example, she stands up for her own rights, speaks in expanded sentences, and really seems to enjoy art.

Making a reliable overall assessment of a single child is not possible based on only one observation. You should have as much information as you can gather from as many different days, activities, and points of view as possible. The best overall records are a compilation from the entire classroom staff. Have each person put a date by the items she has observed. Individuals may want to indicate their checkmarks and evidence with a symbol, initials, or color coding, if everyone is using the same Checklist for all the observations.

After you have decided on Sheila's strengths, you need to look for her areas needing strengthening. We do not call these weaknesses, a negative term, because they are not weaknesses. Words are important, and we should use them carefully. If we talk in terms of negatives, we will think in terms of negatives regarding Sheila and our other children. If we think in terms of areas needing strengthening, we should be able to plan a positive program for Sheila that will help her to continue in her development and improve in areas that need improvement. Put yourself in the same position: Wouldn't you prefer to be involved in a training program that would help you improve in areas needing strengthening rather than a program to overcome weaknesses?

Finally, the learning prescription needs to include specific ideas for helping the child improve in areas needing strengthening by *drawing on her strengths*. Specific ideas for activities can come from your own experience or from the ideas listed in the various chapters after every Checklist item and called "If You Have Not Checked This Item: Some Helpful Ideas." An initial learning prescription for Sheila might read something like the example in Figure 2–6. (See Figure 2–7 later in this chapter for a reproducible copy of a learning prescription form.)

The teachers in Sheila's class will want to continue their observing and recording to evaluate how these activities help Sheila and the other children, as well as to determine what other individual plans are needed.

The chapters that follow in this text can serve as guidelines for you in evaluating children's strengths and needs, and then in planning activities to help individuals or small groups of children with similar needs. The suggestions listed under "Some Helpful Ideas" should prove useful not only in assisting children in their needs, but also in providing the stimulus for your own ideas for activities.

As you study the 11 separate areas of child development included in this observational program, you will note that each of the aspects discussed follows a similar pattern in the growth of the child: from the general to the specific. Children learn to control large muscles before they master small motor control. Children recognize overall patterns of cognitive discrimination before the details become clear, speak single words to include whole categories of things before they learn the names for each, draw a circle to represent a person before they learn to add the details, and pretend in stereotyped roles as mothers and fathers before they add the personal touches identifying specific family members.

This book, on the other hand, proceeds in the opposite direction: specific categories of development are detailed first. We look in some depth at self-identity, emo-

---

Learning Prescription

Name ___Sheila___   Age __3__   Date __10/22__

Areas of Strength and Confidence

1. _Stands up for her own rights_
2. _Speaks in expanded sentences_
3. _Enjoys art & displays art skills_

Areas Needing Strengthening

1. _To separate from mother more easily_
2. _To rely less on adults in classroom_
3. _To play with other children_

Activities to Help

1. _Transition activity when S. arrives: S & Becky could clean the rabbit cage & feed the rabbit._
2. _S. could record her voice & then show Becky how_
3. _S. and Becky could paint large box for class "spaceship" and others could join in_

Figure 2–6   Learning prescription for Sheila

tional development, social play, prosocial behavior, large motor development, small motor development, cognitive development (classification, number, time, and space), spoken language, prewriting and prereading skills, art skills, and imagination.

The child is, of course, a whole being whose development in these areas is proceeding simultaneously. Once you understand the details of this growth, it is possible to make an overall assessment of the developmental skills that each of your children possesses by using the Child Skills Checklist as a whole. Such an assessment then allows you to draw a total picture of the child and formulate individual plans that will promote continued development.

Use of the Checklist by Preservice Teachers and Student Teachers

Preservice and student teachers can use the Child Skills Checklist just as a classroom teacher does, making a series of observations of a single child until all of the items have been noted. In case the observer has no access to live children in a classroom, it is possible to observe and record using videotapes. (See the Videotapes section at end of the chapter.)

For student observers who observe and record live children, you need to rewrite your notes as soon as possible after you have finished your observations. As an experienced observer notes:

> Memory is a notoriously poor recorder, so make it a practice to transcribe your notes soon after you visit a classroom. You are more likely to remember accurately if you rewrite your notes the same day that you observe. As a courtesy, you might offer a copy of your observation notes to the classroom teacher in situations in which sharing would be appropriate. (Benjamin, 1994, p. 190)

To interpret the checked items or blanks, the observer should read the particular chapters that discuss these areas. It is especially helpful for such observers to make a written report or case study that includes an interpretation of the child's development in each of the 11 principal Checklist areas. Such a report should include not only specific information from the observations, but also whatever inferences and conclusions the observer can draw from the observational data collected, based on her knowledge of child development.

In Sheila's case, the observer will want to read Chapter 3, "Self-Identity," to find out what it could mean when the child has difficulty separating from the mother, and why the child shows interest in the classroom activities but does not play with other children. Without a great deal of information, an outside observer often cannot interpret child observations without help from the classroom staff. However, certain inferences and conclusions are possible based on the data collected. The outside observer may even make an important contribution to the understanding of a particular child because of her fresh perspective.

In addition to the written interpretation of each of the 11 Checklist areas, the observer needs to summarize the child's overall development in some detail. A learning prescription similar to Sheila's should be done, followed by an explanation for the activities prescribed.

Case studies such as this can be helpful not only to the preservice or student teacher, but also to the supervising classroom teacher, as well as the parent of the child observed. Supervising teachers need to set up case conferences with individual parents (to which student observers are invited) to discuss the student observers' reports. (See Chapter 14 for more information.)

For students who are unable to observe live children, viewing children on videotape is another possibility. The four-part series *Take a Closer Look: A Field Guide to Child Observation* (ECPDN & Beaty, 1997) offers students the opportunity to view and record children's actions almost as if they were in the classroom themselves.

OBSERVATION OF EACH CHILD

It is important to observe each of the children in this kind of detail during the year. Teachers report they can learn more about each child by stepping back and making a focused observation like this, rather than simply by having the child in their program for an entire year. It is an eye-opening experience to look at one child in-depth from an observer's point of view, rather than from the perspective of a busy teacher involved with the activities of many other lively youngsters.

Child-development students report that in-depth examination of a real child makes textbooks and courses come alive, as well. Parents, too, benefit from the information objective observations provide. Not only do the parents learn new activities to use with their children at home, they also often become involved in the fascinating drama of how their own children develop, why their children act the way they do, and how they, as parents, can best help their children realize their full potential. (Chapter 14 covers this area in more depth.)

REFERENCES

Benjamin, A. C. (1994). Observations in early childhood classrooms: Advice from the field. *Young Children, 49*(6), 14–20.

NAEYC. (1991). Guidelines for appropriate curriculum content and assessment in programs serving children ages 3 through 8. *Young Children, 46*(3), 33.

SUGGESTED READINGS

Martin, S. (1994). *Take a look: Observation and portfolio assessment in early childhood.* Menlo Park, CA: Addison-Wesley.

Nicolson, S., & Shipstead, S. G. (1994). *Through the looking glass: Observations in the early childhood classroom.* Upper Saddle River, NJ: Merrill/Prentice Hall.

Puckett, M. B., & Black, J. K. (1994). *Authentic assessment of the young child.* Upper Saddle River, NJ: Merrill/Prentice Hall.

Schweinhart, L. J. (1993). Observing young children in action: The key to early childhood assessment. *Young Children, 48*(5), 29–33.

VIDEOTAPES

Early Childhood Professional Development Network (ECPDN), with J. J. Beaty. (1997). *Take a closer look: A field guide to child observation* (Four videos: becoming an observer; using observation methods and tools; observing children's development; using observation results). ECPDN, P.O. Box 5574, Columbia, SC 29205-5574.

LEARNING ACTIVITIES

....

1. How can you make yourself unobtrusive in the classroom when you are observing a child? Why is this necessary? What should you do to keep children from finding out that you are observing them? What should you do if they find out?

2. Have two different observers use the Child Skills Checklist to observe the same child at the same time for three days. Compare results. How similar were the observations? In what areas were there differences? How could you improve future observing and recording?

3. Make an anecdotal record for a child after you have observed the child for a half-hour. What inferences can you make about this child based only on your observation? What specific evidence is each inference based upon? Can you make any conclusions? Why or why not?

4. Make learning center logs and place them around the classroom in each of the learning centers. At the end of the day collect the recorded data in each of the logs and transfer it to one or more Child Skill Checklist. How helpful were these logs? What more needs to be done to complete the Checklists?

5. Make a Learning Prescription (see Figure 2–7) for one of the children you have observed listing the child's strengths and areas needing strengthening as well as several activities to help. On what evidence did you base this prescription? Try out one of the activities and record the results.

Learning Prescription

Name _____ Age _____ Date _____

Areas of Strength and Confidence

1. _____

2. _____

3. _____

Areas Needing Strengthening

1. _____

2. _____

3. _____

Activities to Help

1. _____

_____

2. _____

_____

3. _____

_____

Figure 2–7   Learning prescription form

Permission is granted by the publisher to reproduce this form for distribution. Distribution as a hand-out must be free of charge and the form may not be included in a compilation of readings for profit or otherwise.

CHAPTER 3

Self-Identity

SELF-IDENTITY CHECKLIST

- ☐ Separates from parents without difficulty
- ☐ Does not cling to classroom staff excessively
- ☐ Makes eye contact with adults
- ☐ Makes activity choices without teacher's help
- ☐ Seeks other children to play with
- ☐ Plays roles confidently in dramatic play
- ☐ Stands up for own rights
- ☐ Displays enthusiasm about doing things for self

DEVELOPING A SELF-CONCEPT

From the moment of birth, the young human being is engaged in the dynamic process of becoming himself or herself. The child continually develops into a whole person with a temperament, personality, and value-system—with a physical, cognitive, language, social, emotional, and creative makeup that is uniquely his or her own. It is a totally engrossing process that will take a lifetime to complete, but its early stages are perhaps its most crucial, for they set the pattern for all that is to follow.

Among the most important aspects of the child's growing persona is his development of **self-concept**: his sense of self that includes both his **self-image** (his inner picture of himself), and his **self-esteem** (his sense of self-worth). Although these three terms are often used interchangeably, they actually refer to different aspects of the self. A person's self-image is his internal image or picture of himself that includes his looks, his gender, his ethnicity, his standing in the family, and his abilities. A child acquires this image as he grows and sees himself as a separate individual. Self-image is not judgmental, it is descriptive.

On the other hand, self-esteem is an evaluation of these aspects: the child's feeling about his looks, his gender, his ethnicity, his standing in the family, and his abilities. He acquires this sense of self-worth through his interaction with the other people around him as well as his own judgmental view of himself and what he is able to do.

Self-image and self-esteem go together to form a child's self-concept. As Kosnik notes:

> These two areas combine to form our self-concept. Throughout our lives a continuous dialogue exists between these two aspects of self. Our self-concept determines who we are, what we think we are, what we think we can do, and what we think we can become. (Kosnik, 1993, p. 32)

Self-concept formation is a continuous process, but once it has taken some form, it is difficult to change the older the child gets. As the child receives incoming information about the way she is treated by others or her experiences of success or failure, she uses such data to confirm what she already feels about herself. For example, if the child feels good about herself because of the way she is treated in her family, then she will see a teacher's good treatment of her as confirmation of what she already knows. She then acts out these feelings in the classroom by being happy and cooperative. This, in turn, keeps those around her treating her positively.

If, on the other hand, a child has negative feelings about himself because of the way he is treated in his family, even a teacher's good treatment may not change his self-concept readily. Instead, he may rationalize it by thinking that the teacher is being nice to him because she feels sorry for him since he is so bad. He may act out his negative feelings about himself by being aggressive toward other children, disruptive of activities, or else by withdrawing into himself and not participating. Any scolding or other negative response to such behavior only go toward convincing him that he is no good.

How then can a teacher or caregiver of preschool children act to help youngsters become convinced that they are truly worthy people? Teachers must be persistent and consistent in their positive messages to every individual *child every* day. Sometimes we think we have done our duty to greet a child whenever we have time as long as some staff member is at the door to do the greeting in the morning. This is not enough. You personally must deliver your positive messages *every* day to *every* child. As Kosnik continues with her vital message:

> For children to believe that they are valuable members of the community, they must feel individually noticed and they must feel wanted. By getting to know the children and highlighting their abilities, the teacher validates the children. . . . She is one step closer to increasing the children's self-esteem. (Kosnick, 1993, p. 36)

This chapter will discuss some of the developmental progressions that are observable in children three to five years of age as they strive to develop a sense of self in the setting of the child development center or classroom. Although children carry with them their own unique package of genetic traits and home influences, the caregivers they meet and the daily care they receive at the center or classroom have a strong bearing on their future development.

Each item of the Child Skills Checklist will be discussed separately in this and the chapters to follow. Each Checklist item is positive in nature and should be checked if the observer sees the child performing in the manner described. Suggestions for helping and supporting the child's development in the unchecked items will follow the discussion of the item.

The eight items in the Self-Identity Checklist show a progression of steps many children take as they separate from their parents and make the sometimes difficult transition into a preschool or child-care setting. It is important for a teacher to determine at the outset where each child stands in this progression, so that she can assist the children in developing a strong, positive sense of self.

SEPARATES FROM PARENTS WITHOUT DIFFICULTY

Initial Attachment

Most studies of young children agree that a key ingredient to their successful development is a strong initial attachment to a primary caregiver, usually the mother. Without such an attachment babies may seriously lag in their development and in some cases even die. It seems a great paradox, then, to suggest that for successful development to continue, the young human must learn at the same time to separate from the parent. But such is the case. This separation should occur first in the home—not only with the child, but also with the parents, who must encourage the infant to become independent of them, and who must also let go of the infant.

Many current attachment/separation studies are based on the initial work of John Bowlby (1969) and Mary Ainsworth (1978), who talk about children's attachment to their parents as a condition of trust in their parents' reliability. Attachment occurs during the first year or two as a result of many interactions between infants and parents. The first separation of the child from the mother is of course the physical one that occurs at birth. Some psychologists believe that much of life thereafter is the developing being striving to achieve that perfect state of oneness once again with another human (Kaplan, 1978, p. 43).

In the first few months of life, the baby hardly recognizes itself as a separate being apart from its mother or primary caregiver. When she cries, the mother feeds or changes her. When she gurgles or coos, the mother holds her close or smiles. Little by little, as visual memory develops—and "person permanence" occurs—the infant comes to recognize this primary caregiver as being different from everyone else. The child then strives to be near the caregiver or to bring this person close as often as possible. "Person permanence" means that the infant has developed the ability to hold the memory of the person in its mind when the person is out of sight (Damon, 1983, p. 34).

It is necessary, therefore, that this primary caregiver be a consistent one. The formation of a strong attachment becomes complicated if the infant has too many caregivers. If the mother works during the day, for example, she should make arrangements to turn over the secondary caregiving responsibilities to one consistent person while she is away. She can still function as a primary caregiver when she returns from work, if this is the role she has chosen. If she has turned over the role of primary caregiver to the father or to another person from the beginning, then this should be the consistent person whom the infant can turn to at the end of the day. The baby who has developed "person permanence" will welcome this person happily when he or she returns.

This is the beginning of the strong initial attachment that both the infant and caregiver need for later separation to occur successfully. Such an attachment leads to a sense of security and trust on the part of the infant. The lack of such an attachment often interferes with the child's building trust in future relationships. In fact, the failure to thrive in infancy is frequently the result of the breakdown of this initial attachment relationship (Seagull, 1978, p. 8).

Both the primary caregiver and the infant play a part in building this initial attachment. The adult must respond promptly and appropriately to the infant's cries—time after time after time. For example, the adult should feed the infant and not spank her when she cries out of hunger. Some adults don't. On the other hand, the infant should also respond appropriately to the caregiver's actions. For example, the infant needs to stop crying when the adult cares for her needs, or to show delight when the adult plays with her or cuddles her. Some babies don't.

It is difficult for the initial attachment to be strong when the actions of one or the other or both are not satisfactory over a period of time. It takes most of the infant's first year to develop the relationship with a caregiver, in fact (Damon, 1983, p. 29). But without such an attachment, it is difficult for the infant to develop trust in anyone else, and it becomes doubly difficult for the infant or developing child to separate from the caregiver. After all, if she cannot trust her primary caregiver, how can she risk trusting anyone? The attachment between the infant and primary caregiver, in fact, serves as a model for future human relationships.

Initial Separation

The initial separation of the infant from its mother or primary caregiver begins when he first recognizes he is separate from that person. This develops within the first six months of life as the baby recognizes there is a difference between himself and the caregiver—and later, between himself and others. At this time, his first memories—visual in nature—are occurring. Some psychologists call this the "psychological birth" of the baby (Kaplan, 1978, p. 121). It is the first glimmering of self-identity.

Toward the end of the first year, as the infant learns to move about by creeping and finally by her first unsteady steps, an interesting pattern of interaction with the caregiver often emerges. The youngster uses the caregiver as a base from which to explore her environment. She moves out a bit and comes back, moves farther and returns, moves out again, and this time may only look back, making the eye contact that will give her the reassurance to continue exploring. Child-care providers may also notice this same pattern of touching or eye contact between child and parent during the initial school entrance period (Gottschall, 1989, p. 14).

During the last half of the child's first year (or sometimes before), "separation anxiety" also emerges: that is, the infant sets up a strong protest of crying or clinging if the caregiver attempts to leave. This pattern of distress is also exhibited when a stranger appears, making it obvious that the baby recognizes the difference between the caregiver and others.

Thus self-identity develops as the toddler ventures out and scurries back, clings and pushes away, holds on and lets go. But the stronger the initial attachment, the more secure the developing child should feel each time he or she lets go.

The young human learns who he is by the way other people respond to him (how others seem to be affected by his behavior). Hopefully, this response is mainly positive, so that by the time he enters preschool, a child-care center, or Head Start, he already will be feeling good about himself. Table 3–1 summarizes the child's attachment/separation milestones.

Attachment

Preattachment
Birth through first 8–12 weeks
> Responds to people but cannot distinguish one from the other; does not recognize self as separate from primary caregiver

Person permanence
First months
> Learns to distinguish primary caregiver from others

Attachment to caregiver
First months to second or third year
> Seeks proximity to caregiver; shows separation anxiety when caregiver leaves; shows stranger anxiety when stranger appears—most common at seven months

Partnership
Second or third year on
> Comes to understand caregiver's point of view and adjusts own behavior accordingly

---

Separation

Physical separation from mother
Birth

Psychological birth
First six months
> Recognizes self as separate from mother

Exploration of physical environment
Last months of first year to second, third years
> Explores first by creeping, then walking; uses caregiver as base to explore and return

Strengthening of self-identity
Second or third year on
> Gains stronger recognition of self-identity, as child and parent let go of one another for more frequent and longer periods of time

---

Table 3–1   Attachment/separation milestones

Note: This table includes information from Damon (1983).

School Separation

No matter how good the young child feels about herself, the initial school separation from a parent is often difficult. At three years old, the sense of self is still a bit shaky. Although the child has an identity at home, at school the child is in a strange environment. To complicate matters, the parent/caregiver may be experiencing the same "separation anxiety," and the child often senses this.

Each child handles the situation in his or her own way. One child may be used to the home of a loving babysitter, and will take this new "playroom" in stride. Another may cling to her mother and scream whenever the mother attempts to leave. The child used to playing with others may quickly join the group in the block building center. A shyer child may need the teacher's urging to join in. One fussing, crying child may stop as soon as his mother leaves. Another may withdraw into herself and sit in a corner sucking her thumb.

You as a classroom worker hope that children will become adjusted to this separation within a few days or a week or so. Most of them will. One or two may not. How can you help them develop a strong enough sense of self that they also feel free to let go of their primary caregiver?

If You Have Not Checked This Item: Some Helpful Ideas

One or more of the children in your center may have unchecked self-identity checklist items. Because you are aware that each item represents a step in the developmental progression of young children, you may be able to lend children support at the outset by arranging your schedule or setting up your classroom ahead of time to address their problems. Here are some ideas that may help preschoolers separate from their parents with less difficulty.

■ Make Early Initial Contact with Parent/Caregiver and Child

If the child and the parent have met you ahead of time, they may feel less reluctant to separate on the day that school begins. For the child, it is better if this meeting takes place close to the time of school opening rather than the spring before. Memories of a brief visit several months before school begins have little meaning for the young child. An immediate follow-up is more effective. If you visit the child's home, take a camera with you to record the occasion for later use in the classroom to help the child make an easier transition from home to school.

■ Try Staggered Enrollment

Rather than having all of the children in your class begin school on the same day at the same time, you might consider having half of them begin on the first day, and half the second—or half in the morning and the rest in the afternoon. This will allow staff members to devote more time to the individual children and their parents. In addition, the first day may not be so overwhelming for the children if only half of the class is present at once.

■ Create a Simple Initial Environment

The more complex the classroom environment, the more overwhelming it is for certain children. You might plan to have the classroom arranged with fewer activity areas for the first weeks, and less material on the shelves. As the children settle in and become more secure, you can add activities and materials as needed.

■ Use Transition Materials

Children can make the transition from home to school and separate more easily from their parents if familiar materials help bridge the gap. Water is one such material. A water table or basin with an egg beater, funnel, and squeeze bottles may take a child's mind off his parent long enough to get him happily involved in the center. Toy trucks and dolls often have the same effect. Have a special set of little toys you can allow children to take home with them at the end of the day and return again in the morning to make the transition less difficult.

■ Utilize Parent/Caregiver Visits

Allow the parents to stay as long as necessary on the first days, or come in for visits from time to time. The shy child may use her parent as a base for exploration in the classroom, venturing away from the parent and returning just as she did as a toddler at home. If the separation is a difficult one, have the caregiver return early to pick up the youngster. Little by little the children should be able to stay longer without their parents.

■ Show and Foster Acceptance of the Child

Up until now the child's self-identity has evolved from the reactions of his family to him. Now that he is in your classroom, you and your coworkers and the other children will be adding details to the child's interior picture of himself. These details need to be positive, happy ones. You need to support this process first by accepting the child and his family unconditionally. Show your acceptance both verbally and non-verbally. Smile at him frequently. Greet him personally *every* day, telling him how glad you are to see him. Say goodbye to him at the end of *every* day, telling him "See you tomorrow, don't forget!" Demonstrate that you enjoy being near him and having him near you. You are the behavior model for the other children as well. If they see that you accept a child no matter what, they will be more likely to do the same.

■ Read a Book

Children like to hear stories about other children who have feelings the same as they do. Try reading a book about separation to children having difficulty in this area. If the main character of the story is a child from a different culture, all the better. Children learn to accept one another when they see picture books featuring various cultural and ethnic characters. In the book *Will You Come Back for Me?* by Ann Tompert (Morton Grove, IL: Whitman, 1988), Suki is a four-year-old Asian-American girl who has to go to a child-care center while her mother works. Her sensitive mother takes her for a preliminary visit where she meets the teacher, watches the children play, and is invited (but refuses) to join in for a snack. Later Suki tells her mother about the dream she has about taking her teddy bear to school and how the bear cried. The mother helps her overcome her fear of being abandoned by making a red paper heart that Suki takes with her.

Talk to the children about the story and ask them how they felt when they first came to the class. You don't have to point out that Suki is an Asian child. Children see pictures in books and identify with the characters no matter who they are. If there are no characters who look like them, that also plays a subtle role. As Wardle (1995) notes:

> . . . Much of a child's personal identity is determined by the way the environment responds to the characteristics the child has, based on his group belonging (gender, race, family lifestyle, religion). For example, if a program does not support a child's home language, that will impact self-image. If a child does not see pictures, books, and people in his program that look like him, that too will affect his self-image. (p. 45)

DOES NOT CLING TO CLASSROOM STAFF EXCESSIVELY

The next developmental step for the children in your classroom is to build up enough confidence to become involved on their own with the other children and the activities available. Those with a strong sense of self may have no difficulty. Others may not be ready during the first days or weeks. A few may not be ready at all.

Psychologists use the term **significant others** in referring to the people who have the most important influence on our lives (Seagull & Kallen, 1987, p. 13). For the young child this usually means his immediate family. Once he enters your classroom, however, you and your coworkers also become significant others. This means that your reactions toward the child will affect what she thinks about herself. They may reinforce the view of self learned at home, or they may modify that view. Generally positive responses to her will strengthen her feelings about herself as a good person. The opposite, of course, is also true.

The development of a self-identity is thus a subtle but lengthy process. No one knows for sure how long it takes, although it is probably much of a person's life. The early childhood years are the most crucial because they set the course. That is why it is so important for the young self in its most sensitive formative period to receive positive responses from adults.

Many children develop an attachment to one or more of the adults in the early childhood classroom similar to the one they have with their primary caregiver at home. The child needs a consistent caregiver here as well to develop trust in this new environment. It is thus important that the staff of an early childhood center be present consistently throughout the year—not merely dropping in and dropping out.

If the teacher must leave, she should try to have the replacement teacher visit the classroom several times before she departs to allow the children to get to know the replacement. The transition will thus be more gradual and less upsetting for the children. Otherwise, for certain children, changing teachers will be nearly as traumatic as changing primary caregivers.

The child who looks to the teacher as a caregiver may cling to the classroom adult. He or she may not have the necessary trust in the world, or may not have developed a strong enough sense of self yet to let go in a strange new environment. In particular, three-year-olds may relate more comfortably to adults than to other children. After all, much of their life thus far may have been spent in a one-to-one relationship with an adult. A classroom of 15–20 children may be totally overwhelming. How can you help such a child?

If You Have Not Checked This Item: Some Helpful Ideas

■ Display Acceptance

You must accept the child's clinging behavior, knowing that it is a normal step in the developmental progression. But you also need to know ways to encourage and support a child when he is ready to move out. If he feels that you accept his presence near you and will not force him to do something he is not ready to do, then he is much more likely to move out on his own. Forcing a clinging child away from you before he is ready to go may only make him cling more tightly.

■ Have Child Follow Adult's Lead

The child who clings to or "shadows" an adult may follow the adult's lead as well. You could lead her to a table and sit down with her to make a puzzle. If she becomes involved with it on her own, you might try moving on to another group of children. Or you could try playing a role in the dramatic play area and inviting the child to accompany you on some pretend errand or help you accomplish some pretend task. If the child accepts your efforts to involve her, you can freely leave the activity. If she does not, she may not be ready yet to move out on her own.

■ Observe the Child

You may be able to tell when the time is right by your observations of this child. Does he spend a great deal of time watching the others? Is this looking behavior done from the "protection" of your side or does he stand in a "safe" spot and watch? If his eyes seem to be more engaged in following the activities of the others rather than keeping track of you, it may be time to help him become involved with them.

■ Ask the Child to Help an Adult or Another Child

The clinging child will sometimes allow herself to become involved in classroom activities as the adult's helper. Ask her to help you get out the paints or the puzzles . . . to dress a doll in the housekeeping area . . . to feed the guinea pig . . . to deliver a message next door. Little by little, she may venture away from you and then return just as she did with her primary caregiver at home. Or you might ask a second child to join you as a helper. The two of them could then do the same tasks, at which point you could try leaving them on their own.

■ Follow Up on the Child's Interests

One of the most successful techniques for involving the clinging child in classroom activities is to discover what interests him. Your conversations with him may give you a clue. If he is nonverbal, your observations of the things that attract his attention may suggest an activity he could pursue by himself and then later with another child when he feels enough at ease. You might leaf through a magazine with him and ask him to point out pictures of things he likes. He or you could cut these out and he might paste them in a scrapbook to get him started. Or you could use the information you gain about his interests to involve him more directly with similar classroom activities.

If none of these ideas work you should continue to be patient about his clinging. Do not push. When he feels secure enough in the classroom he will venture out on his own. The child who never feels secure enough is probably still not mature enough to handle a classroom situation. If he still continues to cling after several weeks in your program, you may want to discuss with the parent the possibility of keeping him at home for another year, or placing him in a home-type program with fewer children.

MAKES EYE CONTACT WITH ADULTS

Nonverbal cues are among the most important signals people send out about their feelings. Facial expressions, head position, muscle tension, body carriage all reveal a person's state of mind regarding himself and those around him. All of us read these expressions subconsciously. Our subconscious minds process this intake and help our conscious minds make decisions about the people we interact with. We feel that they are friendly, hostile, frightened, or unsure as a result of this constant subconscious processing of visual stimuli.

As teachers of young children, we need to read such nonverbal cues consciously as well because of the important information they can give us about young children. In addition, we need to be aware of how important such information is to young children. Because they are not fully verbal at three, four, and five, young children depend heavily on nonverbal cues from us to make determinations about the people and situations they encounter.

We can say polite words to children and their parents, but if our face is tense and our eyes give out signals of distaste, the child picks up and responds to these. That is why we say children instinctively know which adults to trust. Children read nonverbal signals exceptionally well, partly because children are nonverbal themselves and partly because they are more visually oriented than most adults.

Eye signals are the most important. Eyes give messages of affection, love, happiness, contentment, and humor. They show pain, frustration, anger, fright, and despair. The way the eyes are partly or wholly open, the position of the eyebrows, the size of the pupils, the number of blinks, the length of a stare—all indicate the feelings of a person. Words may not always tell the truth, but eyes do.

Earlier studies assumed that the size of the pupils remained constant if the level of light remained the same. Subsequent research has disproved this notion. What research discovered instead was that the pupils increase in size in the presence of pleasant things and become noticeably smaller if people and situations are disagreeable. Eyes also respond to more than visual cues. Laboratory tests have shown that eye pupils change size in response to voices. Loud, harsh, or scolding voices may cause them to shrink. The size of the pupils is in fact a reliable indicator of a person's feelings (Thompson, 1973, p. 90).

Eye contact between people is important. The first encounter with someone's eyes reveals much about the person's feelings concerning himself. Subsequent contact often tells a great deal about how that person feels toward you. The first actual eye contact itself is a recognition that you exist in a person's world and that person exists in yours. If he feels uncomfortable about himself or you, he often shifts his gaze.

Preschool children are at an egocentric stage in their development when they enter your classroom. They see things mostly from their own points of view. If you asked one to hide so that you would not be able to see her, she might very well cover her own eyes. From her self-centered point of view she believes that you cannot see her because she cannot see you. Children who are initially tense or frightened or uneasy in your presence may use this same subterfuge by refusing to make eye contact: If they do not look at you, surely you will not be able to see them; or if they do not look at you, maybe you won't really be there.

Certain cultures and ethnic groups also condition children not to look adults directly in the eye, considering that disrespectful. You need to decide whether your children avoid eye contact because of cultural conditioning or because they are truly uncomfortable with themselves or you. Eventually you will need to have eye contact with all of your children for them to recognize the freedom and openness of this new environment—to understand that they are worthy human beings in your sight.

When eye contact finally occurs, it often diffuses tense situations. If you can succeed in getting the shy or frightened child to make eye contact with you, you may be able to dispel his fears without saying a word. He or she will see in your eyes the friendliness, sense of humor, and enjoyment he can expect from your presence. But you need to know that your eyes won't fake it. You must truly project to this young developing child that you like him already, no matter what—because you really do.

Research also shows that the more a person likes someone, the more he looks at him (Thompson, 1973, p. 91). This applies to teachers as well as children. It is therefore important that you neither pick favorites nor reject any of your children, because their sensitivity to nonverbal cues will soon tell them this is the case. You will be looking more frequently at the children you like than at the children you do not like. As a professional, you cannot afford to pick favorites or dislike a child. Of course it is human to like one person more than another. But this is not permissible in dealing with children professionally. You must make a concerted effort to correct your feelings if you find yourself responding like this.

If You Have Not Checked This Item: Some Helpful Ideas

■ Accept the Child

Many of the same ideas used to help the child who was not checked for the first two items also apply here. This child either is not sure of himself or has not developed basic trust in the people and world around him. Or she may have a disability of some sort. Autistic children seem to avoid eye contact. Some mentally impaired children have difficulty making eye contact with people outside their family.

To help any child develop a self-identity strong enough to make eye contact with strange adults, you, as the strange adult, must show you accept the child unconditionally. Use both verbal and nonverbal cues. Tell him or her how nice it is to have her in your center. Use his name frequently. Exclaim with delight when he accomplishes something, no matter how insignificant.

■ Make Eye Contact Yourself

You are the model for behavior in your classroom. If you feel it is important for your children to behave in a certain way, then you need to take the lead yourself. Get down at the child's eye level and smile at her. Make eye contact with the shy child at all times. When she finally has the confidence to return the look, she needs to see you smiling at her.

■ Have Patience

Do not force the issue. You must remember that the child's avoidance of eye contact is not a negative action but a clue to you that he may still not be confident enough in your presence to return the look. You need to do all in your power to help him develop that confidence. But sometimes the best thing to do is nothing. Have patience. Forcing the issue will not help. You must have the confidence to know that his refusal to meet your eyes is nothing personal. When he finally feels at ease within himself and within your center, he will return your look.

■ Read a Book

All the children will enjoy the book *What Is Beautiful?* by Maryjean Watson Avery and David M. Avery (Berkeley, CA: Tricyle Press, 1995). But it is especially important to read it personally to the child who has not made eye contact. This simple, colorful story is a cumulative tale starting with Maryjean and what she thinks is beautiful about another person. Then that person replies, telling what he thinks is beautiful about the next person, and so on. Each page has a differently colored background with bright painted words on the left side and a closeup picture of the face of the person on the right. The people are multicultural children, parents, and grandparents. They tell about ears, hair, beard, smile, eyes, hands, nose, mouth, and dimple being beautiful. The last page contains a shiny silver mirror and the question: "What's beautiful about you?" Have the listener look in the mirror and tell you the answer.

All children at one time or another avoid looking at a caregiver. They may be embarrassed or ashamed or feeling foolish about something they have done. But if they can see by the look in your eyes when they finally confront it that you still accept them, then they will be able to return your look with confidence as they continue on their own unique path of development.

MAKES ACTIVITY CHOICES WITHOUT TEACHER'S HELP

One of the next observable indicators of a child's feelings about herself in your classroom is her willingness to choose on her own the activity she wants to engage in. Once she feels confident enough to leave your side, she needs to explore the new environment and try out the various materials and activities on her own. Many children have a strong enough sense of self to go immediately to the activity areas upon first entering the room. Others use the adult who accompanies them as a base for their explorations, going into an area and coming back to the person, much as they did during their initial separation from their primary caregiver when they were infants. Some also use the teacher as this base.

Research seems to imply that having a secure base of attachment facilitates exploratory behavior on the part of two-year-olds in center-based day care (Fein & Schwartz, 1982, p. 88). Three-, four- and five-year-olds also do better when they have this strong attachment. These attachment findings seems to indicate that, just as within the family, the child who is secure in his relationship with a caregiver will also be secure on his own. Thus, as previously mentioned, it is important to help a child build this relationship initially. It is also important to observe which children are able

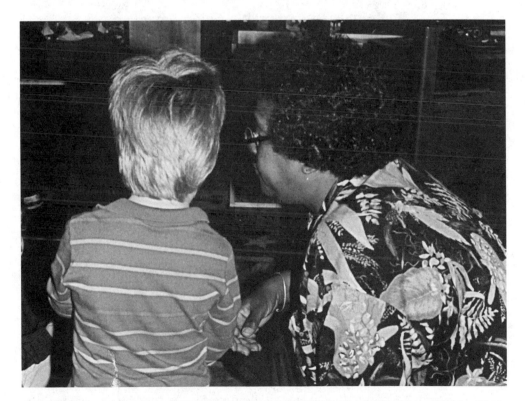

One of the important observable indicators of a new child's feelings about himself is his willingness to leave the teacher's side and become involved in an activity.

to become involved with activities independently—and which are not quite ready, possibly because their sense of self-identity is not yet strong enough.

Your goal for children who do not participate independently in activities will be to help them develop a sense of security with you and within the center. Once they develop this feeling of security, they may take the next step toward self-identity: becoming involved in center activities on their own.

You may need to help the clinging child get started, as mentioned previously. But then you should withdraw. Children need to have every opportunity to express their self-identities on their own. They need to explore the center environment. They need to learn to make their own choices.

It is so tempting for teachers to help children make decisions, and the children to listen. They will even ask for help. They are used to having adults tell them what to do. You must resist the temptation. Invite them to look for themselves, then support them in their exploration. It is so much simpler for you to make up their minds for them, you may argue. But then they will have lost the opportunity to take the next step in their development as a person. Give them this chance.

If You Have Not Checked This Item: Some Helpful Ideas

■ Provide an Explorable Environment

For younger children, your environment needs to be simple with fewer activity areas and a small number of items within each. This applies especially to two- and three-year-olds. Some environments are just too complex for these children to be comfortable. Too many things are going on, and the children respond by refusing to explore or get involved. For this age group you need to simplify your physical environment— at least at the beginning of the year. Later the children will be ready for additional activities.

On the other hand, four- and five-year-olds need the stimulation of complexity, novelty, and variation. This age group tends to be less fearful of new things and more adventurous. A more complex physical environment may encourage rather than discourage their exploration.

■ Give Children Time

Once children feel secure with you and your center, they should be able to make activity choices on their own if you will give them enough time. Let them wander around at first during the free choice period. Don't force them into an activity before they are ready to go. Some children need more time than others. Others need to try out many things before they can settle on one.

■ Act as a Base for Children's Explorations

Sit or stand in an area of the room where children can see you, near but not in any one activity area. Those who still need the security of an adult attachment can make eye contact, receive your smiles of support, and even come over for a moment or so before you encourage them to go off on their own again. The child who is still clinging can explore with her eyes. When she feels secure enough she will join the others, knowing you are nearby.

■ Read a Book

Hearing a book read about a preschool classroom and all of the interesting activities it contains may motivate the insecure child to look around her own classroom and be more willing to make activity choices on her own. *This Is the Way* by Anne Dalton (New York: Scholastic, 1992) shows a family with three children climbing out of bed, getting ready, and finally skipping to preschool where they participate in all the interesting activities in rhyming verses based on the nursery rhyme "Here We Go 'Round the Mulberry Bush." The children are Caucasian but their classmates are a wonderful cultural mix as they work at tables, eat their lunch, play on the playground, and paint their pictures "in a warm and cozy classroom."

SEEKS OTHER CHILDREN TO PLAY WITH

Although this particular item seems to relate more to the child's social rather than emotional development, it actually indicates both. Seeking other children to play with is a part of the progression of the developing self as well as a step on the sequence of socialization.

As the preschool child moves away from the parent to stay by himself in the early childhood classroom, and then, as he moves away from the teacher to make activity choices on his own, his next step in the development of his self-identity should involve joining the other children in play. Yet he often does not join the others, at least not right away. Depending on his previous experience with peers—or lack of it—he may prefer to play on his own at first. In other words, other children do not replace a child's primary or secondary caregivers as objects of attachment. When children finally do seek other children to play with, it is indeed an indication of a stronger self-identity developing.

Children seem to recognize that other children are like themselves; that is, they, too, depend on adult caregivers. From their self-centered perspectives, children may see peers as competitors for the attention of the caregivers as well as for the use of materials and activities.

Through socialization, they will find ways to get along with other children, as well as to share and take turns with materials—and even people—in your center. Through development of their self-identity, children will eventually be seeking contact with others like themselves.

Even as infants and toddlers, children recognize one another and may engage in social behavior. But this contact is not at the same level, type, or intensity as their interactions with adults. Infants' and toddlers' striving for attachment does not involve another child. While infants may look at, imitate, and even vocalize with peers, these interactions are few and far between and are not sustained for long periods. With adults, on the other hand, and especially with their mothers, infants' interactions involve touching, holding, and hugging during more instances, for longer periods, and at a more intense emotional level than anything they do with peers. The most frequent initial contact between two infants, in fact, takes place around toys rather than with one another (Damon, 1983, p. 59).

By the time the young child has entered your class, he or she in most instances has had a number of contacts with peers. Again the interactions are not the same as with adults. Children look to the adult as their base of attachment. They look to their peers as a reflection of themselves. Those children with a strong sense of self will have less difficulty interacting with the other children in your center from the outset. They are indicating by this behavior how far along they are in the development of their self-identities.

Those who need help developing this sense of security within themselves may not seek other children to play with at first. As with the other areas of self-identity, you may need to help the children progress. Don't expect success to occur overnight in this particular area. Some children are just not ready for many days or even weeks to make contact with peers. By looking at and treating each child in your center as an individual, you will begin to elicit clues about each that can help you support their development in this crucial area. As before, you will need to use acceptance and patience whenever a child is slow in moving ahead.

If You Have Not Checked This Item: Some Helpful Ideas

■ Find a Friend

For many young children who are used to dealing with a limited number of people at a time, a roomful of lively peers is overwhelming. You may need to help find a friend for the shy child who may be able to relate on a one-to-one basis with one other child before she can cope with a group. Choose someone who gets along with others and ask the two to do an errand for you—perhaps mix paints or playdough, wash the doll clothes, or get out the cots for nap time. Or you might ask the "friend" to show the shy child how to use the saw or how to record her voice on the tape recorder. Make the activities as personal as possible to attract the shy child's interest and get her to focus on the activity or material instead of on her unsure feelings about herself. Once she successfully relates to one other child, she may begin to seek others to play with on her own.

■ Use Small Groups

Young children are better able to relate to peers when in small groups. You can arrange the physical environment of your classroom so that each of the activity areas accommodates only a certain number of children (say, no more than four). Methods to accomplish this include placing four chairs around a table; using masking tape on the floor to divide the block center into four building areas; providing only four aprons for water play, two saws or hammers for woodworking, three pillows in the book area, and so forth. When you read, read to two to four children rather than the total group.

■ Use a Material or Activity for Two or Three Together

This idea is more often used in European programs to teach children to share, but you might also design or designate a certain material or activity in your classroom as always for use by two or three children together. The use of a saw, for instance, can be set up for three: two to hold the wood and one to saw. You might attach one of your wagons to a trike so that one child must pedal while one rides. Your job chart of daily chores could require that pairs or teams work together to do the jobs. Can you think of other team enterprises?

■ Read a Book

In *Building a Bridge* by Lisa Shook Begaye (Flagstaff, AZ: Northland Publishing, 1993), two little girls experience their first day of school on the Navajo reservation with excitement but also with butterflies in their stomachs. Anna, a Caucasian girl, meets Juanita, a Navajo girl, when their teacher asks Juanita to see if Anna wants to play with a box of purple and green blocks because they're "magical." At first Anna decides to build a bridge with the green blocks and Juanita does the same with the purple ones. But soon the two girls are putting their blocks together to build a huge bridge because it doesn't matter if the blocks are different colors. Differences are magical.

PLAYS ROLES CONFIDENTLY IN DRAMATIC PLAY

Once the young child has begun playing with others in your center, you need to be cognizant of another indicator of his developing self-identity. Is he able to take on and play a role in the pretend situations that abound in early childhood programs? Can he pretend to be father or brother or baby in the housekeeping center? Is she a nurse or doctor or famous skater in the dress-up area? Can he be a race car driver, helicopter pilot, or crane operator on the playground? When a child can play a pretend role with confidence in your center, then he is presenting observable proof that his self-identity has taken on an even more mature aspect.

To play a pretend role, children need to be able to see things from a different point of view than their own. Their perspective, in other words, cannot be egocentric. We mentioned how young children cover their eyes and think you cannot see them because they cannot see you. That view is, of course, highly egocentric. At some point in time, however, three- and four-year-olds seem to be able to step out of themselves and pretend quite realistically to be someone else.

It is not clear whether this ability is stronger or appears sooner in some children because of opportunity, encouragement, and practice at home, or whether certain children are instinctively or temperamentally more imaginative. No matter what causes the behavior, it indicates to the observer of children that a child has reached a milestone in her development of self-identity.

A child's ability to play a role other than her own says a number of things to the observer, including:

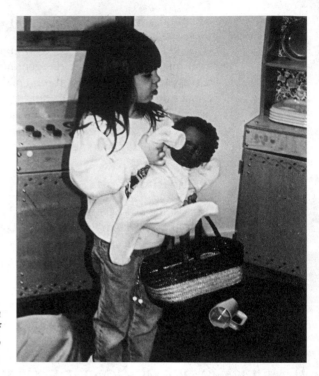

Another observable indicator of a child's good feelings about herself is her playing of roles confidently in dramatic play.

1. The child can distinguish reality from fantasy (i.e., she knows she is pretending).
2. The child is able to symbolize things (i.e., represent a real person or event in a make-believe manner).
3. The child can see things from another person's perspective.
4. The child has a strong enough sense of self to step out of herself and be someone else.

Until all four of these statements are true for the young child, she is really unable to play make-believe roles.

Once she can perform this behavior, then she is able to explore in a wholly new way. She can try out roles. She can see what it's like to be the mother, the older sister, the baby. She can dominate the situation. She can make her "father" or "brother" do what she wants them to. This ability is a heady discovery. Of course in a group situation she herself is often dominated or at least controlled to some extent by the others, and must remain in an assigned or assumed role. If she plays the role "wrong," then she will be reprimanded by those often strict conformists, her peers.

Adults in the early childhood classroom may wonder aloud: "Is this what we want our children to do? Isn't it wrong to encourage fantasizing like this?" Not at all, say child development specialists. This is a natural progression in the young child's development. This "fantasizing" is the way young children explore concepts about people and events in the world around them. While adults look askance at the "Walter Mitty-type" who seems to live in a world of make-believe, it is not only natural but imperative that our children have the opportunity to use their imaginations playfully in exploring their own world (see Chapter 14, "Imagination").

Besides, this playful use of the imagination is the next step developmentally for the young child in creating a strong self-identity. He started as a new human being so attached to his mother that he thought she was a part of him. Then he made the separation in which he not only recognized he was separate, but also realized he could move out from her. Next, he developed enough confidence to come to a new environment and allow other adults to be his caregivers. From these adults he moved out to explore his new environment and interact with his peers. Now he has developed a strong enough sense of himself that he can try out being someone else.

A great deal of power surrounds gaining control over people and situations, even imaginary ones. Up until now, the young child has been virtually powerless in a world controlled by adults. But when she plays a role in dramatic play, she is able to take a stand, be what she wants to be, and make things come out the way she wants them. Her self-identity is thus strengthened as she expands her horizons, gains control over ideas and feelings, and receives immediate feedback from the other players as to how her role affects them.

Also, in playing such pretend roles, the player gets to find out more about himself. The other children's reactions to his role and his own reactions to it help him realize his capabilities and understand his limits. He can explore gender roles more fully—what it's like to be male or female.

Children in our society are treated differently from the moment of birth, it seems, depending on their gender. Now the young pretender can try out being the mother, father, sister, or brother in the family. Because children often play these familiar family roles in a very stereotyped, exaggerated manner—their own interpretation of the way real family members act—the players soon learn which roles are considered the "best" and how the others feel about mothers and fathers, boys and girls.

For a child who did not participate in dramatic play upon first entering your program, now doing so signifies a major step. It means she not only has a strong enough sense of self to try being someone else, but she also now has this unparalleled opportunity to practice her budding interpersonal and communication skills, thus strengthening her self-identity in a manner that was impossible before. Again a paradox exists: once she is able to be someone else, she becomes more of herself. As Davidson notes:

> Although pretend play may look insignificant to the casual observer, there is enormous learning occurring—learning that can be expanded when the adult provides appropriate props, space, time, and guidance. (Davidson, 1996, p. 9)

If You Have Not Checked This Item: Some Helpful Ideas

■ Provide Dramatic Play Materials

Have at least one area of your classroom set up for dramatic play. This section can be a family area with child-size table, chairs, refrigerator, stove, and sink; a bedroom area with doll beds, dresser and mirror, and chest of drawers; a store with shelves of empty food containers and a toy cash register; or any other such setting. If you take your class on a field trip, you should consider setting up a similar pretend area in your room for them to try out the roles they saw enacted on the trip: a doctor's office, a clinic, a laundromat, a barber or beauty shop.

In addition to life-size settings and props, you need miniature toys to encourage role-playing as well. Little cars, trucks, people, animals, boats, and planes can be placed strategically in the block corner, at the water table, and with the table blocks. A box full of dramatic play props can be taken out on the playground. Pictures of people in a variety of roles—from family members to community helpers—can be hung at children's eye level around the room to encourage the exploration of roles. Ask the children what kinds of roles they would like to try out and have them help you assemble the props.

■ Allow Time to Pretend

Because the best dramatic play is spontaneous—even though you may have provided the props—you need to set aside a particular time during the day for free choice activities to occur. Often these activities are scheduled at the beginning of the day, but they can take place any time. Allow enough time for children to become involved in their roles. The length may vary from day to day depending upon the children's interests and yours, but free choice activities should be scheduled to occur at the same time every day so that the children can depend upon a set period for pretending and playing roles.

■ Play a Role Yourself

Sometimes the only way to help the nonparticipant become involved is to play a role yourself. Obviously, if a child is not ready emotionally, your efforts may be wasted. But some children who are ready to play a role may not know how to get started. In that case, you might pretend to be a mother and invite the child to go on a pretend errand with you, ending up in the dramatic play area where the other children are often delighted to see the teacher playing like they are. If the child accepts your lead and becomes involved with the others, you can gradually withdraw.

■ Be an Observer of Pretend Play

It will help you immensely in your understanding of children if you take time out to observe and record the various children's engagement in pretend play. Station yourself unobtrusively in an area of the room where a particular child is playing and jot down as many details as possible in a running record. Do this for several days if possible. Some of the things to look for can include:

1. theme of the play
2. role the child is playing
3. who else is playing and what their roles are

4. type of interaction with other children
5. dialog
6. length of time the child sustains the role

What can you conclude about the child from your observations? Have you learned anything that can help you plan your program differently so that other children will become more easily involved in dramatic play? Could you add props or suggestions to help the children sustain their play? Chapter 13, "Imagination," has additional suggestions.

■ Read a Book

African American Grace, the main character from the book *Amazing Grace* by Mary Hoffman (New York: Dial, 1991), has become a favorite storybook character almost overnight with her vivid imagination and love of pretending. Every page shows a large, vibrant picture of Grace dressed up to be Anansi the Spider, or Aladdin, or a pirate, or a doctor. To help your children get in on Grace's act, many bookstores carry a realistic cloth Grace doll to accompany the book. Be sure to have some dress-up doll clothes handy so your children can create their own pretend characters with Grace.

STANDS UP FOR OWN RIGHTS

For preschool children to stand up for their rights within the classroom, they need to have developed a strong enough self-identity to believe in themselves as individuals with a point of view worth other people's consideration. Thus far in their development of a self-identity they have been able to make the separation from their parents, not cling to the adult caregiver, make eye-contact with classroom adults, choose activities on their own, seek other children to play with, and try out play roles confidently in dramatic play because they could see things from another person's point of view. Now the children are progressing further by developing their own points of view worthy of other children's consideration.

What are some of the classroom rights such a self-confident child might insist on? One is the right of possession. If a child is playing with a piece of equipment, he should be able to continue using it unless some previous turn-taking rule is in effect. Many childhood squabbles take place over objects, often because of children's egocentric perspectives. A child believes he should have a toy because he wants it. The fact that another child is playing with it does not count in his mind. The development of mutual respect is difficult among three- and four-year-olds because many of them lack the ability to understand the other's perspective. The child who feels his right is worth defending will often refuse to give in.

A child's choice of participation is another personal right often established in early childhood classrooms. If a child opts to join or not join a particular activity, you and the other children need to honor her choice. Use enticements rather than force if you feel the child should be involved when she chooses not to be.

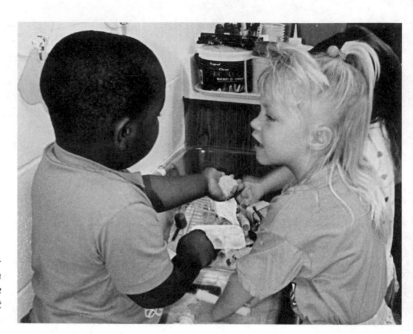

When you observe children standing up for their own rights in an interpersonal situation, you realize they are feeling positive about themselves as worthy persons.

Completing independent projects her own way is a right that self-confident children will defend. If a child is doing a painting, modeling clay, constructing a building, or dressing a doll on her own, she should be able to do it as she sees fit so long as she is not interfering with others. Similarly, others should not be allowed to interfere with her. The child with the strong self-identity will continue in her own manner disregarding or rejecting the attempts of others to impose their will.

Protecting property is another right that self-confident children will insist on. Toys or games they have brought from home are often the focus of conflict. You need to provide a private space like a cubby for each child to store his possessions. Block buildings are also important to the children who have built them. The child who insists on saving his building may want help in making a sign informing others: "Please Leave Jeffrey's Building Standing."

Children may stand up for their own rights in a number of ways. They may physically prevent another child from doing something or making them do something. They may verbalize their position with the child. They may tell the teacher. Some of their actions may not even be acceptable in a classroom full of children. Use of power or aggression is not appropriate. You need to help such children find more acceptable means for making their point.

As you observe your children on this particular item, look to see which ones do not allow another child to urge or force unwanted changes on them, and which ones do not back down, or give up a toy or a turn. At the same time, take note of children who always give up or give in to the demands of another. They also need your support in the strengthening of their self-confidence.

If You Have Not Checked This Item: Some Helpful Ideas

■ Model Behavior

You need to model the behavior you want your children to follow. Stand firm on your decisions. Let your children know why. If you are "wishy-washy" or inconsistent in your treatment of them, they may have trouble standing firm themselves.

■ Allow Children Choices

One way to help a child learn that his rights can count is to give her a chance to make choices that are important to her. Let her choose a favorite activity to participate in or a toy to take home, rather than forcing your choice on her.

■ Stand Up for the Child

When it is clear to you that a child's rights have been infringed upon by another child, you should take a stand yourself supporting the child, and at the same time letting the others know "why Karen can finish her painting now and Bobby can't," for example.

■ Read a Book

In *Bet You Can't* by Penny Dale (New York: Lippincott, 1987), a big sister and little brother have a clash of wills in a simple story of two African American children struggling with bedtime pickup of toys in their room. They each stand up for themselves and are able to complete the pickup at last in a fun way.

DISPLAYS ENTHUSIASM ABOUT DOING THINGS FOR SELF

The lifelong quest to develop an identity is, in the final analysis, a struggle for autonomy. If young children are successful in this quest, then they will be able and willing to behave independently in many ways. Louise J. Kaplan (1978) describes the importance of the struggle:

> In the first three years of life every human being undergoes yet a second birth, in which he is born as a psychological being possessing selfhood and separate identity. The quality of self an infant achieves in those crucial three years will profoundly affect all of his subsequent existence. (p. 15)

Your observations in the area of self-identity will help you determine which children in your class are well on the road to developing strong self-identities and which ones are not. The most successful children will be those who can and want to do things for themselves. They will have achieved enough self-assurance about their own abilities to be able to try and eventually succeed in doing things on their own. Achieving this competence will then allow them a measure of independence from the adults around them.

What are some of the activities you may observe such children performing independently in your classroom? Here is a partial list:

dressing and undressing	painting with brush
tying or fastening shoes	mixing paints
using own cubby	getting out toys
toileting	putting toys away
washing hands and face	returning blocks to shelves
brushing teeth	dressing dolls
setting table for eating	handling hammer, saw
pouring drink	cutting with scissors
dishing out food	cutting with knife
handling eating implements	mixing dough
eating	using climbing equipment
cleaning up after eating	making puzzles
using computer	using tape recorder

The adeptness of three- and four-year-old children in these various activities depends on their own sense of self, the practice they have had at home or elsewhere, and on the encouragement or discouragement the adults around them have offered. This author has noticed that children from low-income families are often more adept at accomplishing many of the self-help skills than children from middle- and upper-income families. We might infer that children in low-income families have had to do many self-help activities on their own and thus become more skilled sooner than their middle- and upper-income counterparts.

Similarly, children who have always had things done for them by the adults around them often give up the struggle for autonomy. You and your coworkers need to beware of the temptation to "help" the little children in your care more than necessary. Children can do many more things for themselves than we realize. You need to allow time for children to learn to zip up jackets and pour their own drinks. Otherwise you are denying them an unparalleled opportunity to develop their own independence.

The way adults behave toward children during these formative years can indeed make a difference in children's feelings about themselves and thus in the way they behave. Research regarding gender stereotyping has found that mothers and fathers treat their young daughters differently from their sons when it comes to independent behavior. Parents often allow and encourage boys to behave independently earlier than girls in such areas as using scissors without adult supervision, crossing the street alone, playing away from home, and riding the bus. When girls ask for help they often get it, but boys more often receive a response telling them to do it themselves. Boys are encouraged to manipulate objects and explore their environments, while girls are more often discouraged. Thus it seems that parents value independence in boys more than in girls.

This type of discriminating behavior may of course result in girls feeling less capable than boys, and therefore attempting fewer things on their own. Or this behavior may cause girls—and therefore women—to become dependent on men and less willing to risk using their own capabilities.

You and your coworkers need to take special care that stereotyped attitudes about the roles of men and women do not color your behavior toward the boys and girls in your center. As in all areas of development, your goal should be to help each child become all he or she is capable of being. When each shows enthusiasm about doing things independently, then you know they are well on their way to developing a strong sense of self-identity.

If You Have Not Checked This Item: Some Helpful Ideas

■ Assess Your Center for "Independent" Possibilities

What can children do on their own in your center? It gives them great satisfaction to accomplish difficult tasks. Walk around your physical area and make a list of things that children can do. Items on your daily job chart for individuals or teams to choose can include:

feeding the rabbit	taking own attendance
cleaning the aquarium	getting out playground toys
watering the plants	sweeping the floor
scraping carrots for snack	sponging off the tables
delivering mail to the office	getting out cots for naptime
tape recording a story	turning on and using the computer

■ Encourage Performance of Self-Help Skills

Teach children how to tie their shoes when their small motor coordination allows them this capability. Or have another child help them get started with buttons or zippers or Velcro tabs. Allow enough time for even the slowest child to perform this task on his own.

■ Help Children Get Started

Sometimes the first step is all a child needs to start her on her way to independence. Sit next to the child who tells you she can't make the puzzle, and put in a piece yourself. Then ask her to look for the next one. Stay with her until she completes the puzzle if need be. Then ask her to try it again on her own. Give her positive verbal support all the way, but refrain from helping this time.

■ Be Enthusiastic Yourself

Enthusiasm always scores very high on lists of the competencies of successful teachers. You as a behavior model in your classroom need always to be enthusiastic and positive about everything you do. If children see you acting on your own with vigor they will be encouraged to do likewise.

■ Read a Book

Gah-Ning, the Chinese Canadian heroine of *Where Is Gah-Ning?* by Robert Munsch (Toronto: Annick Press, 1994), is the most independent, strong-headed, hilarious little girl your youngsters will ever meet. She is bound and determined to go to Kapuskasing regardless of her father's strong objection. So off she starts: first on her bike (but her father intercepts her); then on roller blades (but her father intercepts her again). Finally she goes to the library instead where a clown is giving out balloons. Gah-Ning takes 300 and finally floats to Kapuskasing! Ask your children what impossible tasks they were able to find a way to do.

OBSERVING, RECORDING, AND INTERPRETING SELF-IDENTITY

Self-identity was chosen as the first topic on the Child Skills Checklist because this is the first area of child development a teacher should be concerned with when she meets new children in her center for the first time. To determine how children feel about themselves in their new environment, and which children may need help in making the transition from home to school, you may want to observe and record the behaviors of all the children in your class at one time.

To do this, use one sheet of paper listing the names of the children down the left side and the checklist items along the top. Draw lines horizontally and vertically to section off the names and items. Now you can mark the items you have seen each child performing under "Self-Identity." When you find a number of blank spaces for a particular child, you may want to observe this child in more detail, using the entire checklist.

You will then be able to design a learning prescription for the particular child, as was done for Sheila in Chapter 2. The Checklist results will tell you which areas of strength and confidence the child displays, as well as which areas may need improvement. Then you can begin planning for the individual by listing several activities to help the child based on his or her strengths. Such activities can come from your own repertoire or from those suggested in the chapter.

Be sure that observation of such children is an ongoing process in your center. Do a follow-up of children who seem to need special help. Has your learning prescription been helpful? Did the activities you planned really help this child? Share your observations with your classroom team and with the child's parents. Ask them to make similar observations. Include their ideas, as well, in your individual plans for each child.

REFERENCES

Ainsworth, M. D. S., Bell, S. M., & Stayton, D. J. (1974). Infant-mother attachment and social development. "Socialization" as a product of reciprocal responsiveness to signals. In M. M. Richards (Ed.), *The integration of a child into a social world.* London: Cambridge University Press.

Bowlby, J. (1969). *Attachment and loss: Vol. 1. Attachment.* New York: Basic Books.

Bowlby, J. (1973). *Attachment and loss: Vol. 2. Separation anxiety and anger.* New York: Basic Books.

Damon, W. (1983). *Social and personality development: Infancy through adolescence.* New York: W. W. Norton.

Davidson, J. I. (1996). *Emergent literacy and dramatic play in early education.* Albany, NY: Delmar Publishers.

Gottschall, S. (1989). Understanding and accepting separation feelings. *Young Children, 44*(6), 11–16.

Kaplan, L. J. (1978). *Oneness and separateness: From infant to individual.* New York: Simon and Schuster.

Kosnik, C. (1993). Everyone is a V.I.P. in this class. *Young Children, 49*(1), 32–37.

Seagull, E. A. W., & Kallen, D. J. (1978). Normal social and emotional development of the preschool-age child. In N. B. Enzer & K. W. Goin (Eds.), *Social and emotional development: The preschooler.* New York: Walker & Co.

Thompson, J. J. (1973). *Beyond words: Nonverbal communication in the classroom.* New York: Citation Press.

Wardle, F. (1995). How young children build images of themselves. *Child care information exchange.* #7, 44–47.

SUGGESTED READINGS

Balaban, N. (1985). *Starting school: From separation to independence, a guide for early childhood teachers.* New York: Teachers College Press.

Beaty, J. J. (1996). *Skills for preschool teachers.* Upper Saddle River, NJ: Merrill/Prentice Hall.

Briggs, D. C. (1970). *Your child's self-esteem.* Garden City, NY: Doubleday.

Curry, E. E., & Johnson, E. N. (1990). *Beyond self-esteem: developing a genuine sense of human value.* Washington, DC: NAEYC.

Solomon, J., & George, C. (1990). *Conflict and attachment: The experience of disorganized/controlling children.* Paper presented at the International Conference on Infant Studies, Montreal, Quebec, Canada. ERIC, #ED 319 496, pp. 1–15.

VIDEOTAPES

Magna Systems, Inc. (1993). *Self-identity and sex role development.* Magna Systems, Inc., 95 West Country Line Road, Barrington, IL 60010.

National Association for the Education of Young Children (NAEYC). *Building quality child care: Independence.* NAEYC, 1509 16th St. NW, Washington, DC 20036-1426.

LEARNING ACTIVITIES

1. Observe all the children in your classroom each morning of the first week of school, using the items in the self-identity checklist as a screening device. Note which children can separate without difficulty from their parents and which children cannot. Make a written Learning Prescription for a particular child to help him or her overcome this initial anxiety. Discuss the plan with your supervisor and then implement it. Discuss the results.

2. Choose a child who seems to have difficulty getting involved with other children or activities. Make a running record of everything the child does or says during three different arrival periods. Transfer this information to the Child Skills Checklist under "Self-Identity." How do you interpret the evidence you have collected? Can you make any conclusions yet about this child?

3. Meet with one or more parents of children in your classroom. Discuss how children develop their self-identities, and give the parents ideas that can be used at home to help strengthen their child's self-concept. Ask them for suggestions about how they would like you to work with their child. If you are not in a classroom, make a written report of how you would do this.

4. Observe a child playing a role in dramatic play for three days. Keep a running record of everything the child does or says. Pay special attention to the characteristics of play listed on p. 76.

   Can you make any conclusions about the child's self-identity based on these observations?

5. Choose a child for whom you have checked "Displays enthusiasm in regard to doing things for self." Observe this child during the first half-hour of class for three days. Which of the other items can you check for this child based on your observations? What is your evidence for each checkmark? What conclusions can you make about this child based on these observations?

CHAPTER 4

Emotional Development

EMOTIONAL DEVELOPMENT CHECKLIST

- ☐ Allows self to be comforted during stressful time
- ☐ Eats, sleeps, toilets without fuss away from home
- ☐ Handles sudden changes/startling situations with control
- ☐ Can express anger in words rather than actions
- ☐ Allows aggressive behavior to be redirected
- ☐ Does not withdraw from others excessively
- ☐ Shows interest/attention in classroom activities
- ☐ Smiles, seems happy much of the time

DEVELOPING EMOTIONS IN YOUNG CHILDREN

The emotional development of the preschool child is somewhat different from other developmental aspects. Although emotional growth happens simultaneously with physical, social, cognitive, language, and creative development and is interdependent on them, it seems as if youngsters do not stay developed. They seem to repeat the same sequences of emotional development over and over until they get it right—throughout life.

In some respects this observation is true. Emotional development does have a physical and cognitive basis for its expression, but once the basic human abilities are in place, emotions are much more situational.

If we agree that emotions are particular reactions to specific stimuli, then we note that these reactions may not change much in a developmental sense over a person's lifetime. Many of us get red in the face when we are angry and cry when we are sad, both as infants and as adults. In other words, it is the situation—the stimulus—rather than our developmental level that seems to govern our emotional responses.

Actually, emotional development is even more complex. Whereas physical and cognitive development seem to be based on the genetic traits children inherit plus the environment in which they are raised, Izard (1977, 1991) suggests emotions have three internally interacting dimensions:

1. the conscious feeling or emotional experience
2. the process in the brain and nervous system
3. the observable expressive patterns or reactions

Obviously, the brain and nervous system, because they are physical, can exhibit inherited traits. But can emotions themselves be inherited and then develop through maturation and surroundings just like the ability to think? Many psychologists have trouble accepting the idea that emotions are at all biological and based on maturity. However, developmental researchers must admit that certain emotional responses— separation anxiety, for instance—occur at about the same time and for the same reasons in infants and toddlers around the world. Similarly, other types of emotions seem to trigger universal fight or flight response in humans at all ages.

Developmental psychologists studying universal responses talk in terms of the functions of emotions (i.e., how they help the human species adapt and survive). These scientists note that certain emotions that trigger necessary survival responses in infants have outlived their usefulness when they occur in older children and adults. The acute distress the infant feels and expresses in tears and screams when mother leaves the house, for example, has outlived its usefulness if it is a daily occurrence for a four-year-old whose mother leaves him at the child care center. Although such basic emotions seem to serve in helping to preserve the self or the species, the higher emotions serve social purposes, and their appropriate responses must be learned in a social context.

Thus we should focus on the response—not the emotion itself—when we speak of emotional development in preschool children. And what most concerns us is not the development, but the child's control of the response. In the areas of physical and mental development we want the young child to grow, mature, and extend his abilities to the utmost. With emotional development, we want the child to learn to make appropriate emotional responses, and especially to control negative responses. An emotionally disturbed child is, after all, often one who is out of control.

This chapter, then, looks at observable emotional responses of young children in eight different areas, followed by suggestions for improving the child's behavior if the particular item is not demonstrated. Each of the checklist items refers to a particular emotion. It should be noted, however, that the order in which the items are listed is not a developmental sequence, because sequence as such does not seem to be an important factor in emotional development.

Many psychologists recognize either 8 or 10 basic emotions and their combinations. These are sometimes listed as interest-excitement, enjoyment-joy, surprise-startle, distress-anguish, anger-rage, disgust-revulsion, contempt-scorn, fear-terror, shame/shyness-humiliation, and guilt-remorse. The emotional responses of preschool children seem to be involved principally with the following seven emotions (plus one response):

1. distress
2. fear
3. surprise
4. anger
5. aggression (a response)
6. shyness
7. interest
8. joy

To help children develop emotionally, the preschool teacher should be concerned with promoting positive responses and teaching control of inappropriate responses. Although techniques to accomplish this control may vary depending upon the emotion and the situation, the following five strategies can be used in helping children control their inappropriate reactions:

1. Remove or reduce the cause of the emotion.
2. Diffuse the child's negative response by allowing him to "let it out" through crying, talking, or transferring his feelings into nondestructive actions.
3. Offer support, comfort, and ideas for self-control.
4. Model controlled behavior yourself.
5. Give children the opportunity to talk about feelings in a nonemotional setting.

Your goal for the children should be the same as in the other aspects of their development—for them to gain self-control. To help children acquire this control, you first need to find out where they stand in their present development. Do they cry, whine, or complain much of the time? Do they ever smile? Do they show anger or aggression toward others? The Child Skills Checklist lists eight representative items of emotional behavior that can be observed in preschool children. Each item represents one of the eight emotions listed above. Observe the children in your class to determine which youngsters have accomplished the emotional self-control described in the checklist. Children who have not exhibited these checklist behaviors may benefit from the ideas and suggestions discussed in the remainder of the chapter.

 ## ALLOWS SELF TO BE COMFORTED DURING STRESSFUL TIME

Distress

Children who do not allow themselves to be comforted during stressful times are often exhibiting the emotion known as distress. At its lower extreme, distress may result from physical discomfort due to pain, extremes of temperature, or noise; at its upper level, distress may take the form of anguish, grief, or depression due to the loss of a loved one. A basic cause of distress throughout life is physical or psychological separation, especially from a loved one. Children who perceive themselves as having been abandoned by an adult, even when this is not the case, experience the same emotions as children who actually have been abandoned.

Children express distress by crying, whining, or showing a sad face. Sometimes they cling to an adult caregiver. Distressed children may feel uncomfortable, disappointed, lonely, sad, or rejected.

Since distress is not the most severe negative emotion found in children, adults do not always take it seriously. They should. Distress is an indication that all is not well with a child. Failure to reduce the distress or its causes over time tends to break down the child's trust in adults. Furthermore, she may learn to become unsympathetic to others who are distressed because that is the way she has been treated.

Every human being endures the initial distress of the birth experience, which is not only a physical discomfort but also a separation ordeal in the extreme. As such, birth is greeted with lusty crying by the distressed infant. Psychologists believe that distress, whenever it occurs, thus serves as a warning to others that something is wrong with this person and something should be done about it. Because it concerns separation, distress also seems to serve as a device to keep one's group (e.g., family, clan) together.

What are the principal causes of distress in the child-care setting? For many youngsters, separation from their mother or primary caregiver is the greatest stressor. Physical discomfort or pain, rejection by peers, dissatisfaction with a performance, and lack of a skill are other causes of distress. A stressful situation in the family, such as the birth of a new baby, a death, a hospitalization, a move, or a divorce, may also be carried over into classroom behavior by the child who is disturbed by it.

The Teacher's Role

How can you help? Your principal role in the children's emotional development should be to help them master their feelings. You should not be the controlling device yourself, but instead you should help them find a way to control their feelings from within. Adults are often tempted to take control of an emotional situation. Young children, in fact, look to you to solve the emotional problems that so often overwhelm them. You do children a disservice if you comply. Your role should be that of a facilitator, not a controller. Otherwise, without you, the children will be no better off the next time the emotional situation occurs. As with all other aspects of development, your overall goal for children should be to develop their emotional independence—in other words, emotional self-control.

Although the particular situation may determine your response, distress most often requires that you first give comfort to the child. She is upset and uncomfortable; she may be whining or crying. You can show your concern through comforting words and actions such as holding or hugging. As noted by Raikes (1996):

> Teachers who are close to their children often report child anxiety during such times as a divorce, the birth of a sibling, or family illness. During times of child stress, teachers may give extra hugging, holding, or one-on-one time. (p. 62)

Requiring a child to stop crying right away is not usually the way to help him master his emotions. Venting through tears is, after all, a catharsis. He may think you are not sympathetic to his plight if you insist he stop crying. He may in fact stop on his own when he hears your comforting words or feels your touch. Recent studies have found that crying is of therapeutic value not only psychologically, but also physically. Chemical toxins that build up during stress are released in tears. Even blood pressure, pulse rate, and body temperature seem to be lowered by crying (Frey & Langseth, 1985). As psychologist Aletha Solter (1992) points out:

Crying is not the hurt, but the process of becoming unhurt. . . . A child who has been allowed to cry as long as needed will feel happier and more secure at school, in the long run, than a child who has been repeatedly distracted from her feelings. (p. 66)

Once the child can verbalize, she can begin to take charge of her emotions. She may be able to tell you what happened or how she feels. This is the first step toward self-mastery of emotions. She might even be able to tell you what would make her feel better.

If the situation is too overwhelming for a child to stop crying or to verbalize his feelings, your best strategy may be to redirect his attention when the time seems right: after he has stopped crying. If he was injured on one leg, perhaps you can get him to show you the other leg. How does it look? How does he think it feels? Maybe together you can do something to make the injured leg feel like the uninjured one. Distress, then, can often be relieved when you

1. give comfort
2. allow child to cry
3. redirect attention
4. help the child to verbalize

As for mastering distress so that it will not happen again, this is probably not possible and certainly not appropriate. Distress may be relieved and perhaps controlled to some extent, but not completely mastered. Nor should we want it to be. Distress is a necessary symptom signaling that all is not well with the individual. In your child-care program, you should hope to relieve, not prevent, distress in a child. If you are successful, then a distraught child will allow herself to be comforted or redirected. But if her sense of self is not strong enough or if the distress is too overwhelming, she may not even allow this. What can you do to help such a child?

If You Have Not Checked This Item: Some Helpful Ideas

■ Hold and Rock

It's a good idea to have an adult-size rocking chair in your center. Sometimes the best help for a distraught child is to hold and rock him.

■ Have the Child Hold a Huggable Toy

A child is often comforted by holding something soft. That is why toddlers carry "security blankets." Your classroom should have cuddly stuffed animals or similar toys available, not only for play but also for stressful situations. The child who does not allow you to comfort her may help herself by holding such a toy. Be sure the toy is washable so it can be cleaned for use by other children.

■ Use a Material with Soothing Properties

Water play and finger painting are activities with soothing qualities. Distressed children can take out their frustrations by moving paint around a surface with their hands or by swishing water and squeezing sponges, thus transferring their negative energy in a harmless fashion.

■ Have the Child Talk to a Puppet

Verbalizing distraught feelings is one of the best ways to defuse and control them. You could designate one of the puppets in your room as a "feelings" puppet and keep it in a special place for the times when children are feeling sad or upset. They can talk to the puppet about how they feel and ask the puppet how it feels. Model the use of this puppet yourself when upsetting occasions arise so that the children can follow your lead when they feel bad.

■ Read a Book

Sometimes distraught children will allow you to read a favorite book to them. You might also keep particular books for them to look at on their own during troubling times. The following books are especially suitable for stressful situations.

Feelings
Double-Dip Feelings by Barbara S. Cain (New York: Magination Press, 1990) shows young multicultural children expressing a variety of feelings: sometimes cheerful, sometimes sad, and sometimes cheerful and sad together. Playful, mad, proud, scared, and happy are some of the feelings illustrated.

My Dad Takes Care of Me by Patricia Quilan (Toronto: Annick Press, 1987) tells the story of Paul and his dad, who is out of work and staying home to take care of Paul. Emotions are expressed, including the father's crying, but the loving, accepting atmosphere makes it an upbeat story.

Mama, Do You Love Me? by Barbara M. Joosse (San Francisco: Chronicle Books, 1991) is a beautifully illustrated story of a little Inuit girl asking her mother how much she loves her. Every answer by Mama introduces various Arctic animals. Then the girl plays a what-if game with her questioning, still testing her mother's love. It comes shining through even when Mama is sorry, angry, worried, sad, surprised, and scared.

Separation
Sarah loses her doll, Abigail, in the shopping mall and mama loses Sarah in *Don't Worry, I'll Find You* by Anna Grossnickle Hines (New York: Dutton, 1986). But the lost ones stay put as directed and are finally found.

In *Friday Night Is Papa Night* by Ruth A. Sonneborn (New York: Puffin Books, 1970), Pedro, a little Hispanic boy, waits with apprehension for his businessman father to come home on the weekend, which he finally does.

In the large, vividly illustrated *At the Crossroads* by Rachel Isadora (New York: Greenwillow Books, 1991), South African black boys wait all night at the crossroads for their fathers to come back from 10 months of working in the mines.

Moving

The Leaving Morning by Angela Johnson (New York: Orchard Books, 1992) is a wonderfully illustrated story about an inner-city African-American boy and his sister who are saying goodbye to their friends in their apartment building and neighborhood on the morning they leave.

Gila Monsters Meet You at the Airport by Marjorie Weinman Sharmat (New York: Macmillan, 1980) shows the hilarious misconceptions that a New York boy moving to Arizona and an Arizona boy moving to New York have of each of these places because they are afraid of moving there.

In the hospital

Going Home by Margaret Wild (New York: Scholastic, 1993) tells the story of Hugo, an Hispanic boy who has finished his stay in a hospital near a zoo and wants to go home. Each night he puts on his magic slippers and pretends to take off for an adventure with one of the zoo animals. Each day he makes an animal puppet or mask for his sister, who comes to visit him until he finally gets to go home.

Death

The Tenth Good Thing About Barney by Judith Viorst (New York: Atheneum, 1971) is the classic story about a sad little boy whose cat, Barney, dies. The boy's mother tries to comfort him by having him think of 10 good things to say about Barney when they bury him in the backyard.

You Hold Me and I'll Hold You by Jo Carson (New York: Orchard Books, 1992) tells the tender story in the words of a little girl whose father cares for her because her mother has left. The father and daughter go to a family funeral at Grandpa's where she sees people feeling sad and crying. During the service her father takes her in his arms saying, "You hold me and I'll hold you," and she finally feels better.

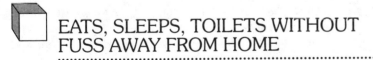

EATS, SLEEPS, TOILETS WITHOUT FUSS AWAY FROM HOME

Fear (Anxiety)

Children who have difficulty eating, falling asleep, or using the toilet in your center or classroom behave this way because of tension. This tension is most often produced by anxiety, which is one of the most common expressions of fear.

Fear first appears as an emotion in the second half of the first year of infancy, according to many psychologists. Somewhere between five and nine months of age, babies begin to recognize an unfamiliar face and are afraid of it. Before that point, their physical and cognitive development have not progressed to where they can distinguish between friend and stranger. After that recognition occurs, infants see unfamiliar faces as a possible threat—until they learn differently.

Thus, the emotion of fear is caused by the presence of something threatening or the absence of safety and security (Izard, 1977, p. 356). Fear may result when the possibility of harm appears, when a strange person, object, or situation is confronted, and when specific fright-producing elements—heights, the dark, thunderstorms, particular animals such as dogs and snakes—are present. When humans are afraid, they feel anxious and alarmed. They may tremble, cower, hide, run away, cling to someone, or cry, depending on their degree of fright. They often seek protection.

Fear is in some ways age-related. Young children are generally not afraid of heights, the dark, or animals before their second year. It is as though they really don't know enough to be frightened before then. As they grow older, children add new fears to their repertoire and drop some of the old ones. Fear, like distress, seems to serve as a warning signal for the human species: Reduce the threat or seek protection. When this warning feeling persists but is no longer useful to the young human, you as a child-care worker or teacher need to intervene.

We know of course that extreme fear can be paralyzing, but we need to realize that even lesser fears like anxiety produce tension of some sort: a tightening up of the body and the mind. Anxiety "is the most constricting of all the emotions" (Izard, 1977, p. 365). The anxious person has trouble relaxing and feeling at ease in tense situations and unfamiliar settings that somehow pose a threat.

For young children used to the security of home, the early childhood classroom can be such a tense setting at first, no matter how relaxing and nonthreatening you have made it. Some children may view the setting as a threat for three reasons: (1) the setting is unfamiliar, (2) they lack initial trust in the setting and the people there, and (3) their parents or caregivers have left them.

Most children display some anxiety when they first experience an early childhood classroom. It is a natural reaction to being left in a strange place. But if they have a strong enough sense of self and sense of trust in the world and the people around them, the children should soon come to feel perfectly at ease in your center. For children who do not achieve this sense of ease, you may need to provide special attention to help them overcome their anxiety.

The routine functions of eating, sleeping, and toileting and how they are carried out can often provide the careful observer with clues concerning who is at ease in the classroom and who is not. Because these routines are of such a personal nature and so closely connected with the home and the primary caregiver, eating, sleeping, and toileting are deeply significant to the child. From her earliest memories she is used to having her mother feed her or help her to feed herself. She expects her mother to tuck her in and kiss her goodnight. She is at ease in using the toilet—a rather formidable piece of equipment for a young child—in her own home, because she has learned it will not flush her away.

Suddenly the child is thrust into a new and unfamiliar environment where these very personal processes are to be directed by strangers. Even the most secure and experienced young explorer may have moments of anxiety in the beginning. Anxiety produces tensions in which muscles actually tighten up, whether or not the tense person is aware of it. Unless the tense child is able to relax, he or she may certainly experience difficulty in eating, falling asleep, or using the toilet.

The anxious child in your classroom may not have difficulty with all three of these acts. One or the other may be more meaningful in his life at home and thus cause more problems for him away from home. His difficulty may also have causes other than anxiety. A health problem, for instance, could also cause a disruption in his normal functioning. If a child exhibits persistent difficulty in eating, sleeping, or toileting at any time while he is in your care, however, the cause may be anxiety and the child may need your help to overcome the negative effects of this emotion.

Eating

Eating is the act most closely connected with the child's mother. From babyhood when he nursed at his mother's breast or was held close to her while being bottle-fed, the child not only received life-sustaining nourishment but also comfort and love. It is not surprising, then, that he makes a connection between food and comfort. Later, as he is weaned from breast or bottle and learns to take solid food, he may perceive this either as a happy experience or a battle of wills if force is used to make him eat. By the time he enters your center, the child has had at least three years of experience with the emotional nature of eating. You hope this has been positive. No matter what, you need to make sure eating is a positive experience for the child in your program.

Once you are aware of the emotional nature of eating and how a child's anxiety can interfere with his eating habits, you will be better prepared to deal with children who refuse to eat. Be sure at the outset that your meals take place in an atmosphere of friendliness and relaxation. Are meals served family style in your classroom around small group tables? School cafeterias are too large, noisy, impersonal, and rushed for children this young. If you have been assigned to a cafeteria, talk with the supervisor and explain the needs of young children; ask whether the food could be carried to your room instead.

Do you eat at the table with the children? It is important in family-style eating that a member of the staff sit at each table to converse informally with the children, answering their questions about the food and assisting them in their own pouring and serving. Help the children take a little of everything. If their portions are too large, they may not even want to begin. Involving them in dishing out and passing the food, however, is a physical step that psychologically connects them to eating.

What about rules concerning food? Mealtime should be pleasant and relaxing. Too many rules about portions, second helpings, and dessert may create tension even in relaxed children. Is withholding of dessert used as a punishment for children who have misbehaved? No matter how food is used in the homes of your children, it should never be used in a punitive manner in your center. All of the food served, including dessert, should be nutritious, appealing, and available to all of the children all of the time.

Are you a good eating model yourself? "Practice what you preach" is a cliché worth repeating when it comes to eating. Your children should see that you take a reasonable-sized portion of each food, eat all your food, talk about how good it tastes, ask politely for seconds if this is appropriate, refrain from nagging, and make positive comments about the children who have cleaned up their plates.

If You Have Not Checked This Item: Some Helpful Ideas

■ Refrain from Pressure

Do not use force or pressure to get a reluctant child to eat. Force probably will not work anyway, but more importantly, it will certainly not reduce the anxiety and tension that may be the cause of a refusal to eat in the first place. All attempts to resolve the problem should be positive in nature, aimed at removing or reducing the cause for the emotion and helping the child gain inner control over her reactions. Sometimes patience alone is the only solution. When the child feels at ease in your program, she will eat.

■ Talk with Parents

Ask parents what they expect of their child and what they hope he will gain from your program. Talk about food habits and how the child eats at home. But be aware that the basic problem may not be food but anxiety and how the child reacts to it. Is the child under pressure at home? How does he react to pressure? How can you and the parents relieve him of this pressure?

■ Read a Book

Perhaps a lighthearted approach will work to encourage eating. If you think the reluctant eater can deal with food in a playful manner, you might try reading together one of the following books.

Gregory, the Terrible Eater by Mitchell Sharmat (New York: Scholastic, 1980) is the story of little goat Gregory, who will not eat the goat food his mother serves (tin cans, rugs, bottle caps). He only wants fruits, vegetables, and eggs——"Good stuff like that." When junk food gets too much for him, he and his family finally reach a compromise.

Eat Up, Gemma by Sarah Hayes (New York, Mulberry, 1988), a story about an African-American baby who won't eat, told by her little brother, shows Gemma throwing her breakfast on the floor, squashing the grapes that her mother gives her, feeding her picnic cookie to the birds, and giving her pizza to the dog when no one is looking. Then her brother notices how she tries to eat the plastic fruit off a lady's hat in church, and finally figures out how to get Gemma to eat up.

Sleeping

If the children spend all day in your center, then you must provide them with a nap period in the afternoon. For some children this is a relief from the exuberant activities of the morning. They welcome the chance to rest and will promptly fall asleep. For others, naptime involves tossing and turning, whispering and squirming, disturbing other children and the teacher. Some children may have outgrown naptime. Others may be so wound up they need to relax before they can fall asleep. A few may be the anxious children we have been discussing, who cannot fall asleep because of tension.

First, you need to prepare all of your children for naptime. They can help by getting out the cots or mats. They can choose their own area of the room to sleep in. They need to know that when the lights are turned out or the curtains pulled, it is time to close their eyes. You might try playing dreamy music at a low volume on the record player. Or you could read a story in a monotone or whispery voice. You might read a sleep story such as Margaret Wise Brown's classic *Goodnight Moon* (New York: Scholastic, 1947), or the Native Alaskan bedtime story *Northern Lullaby* by Nancy White Carlstrom (New York: Philomel Books, 1992), or the animal bedtime story *Asleep, Asleep* by Mirra Ginsburg (New York: Greenwillow Books, 1992).

For some children, rubbing their backs helps them to let go and fall asleep. If you rub backs for some, however, be sure to do it for all who want it. Children like you to trace their names on their backs with your finger. What if some children still do not fall asleep?

If You Have Not Checked This Item: Some Helpful Ideas

■ Naptime Toys

If, after 10 or 15 minutes, certain children show no signs of falling asleep, you may decide to allow them to play quietly on their cots with some sort of naptime toy, perhaps a tiny car or doll from a basket you pass around to the nonsleepers. Because they do not move from their sleeping quarters, the nonsleepers still have the chance to fall asleep if they want. On the other hand, some teachers prefer to have a different area where nonsleepers can go to play quietly.

■ Reduce Tension

If some children are still too anxious and tense to allow themselves to fall asleep, you may need to try a variety of methods for reducing tension. Can these children take a teddy bear to bed? Ask them how they can help themselves get sleepy. Will rocking help? What do they do at home? In the end, your acceptance of them as worthy persons should eventually help them to relax and take a nap if their bodies have the need for it.

Toileting

Children's bathroom habits are as different from one another as their eating habits. Children will probably learn the most about what is expected of them in your center from their peers. But you also need to be aware of what the children expect or need from you. Do you have a single classroom bathroom or a public-type bathroom with several stalls? Are the children used to being in a bathroom with other children? Can they handle their clothing, clean themselves, and wash their hands by themselves?

You may need to talk to newcomers in the beginning about what they can expect and ask them what they are used to. You may need to go in the bathroom with them at first to help them and get them used to the equipment.

If parents tell you their children are not using the center facilities or if the children begin to have accidents in the classroom, you will want to talk with them about it as gently as possible. Because toilet training—unfortunately—is controlled in some homes through the negative method of shaming, you need to be careful that your concern will not make the child feel ashamed.

Is the child too shy to use the bathroom with other children? You may need to accede to his feelings at first until he is used to your center and his peers.

If You Have Not Checked This Item: Some Helpful Ideas

■ Use Rewards

The behavior modification idea of giving a reward is always controversial, but for some children it works. An external reward can become an internal behavior if the child plays her part. Try keeping a private chart on which you put a check or smiley face each time the child uses the toilet. Once a child is in the habit or has overcome her anxiety about using your facilities, the use of the chart should fade away.

■ Display Acceptance

Use every strategy you know to show the child you accept him. Nonverbal cues such as smiles or hugs and friendly words, special activities, and jobs or errands make a child feel accepted. Help him to be accepted by the other children as well. Once anxiety about your center and its inhabitants is lessened, a new child should not be so tense about using the bathroom facilities.

■ Read a Book

An especially good book about using the toilet is *Toilet Tales* by Andrea Wayne von Konigslow (Toronto: Annick Press, 1985). This hilariously illustrated story tells why big boys and girls can use the toilet and why animals like elephants, lions, snakes, and beavers cannot. When your children are finished laughing, most of the tension about using the toilet should be gone!

HANDLES SUDDEN CHANGES/STARTLING SITUATIONS WITH CONTROL

Surprise (Startle)

Surprise is different from the other emotions in that it lasts only for a moment, although its results may continue for some time with young children. A sudden or unexpected external event causes a reaction of surprise, or startle. The event could be a loud noise such as an explosion or clap of thunder at one extreme, or the unexpected appearance of a person at the other extreme. A startled person's mind goes blank for an instant and his muscles contract quickly. He may even jump or let out a scream if the incident is surprising enough. Depending upon the situation, the person may be shocked, bewildered, confused, or embarrassed because of his reaction. Or he could be delighted.

Although a startle reflex appears in babies a few hours after birth, this reflex does not seem to be the same as the emotion of surprise, which occurs in infants between the fifth and seventh month. By that time, enough cognitive development has occurred to enable the infant to form expectations (Izard, 1977, p. 283).

Because everything is new for the child, there will be many startling events in her young life. If most of her surprises are pleasant ones, she will come to view surprises positively. If the opposite is true, then surprises may cause the child to cry or exhibit defensive behavior.

Many mothers help prepare their children for surprises, perhaps unintentionally, by playing low-key surprise games such as peekaboo with their children. The surprise is always a pleasant one: the revealing of mother's hidden face. But if children are scolded or ridiculed too severely at home when they cry or make a fuss over unexpected happenings, they may become fearful of anything different whether or not it is sudden.

Research shows that most adults view surprise as pleasant. Their experience has taught them this. Young children, on the other hand, do not necessarily show the same response. Perhaps because their experience is limited, or because the occurrence of sudden happenings leaves them overwhelmed, they tend not to greet unexpected things as adults do. Most young children, for instance, do not react happily to surprise birthday parties. Young children are, in fact, more likely to cry or withdraw. It may take some time for the shock to wear off and for them to become their pleasant selves again. Sensitive adults will not impose such startling events on children. Children enjoy the pleasant anticipation of parties, rather than startling surprise.

What about the children in your center or classroom? How do they respond to the unexpected? They need to be prepared for it in their lives, and they need to be able to control their responses. Like the other emotions, surprise/startle cannot be eliminated, nor should it be. It serves the useful function of preparing an individual to deal with an unexpected event. But if a child's reaction is one of such alarm as to immobilize her, then you need to help her deal with it in a better way.

What are some startling events you might anticipate? Most centers have fire alarms that they may or may not be able to control. Ask your building supervisor if your children can have a chance to practice a fire drill with the alarm until they are able to do it with ease. Practicing simulated emergency situations is one of the best ways to learn to deal with real emergencies.

In addition to practice, the children can learn to handle sudden changes or surprising events by acting the way you do. You need to be calm and collected yourself, modeling the behavior you would like the youngsters to emulate.

Some children go to pieces when they are startled. They may be the ones who have not developed a strong enough sense of self or a sense of trust in the people around them. These children may cry, cling, or withdraw long after the event is past. How can you help them?

If You Have Not Checked This Item: Some Helpful Ideas

■ Read a Book

Children may be helped to overcome their negative responses if they hear how others like themselves deal with surprises. Books about startling situations should be read not only to a group of children, but also to individuals who have exhibited a poor emotional response to a surprise.

Jim Meets the Thing by Miriam Cohen (New York: Greenwillow Books, 1981) can be reassuring to many young children who are startled and frightened by the things they see on television. In this story, young Jim seems to be the only one in his class who is scared by the monster movie on TV the night before. But when the children play superheroes on the playground, only Jim stays calm when a praying mantis suddenly lands on Danny.

Storm in the Night by Mary Stolz (New York: Harper, 1988) tells, with illuminating words and illustrations, how a little African-American boy, Thomas, his grandfather, and his cat Ringo deal with a frightening thunderstorm that puts out their lights.

Dinosaur Days by Linda Manning (BridgeWater Books, 1993) is a what-if, days-of-the-week book in which seven different dinosaurs slip, pop, roar, slide, crash, roll, and take over the household of a little girl in surprising fashion every day of the week. What should she do? Turn each page and see.

 CAN EXPRESS ANGER IN WORDS RATHER THAN ACTIONS

Anger

Anger is the emotion of most concern not only in the child-care center, but also in society at large, perhaps because anger has the potential for such harm. We are very much concerned that people learn to control their anger. Therefore we begin teaching what to do—or rather what not to do—very early. We are usually not very successful. There is, however, a positive approach to controlling anger that can diffuse the anger so that children do not turn it against others or themselves.

First, we need to look at the emotion itself to understand what it is, what causes it, and what purpose it serves. Anger is the emotion or feeling that results when we are physically or psychologically restrained from doing something, frustrated in our attempts, interrupted, personally insulted, or forced to do something against our will. We feel hurt, disappointed, irritated. We frown, our face gets hot, our blood "boils," our muscles tense, our teeth clench, our eyes stare. At anger's highest level we feel rage that threatens to erupt in an explosive manner. At the other extreme we feel hostility, a cold type of anger.

With anger comes a sense of physical power and a greater self-assurance than with any other negative emotion (Izard, 1977, p. 331). The body, in fact, rallies its resources in readiness to strike out against the cause of the anger. In primitive humans anger mobilized the body's energy quickly and was important for survival. In modern humans the anger still appears but its primary purpose has all but vanished.

Here we are, then, ready to turn this rush of physical energy against the "enemy." What should we do with it? This energy needs to be released or somehow diffused, otherwise we will turn it against ourselves. Repressed anger has been implicated as one of the causes of skin diseases, ulcers, migraines, hypertension, and certain psychological disorders (Izard, 1977, p. 351).

Most parents teach their children from the start not to display anger. When they allow angry feelings to begin to show on their faces, children sense their parents' displeasure. Many children soon learn to conceal or disguise anger. Others let anger out in acts of aggression. Neither response is satisfactory, yet many of us carry these responses throughout life.

Instead, we need a positive approach that teaches children from the start what they should do (expression) rather than what they must not do (repression). Anger definitely calls for some sort of release, but children and adults need to "let off steam" harmlessly.

One of the most satisfactory methods used by many preschool teachers coaches children to verbalize their feelings. Verbalizing involves neither yelling nor name-calling, but expressing in words how the child feels about whatever is causing the anger. This approach has at least two advantages: It gives children an acceptable release for their strong feelings, and it puts the children in control. They—not adults—deal with the situation. And solving the problems on their own strengthens the children's sense of self.

Strong feelings such as anger overwhelm and thus frighten young children. A method for learning control from the inside and not being controlled from the outside will help children in the future when adults are not around. The anger emotion calls for action. But if children learn to speak out rather than strike out, they will not have to suffer the guilt or remorse afterward for an unacceptable act. As child development specialist Robert A. Furman (1995) recommends:

> The identification and verbalization of feelings can be taught or reinforced in schools, child care centers, and family child care homes as an important part of the early childhood educator's job. (p. 37)

Expressing anger in words is not easy in the beginning. It does not come naturally for young children whose communication skills are still limited. It is even more difficult for the child caught up in the throes of an overwhelming emotion who finds it simpler to strike out physically, shout, or cry. Yet three-, four-, and five-year-olds can learn the response of telling how they feel in words.

How do you teach them? First, you need to model this behavior yourself. When you become angry, tell the individual or the group how you feel and why you feel this way: "I feel very upset to see you dropping the tape recorder on the floor like that! If you break it no one can enjoy the music any more," or "Paul and Gregory, I am so angry to see you ganging up on Leslie again! Two against one is not fair!"

You must also convey to your children that their actions—not them as individuals—make you angry. You must show you still respect and like the children no matter how angry they get or how upset you feel over their actions. Show the children both verbally and nonverbally that you still accept them as good people.

You also must intervene *every time* the children display temper, and you must help them repeatedly to express their feelings in words: "Sarah, tell Jessica how you feel when she takes your book." "Roberto, don't hit Luther. Tell him how you feel."

Make eye contact with the children. Help them to make eye contact with one another to help diffuse their anger: "Roberto, look Luther in the eyes and tell him."

Teaching children to express anger in words is a time-consuming process, but so is all learning. If you believe children must gain inner control over their anger, and if you understand they must have some acceptable way to vent their feelings, then you will find it worthwhile to put in the time and effort necessary to divert anger's destructive energy into words. You will know you have been successful when the children begin telling one another, "Don't hit him, Jamar, tell him!"

If You Have Not Checked This Item: Some Helpful Ideas

■ Talk About Feelings

Establish a "feelings" corner in your room with pictures of people looking sad, angry, and glad. Ask the children to tell you what they feel when they look like that. If you have no pictures, make photocopies of feelings pictures from books. Provide a feelings hand puppet that the children can hold and talk to about the feelings they have.

■ Read a Book

Read books about feelings to a child or small group at any time of day, not only when tempers are short.

Feelings by Joanne Brisson Murphy (Windsor, Ontario: Black Moss Press, 1985) shows large, full-color illustrations of a boy and his family experiencing the feelings of pride, frustration, excitement, fear, anger, surprise, and happiness.

Sometimes I Feel Like a Mouse by Jeanne Modesitt (New York: Scholastic, 1992) is a simple story of a child comparing his feelings to different animals being shy, bold, sad, happy, scared, brave, excited, calm, mad, ashamed, and proud.

When Emily Woke Up Angry by Rachel Duncan (Hauppauge, NY: Barron's, 1989) shows a little girl getting up on the wrong side of the bed and trying to work off her anger as various animals might.

 ## ALLOWS AGGRESSIVE BEHAVIOR TO BE REDIRECTED

Aggression

Aggression is not an emotion but rather the expression of one. It is the action an individual commonly takes as a result of anger or frustration. Hostile actions or angry

When young children allow their aggressive behavior to be redirected, they are showing positive indications of their emotional development.

words are intended to harm or defeat or embarrass the person who caused the anger. Aggressive behavior in the classroom most commonly takes the form of hitting, throwing things, name-calling, spitting, biting, kicking, pushing or pulling, physically forcing someone to do something, restraining someone, destroying property, or forcefully taking someone else's possessions or turn.

Young children who have not learned to control their negative emotions often resort to aggressive behavior. Children who have been neglected or treated harshly sometimes use aggression to strike out at the world around them. Children who have had to fend for themselves among older peers without much adult guidance may have learned aggressiveness as a survival strategy. Other children with highly permissive parents may have learned certain aggressive acts to get their own way—hitting and name-calling, for instance.

Research tells us that boys are more aggressive than girls. Since Helen Dawe's early observational study of the quarrels of preschool children in 1934, most findings have shown boys to be more aggressive (Brooks-Gunn & Matthews, 1979, p. 130). We can blame boys' aggression on genetics—physical development and hormones— but we also need to look at society's expectations for boys and girls as well as adult interpretations of their behaviors.

Adults tend to read different messages into the nonverbal behavior of girls and boys. In talking about gender differences in her class of four-year-olds, Ilene described how some parent volunteers attributed angry or aggressive intent to boys' behavior, while interpreting the same kind of behavior quite differently in girls—for example, "She must be upset today" (Hyson, 1994, p. 66).

Society expects boys to be more aggressive than girls; thus boys are *allowed* to be more aggressive. If aggressiveness were considered a feminine trait, then no doubt the findings would quickly change.

How can you as a preschool teacher help children of both genders control unwanted aggressive behavior? Putting negative feelings into words helps achieve inner control, as previously mentioned. But if their actions are already aggressive, then children need to be redirected into a less destructive activity.

Certain classroom activities lend themselves to the redirection of out-of-control children. Children who strike out aggressively can be redirected to pound a ball of clay or play dough with their hands, to throw a beanbag at a target, to punch a pillow, to pound with a hammer, to hit a tetherball, to kick a soccer ball, or use rhythm band percussion instruments. Activities that will calm overwrought children include finger painting, water play, sand play, working with playdough, mixing dough, or listening to music or a story.

If You Have Not Checked This Item: Some Helpful Ideas

■ Hold the Child on Your Lap

Sometimes you must physically restrain a child from hurting others. Because you are bigger, you can hold the child so she cannot hit or kick, until she calms down enough to control herself.

Hold the child on your lap and restrain her from using her arms. If she also kicks, you may need to remove her shoes. This child is totally out of control and needs your help to restore herself to normalcy. Do not lose control yourself. Children are afraid of their own overwhelming emotions. They need you to remain calm and to prevent them from doing damage. If you are in a rocking chair, rock back and forth, humming a tuneless song over and over. Finally ask the child if she feels calm enough for you to let her get up. If she can't tell you, she is not ready yet.

■ Read a Book

At a later time, some children who use aggression to solve problems may want to listen to books about others who do the same.

The Grouchy Lady Bug by Eric Carle (New York: Crowell, 1977) is a time-counting book about a ladybug who challenges one after another of the animals all around the world to a fight. When each agrees, the ladybug flies off, telling them they are not big enough. Finally the whale, without even knowing it, slaps some sense into the grouchy ladybug.

Bootsie Barker Bites by Barbara Bottner (New York: Putnam's, 1992) tells the tale of the dominating Bootsie who comes with her mother to visit the little girl narrator's mother and always ends up playing so roughly as a ferocious dinosaur it frightens the little girl. She finally resolves the problem next time, scaring Bootsie by pretending to be a dinosaur-hunting paleontologist.

Angel Child, Dragon Child by Michele Maria Surat (New York: Scholastic, 1983) tells of the difficult time the little Vietnamese girl Ut has at her first American school when the children use words aggressively, making fun of her, with Raymond even throwing snowballs at her. Raymond's aggressive attitude and Ut's "dragon child" response are turned around when understanding of one another finally creeps in.

 # DOES NOT WITHDRAW FROM OTHERS EXCESSIVELY

Shyness (Shame)

As you observe the children in your classroom at the beginning of the year, you may note that certain ones seem to stay by themselves. They may stand apart or sit apart. If you try to get them involved, they may lower or avert their eyes, turn their heads, or even suck their thumbs. They seem to want to shrink into invisibility if only they could. They seem, in fact, to be exhibiting all of the indications of painful shyness.

Shyness is one of the least studied of the negative emotions. Yet nearly all humans experience shyness at one time or another. Early childhood is a common time for such an occurrence. Shyness results from a heightened degree of self-awareness in which the individual feels exposed, helpless, incompetent, and somehow shameful about it all.

As with so many of our feelings about ourselves, shyness seems to come from a combination of inherited traits plus first-year experiences. The earliest "shame" feelings that infants experience occur when they first recognize the face of a stranger about the age of five to seven months. Previously they have been fascinated with the human face. It has been a stimulus for excitement and joy. They want contact with it. They want some kind of interaction.

Then something occurs within the cognitive development of infants that allows them to discriminate one face from another. Suddenly, when a stranger appears, they realize they are not looking at a familiar, friendly countenance. They no longer respond joyfully, but instead, seem to realize their mistake and thus suffer their first embarrassment. They may cry, become red in the face, or try to get away.

If children have a series of negative experiences with strangers at this time, then they may learn that they are subject to this sort of shame whenever they meet a stranger (Izard, 1977, p. 395). Highly sensitive children seem to exhibit such embarrassment whether or not their experiences have been negative.

Something else is happening within children at this time. They are becoming aware of themselves as separate beings. This awareness has to happen before embarrassment—and therefore shyness—can occur. The shyness emotion is, after all, the feeling of exposure of self, of extreme self-consciousness, in which a person feels that all eyes are on him and he is uncomfortably out of place. According to research, these feelings occur most frequently in large groups, in new situations, and with strangers (Izard, 1977, p. 399).

Is it any wonder, then, that certain children exhibit this emotion in your classroom, especially at the beginning of the year? These children may be the sensitive ones, or the ones whose parents have used shaming as a method of discipline. Or they may be children who have not yet developed a strong enough sense of self to be comfortable among strangers. Shyness can be emotionally crippling to a child. It can prevent her from enjoying the best of herself and of others in your center. You need to find a way, using the utmost tact and sensitivity yourself, to help the shy child.

Children have no need to feel ashamed. They often do so because they are not able to live up to their expectations of themselves. They look around at other people and see themselves as a shameful example of what they would like to be. To help them change this inaccurate perception, you need to let them know how good they really are. Tell them verbally, show them nonverbally, and involve them actively in important duties and projects. You need to engage these children in activities where they will find out for themselves how worthy they are. But never at any time should you use shaming or ridicule as a method of discipline or scolding (e.g., never say anything like "Look what you did to the paints! How could you be so clumsy!").

The shyness/shame emotion does have a use in human development. Shame is the emotion—and a very powerful one—that keeps us from acting shamefully among others so that we do not invite ridicule. Rules for behavior (such as manners) are one result of this emotion. People who lack a sense of shame may commit such shameful acts as incest or child abuse. On the other hand, people who are overcome with an irrational sense of shame may also be emotionally crippled by it.

Some young children have this irrational feeling of shyness/shame. Because shame results from a real or perceived put-down of the self, and not just from an act the self has performed, there is real danger in allowing the child to feel that he is not good. If you do nothing to help the child correct his negative perception of himself, he may come to believe it. He may express his belief by withdrawing from others excessively. Thus you must make a concerted effort to correct the situation.

If You Have Not Checked This Item: Some Helpful Ideas

■ Focus on the Child's Strengths

Because the shyness emotion expresses the feeling that a child has not accepted herself, you can best help a shy child by finding ways for her to feel good about herself. Is she wearing a brightly colored dress? Maybe she could cut out pictures from a magazine of other dresses the same pretty color as hers. Or have her look at her pretty hand (she may be too sensitive to look at her face in a mirror at first). Could she trace around her fingers and then color the hand and cut it out? Perhaps she will allow you to display it on the classroom wall.

■ Do Not Dwell on Shyness

Reading books about shy children may not be a good idea. Shy children are already painfully aware of how they feel. To point out this shyness by reading a book about it may only make it worse.

■ Pair with Another Child

If one other child accepts him, the shy child may find it easier to accept himself and become involved with others. You may need to take the initiative in this case, asking another child to work with the shy child on a puzzle or go on an errand for you together.

■ Talk with Parents

Does the child exhibit this same behavior at home? Maybe not. Many children act completely differently at home than at school. This may mean that the child feels self-conscious and thus exhibits shyness in your classroom. In that case, continue your activities to show acceptance and help her accept herself. But if the parents admit that the child behaves the same at home, you may want to discuss tactfully with them the methods of discipline they are using. If shaming or ridiculing are involved, perhaps the parents could learn another way. You might consider having a meeting for all parents in which a speaker or film discusses the discipline issue.

SHOWS INTEREST/ATTENTION IN CLASSROOM ACTIVITIES

Interest (Excitement)

Interest is the most frequent and pervasive positive emotion that human beings possess. Children show interest by directing their eyes toward an object or person that catches their attention, and then exploring it with their eyes and, if possible, their other senses. Interested people are alert, active, self-confident, and curious. Interest is the motivator for much of children's learning, as well as for their development of creativity and intelligence. Thus it is crucial for growing children to have their interest stimulated by the interesting people, materials, and ideas in their environment.

Psychologists believe that change or novelty is the basis for the interest emotion. The novelty of an object first attracts the person's attention. Once he is aroused and curious, he is motivated to find out more about the object, thus increasing his knowledge, skill, and understanding. Interest, in other words, is the impulse to know, which then sustains our attention in the things we are curious about. Excitement is the most intense form of interest.

For an infant to perceive an object, she must first pay attention to it for a time. It is the emotion of interest that keeps her attention. Without this emotion she may become passive, dull, and apathetic, with little initiative or movement. The final result may be developmental lags or even retardation.

The interest emotion appears very early in an infant's life. Interest is evident in the attention she shows to the human face; eyes riveted to her mother's face and turning to follow it. Objects such as rattles, bottles, mobiles, her own fingers and toes are fascinating fields for exploration with her eyes and then her mouth. Later she shifts from external exploration to manipulation. What will objects do when you kick them, throw them, drop them?

When he throws his cereal dish on the floor, the child is not being naughty, only normal. He finds out about his world this way. Acts like this against physical objects obviously teach the child many additional things about the feelings of the people around him. If the family is strict or harsh or punitive about his actions, this will inhibit such interest-motivated exploration. If the child is punished too many times, he may cease exploring altogether, which poses dire consequences for his future development. On the other hand, encouragement to explore, play with things, and be curious will stretch his mind, his senses, and his physical skills.

Poverty frequently interferes with the development of strong interests because the variety of objects or activities available in the child's environment is often limited. In cases where the parents must also spend much of their energy struggling to survive, they may have little or no time to interact with their youngsters. The parents may, in fact, actively discourage them from exploratory endeavors. If, in addition, negative emotions dominate the atmosphere, interest quickly fades away.

Thus it is important for you to know which children in your classroom have retained their native curiosity and which have not. The interest and attention individual children pay to classroom activities may give you a clue. But you need to remember that interest is stimulated by novelty and change, so a truer test might be to set up a new activity area and observe which children notice it, who plays in it, and for how long. Because interests by now are very much individualized and personalized, what interests one child will not necessarily cause a flicker of attention in another. For this reason you must provide a wide range of activities and materials for your group. Remember to add something new once in awhile.

The basic interest emotion also affects attention span. Children must first be attracted to an activity through interest that is activated by change or novelty. If they find the activity interesting, they are likely to spend more time doing it and pay more attention to it. Although we know that age and maturity have a great deal to do with how long a child's interest can be held (i.e., the older, the longer), we can also increase the attention span by providing highly attractive materials and activities. Because children must attend (i.e., pay attention) to learn, the length of attention span is crucial in every learning situation. Teachers thus need to know what kinds of things three-, four-, and five-year-olds find attractive.

If You Have Not Checked This Item: Some Helpful Ideas

■ Focus on the Self

Although children's interests are widely varied, all humans—especially egocentric youngsters—have a basic interest in themselves. Think of something new and different about the child who shows little interest in center activities. Make it some kind of question, problem, or challenge that is intriguing and fun. Then turn the child loose with it. For instance, have a Slappy Shoe Contest. The child who shows little interest can start. Have her make some kind of paper design that she can tape to the top of her shoes. This makes her Ms. Slappy Shoe for the day. Then have her slap out a rhythm with her shoes, which you tape record. Play the tape. Let other children try to copy it and tape record their shoe slaps. Let her choose who will be the next Mr. or Ms. Slappy Shoe.

■ Arouse Curiosity

Children love mysteries. Invite a mystery guest (an adult dressed in a costume and mask) to visit the classroom. Let children guess who it is. Or bring a big stuffed animal in a bag and let the children guess what it is. Give them hints about what it eats or the noise it makes. Maybe the slow-to-respond child would like to think of a name for it once it is out of the bag.

■ Read a Book

My Head Is Full of Colors by Catherine Friend (New York: Hyperion Books, 1994) should stir even the most apathetic child to notice the exuberant pictures in this story about Maria, who wakes up one morning and finds her head full of not brown hair, but fire red, sky blue, emerald green, lemon yellow, and cotton candy pink colors! Her mother thinks she has slept on a rainbow. Maria paints up a storm. Then one day she wakes up with her head literally full of books, and another day with her head full of. . . . Have the children guess what comes next and what Maria intends to do about it.

Animals attract children's interest too, and *Edward the Emu* by Sheena Knowles (New York: HarperCollins, 1988) should quickly delight them with the zany zoo antics of this big flightless bird who is not satisfied with being an emu because it is so boring. So Edward becomes a seal, then a lion, then . . . what next?

SMILES, SEEMS HAPPY MUCH OF THE TIME

Joy (Enjoyment)

Joy, the most positive of the emotions, is also the most elusive. Seek it and you may not find it. Try to experience it directly and it may elude you. But live a normal life and it will appear spontaneously. Joy does not occur so much on its own as it does as a by-product of something else: a pleasant experience, a happy thought, a good friendship. In other words, this emotion is indicative of feeling good about oneself, others, and life in general.

The absence of joy tells us that the child is not feeling good about these things. We need to observe children carefully to see where they stand in regard to this important indicator of inner feelings, and we need to take positive actions if this emotion is missing.

Joy is the feeling of happiness that may precede or follow a pleasant experience: sensory pleasure such as a hug, a kiss, or a back rub; psychological pleasure such as

A happy smile is usually an indication that a child feels good about herself, others, and life in general.

the remembrance of good times; and the anticipation of seeing a loved one or of having fun with friends. People express joy with smiles, laughter, the lighting up of eyes, increased heartbeat, an inner feeling of confidence, a sense of well-being, or a glow. The emotion itself is fleeting, but the good feeling it creates may color a person's actions and responses for many hours.

As with the other emotions, the capacity for joy is inherited and is different for each individual (Izard, 1977, p. 239). Its development, however, depends greatly on how the mother or primary caregiver responds to joy in the infant. A person cannot teach another person to be happy, but she can influence the occurrence of happiness by creating a pleasant environment in the first place, then responding positively when joy occurs.

Babies may smile during the first days of life. At first they smile in revery or dreams, then during waking hours when a pleasant, high-pitched voice talks to them, and finally, by the fifth week at the sight of a friendly face coming close (Izard, 1977, p. 239). The first smile, in fact, is almost a spontaneous reflex coming 2 to 12 hours after birth. The elicited smile that comes as a result of a voice occurs soon afterward within the first week. By the second or third month, infants are smiling spontaneously without seeing or hearing anyone—that is, if they have been responded to pleasantly by their caregivers. But the human face remains the single most effective stimulus to smiling (Izard, 1977, p. 248).

Laughter has its own developmental sequence. It first occurs between five and nine weeks, usually in response to patty-cake-type games or tickling. Scientists believe a child's motor development has some relationship to development of laughter. But both laughter and smiling can be stimulated by the same expressions of joy on the part of another.

Situations that discourage or prevent the emotion of joy from occurring include poor physical health, fatigue or boredom, harsh treatment or neglect, conditions of poverty that limit a child's possibilities, and lack of joy on the part of caregivers.

Recognition of a familiar person, object, or situation helps stimulate or encourage the expression of joy. Whereas change and novelty seem to stimulate the emotion of interest, familiarity and being comfortable with things set the stage for joy. Keep this in mind in your child-care center. A little change is challenging, no change at all is boring, and too much change is overwhelming for young children. They need a stable schedule of daily events they can depend on and a physical arrangement of equipment that does not change too drastically overnight. Then they can look forward with joy to coming to the center every day.

If You Have Not Checked This Item: Some Helpful Ideas

■ Talk with Parents

Children who express no joy probably are not very happy. You will need to converse with the joyless child's parents in a sensitive manner, trying to elicit how the child reacts at home, whether any particular problems or pressures are affecting him, and what his basic personality is like. Is the child fundamentally happy? What are his favorite foods, colors, toys, activities? What makes him laugh? Perhaps you can use some of these favorites as a focus for an activity to make him feel joyful.

■ Be a Joyful Person

Children and others feel joy when they meet a person who thinks they are delightful and wants to be around them. Make yourself that kind of person.

■ Read a Book

Fun Is a Feeling by Chara M. Curtis (Belleview, WA: Illumination Arts, 1992) illustrates wonderfully what the feeling of fun (or joy) can be for a child, especially when the child pretends.

It Wasn't My Fault by Helen Lester (Boston: Houghton Mifflin, 1986) tells the hilarious story of Murdley Gurdson, who is always bumbling into things that turn out to be his fault. Then one day while he is out walking, someone lays an egg on his head. As he confronts one comical animal after another to find out whose fault it was, your children should be filled with laughter over the absurd situation and its final solution. It is a joyous experience.

Table 4–1 helps you see at a glance the causes and results of these common feelings. Such awareness can assist you in helping children develop more positive responses in emotional situations.

Table 4–1   Childhood emotions in the classroom

Emotion	Common Cause	Possible Results
Distress	Separation from loved one; abandonment	Crying; whining; clinging
Fear (anxiety)	Presence of threat; absence of safety	Tightening of muscles; refusal to eat, fall asleep, go to toilet
Surprise (startle)	Loud noise; unexpected appearance or event	Crying; withdrawing; clinging
Anger	Physical or psychological restraint; interruption; insult	Red face; loud words or screaming; physical aggression
*Aggression	Anger; frustration	Hitting; throwing; biting; kicking; pushing
Shyness (shame)	Heightened self-consciousness; exposure	Red face; crying; withdrawal
Interest (excitement)	Change; novelty	Looking at something; exploration with senses; wide eyes
Joy (enjoyment)	A pleasant experience; happy thoughts; friendship	Smiling; laughing; lighting up of eyes; talking happily

*NOTE: Not a true emotion

OBSERVING, RECORDING, AND INTERPRETING EMOTIONAL DEVELOPMENT

To understand and interpret the emotional growth of individual children, it is helpful to fill out the emotional development section of the Child Skills Checklist for specific children. Using data gathered during observations, her teacher filled out this section of the Checklist for Sheila, the child discussed in Chapter 2, as shown in Figure 4–1.

Sheila shows confidence in her use of language, as well as in her eating, sleeping, and toileting away from home without a fuss. This seems to indicate she is at ease in the classroom setting. However, she does not seem to be all that comfortable with the other children: She does not play with them yet, and she runs to the teacher whenever anything upsetting happens. The other important indicator is the fact that she does not smile or seem happy. Perhaps Sheila does not display happiness because she is ill at ease with the other children.

This observation was made at the beginning of the school year before all of the children were used to each other and to the center. Some of the activities listed

Child Skills Checklist

Name _Sheila — Age 3_   **Observer** _Connie R._

Program _Head Start_   **Dates** _10-22_

Directions:

Put a ✔ for items you see the child perform regularly. Put *N* for items where there is no oppor-

tunity to observe. Leave all other items blank.

Item	Evidence	Date
2. Emotional Development		
✔ Allows self to be comforted during stressful time	Lets teacher calm her down when Beth takes her crayon	10/22
✔ Eats, sleeps, toilets without fuss away from home	Always does these things with ease on own	10/22
____ Handles sudden changes/ startling situations with control	Cries or runs to teacher when upsetting things happen	10/22
✔ Can express anger in words rather than actions	When Beth takes crayon she says to her: "That's not fair!"	10/22
✔ Allows aggressive behavior to be redirected	Allows teacher to involve her in other activities	10/22
____ Does not withdraw from others excessively	Does not play with other children	10/22
✔ Shows interest/attention in classroom activities	Goes around room trying out everything	10/22
____ Smiles, seems happy much of the time	Rarely smiles; does not give evidence of being happy	10/22

Figure 4–1   Emotional development observations for Sheila

under "If You Have Not Checked This Item: Some Helpful Ideas" may help Sheila feel more comfortable with the others. The fact that Sheila goes around the room trying out everything is a sign that she will eventually want to get involved in everything. Perhaps Sheila can do an art activity with another child. Her teacher may want to pair Sheila with a child who is already at ease and will thus help Sheila feel more at home in the classroom.

REFERENCES

Brooks-Gunn, J., & Matthews, W. S. (1979). *He & she: How children develop their sex-role identity.* Upper Saddle River, NJ: Merrill/Prentice Hall.

Frey, W. H., & Langseth, M. (1985). *Crying: The mystery of tears.* Minneapolis: Winston.

Furman, R. A. (1995). Helping children cope with stress and deal with feelings. Young Children, 50(2), 33–41.

Hyson, M. C. (1994). *The emotional development of young children: Building an emotion-centered curriculum.* New York: Teachers College.

Izard, C. E. (1977). *Human emotions.* New York: Plenum.

Izard, C. E. (1991). *The psychology of emotions.* New York: Plenum.

Raikes, H. (1996). A secure base for babies: Applying attachment concepts to the infant care setting. *Young Children,* 51(5), 59–67.

Solter, A. (1992). Understanding tears and tantrums. *Young Children,* 47(4), 64–68.

SUGGESTED READINGS

Beaty, J. J. (1995). *Converting conflicts in preschool.* Ft. Worth, TX: Harcourt Brace.

Beaty, J. J. (1996). *Skills for preschool teachers.* Upper Saddle River, NJ: Merrill/Prentice Hall.

Curry, N. E., & Arnaud, S. H. (1995). Personality difficulties in preschool children as revealed through play themes and styles. *Young Children,* 50(4), 4–9.

Kuebli, J. (1994). Young children's understanding of everyday emotions (Research in review). *Young Children.* 49(3), 36-47.

Schickedanz, J. A. (1994). Helping children develop self-control. *Childhood education,* 70(5), 274–278.

VIDEOTAPES

Magna Systems, Inc. (1994). *Preschoolers: Social and Emotional Development.* Magna Systems, Inc., 95 West County Line Rd., Barrington, IL, 60010.

LEARNING ACTIVITIES

1. Observe the children in your classroom for a week in the eight areas of emotional control. Which children exhibit behavior that seems to show emotional control? Which ones have not yet learned inner control? How can you help them? Write out and discuss a plan with your supervisor.

2. Choose a child who has trouble allowing his or her aggressive behavior to be redirected. Observe the child for three mornings, making a time sampling of the behavior. Use a behavior modification idea as discussed in Chapter 1 to see if you can reduce the number of times this negative behavior occurs. What are the results of your follow-up observation?

3. Choose a child who has trouble either eating, sleeping, or toileting in your center. Observe the child, making a running record of behavior on three different days. What other indications of tension do you find? What suggestions do you have for alleviating the tension?

4. Work with one of the children in your classroom who has difficulty expressing his or her anger in words. What actions can you take to help the child? Observe and record the results.

5. Choose a child for whom you have checked "Smiles, seems happy much of the time." Observe this child on three different days. Which of the other items can you check on the Checklist based on your observations? What is your evidence for each checkmark? What conclusions can you make about this child based on these observations? Do you need any additional evidence to make conclusions?

CHAPTER 5

Social Play

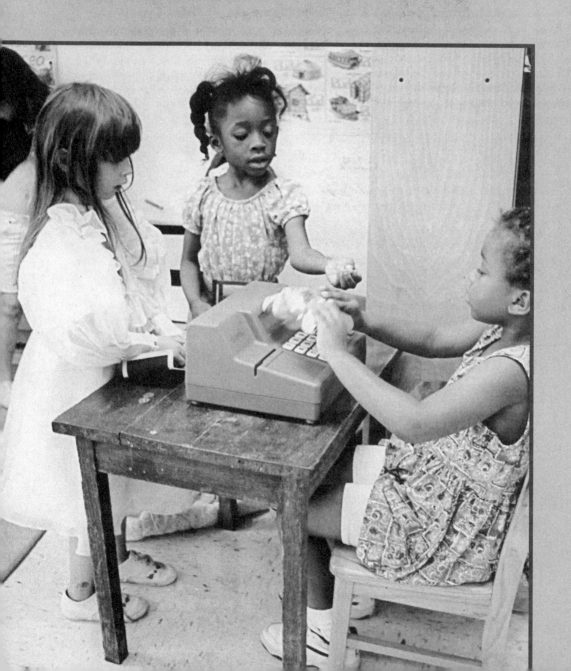

SOCIAL PLAY CHECKLIST

☐ Spends time watching others play

☐ Plays by self with own toys/materials

☐ Plays parallel to others with similar toys/materials

☐ Plays with others in cooperative play

☐ Makes friends with other children

☐ Gains access to ongoing play in positive manner

☐ Maintains role in ongoing play in positive manner

☐ Resolves play conflicts in positive manner

DEVELOPING SOCIAL PLAY SKILLS

The social development of the preschool child is revealed in how he or she gets along with peers. Often, we think of social actions as manners and politeness, but in the study of young children, social actions refer to how children learn to get along with their peers. Getting along for this age group rarely involves manners and usually is not very polite. Young children, in fact, frequently struggle to develop social skills.

Children start out completely self-centered, which seems to stem from a survival mechanism in infancy. Chapter 3 discussed how infants do not even recognize themselves as different from their primary caregiver in the beginning. Then, little by little, infants begin to discover their own self-identities. By the time they arrive in your classroom, children have begun to know themselves as individuals but mainly in relation to their adult caregivers.

Children who have already developed strong self-identities should do well away from home. They will be able to let go of their primary caregiver more easily and will be more willing to try new things and to experience new people. Reviews of current research support this point of view: "The quality of the child's attachment relationship with his mother in infancy has been found to predict the child's social acceptance in preschool," according to the studies examined by Kemple (1991, p. 51). In addition, if the children have siblings at home, they will have learned to respond and react to other children.

Peers in the early childhood classroom, however, pose a different problem for the young child. Many, if not most, three- and four-year-olds simply have not developed the social skills for making friends or getting along with others. The focus of these children is on themselves. Everything has been done for them up to this time. Even if a new baby has replaced them as the youngest in the family, they still struggle to be first in the eyes of their parents.

This egocentric point of view does not serve them well in the world at large, because sooner or later they must learn to deal with others and be treated as part of a group. They may have been enrolled in your program to learn precisely this. The purpose of many preschools, especially nursery schools, is to help young children develop basic social skills.

What do these preschoolers need to learn? If socialization is not concerned with politeness and manners, then what social actions are involved in the early childhood classroom? Some important aspects include:

1. learning to make contact and play with other children
2. learning to interact with peers, to give and take
3. learning to get along with peers, to interact in harmony
4. learning to see things from another child's point of view
5. learning to take turns, to wait for a turn
6. learning to share with others
7. learning to show respect for others' rights
8. learning to resolve interpersonal conflicts

Preschoolers' success in developing these skills, either on their own or with your help, may make the difference in how they get along for much of the rest of their lives.

This chapter is particularly concerned with the young child's ability to make contact, interact, and get along with peers. To determine where each of your children stands in the development of these skills, you need to be aware of behaviors that indicate their development level. Because children engage in play—often together— and because play is an observable activity in the preschool classroom, we will focus on observing social play in this chapter. Stone (1995) and other researchers agree that playing with others offers young children the best opportunity to learn social skills:

> Play is the primary mode for children's social development. Play encourages social interaction. Children learn how to negotiate, resolve conflicts, solve problems, get along with each other, take turns, be patient, cooperate, and share. Play also helps children understand concepts of fairness and competition. (p. 49)

EARLY RESEARCH

Many early childhood specialists have been interested in determining how children develop the skills to get along with one another. Social play has been the focus of such research since Mildred Parten first looked at "Social Participation Among Pre-School Children" in the late 1920s and published her findings in 1932. She found that social participation among preschoolers could be categorized and the categories correlated closely with age and maturity.

Parten (1932) identified six behavior categories that have since served as a basis for determining children's social skills level in several fields of study. Her categories include:

1. *Unoccupied behavior:* The child does not participate in the play around him. He stays in one spot, follows the teacher or wanders around.

2. *Onlooker behavior:* The child spends much time watching what other children are doing and may even talk to them, but he does not join or interact with them physically.

3. *Solitary independent play:* The child engages in play activities, but he plays on his own and not with others or with their toys.

4. *Parallel activity:* The child plays independently but he plays next to other children and often uses their toys or materials.

5. *Associative play:* The child plays with other children using the same materials and even talking with them, but he acts on his own and does not subordinate his interests to those of the group.

6. *Cooperative play:* The child plays in a group that has organized itself to do a particular thing, and whose members have taken on different roles. (pp. 248-251)

Since 1932, many other researchers have used Parten's categories and find them still "observable." Researchers like to use Parten's "play categories" when observing children at play because these behaviors really can be seen in the play interactions of young children. Yet since Parten's day, a great deal of new information about the social development of young children has surfaced. Today we acknowledge that these early play categories are indeed a valuable beginning point for gathering observational data about a young child's social development, but we also need to incorporate other up-to-date information. Thus, the Child Skills Checklist uses four of Parten's play categories under Social Play, but then uses four categories relating to children's play behavior in making friends, gaining access to ongoing play, maintaining a play role, and resolving play conflicts.

SOCIAL PLAY DEVELOPMENT

Because development of social play is very much age-related, the preschool child-care worker can observe it in a particular sequence as children progress from solitary play through parallel play to cooperative play. "Age-related development" thus signifies that the child's social skill level depends upon cognitive, language, and emotional maturity. It also infers that the older a child is, the more experience he probably has had with social contacts.

Observers have noted that infants first begin to imitate one another in play toward the end of their first year. Early in their second year, they are already engaging in peer play whenever they have the opportunity (Smith, 1982, p. 132). Two-year-olds often begin peer play by playing alongside another toddler in a parallel manner. If they interact with an agemate, it is only with one. Two-year-olds have difficulty handling more than one playmate at a time. A threesome does not last long for children of this age.

Three-year-olds, as they become more mature and experienced, are able to play with more than one other child at the same time. As they become less egocentric and

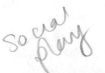

more able to understand another child's point of view, three-year-olds have more success with social play. Using more mature language, listening to their play partners, and adjusting their behavior to the situation all support such play.

Access Rituals

The trick for many children in your center, you will note, is to gain access to play already in progress. Sociologists call these maneuvers "access rituals." Children new to the group may try different strategies to get involved: (1) the youngest children may use nonverbal appeals such as smiles or gestures of interest as they stand nearby and watch, hoping a player will take note and invite or allow them in; (2) other children may walk around and watch, or stand and watch, waiting for an opportunity to insert themselves; (3) they may engage in similar play parallel to the original players, hoping to join the original players if their own parallel play is accepted; (4) they may intrude in a disruptive manner claiming that the space or the toys are their own; (5) the oldest preschoolers often use words, asking "Can I play?" or "What are you doing?" to gain access.

One successful strategy for a child to gain access to ongoing play seems to be engaging in parallel play. The least successful strategy is to be disruptive (Smith, 1982, p. 130). Researchers have noted that parallel play among preschoolers decreases as group play increases. Still, parallel play seems to be one of the principal modes of social play for three- and four-year-olds in most centers and classrooms.

THE TEACHER'S ROLE

Many children learn how to interrelate and play with peers in an early childhood program without the teacher's assistance. Others, however, need your help. Newcomers, shy children, immature children, and others often have difficulty on their own. If yours is a multiage classroom, it is often the youngest children who have difficulty gaining access to group play, sustaining their role in the play, or resolving conflict when it appears. These children definitely need your help.

Yours is a special role in helping children develop the social skills for peer acceptance. It involves several steps:

1. Set up the physical arrangement of the classroom to accommodate small group activities.
2. Observe and record the social skills of the children to determine: (a) who is unoccupied, (b) who watches, (c) who plays alone, (d) who plays parallel to others, (e) who initiates play activities, (f) who gains access to play, (g) who can maintain his play role, and (h) who can resolve conflict.
3. Help children initiate contacts with other children.
4. Help children gain access to ongoing play.
5. Help children maintain their play roles.

6. Help children learn to resolve conflicts with others.

How the teacher carries out this important role in children's social skills development is discussed under each of the Checklist items to follow. All four of the Checklist items—onlooker, solitary, parallel, and cooperative play—are, of course, descriptive, rather than judgmental. We are interested in observing individual children on each item to try to discover the child's level of social skills. We must be careful not to judge a child negatively if we do not check a certain item. The items themselves are neither negative nor positive; they merely describe behavior. What we infer from the checkmarks or lack of them will be more meaningful if we also look at the recorded evidence on which the checkmarks or blanks are based. It is just as important to record descriptive evidence on *items not checked* as on those items you have checked.

SPENDS TIME WATCHING OTHERS PLAY

By using the Child Skills Checklist to determine the social play level for the children in your classroom, you can identify children who have not yet become involved in play with others. These may be some of the children described in Chapter 3 who have had difficulty letting go of mother or their primary caregiver, especially at the beginning of the year. The shyness of children and the newness of the environment may also cause some children to hold back at first.

If the youngsters have not had experience with other children their age, a large group of peers can be overwhelming. This lack of experience with other children may deter them from gaining access to group play. Three-year-olds, especially, have usually had more experience with adult caregivers than with other children their age, and may not know how to behave in a peer group.

Some children who are new to a program begin by watching. They may walk around the room to see what is going on, but not join in. Parten (1932) describes the **onlooker** this way:

> The child spends most of his time watching the other children play. He often talks to the children whom he is observing, asks questions, or gives suggestions, but does not overtly enter into the play himself. This type differs from the unoccupied in that the onlooker is definitely observing particular groups of children rather than anything that happens to be exciting. The child stands or sits within speaking distance of the group so that he can see and hear everything that takes place. (p. 249)

Onlooking behavior is often the first step toward group participation. Some children take longer than others to become involved with group play. They need to know what is going on around them, who is doing what, and how they can enter this play. If the child seems engaged in watching a group at play, it may be best to leave him alone at first. He may join the others once he is at ease in the center. On the other hand, some children do not seem to know what to do or say to get others to play with them or to allow them to join in.

If You Have Not Checked This Item: Some Helpful Ideas

■ **Arrange Parts of the Room for Two Children**

Set up a few small tables, especially at the beginning of the year, for two children to participate in an activity: two puzzles, two table games, two sheets of paper and boxes of crayons, two individual chalkboards and colored chalk, two books to look at, two easels next to one another. This may be all it takes for the unoccupied child to become involved as soon as she feels comfortable. Playing with one other child is not so overwhelming as a whole group. Furthermore, since children imitate one another, the immature child can actually learn how to play in this new environment by copying her table mate.

■ **Suggest an Initiating Activity**

New children need to establish connections with other children in the classroom. They can do this by initiating a conversation with another child. If the onlooking child has not done so, you can suggest that he or she go over to another child and tell him what he would like to do. "Tell Paul you like to play with blocks. Say to him: 'Let's build a house with the blocks.'"

■ **Suggest Parallel Play**

If, after some onlooking time has elapsed, the child still has not joined in with the others, you may want to suggest that he erect a building next to Paul's, or play with clay at Ricardo's table, or drive his toy car through Sondra's tunnel after he asks her permission. As mentioned previously, parallel play like this is one of the most successful strategies for a child's gaining access to ongoing play.

 # PLAYS BY SELF WITH OWN TOYS/MATERIALS

Many young children, when they first enter a preschool program, start out playing by themselves. This may occur because of the strangeness of the situation or their lack of self-confidence with unfamiliar children. Solitary play also occurs because children are attracted by the toys and materials and want to try them out by themselves. Some solitary play may occur because certain programs encourage it or because children have an independent project they want to accomplish. You will need to observe and record the child's actual activity during solitary play, as well as the youngster's overall involvement or lack of it with other children. Even after children have advanced to cooperative play, many continue playing by themselves on projects of their own, and should not be discouraged from doing so.

Parten (1932) describes "solitary independent play" as follows:

The child plays alone and independently with toys that are different from those used by the children within speaking distance and makes no effort to get close to other children. He pursues his own activity without reference to what others are doing. (p. 250)

For some children, solitary play is truly a beginning level of social play that precedes their becoming involved in playing with others. If your children do not play at all with others or only play parallel to them, then you might consider solitary play as a beginning level of play for such youngsters.

More recent research by Sara Smilansky in the 1960s and Kenneth H. Rubin in the 1970s and 1980s has looked at children's play in terms of their cognitive development in addition to their social skills. They maintain that levels of play are determined not only by whether children play by themselves or with others, but also by what children do during play.

To determine whether your solitary players are, indeed, at a beginning level of social play, you should note in your observational data what they are doing. If children are manipulating toys and materials or trying them out to see how they work, then they are at a beginning level of play. In block play, for instance, beginners often pick up a block, put it down, pound with it, or put it in a container and then dump it out. More mature players stack blocks into towers, line them up into roads, or build buildings with them.

Research has also revealed that children from low-income families spend more time doing this sort of manipulative play than middle-income children (Rubin, 1977, pp. 16–24). Can we infer that such children are less socially and cognitively mature than their middle-class peers? Or should we wonder whether their solitary play has to do with the fact that they may have fewer play materials in their homes and thus must spend more time in a solitary manner in your program, manipulating these materials to find out how they work? Whatever the case, we need to provide a wide range of learning materials to encourage children to become involved on their own, as well as with others.

If you observe a child constructing or creating something by herself, this may indicate something altogether different than the beginner who is manipulating materials alone. If she is purposefully using materials toward some end, for instance, making a building, a painting, or a playdough creation, she may be exhibiting higher-level creativity skills. This higher level of skill development may have enabled such children to get satisfaction out of making something on their own. Instead of discouraging these children from solitary constructive play, you should provide them with many opportunities for expressing this creativity. Such children will join in group play again when the time is right for them.

Particular programs, such as Montessori's, have an approach that features one-person problem-solving materials. Such programs have a great deal more solitary play going on and less group play than other programs. Thus it is important that you take note of a program's goals and curriculum during your observations, as well as how the child uses the available materials.

If a child is neither engaged in solitary play nor any other kind of play during the free choice period, however, you can help him in several ways.

If You Have Not Checked This Item: Some Helpful Ideas

■ Give Child a Familiar Material

Many children are familiar with dough at home but have not had an opportunity to play with it. Have the nonplaying child help you mix a bowl of "playdough." Then give him some implements such as a small rolling pin and cookie cutters, and let him play.

■ Read a Book

Read a book about a child in a preschool such as *Chatterbox Jamie* by Nancy Evans Cooney (New York: Putnam's, 1993), about Jamie, a little boy who feels out of place when he first comes to school because he is alone without his Mom and Dad. At home he is a regular chatterbox, but at nursery school he is silent. On the first day he watches all of the different activities but doesn't join in the play of his multicultural classmates. The second day he starts playing on his own, and finally joins in. But it takes several weeks before he finally talks at school.

PLAYS PARALLEL TO OTHERS WITH SIMILAR TOYS/MATERIALS

Parallel play is a fascinating phenomenon. If you are unfamiliar with this type of play, you have to see it to believe it. Parallel play often involves two children who seem to be playing together. As you get close enough to witness what is going on, you find that each child is actually playing a different game from a different point of view. If language is involved, the two children seem to be talking to themselves rather than each other. Parten (1932) describes parallel play this way:

*Observe children playing next to one another to determine whether they are actually playing together or instead engaging in **parallel play,** a common early childhood phenomenon.*

The child plays independently, but the activity he chooses naturally brings him among other children. He plays with toys that are like those which the children around him are using, but he plays with the toy as he sees fit, and does not try to influence or modify the activity of the children near him. He plays *beside* rather than *with* the other children. There is no attempt to control the coming or going of children in the group. (p. 250)

All kinds of parallel play goes on in the preschool setting. More seems to occur with younger than with older children. Parallel play, as previously mentioned, seems to enable younger children to learn to play cooperatively with others in an early childhood center. This idea makes a great deal of sense when you consider that your center consists of a large group of highly egocentric youngsters who are strangers for the most part. They come together in a physical setting full of toys and activities just for them. How are they to deal with such a setting?

They begin by trying out things on their own. Then they play side by side using the same materials but playing a different game. Finally the children begin to cooperate, to interchange ideas, and to come together to play as a group with self-assigned roles and tasks. Once children have learned to play cooperatively, they may abandon parallel play altogether.

If You Have Not Checked This Item: Some Helpful Ideas

■ Try Fingerpainting for Two

Set up a small table where two can sit side by side, and put out finger paints to be shared. Invite one of your reluctant participants and one other child to paint. Do not force the reluctant child. Perhaps you could first involve him in a solitary manner and then ask him if another child could work next to him. This time he will be working not only parallel to the other child, but with the child, because the paints have to be shared.

■ Set Up Tape Recording for Two

It is important to have two cassette tape recorders in your program. They are invaluable because they provide an opportunity for two people to play individually with the same materials in a parallel manner. Tape recording is personal and fun. Even the shy child can talk as softly as she wants as long as she holds the mike up close. She can say anything about herself she wants: her name, the names of her brothers or sisters or pets, her favorite foods, or where she lives. Then comes the fun of listening to what she has spoken. Two children can record at the same table if they each talk into their own microphones. They may eventually want to talk into each other's mikes.

■ Read a Book

The story *Building a Bridge* by Lisa Shook Begaye (Flagstaff, AZ, Northland Publishing, 1993) mentioned in Chapter 3 can help children understand how two children who are playing separately but parallel to one another can come together. The Navajo girl

Juanita and the Caucasian girl Anna each build their own bridge with different-colored blocks, but then decide to put them together to build a bigger and better structure.

 ## PLAYS WITH OTHERS IN COOPERATIVE PLAY

When children play together in a group using the same materials for the same purpose or doing pretend play around a common theme, we say they are engaging in cooperative play. A great deal of cooperative play occurs in most early childhood programs, although not every child joins in. The observer can often spot children engaged in cooperative play in the block center where they are building structures together or in the dramatic play center where they are playing house or doctor. Early childhood specialists note that:

> Cooperative play involves sophisticated efforts to negotiate joint play themes and constructions with peers, and is characterized by children stepping in and out of their play to establish roles or events. For example, three children playing restaurant may alternate their roles in the play as customer, cook, and waiter with comments about the plot made from outside the play such as, "And pretend the hamburger got burned." (Van Hoorn, et al., 1993, p. 39)

Cooperative play like this is the principal activity for many children during free play time, while others have not yet learned the social skills necessary to enter the play or sustain their roles. They are the children often engaged in parallel play alongside the cooperative players. Some children are perfectly content to play alongside others without joining in, while other youngsters may need your help to join the fun.

Whatever you do, don't force the issue. Some children are not yet at ease enough in the classroom to join in with others in their cooperative play schemes. Give them a chance to get used to the program. Children fare very well on their own, and most will join in their own good time. Because this is the most sophisticated type of play in preschool, many children need time to play on their own or in a parallel situation. They need to become acquainted with the other players and perhaps make friends among them. They also need to have an interest in what the group is doing.

Your role should be to encourage cooperative play by giving children the opportunity for it to occur during the free choice period; by supporting children in their own play schemes or giving them ideas for new play projects from time to time; by giving them plenty of time to carry on this play; and by inviting anyone interested to join the play.

For children who want to play but do not know how to join in, see the suggestions under *Gains Access to Play in Positive Manner.*

If you do not see much cooperative play of any kind occurring in the classroom, you may need to take stock of your room arrangement or materials. Is your classroom divided into learning centers or curriculum areas with enough space for several children in each area? The block area should have room for at least six to eight children to create structures on the floor, but not be so large or open that all of the children try to occupy it at once. Block shelves can be pulled away from the walls to partially enclose the area. The shelves themselves should be filled with wooden unit blocks, enough for groups of children to build really large structures. Building accessories can include people, animals, small vehicles, and dollhouse furniture.

Many children first come together in cooperative play in the block center. They may start by playing with blocks by themselves, then build parallel to other builders, and finally join in with a group. Do your space and materials allow for this to happen?

A second area highly conducive to cooperative play is the dramatic play center. Most classrooms have a housekeeping area with child-size kitchen furnishings, a full-length mirror, dolls and dress-up clothing. In addition, you can add shelves, a desk and toy cash register, empty containers and bags for creating a pretend store. If there is space enough for several children and materials enough for several play themes, you may see more than one cooperative play group in operation at once.

If You Have Not Checked This Item: Some Helpful Ideas

■ Follow-up Field Trips

Whenever you go on a field trip, whether near or far, be sure to set up in one of the learning centers some trip-related props for children to play with cooperatively. Children can then spontaneously re-create the trip or play out some aspect of it that interests them. For example, put out firefighters' gear (hats, raincoats, boots) in the dramatic play center; or put out little fire trucks, plastic tubes for hoses, and figures of people in the block center.

■ Follow-up Book Readings

Another way to initiate spontaneous group play is to read a favorite story and then put out props for children to reenact or follow up some aspect of the story. *Feast for 10* by Cathryn Falwell (New York: Clarion Books, 1993) is a simple, vividly illustrated story of an African American family with five children, mother and father, grandparents and a friend joining together for a wonderful feast. It is a counting story in rhyme with the mother and children buying the necessary food in the grocery store, loading it in the car, preparing the meal, and finally sitting down to eat. You can follow up by putting out plastic food props in the dramatic play area along with bags and cash register, pans, ladles, hotpad gloves, and dishes in the house area just like the book characters used.

In *Tar Beach* by Faith Ringgold (New York: Crown, 1991) another African American family goes to the "beach" on the roof of their apartment building during hot summer nights in New York City. Little Cassie, the narrator, lies on a blanket and looks up at the George Washington Bridge and other lighted buildings. Then she takes off in her mind and flies over the city. This book also comes with a doll figure of Cassie that can be used as a prop in your block center along with black squares of paper for the "tar beach" roofs of your own block buildings, and dollhouse furniture such as tables and chairs. Can your children build tall buildings with black rooftops? Put the book and Cassie doll in the block center after reading this story and watch to see what group play ensues.

Children of every race enjoy pretending to be book characters. Whether or not you have African American children in the class, your youngsters can identify with book characters like Cassie and thus feel good about such children. That is why it is so important to have picture books showing people of many races and cultures available for your children to look at. As noted by early childhood specialist Patricia G. Ramsey (1991):

> When children role play situations and characters in a book, they learn how to perceive situations from a variety of perspectives and literally be "in another person's shoes . . . " By engaging children in stories, we enable our young readers and listeners to empathize with different experiences and points of view and experience a wide range of social dilemmas. (pp. 168–169)

MAKES FRIENDS WITH OTHER CHILDREN

Is making friends with peers really important to young children, you may wonder? For instance, are they worried about finding a friend when they first come to school? Whether they express this idea openly, it is often uppermost in the minds of many youngsters when they first come into the unknown environment of the preschool classroom. Will the other children like them? Will there be a friend waiting for them? Just like human beings everywhere, young children also need to feel welcomed and accepted wherever they go.

This is part of being human. All of us as human beings need to be accepted as part of a group outside of our families. And within that group we need at least one other person we can relate to and who relates to us as a friend. The needs of preschool children are no different. But they are different in their ability to make friends. How does one go about making a friend when one is three or four or five?

Some children have no difficulty. Others seem to bumble about without much success. A few others don't even try. Not so many years ago this whole idea of friendship was the main reason that parents enrolled their children in preschools. They called it "socialization." They wanted their children to learn socialization skills before they went to elementary school. In other words, they wanted their children to learn to get along with other children.

Somehow, in the intervening years, many people have changed their goals for preschool children. When parents and some preschool teachers talk about preparing children for elementary school, they seem to mean their learning of preacademic skills such as reading, numbers, letters, and the cognitive concepts of shapes and colors. What happened to the social skills of making friends and learning to get along with peers? Don't children still have to learn that?

This textbook takes the point of view that all development occurs simultaneously. Social skills are just as important as cognitive skills, and support for their development should not be neglected. For preschoolers who do not develop competence in interpersonal social skills, the results can be disastrous in later years. Various studies have correlated poor peer relationships in early childhood classrooms with later delinquency, as well as emotional and mental health problems.

As children move away from their families by coming to preschool, they necessarily form new relationships with the people around them, especially their peers. Although such relationships are usually thought of as friendships, they are quite different from the friendships of older children or adults. Being preoccupied with their own interests and needs makes it difficult for preschool children to form friendships based on personality. They are more likely to look upon a friend as a momentary playmate who is doing something interesting or is fun to play with. As Ramsey (1991) notes:

> During preschool, children form "playmateships" in which children think of their most frequent companions as their friends. Friendships are defined by the current situation. Children sometimes say "I can't be your friend today" when they really mean "I'm playing with somebody else right now." Because frequency of association is often determined by availability and proximity, some friendship choices may reflect convenience more than personal preference. (p. 21)

Until children can truly see things from another person's perspective, their relationship with that person will always be somewhat one-sided. For the egocentric child of three to about six years, friendship is more of a one-way street than a two way relationship with each partner contributing. Young children are preoccupied with their own needs. They believe that others want what they want. That is the reason that play among preschoolers may so suddenly break down into conflict, because the players cannot see things from the other person's point of view.

How does friendship come about, then, among young children? When toddlers and the youngest preschoolers talk about a friend, they usually apply the word to any special person who has been called this for them. They do have favorite peers and can form strong attachments, but the concept of friendship itself does not have much meaning for them at first.

With older preschoolers, friendship often starts with two children (sometimes more) coming together. Each needs to be recognized as a person by the other, and then accepted. Still, preschooler concepts of friendship are

> self-centered, present-bound, and focused on the concrete and external. A friend is someone whom the self likes "right now." Friends play together and share food, toys and other valued resources. They are close in terms of physical proximity or even looking alike. (Edwards, 1986, p. 117)

These children may indeed be true friends, but often the reason for their friendship in preschool is based on playing together rather than liking one another's personality. The most important aspect of this type of friendship in an early childhood program is whether the child is *included* in the play with a partner or a group.

Teachers can best help young children make friends with others in the classroom first by observing and recording the children to determine who has been included in and excluded from group activities. Keep your eye on disruptive children who often engage in verbal and physical aggression. They may well be children who have not found friends. They may wander around the room, hovering close to others but not really included. Other onlookers may be shy or withdrawn children who have not been rebuffed but ignored by their peers. And still others may be children who are new to the class and have not yet found a way to be included by others. Children who are perceived by others to be different because of looks, language, age, or a physical disability are also sometimes excluded.

Once you have determined which children do not seem to have a friendly attachment to anyone in the group, you can decide whether such youngsters need to resolve their own friendship problems or if you should intervene to help them. If children come to you or cling to you, it may be a sign for you to bring them together with one other child. On the other hand, if an onlooker seems content to play parallel to the others, she may need more time to become comfortable with the activities and children before finding a friend on her own.

Children with disabilities may also need your help to find a friend. As Honig and Wittmer (1996) note:

> Children with disabilities need your inventive interventions to learn how to make a friend, use positive and assertive techniques to enter a play group, and sustain friendly play bouts with peers. (p. 65)

If You Have Not Checked This Item: Some Helpful Ideas

■ Help Children Find Partners

Play singing games, or circle games where children have a partner to participate with. Do not ask children to go around choosing a partner, because some children will be left out. Instead, the teaching staff can help children pair up quickly and quietly without a fuss. Playing partner games like this every day may help outsiders feel included enough to begin playing with their partner in an unstructured activity afterwards.

■ Do Not Make a Fuss About Friends

Teachers who talk a great deal about which children are friends with which other children may unknowingly be putting pressure on children who do not have identifiable "friends." Finding a personal friend is not the point in preschool. Most children have not yet developed to this level. Having a playmate is more important, but talking about it is not.

■ Model the Contact Behavior

If the child seems unable to make any contact with someone to play with, you can model the behavior yourself. "C'mon, Rodney, you take that car and I'll take this car. We're going to build a garage for our cars. Let's see if we can get someone to help us. Let's ask Eric. "Hi, Eric. We're going to build a garage for our cars with the blocks. Want to help us?"

You should be successful because children enjoy playing with the teacher and like to be chosen by the teacher to do things. However, if Eric refuses, then approach another child with the same request. This helps Rodney learn what to do should he be refused. You can extract yourself unobtrusively from this play once the children are engaged.

■ Read a Book

Some preschool children may have an imaginary friend at home, but seldom does this "friend" come to preschool. In *Jessica* by Kevin Henkes (New York: Puffin, 1989), little Ruthie has an imaginary friend named Jessica who goes wherever she goes and does whatever she does. Her parents tell her in no uncertain terms, "There is no Jessica!" But for Ruthie there is. When Ruthie turns five and goes to kindergarten, Jessica goes along reluctantly just like Ruthie. But when the children in school line up with partners, another girl comes and stands by Ruthie. Her name is Jessica, and they end up being good friends.

Margaret and Margarita by Lynn Reiser (New York: Greenwillow 1993) are two little girls who meet in the park. One speaks English and the other Spanish, saying exactly the same things on opposite pages. They sit with their mothers at opposite ends of a park bench, but soon come together because one has a toy rabbit named Susan and the other a toy cat named Susana. Soon they are learning to say words in each other's language and having a party with their toys, just like friends everywhere.

GAINS ACCESS TO ONGOING PLAY IN A POSITIVE MANNER

Next, children need to find a way to enter ongoing play. Some have no difficulty. Others may need your help. As mentioned previously, disruptive actions are the least successful. In her survey of research on preschool children's peer acceptance, Kristen Kemple (1991) found that:

> Researchers have recognized for a long time that generally positive behaviors, such as cooperation are associated with being accepted by peers, and generally antisocial behaviors such as aggression, are associated with being rejected. (p. 49)

Children who successfully enter ongoing play seem to have adopted such positive strategies as (a) observing the group to see what is going on, (b) adopting the group's frame of reference as in parallel play, (c) contributing something relevant to the play, and especially, (d) asking again if they are denied access (LeBlanc, 1989, p. 30). Communication skills seem to play an important role in children's gaining acceptance in group play. They need to talk with the players, understand what their replies are, then respond again, replying to their concerns.

If the group is pretending to take their babies to the doctor's, for example, a successful strategy Charlene might use for gaining entrance is to get a doll from the housekeeping area and bring it along with the others, saying, "My baby needs to be examined, too." In this case, she has adopted the group's frame of reference (doctor play) as well as contributing something relevant to the play (bringing her baby to be examined). But just as important, she uses words and does not crash unannounced

Teachers should observe to see how outsiders gain access to ongoing play, an indication of their social play development.

into the play. Instead, she gets a doll, brings it along with the others, and then communicates clearly: "My baby needs to be examined, too."

Had she merely asked, "Can I play?" it would be easy for the group to reject her. Had she taken one of the other children's dolls or tried to take over the role of the doctor, she would probably have been rejected. Children who have difficulty seeing things from another person's point of view may not understand what is required of them to join ongoing play. Then it is up to you to help.

Rosa, a shy little girl in Head Start, had trouble gaining access to much of the group play because she tended to be so unassertive. She would watch the others play, but whenever she shyly asked, "Can I play?" she was usually refused. Then she went off by herself. She should not have given up so easily. Over half of the requests made to join preschool play groups are denied, Corsaro (1981) discovered. But because group play in preschool is so fluid and brief, outside children have many opportunities to join in during a typical day. Just because a child is denied access once does not mean she will be denied if she tries again.

Many children like Rosa do not try again. Then it is up to the teacher to coach them on their next step, or to model a more successful strategy that they might try. If nothing seems to work for Rosa, and the group itself will just not accept her, then the teacher may want to spend some time coaching the group later on how to admit an outsider.

The teacher, however, should not herself force the child on the group. Being the adult in charge, the teacher has the power to make the group accept Rosa, but she will not be solving Rosa's problem by doing so. Instead, the group may become resentful toward Rosa, who was forced upon them by the teacher. The social dilemmas preschool children face are actually important learning situations for them. If the teacher solves the problem, the child has missed the opportunity to try to work it out for herself. Whenever a teacher intervenes, it should be as a last resort after a child has had more than one chance to attempt the resolution herself.

If You Have Not Checked This Item: Some Helpful Ideas

■ Use Puppets with the Child and/or the Group

When it seems appropriate, bring out two hand puppets and introduce them to Rosa with names such as Ollie Outsider and Purely Personal. Tell her that Ollie wants to play with Purely, but Purely won't let her. Ask Rosa what she thinks Ollie can do to get Purely to let her play. Whatever Rosa suggests, you can try out with the puppets. Let the Ollie puppet succeed if Rosa's suggestions seem appropriate. Give your own suggestions if nothing of Rosa's seems to work.

Use this same sort of puppet play to coach a group that will not let an outsider join. First ask the children how they think Ollie feels when Purely won't let her play. Then ask the group why they think Purely won't let Ollie join in. Finally ask the group what Ollie can do and what Purely can do so that everyone can play together. Then act out with a puppet on each hand the suggestions given by the group. Finally, let a child be one of the puppets while you play the role of the other one in a repeat of this social role play.

■ Provide a Time for Everyone to Join a Group

It is much easier for children to join a play group at the outset. Once the group has started, the outsider usually encounters resistance entering an established group. Therefore, it is important for the preschool teacher to provide a time and opportunity for everyone to become involved in playing with someone else. This can be at the beginning of the free choice period. Perhaps a brief circle time can acquaint the children with the activities available. Then each child can join the activity group of his choice.

Be careful that you do not choose the activity for the child and force him into it. The child must learn on his own how to gain access to a group. If a certain child holds back and does not join with any others, you can make a suggestion. You can urge the child to choose an activity or a partner. But do not pressure. He may not be ready yet.

■ Read a Book

In *I'm Calling Molly* by Jane Kurtz (Morton Grove, IL: Whitman, 1980) Christopher, an African American boy, lives next door to his playmate, redheaded Molly. One day when Christopher calls her, Molly refuses to come over and play because she is making gorilla stew with Rebekah. Then the girls dress up and walk by Christopher's house saying "We don't know you." He imagines all sort of outrageous things happening to Molly until Rebekah's mom drives up to get her, and soon Molly is calling him once again.

MAINTAINS ROLE IN ONGOING PLAY IN A POSITIVE MANNER

Developing the skill to enter ongoing play is not the end of social skill development for the preschool child, but rather the beginning. He must also be able to continue playing with the others. If the play situation is a pretend one, then the child needs to get along with others in the role he has chosen or been assigned. If he is building a block structure with another child, then the child needs to be able to cooperate with his play partner and complete the building. This give-and-take among preschool youngsters is not always smooth. To maintain his role in ongoing play, a child needs to be able to:

1. carry on a conversation
2. maintain eye contact when speaking
3. listen to and watch other speakers
4. adjust own conversation content in order to be understood (Smith, 1982, pp. 135–136)

In a spontaneous dramatic play situation, the child must also be able to pretend, take a role, take turns, and show respect for others' roles—all within a playful framework. Quite a complex agenda for three-, four-, and five-year-olds. No wonder not all children are successful at it.

Yet being successful at group dramatic play helps young children to practice and learn the social skills necessary *to be successful in life.* That is why group dramatic play in the preschool classroom is one of the most important activities. Some of the social skills children can learn through group dramatic play include:

- adjusting their actions to the requirements of their role and the group
- being tolerant of others and their needs
- not always expecting to have their own way
- making appropriate responses to others
- helping others and receiving help from them

Most centers and classrooms provide a place for group dramatic play; that is, the taking of spontaneous roles in an imaginary situation made up by the children during free play. Rubin (1977) found that these situations mainly involve topics revolving around house, store, doctor, firefighter, and vehicle play.

A clear sequence of pretend play in young children has emerged over the past 20 years of research. By age two, children can pretend and often play with imaginary objects. The more complex group dramatic play mentioned here cannot happen until children can articulate verbally, which occurs between two and four years of age. Such play gradually becomes more complex with five-year-olds in kindergarten until about age six, when the frequency of group dramatic play begins to decline. By age seven, games with rules are more prominent, and group dramatic play seems to disappear altogether (Smilansky, 1968, pp. 10–11).

Thus, the early childhood classroom needs to take advantage of this recognized sequence of children's activities, and to provide the materials, equipment, space, and time to allow and encourage children to engage in group pretend play: the practice field for the social skills of life itself! Chapter 14 discusses the development of the child's imagination and themes he or she chooses when making up the roles and situations for group dramatic play. Here we are concerned with the young child's personal interactions with peers that will allow him to continue his play with them. Engaging in group pretend play like this helps to transform a preschool child from an egocentric being who is the center of all attention into a socialized human being who recognizes the existence of others' points of view and can respond appropriately.

If You Have Not Checked This Item: Some Helpful Ideas

■ Make Prop Boxes for Field Trip Pretend Play

You will be taking your children on field trips to stores, farms, fire stations, hospitals, laundromats, parks, zoos, pet shops, and construction sites. Upon your return you will want to provide a variety of ways for children to represent and talk about their experiences. An excellent activity involves providing props for them to play the roles seen at the field trip site. Many teachers make up a prop box after every field trip, filled with paraphernalia to be used in pretending the different roles. A trip to the post office, for instance, could produce a prop box with stamps (cancelled postage stamps or stickers of some sort), a stamp pad and stamper, envelopes, a mail bag (tote bag), a mail carrier's hat, and a picture book about a mail carrier. Label each box with a picture and words the children will soon recognize. Allow the children to take such boxes from the shelf and play with the equipment during free choice period. If children have shown interest in the field trip, they are more likely to become involved with pretend play afterward.

■ Change Your Dramatic Play Area from Time to Time

Everyone is stimulated by change. If you have had housekeeping equipment in your dramatic play period for a number of weeks, try converting the area to something else: perhaps a store or a beauty/barber shop. Talk with the children and have them help stock it with empty or discarded items from home.

■ Put New Accessory Items in the Block Area

Group pretend play takes place in areas other than the dramatic play corner. Children can do their follow-up pretending after a field trip in the block corner as well. Mount pictures of the field trip site at eye level on the wall to give children seated on the floor ideas for creating new kinds of buildings. Add appropriate accessories to the shelves within the block area as well. If you have been to a construction site, put out little trucks, figures of people, string (for ropes and wires), plastic tubing, even stones if you want to be very realistic. Accessories can also be put at the sand or water table, although pretending in these areas is more often solitary or parallel than group play.

RESOLVES PLAY CONFLICTS IN POSITIVE MANNER

Not only does group play teach children the social skills of gaining access and maintaining a role in the playing, but more importantly, it gives young children the opportunity to learn to get along together. This is not always easy. Conflicts of all kinds occur with high frequency in an early childhood classroom. Children need to learn how to resolve such disagreements in a positive manner. During group play, major conflicts often focus on:

- roles
- direction of play
- turns
- toys

Pretend roles are important to the children who take them. In spontaneous dramatic play, certain children often insist on being mother, or father, or doctor. If several children want the same role, a conflict often results. This does not necessarily mean a physical fight, but usually an argument and sometimes tears. If the children involved cannot resolve the conflict quickly, play is disrupted and sometimes disbanded.

Conflict also occurs over play themes in dramatic play (e.g., "Let's play doctor." "No, let's play superheroes.") as well as the direction of the action, which is generally made up on the spot. Egocentric young players often want their own way, and frequently disagree over who will do what, what are they going to do, and what's going to happen next.

"It's my turn!" or "It's my toy!" are other comments frequently heard during group play in early childhood classrooms or playgrounds. Youngsters three, four, and five years old are still for the most part focused on themselves and their desires. It is most annoying for them to find that someone else got there first, or has what they want, or won't listen to them.

Often children turn to the teacher to resolve these conflicts. You need to be aware, however, that the youngsters themselves have the capability to resolve social play conflicts on their own. That, in fact, should be your goal for the children: to help them resolve play conflicts by themselves in a positive manner. How do you do it? To begin with, your observation of individual children will tell you which youngsters are able to resolve conflicts on their own and which ones are not.

Rather than focusing on the negative behaviors during such conflicts, spend some time observing how certain children are able to settle their disputes positively. We can learn a great deal from children if we are willing to try. Consider the following running record that looks at four-year-old Alex:

> *Alex, Calvin, and Dominic are on top of the indoor climber pretending to be astronauts in outer space. Alex is the captain of the space shuttle. All three boys make zooming noises and motions. Alex pretends to steer. Two other boys climb up the ladder to try to join the group but are ignored and finally leave.*
>> Alex: "Duck! There's a meteor!"
>> Calvin: "It's my turn to be captain, Alex."
>
> *Alex ignores Calvin and continues steering.*
>> Dominic: "No, it's my turn. I never get a turn."
>> Alex: "We're being bombarded by meteors! You need to duck!" *(He ducks his head.)*
>> Calvin: "I'm captain now."
>
> *Alex ignores Calvin and continues steering.*
>> Dominic (to Calvin):   "You can't be captain. Alex is still captain."
>> Alex: "You can be copilot. They always have copilots."
>
> *Calvin begins pretending to steer.*
>> Alex: "Bang! We've been hit by a meteor! Abandon ship!" *(He slides down slide to floor and runs across room; other boys follow.)*

This exciting adventure in outer space is typical of the vigorous dramatic play preferred by four-year-olds. It should also be exciting for an observer to see a four-year-old like Alex handle a role conflict with such composure and success. Alex is often the leader in such play, and from the way he uses ideas and words, it seems obvious that he is an experienced player. Children who play together a great deal learn by trial and error what works in resolving conflicts and what doesn't. They also find out what works with particular children and what doesn't work.

The first strategy Alex uses is *ignoring*. Alex ignores the boys who try to join his ongoing space shuttle play. They finally go away, so he certainly notes that this kind of ignoring is a successful way to keep out certain unwanted players. Then another potential conflict emerges: Calvin wants a turn to be captain. At first Alex ignores this request as well. Then Dominic joins in and also wants to be captain. Now Alex tries another strategy: *distracting*. He tells them that they are being bombarded by meteors and wants them all to duck. A strategy like this may sometimes work. In fact, here it seems to work with Dominic, who gives up his own demand to be captain, and *cooperates* with Alex. But it does not work with Calvin because he has not given up his demand. So Alex tries another strategy: *negotiating*. He offers Calvin another role: copilot. Calvin accepts and the play continues. This does not mean that either boy knows exactly what a copilot is. But it must sound satisfactory to Calvin because he *compromises* his demand to be captain, accepts the new role as copilot, and plays the role the same as Alex plays the captain's role.

Alex may very well have known that he had to do something to satisfy Calvin, or perhaps Calvin would have: (1) gotten up and left or (2) continued his complaints and disrupted the play. Obviously Alex wanted the play to continue and wanted to keep his own role as captain and leader. He was successful in *negotiating a compromise*.

Did all of this actually happen in so short a dramatic play incident, you may wonder? Yes, it did. Observe a child involved in group play for yourself and record everything that happens. Then step back and interpret what you have seen. Obviously the children do not talk or think in terms of strategies. These are adult interpretations. Young children do not conceptualize in this manner. They just do it. Trial-and-error has taught certain alert youngsters what works for them and what doesn't when conflict arises. Children who are successful in resolving play conflicts in a positive manner often use strategies such as:

- ignoring
- distracting
- reasoning
- negotiating
- cooperating
- compromising

If your observations turn up children who do not seem to know how to resolve play conflicts like this, then you may want to consider some of the following solutions:

If You Have Not Checked This Item: Some Helpful Ideas

■ Have Child Observe and Discuss Play with You

For a child who often tries to resolve play conflicts by hitting or shouting, you can have him observe a group play situation with you and then discuss it. If the child had sat next to you as you observed and recorded the Alex-Calvin-Dominic play incident, you might say to him:

> *Alex is captain of the space shuttle, isn't he? But Calvin wants to be captain, and so does Dominic. What does Calvin do? Yes, he tells Alex that he wants to be captain. Does Alex let him? No, he doesn't pay attention to him. So then what does Calvin do? Does he yell at Alex? No. Does he hit Alex? No. He tells him again that he wants to be captain. Does Alex let him? He lets him be a copilot. Is that like being captain? What would you do if you were on the space shuttle with Alex, Calvin, and Dominic? Do you think your ideas would work?*

If the play situation you observe with the child contains some aggressive behavior, ask the child what the result of the behavior was. Most children will not continue to play with peers when they act aggressively. Often they won't allow such peers in their play groups in the first place.

■ Use Puppets

For a child who gets into arguments frequently with his playmates, try using two puppets to enact a similar situation. Name your puppets something like Tong-Talk-Back and

Fronz-Friendly. Put one on each hand and enact a play situation where Tong argues with Fronz over something, with the result that the playing is discontinued. Ask the child what Tong could have said to keep the play going. Ask what the child would have done.

■ Coach the Child on How to Act

Sometimes you need to go to a child and coach him or her on how to act or what to say in a situation. You must make it clear to children that you will not let them hit anyone or hurt anyone or call them names. When they are upset about something, children must learn to express their feelings in words. You may need to coach those who do not know how:

> *Tell Jenny how you feel, Teresa, because she took your egg beater. Don't call her names. Tell her why you are upset. Say it in words. Say:"Jenny, you took my egg beater. That makes me feel bad. I wasn't finished using it. Please give it back."*

■ Do a Group Role Play

Sometimes the play group itself doesn't know how to resolve conflicts peacefully. In that case, you can consider having a group role play sometime after the children have settled down. The players should be other children, so that the children having conflicts can watch. Take a role yourself if it seems appropriate. Then you can help direct the play. Give a few other children names and roles to play. Describe a brief conflict situation. Then have the children act it out. Stop the play at any time to discuss what has happened, and whether there is a better way to resolve the conflict. Try each of these techniques to see which ones work best with your particular children.

■ Read a Book

There are other ways to get what you want besides aggressive actions. Read to one or two children at a time *Move Over, Twerp* by Martha Alexander (New York: The Dial Press, 1981) about little Jeffrey, who is finally big enough to ride the bus to school, but the big boys won't let him sit where he wants to. Jeffrey's family members give him advice on what to do, but it is Jeffrey's own clever strategy that finally helps him get his way. Ask your children what they would do. Could any of them apply a strategy like Jeffrey's to anything that happens in your classroom?

OBSERVING, RECORDING, AND INTERPRETING SOCIAL PLAY

How should you use the Social Play Checklist section with your children? The following description shows how one classroom team put the checklist to use:

When three-year-old Lionel entered the classroom as a new child in January, he seemed to have a great deal of trouble interacting peacefully with the other children. By the end of the third week he still had not joined any of the group activities. The staff members decided to make a running record of Lionel during the free play period for several days and then transfer the results to the Child Skills Checklist. Here is a typical example of a running record made on Lionel:

Lionel gets two little cars from box in block corner & sits on floor moving cars around, one in each hand. Makes car noises with voice. Plays by himself with cars for five minutes. Moves closer to block building that two other boys are constructing. Plays by himself with his cars. Then L. tries to drive his cars up wall of building. Boys push him away. L. waits for a minute, then tries to drive car up wall of building again. Boys push him away. L. crashes one car into building & knocks down wall. One of boys grabs L's car & throws it. Other boy pushes L. away. L. cries. Teacher comes over & talks with all three. L. lowers head & does not respond. Boys say: "He was trying to knock down our building with his cars." and "We don't want him to play with us."

When the staff members reviewed the running records and checklist information recorded for Lionel (see Figure 5–1), they concluded that he knew where to find

Child Skills Checklist

Name _____ Lionel _____   Observer _____ Barb _____
Program _____ Preschool—K 2 _____   Dates _____ 1/20 _____

Directions:
Put a ✔ for items you see the child perform regularly. Put *N* for items where there is no opportunity to observe. Leave all other items blank.

Item	Evidence	Date
3. Social Play		
_N_ Spends time watching others play	L. is beyond this level of play	1/20
✔ Plays by self with own toys/materials	Plays with little cars	1/20
✔ Plays parallel to others with similar toys/materials	Moves close to block building with his cars	1/20
____ Plays with others in cooperative play		1/20
____ Makes friends with other children		1/20
____ Gains access to play in a positive manner	Tries to gain access by driving cars up bldg then crashes car	1/20
_N_ Maintains role in ongoing play in a positive manner	Does not gain access	
____ Resolves play conflicts in a positive manner	Crashes car into bldg. when boys won't let him play	1/20

Figure 5–1   Social play observation for Lionel

materials and toys in the classroom and how to use them. They also interpreted his Social Skills Checklist results to mean that Lionel was beyond onlooker behavior, and that he played by himself and in parallel play as closely as possible to other children because he wanted to join them. His methods for gaining access to a group (e.g., driving his car up the block building wall and crashing his car into the wall) were neither successful nor acceptable. Nor was his language development as advanced as many of the children in the classroom, they determined from the Language Skills Checklist results. That may have been the reason he did not express his wants verbally. Perhaps because he was a new outsider, he had not made friends with the other children and his aggressive actions had prompted some of the boys to keep him out of their play.

The staff decided to try pairing up Lionel with Adrian, a more mature player, who might help Lionel get acquainted with the others and gain access to their play. They asked Lionel and Adrian (who also liked cars) to build a block garage for the little cars, and said they would take a photo of it. Eventually two other boys joined them in this activity.

This type of observing and recording can assist individual children in their development of social play skills and help them grow and learn in your program.

REFERENCES

Corsaro, W. (1981). Friendship in the nursery school: Social organization in peer environment. In S. R. Asher & J. M. Gottman (Eds.), *The development of children's friendships*. New York: Cambridge University Press.

Edwards, C. P. (1986). *Social and moral development in young children*. New York: Teachers College Press.

Honig, A. S., & Wittmer, D. S. (1996). Helping children become more prosocial: Ideas for classrooms, families, schools, and communities. *Young Children, 51*(2), 62–70.

Kemple, K. M. (1991). Preschool children's peer acceptance and social interaction. *Young Children, 46*(5), 47–54.

Parten, M. B. (1932). Social participation among preschool children. *Journal of Abnormal and Social Psychology, 27*, 243–369.

Ramsey, P. G. (1991). *Making friends in school: Promoting peer relationships in early childhood*. New York: Teachers College Press.

Rubin, K. H. (1977). Play behaviors of young children. *Young Children, 32*(9), 16–24.

Smilansky, S. (1968). *The effects of sociodramatic play on disadvantaged preschool children*. New York: John Wiley & Co.

Smith, C. A. (1982). *Promoting the social development of young children: Strategies and activities*. Palo Alto: Mayfield Publishing Company.

Stone, S. J. (1995). Wanted: Advocates for play in the primary grades. *Young Children, 50*(6), 45–54.

Van Hoorn, J., Nourat, P., Scales, B., & Alwood, K. (1993). *Play at the center of the curriculum*. Upper Saddle River, NJ: Merrill/Prentice Hall.

SUGGESTED READINGS

Beaty, J. J. (1995). *Converting conflicts in preschool*. Ft. Worth, TX: Harcourt Brace.

Beaty, J. J. (1996). *Skills for preschool teachers*. Upper Saddle River, NJ: Merrill/Prentice Hall.

Gowen, J. W. (1995). The early development of symbolic play. *Young Children, 50*(3), 75–84.

Greenberg, J. (1995). Making friends with the Power Rangers. *Young Children, 50*(5), 60–61.

Howes, C. (1992). *The collaborative construction of pretend: Social pretend play functions*. Albany, NY: State University of New York Press.

Montagu, A. (1995). Friendship—loving: What early childhood education is all about. *Child Care Information Exchange.* #106, 42–44.

Schickedanz, J. A. (1994). Helping children develop self-control. *Childhood Education, 70*(5), 274–278.

Wintre, M. G. (1989). Changes in social play behavior as a function of preschool programs. *Journal of Educational Research, 82*(5), 294–300.

VIDEOTAPES

Magna Systems, Inc. (1994). *Preschoolers: Social and emotional development*. Magna Systems, Inc., 95 West County Line Rd., Barrington, IL 60010.

LEARNING ACTIVITIES

1. Use the Child Skills Checklist, Social Play, as a screening tool to observe all of the children in your classroom. Which ones engage mainly in solitary play? In parallel play? In cooperative play? Are any unoccupied or onlookers?

2. Choose a child whom you have observed engaging in solitary play. Do a running record of the child on three different days to determine what kind of solitary play was performed. How could you involve the child in the next level of play? Should you do it? Why or why not?

3. Choose a child whom you have observed engaging mainly in parallel play. What kind of play does the child do? How can you help the child get involved in the next level of play? Use one of the suggested activities and record the results.

4. Choose a child who is not able to gain access to ongoing group play, and use one of the activities described to help the child enter and play with a group.

5. Make a running record of a child observed in group pretend play. Afterwards, determine which of the strategies discussed the child used to resolve conflicts. If the child is not successful, describe why and how you would propose to assist him.

CHAPTER 6

Prosocial Behavior

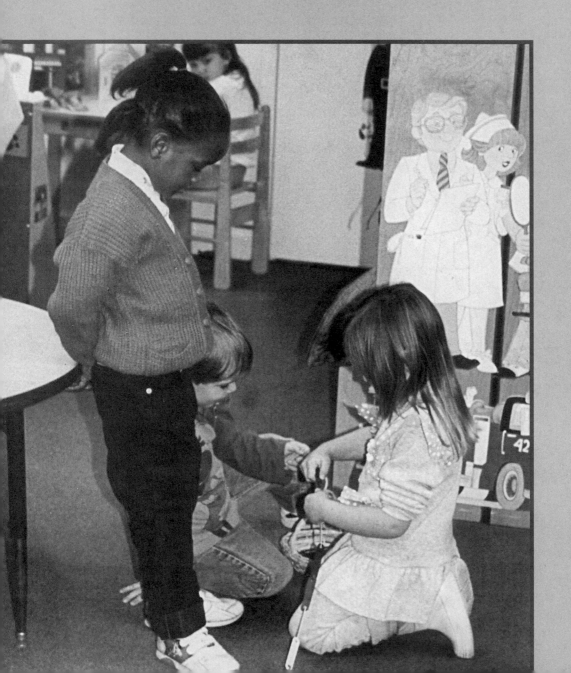

PROSOCIAL BEHAVIOR CHECKLIST

☐ Shows concern for someone in distress

☐ Can tell how another feels during conflict

☐ Shares something with another

☐ Gives something to another

☐ Takes turns without a fuss

☐ Complies with requests without a fuss

☐ Helps another do a task

☐ Helps (cares for) another in need

DEVELOPING PROSOCIAL BEHAVIOR

A second area of young children's social development that is of great concern to early childhood caregivers is the positive aspect of moral development, better known today as **prosocial behavior**. It includes behaviors such as **empathy**, in which children express compassion by consoling or comforting someone in distress or by expressing how another child feels during interpersonal conflict; **generosity**, in which children share or give a possession to someone; **cooperation**, in which children take turns willingly or cooperate with requests cheerfully, and **caregiving**, in which children help someone complete a task or help someone in need.

These are some of the characteristics that help people get along in society, motivate people to interact with one another, and help make us human. Young children are not in the world alone. They are part of a family, a clan of relatives, a neighborhood, a community, a country, and a world of similar beings. To be an integrated member of the "human tribe," the young child needs to learn the tribe's rules of behavior from the beginning.

This learning, you may argue, should happen in the home, and it certainly does in an informal manner, whether or not parents realize they are teaching their children pro- or antisocial behavior. Children absorb everything that happens around them: what mom does when the baby cries, what dad does when someone upsets him, and what family members do when they disagree. Every emotional situation presents the young human with forceful patterns of behavior he can model. We know only too tragically that adult child abusers often come from families where they were abused as children.

Prosocial behavior can be modeled as well. Both the home and the school should be aware of the powerful lessons taught by behavior modeling, which the child absorbs so readily at this early age, especially in emotional situations. What does the teacher do when out-of-control children upset her? It is so important for the other young children around her that she does not let her negative feelings burst out.

The actions of adults in emotional situations can be used to demonstrate the prosocial feelings of caring, sharing, and consoling, too. Or, as William Damon says in his book *The Moral Child,* (1988):

> The social guidance that helps children refine their early moral emotions can come in many forms: as a conscious program of moral instruction offered by parents, teachers, and other adults; or as a spontaneous comment on one's conduct by friends, siblings and other peers. In each case, children learn to know and interpret their own moral emotions in light of the moral reactions of others. (p. 29)

Children also learn behavior by methods other than example both in the home and the preschool. Formal—often restrictive—rules for "proper behavior" have been drummed into children from time immemorial. Children are scolded or punished when they behave in an unacceptable manner. They may cry, sulk, or slink away, or they may try to behave correctly next time. But just as often, they stick out a tongue in defiance and grumble, "try and make me!"

There is a better, easier way. Many early childhood specialists these days are turning to focus on the so-called **prosocial behaviors** in a search for ways to raise more humane members of the race. Not only does the learning of prosocial behaviors promise positive results, but it also offers more satisfying responses for both the child and the caregiver. Those who have tried this positive approach claim it is more effective than the negative method, and that as children learn prosocial ways to behave, negative behaviors seem to fade away. As noted by Honig and Wittmer (1994):

> Emphasizing and encouraging prosocial behaviors made a difference in how children learned to interact and play with each other. (p. 5)

Empathy, generosity, cooperation, caregiving: How do you teach such behaviors, anyway? They sound so elusive. Aren't some children just "good" naturally?

If children seem to be good, they probably are mature and have a good "home start." You can reinforce that maturity and home influence by the way you treat children in the early childhood classroom and by the way you model behavior yourself. But first, as with other areas of development, you should know where each child already stands concerning his or her development of prosocial behaviors. You will need to observe every child on the eight Checklist items and then make plans to provide individual support or activities.

Each of the Checklist items in this chapter is an observable behavior that shows if the child possesses a particular prosocial capacity.

SHOWS CONCERN FOR SOMEONE IN DISTRESS

Empathy

Empathy is the capacity to feel as someone else feels. A person with empathy is able to understand another person's emotional response to a situation and to respond in the same way—in other words, "to feel for him." Empathy is a step beyond mere sympathy in which one person can respond emotionally to another but from his own perspective. With empathy, you respond from the other person's perspective and participate in his feelings.

Some psychologists believe empathy is the basis for all prosocial behavior. Without this capacity, a child will be unable to behave naturally in a helping, sharing, compassionate manner. Obviously, the child can be forced to perform prosocially whether or not she understands what she is doing. But this forced performance is not empathy. Forced behavior has little to do with the prosocial skills of our concern. Behavior must be natural and spontaneous to show that children possess empathy.

Are children born with empathy, or do they learn it? Probably a little of both. Researchers have determined that capacities such as empathy have at least two different aspects to consider (Damon, 1983, p. 129). Empathy has an affective side, which is the emotional response to another's distress or joy, and a cognitive side, which allows the child to see things from another person's perspective.

Until this cognitive development has occurred (as discussed in Chapter 3), the child may have difficulty expressing empathic concern for others because he still will be too egocentric and therefore unable to see things from another person's point of view. Because they lack this empathy, infants and toddlers often mishandle their animal pets. The youngsters have no idea that pulling a puppy's ear or squeezing a kitten might hurt. If these actions do not hurt the children, they think, why should the pulling or squeezing hurt their pet? This egocentric point of view eventually changes with cognitive maturity and experience, but until a child can view things from another's perspective, he may have difficulty showing empathic compassion for another's distress.

When does this change take place? It happens gradually, of course, as does all development. Yet, some part of the human capacity to respond to distress must be built in, for even infants one day old will become upset and cry when a nearby baby starts crying. Then, somewhere between one and two years of age, the cognitive change takes place. Toddlers, although they may not act appropriately, begin to show genuine concern for others. These youngsters have been observed giving up their favorite stuffed animal to an older sibling who is crying. They feel comforted by the animal, so why not give it to another in distress? The act of giving demonstrates their developing capacity for empathy.

From two to around six years of age, children begin to react more appropriately to the distress of others around them. The ages of the children in your class fall within this range. You will be observing them to determine which ones show concern for another child in distress. Distress may be displayed by someone who is hurt, sad, or sick. She may be crying or even screaming. It also could be less dramatically disclosed by a child who puts her head down on a table, goes into a corner, or leaves the room after an upsetting incident.

You will note that some children immediately come to the side of the upset child. Others do not. The children who display this empathic concern, of course, may be special friends of the upset child. On the other hand, highly sensitive children who have no particular friendship with the child also will come close. Some youngsters just stand by the side of the distressed child and look at him or her, or look for the teacher. Others actively console the child, touching or speaking to him or her.

If a teacher causes the distress, a similar thing may happen. A child being reprimanded or scolded often will attract a circle of observers. In this case you will have more difficulty determining empathic behavior because some of the observers are more concerned for themselves and how the teacher feels about them. Others are simply curious. Before you check this item about them, watch and see who comforts the child after the teacher leaves. The children who comfort the child are not necessarily taking the distressed child's side against the teacher. If they stay with the child after the teacher leaves, they more than likely have true compassion for the child.

The classroom worker should know that family life and cultural background have a definite influence on empathic response in children. If families stress prosocial behavior, then their children will exhibit it more than children from families who do not teach or demonstrate it.

Some cultures stress consideration of group members more than others. Communal-type cultures, such as the Native American, Pacific Island, or Asian cultures often stress concern for group members more than the mainstream U.S. culture does. Our culture seems to stress competition among individuals more often than cooperation. The individual is glorified in our society, sometimes at the expense of the group. As a child caregiver in the multiethnic, multicultural society that makes up the United States, you need to be aware of such differences.

Research has shown that community size and the role of women also influence a child's prosocial inclinations. Children from a rural rather than urban setting, from a small rather than a large city, or from a society where women have an important economic function outside the home are more inclined to show concern for others (Damon, 1983, p. 132). If the mother works outside the home, the children often learn to take on responsibilities at an early age. Learning helping and caretaking tasks so early obviously inclines children toward prosocial behavior. Thus, the teacher needs to know something about the individual child's background to assess the child's behavior accurately.

Individual differences in children also influence behavior, as Damon (1988) notes:

> Like the capacity for empathy itself, such individual differences in empathic responding show up very early in life. Children as young as one and two respond differently to others' distress. Moreover, these differences between individual children endure, at least through the early childhood years. (p. 18)

If you have not checked this item for many of your children, do not be alarmed. Showing concern for someone in distress is one of the more difficult prosocial behaviors for preschoolers to learn. Distressful situations that happen to others upset onlookers, too. Before the onlookers can respond, they often need to overcome their own anxieties. They thus are more apt to step back and let the adult show the concern. You, however, can involve your children in this humane act.

If You Have Not Checked This Item: Some Helpful Ideas

■ Model Empathic Behavior in the Classroom

You must serve as a model for the children. When something distressful happens to someone, you should show your own concern by going to the person; touching, hugging, or holding the person if this is appropriate; talking to the child; and giving the youngster time and space to feel better again.

A second way to model this behavior is through your actions in distressful situations that happen outside the classroom. If someone is hurt or dies, if a tragic event is shown on television, or if something upsetting happens within their families, then you must let the children know you are concerned, too.

■ Help the Children Show Their Own Concern

Talk to the children both privately and in a group about distressful happenings that have occurred. Encourage the children to ask questions about things they do not understand. Show them that it is all right to cry and express emotions openly. When a class member is in the hospital, have the class make and send a card.

When children are pretending in dramatic play about people or pets being hurt, listen to see if the youngsters express compassionate feelings even in pretend. You can model a concerned role in pretending too, by expressing your own sympathy when one of the players is pretending to be hurt, or a baby is getting a shot from the doctor.

■ Read a Book

Maybe a Band-Aid Will Help by Anna Grossnickle Hines (New York: Dutton, 1984) is a beautifully illustrated first-person narrative of little Sarah's concern and help for her doll Abigail when its leg comes off.

Don't Worry I'll Find You by Anna Grossnickle Hines (New York: Dutton, 1986) is a follow-up story about Sarah and Abigail, both of whom get lost when they go shopping in the mall. Sarah's concern for her doll and Mama's concern for Sarah are cleverly demonstrated.

I Have a Sister My Sister Is Deaf by Jeanne Whitehouse Peterson (New York: Harper, 1977), is a first person narrative by a young girl about her younger sister, who is deaf. The girl tells all the things her sister can—and cannot—do in a manner showing great concern and sensitivity.

Daniel's Dog by Jo Ellen Bogart (New York: Scholastic, 1990) tells the story of young African American Daniel who at first feels a bit left out when his new baby sister comes. But then he gets an imaginary dog, Lucy, who keeps him company when he is lonely. His Hispanic friend Norman feels lonely, too, because his dad is away. Daniel puts a comforting arm around him and tells him that Lucy has an imaginary dog friend named Max who will come to be with him at bedtime that night. That makes it okay.

CAN TELL HOW ANOTHER CHILD FEELS DURING CONFLICT

Empathy

Empathy for another child is sometimes difficult to feel when one youngster is in conflict with another. But you can actually *teach* children to become aware of what another child feels to convert the conflict to positive feelings. This new approach to conflict resolution often works when no other behavior management strategy succeeds.

"Feel what the other child feels." Can a young child actually do this? Researchers have found that

> . . . with the beginning of a role-taking capability, at about 2 or 3 years, children become aware that other people's feelings may sometimes differ from theirs. . . . More important, because children now know that the real world and their perceptions of it are not the same thing, and that the feelings of others are independent of their own, they become more responsive to cues about what the other is feeling. (Hoffman, 1983, p. 23)

Most conflicts in preschool revolve around possession disputes. Someone wants something that another child is playing with, or someone takes something away from another child. Most such conflicts are brief interruptions in play, resolved by the children themselves, as they should be. Occasionally the conflict becomes so overpowering an adult must intervene. When hitting, fighting, throwing things, or crying break out, it is time for an adult to take action.

Suppose Samantha has been playing with the baby buggy; Kimberly takes it away from her; Samatha hits Kimberly, and she cries. What will you do? You might try "conflict conversion," an effective new form of behavior management. Take the two girls aside, and when they are calm enough to talk, ask each to tell you what happened. Accept whatever they say. Samantha will talk about her buggy being taken, and Kimberly will complain that Samantha hit her. Accept both these points of view.

Then convert the conflict to a feelings solution by asking each girl in turn to tell you how she thinks the other girl feels. "Look at her face, Kimberly. What does that tell you about how she feels?" "She's been crying, Samantha. How do you think she feels?"

Many children are surprised to find another side to the conflict. Most have never been asked to consider the other child's feelings. But when they realize this is what you want them to do, they are relieved to find that you do not blame them and are not going to punish them. Instead, you are asking them to consider the other girl's feelings, then decide what will make the other girl feel better.

Each child has attention focused on her in a positive way. You have listened to her side of the conflict. You are asking the other child to look at her and tell how she feels. Then you are asking the other child to think of something that will make her feel better. Just taking this action makes her feel better already. The same focus then switches to the other child, and she also begins to feel better.

Finding out about another child's feelings is often a great revelation to young children. Nobody has asked them to do such a thing before. Preschool children are extremely sensitive to feelings because they are so open with their own feelings and have not yet learned to conceal them as older children and adults do. When you point out to them that other children have feelings that can be hurt, most youngsters are willing to try to make amends. Nobody is being blamed for the conflict. They are only being asked to consider the other child's feelings, then to do something that will make the other child feel better. Many converted conflicts like this end up with a hug.

Teachers can help children become more responsive to cues of what the other child is feeling by directing the attention of the children in conflict to each other's faces as noted above. "How do you think Samantha feels, Kimberly? Look at her face." She should have no trouble identifying a basic emotion. Research has found that even infants as young as six weeks of age can distinguish between one facial expression and another, while children two and three years old have no trouble associating basic emotions with facial expressions (Hyson, 1994, p. 52).

As teachers start helping children become aware of other's feelings, many will find a new consideration of others developing within their classrooms:

> A preschool teacher kneeled to be at eye level with a child who had just socked another child during a struggle for a bike. The teacher pointed out the feelings of the other child: "He's very sad and hurt. What can you do to make him feel better?" The aggressor paused, observed the other child's face, and offered the bike to the crying child. (Wittmer and Honig, 1994, p. 7)

Children may, however, have difficulty with the words for expressing emotions because of their limited verbal skills. Here is where you come in. Be sure to spend time talking to individuals and small groups about their feelings. Read books about feelings as suggested in Chapter 4 and mount pictures around the room of children's faces expressing particular feelings. Can children name the feelings they see? With your support they can develop this ability to verbalize feelings. As Ramsey (1991) notes:

> Because even very young children resonate to others' emotions, children can empathize and communicate on an emotional plane before they are consciously aware of others' perspectives. (p. 18)

If You Have Not Checked This Item: Some Helpful Ideas

■ Use Mirrors

Bring in several small hand mirrors and place them on a table set for four to six children. Let children look in each mirror and make faces of their own. Have them make a happy face, a sad face, an angry face, a surprised face. Then have them make a face for their tablemates and let the others guess what kind of face they are making.

■ Use Puppets

Put a hand puppet on each of your hands and let them engage in a conflict over a toy. You can be the voice for each puppet. Then you can stop the conflict as the teacher and ask each puppet

What happened?
How do you think the other puppet feels?
What would make the other puppet feel better?

Ask the children in your small group to join in, too. Ask them how they think each of the puppets feels and what would make them feel better.

■ Read a Book

In *If I Ran the Family* (1992) by Lee and Sue Kaiser Johnson (Minneapolis, MN: Free Spirit) Debbie Dundee tells in her own words what she would do if she ran her multi-ethnic family and lets her do so for a day. Double-page illustrations show the vivacious Debbie dealing with various emotional situations: comforting, crying, being angry, being afraid, getting hugs, saying no, keeping secrets, being scared of the dark. Have your listeners tell you how they would feel in situations like Debbie's and what they would do about it. Can they tell by the faces of the children in the family how they are feeling on the different pages?

 SHARES SOMETHING WITH ANOTHER

Generosity

Sharing and helping may be the easiest prosocial behaviors for young children to learn because these behaviors occur most frequently in the early childhood classroom, which is understandable when you consider the many opportunities children in a group have to learn to share materials with one another. Sharing also is easier to do than some of the other prosocial acts because the child only suffers a temporary loss. The youngster must give up something, but only temporarily.

Again, the child's ability to perform such an action depends upon her cognitive maturity as well as the lessons she has learned from those around her. The younger the child, the more inclined she is to consider the toy she is playing with as her personal possession, whether it is or not. Children still retaining this egocentric view also will try to take the toys they want away from others, and they will be upset if the others do not comply. The fact that these egocentric children want the toy makes it theirs, according to their reasoning.

William Damon's study of the development of a child's sense of justice involved findings about what children considered to be fair in sharing or dividing up candy. The younger children (ages four and five) gave themselves more candy than the older children gave to themselves. A scale Damon derived to indicate children's levels of positive justice showed children age four and under justifying their choices simply on the basis of their wishes: that is, they should get something because they want it.

Children at the second level of the scale (ages four and five) justified their actions on the basis of their size, gender, or whatever characteristic would get them the most candy. The next level of children (ages five through seven) preferred to share equally to prevent squabbles. Thus older children must realize that preserving the peace is more important than getting an extra piece of candy (Damon, 1983, p. 136).

To prevent squabbles, early childhood teachers need to establish rules governing "property rights" at the outset. When children first enter the classroom, they are confronted with a treasure trove of materials to enjoy. The youngsters need to understand that these materials belong to the center, not to specific children. Individuals can use the materials, but the items must be shared, which means letting other children use the items either at the same time (as with paints), or one after another.

Nevertheless, some squabbles over equipment can be expected. The primary way young children learn rules is to test them out. Who gets the favorite toy first? Favorites are often trikes and eggbeaters. Some teachers consider it best to have several favorites to avoid problems. Other teachers believe that such problems afford good opportunities for children to learn how to share and take turns.

Researchers find that older children are more likely to share than younger ones. Sharing with peers, in fact, increases dramatically between the ages of 4 and 12 (Damon, 1983, p. 128). If a toy belongs to the center, young children are more likely to share the item than if it belongs to them personally. Most teachers ask children to keep toys from home in their cubbies. The youngsters can show the toys to the class at circle time, but afterwards, the toys must be put away until it is time to go home.

Because sharing is such an important prosocial skill in the preschool center, everyone must spend time helping individuals learn the skill. You may want to start by observing the prosocial behavior of every child in your class to see which children already know how to share and which ones may need help in learning this skill. Some children will share toys, food, and turns when asked by another child, but many still need the teacher to make the request.

More children will share if the teacher makes sharing important for everyone. As noted by Honig and Wittmer (1996):

> Sharing increases among preschool children whose teachers give them explanations as to why sharing is important and how to share. (p. 64)

If You Have Not Checked This Item: Some Helpful Ideas

■ Model Sharing Yourself

Sharing is one of children's behaviors that definitely reflects adult modeling behavior. Adults often ask children to share with their peers, but how often do adults ask a child to share with them? Try it. Set up a situation where a child who has had difficulty in sharing must share a seat, a piece of equipment, or an activity with you. For example, invite him to paint at your table. Then, set out one jar of paint that the two of you must share. Verbalize as you work on your painting. Let the child know he is doing well in sharing the paint.

■ Use Group Toys

Encourage a small group of two, three, or four children to construct a building using one set of Lego blocks. Have several children work on a large puzzle together. Have one child hold the wood while another saws at the woodworking table. Tie a wagon to the trike and let one child pedal while another rides in the wagon.

■ Set Up a Food-Sharing Experience

Bring in one apple, one orange, or one melon for each small group at your snack tables. Discuss with the children how they can share the piece of fruit. Let them help you divide it equally.

■ Videotape Sharing

Use a camcorder to capture an incident of children's sharing on a videotape. Then play it back to one small group at a time and talk about it with them. Children remember visual images like this.

■ Read a Book

Sharing (1981) by Taro Gomi (South San Francisco: Heian International) is a simply illustrated book of two little girls who find ways to share an apple, colored paper, a ribbon, toys, and a love of their cat.

When This Box Is Full (1993) by Patricia Lillie (New York: Greenwillow) shows in large sensitive illustrations an empty box filled month by month on each double page with a particular item associated with the month (e.g., a wishbone for November) until it is full. On the last page, an African American boy says: "I will share it with you."

Just Not the Same (1992) by Addie Lacoe (Boston: Houghton Mifflin) shows three sad-looking sisters who have trouble sharing everything, with the result that their mother or father makes compromises so that each one will get exactly the same, but it is "just not the same." They finally have to learn to share when they are given one puppy.

 # GIVES SOMETHING TO ANOTHER

Generosity

A great deal of research has been done on this aspect of prosocial behavior, perhaps because researchers find it easy to measure whether children are willing to give one of their possessions to someone else. Most studies show that as children increase in age, their generosity also increases. What is not so clear is why.

We assume that as children become cognitively more mature they will be less concerned with themselves as the center of everything, and more aware of others and their needs. We also expect that as children grow older they will have more experiences with social customs through the teachings of their family, friends, school, and church. In other words, children will have learned how society expects them to behave.

Other things also affect young children's giving. Length of ownership is one. Children seem more willing to give up a possession they have had awhile than something they have just obtained (Smith, 1982, p. 210). Perhaps the novelty eventually wears off.

The item they are giving also makes a difference. It may be a toy, an item of food, a piece of candy, or money. Whether they have more of the same also makes a difference. Reasons for the giving have a bearing, too. Is the item given out of friendship, because someone asks, because someone has a need, or because an adult suggests that it might be a nice thing to do? Older children are more apt to respond to adult suggestions or pressure.

Children are more likely to share a favorite toy rather than give it up totally. Formal occasions for giving, such as birthdays or religious holidays, teach children about giving. The child's egocentric nature often shows itself when he or she wants to give mom a toy truck or doll for her birthday.

Teaching generosity, however, is tricky in our society. We send children mixed messages. We tell them it is a good idea to give to people in need, but then the youngsters see us turn away charity solicitors at our front doors. Children hear us refuse to lend a lawn mower or power tool to a neighbor who has a need. "Let him buy his own," we say, "Let him work as hard as we did to buy this one."

Ours is a very material possession–oriented culture. Children learn this from television and our responses to the messages TV sends. Children witness how strongly we feel about our cars, stereos, and microwave ovens. It is an interesting commentary on our values to see families with fewer material possessions being much more generous with them.

Not all cultures value personal material possessions so highly. Native Americans and Pacific Islanders, for instance, teach their children that giving is more important than possessing. These people practice what they preach by simply giving a possession to a neighbor or relative who admires or has need of it. These people believe they are enhanced by the person accepting something from them.

Nevertheless, as preschool teachers we need to be aware of how this prosocial behavior works with children in our classroom, regardless of our society's confusion over the issue. Use the Child Skills Checklist to determine which children will give a possession to someone else. Are these the same children you have checked on the other prosocial behaviors? What other characteristics do these children share? Do they come from families where they have been given a great deal of responsibility? Prosocial behavior such as generosity is often more evident in such children. Do these children seem more mature in all areas of development? We know that generosity increases with age and maturity.

If You Have Not Checked This Item: Some Helpful Ideas

■ Be a Model of Generosity

Let children see you give up something to someone in need: an item of clothing, a book, food, or money. How do you feel about this? As adults, we are often reluctant to begin this kind of giving ourselves. Will it get out of hand? Will people take advantage of us? How genuine is your own generosity? We have been conditioned to acquire material possessions and guard against losing them.

■ Articulate Generosity

When situations arise where giving is appropriate, talk to your children about it. Maybe they could donate some money or services to help someone in need. Perhaps you could put up a box for pennies to be given to fire, storm, or flood victims.

■ Read a Book

In *Jamaica's Find* (1986) by Juanita Havill (Boston: Houghton Mifflin), a little African American girl, Jamaica, finds a stuffed dog in the park and takes it home for her own until her family helps her to reconsider that another girl like herself might have lost it. Jamaica returns the dog to the park lost-and-found, by chance finds the girl who lost it, and then shares the girl's delight over the recovery of her favorite toy.

Maebelle's Suitcase (1987) by Tricia Tusa (New York: Macmillan) is a whimsical story about 108-year-old African American Maebelle, who lives in an exotic treehouse she has built because of her fascination with birds. Maebelle makes hats to sell, but also to enter in the town's annual hat contest. When her bird friend Binkle asks for her suitcase to take on his trip south, Maebelle gives it to him without hesitation. But when Binkle loads it too heavily to lift, she invites him in to watch her make her contest hat. Somehow all of the decorations she needs can be found in Binkle's suitcase, which he gives to her one-by-one, including the suitcase. Her hat does not win the contest but is chosen for the town museum. Both of them are proud and happy: Maebelle because she gave up her real hat to help her bird friend, and Binkle because he gave Maebelle the contents of the suitcase to make the hat.

Alejandro's Gift (1994) by Richard E. Albert (San Francisco: Chronicle Books) tells the story of the Alejandro, an Hispanic man who lived by himself in a little adobe house in the desert but felt very lonely until he made himself a garden. Wild creatures came to share it, so he dug them a water hole and many more came.

A Birthday Basket for Tia (1992) by Pat Mora (New York: Simon & Schuster) is the story of Cecilia's gathering of gifts for her Great-Aunt Tia's surprise birthday party. She goes through her house choosing items that she and Tia have enjoyed together, putting them in a birthday basket. When Tia comes to the surprise party, Tia shows her appreciation for each item.

 ## TAKES TURNS WITHOUT A FUSS

Cooperation

Cooperation includes a wide range of prosocial behaviors including turn-taking;, alternating the use of toys, equipment, or activities; complying with requests; coor-

Taking turns without a fuss is an indicator that children are developing prosocial behavior.

dinating actions to accomplish goals; accepting other children's ideas; and negotiating and compromising in play. Certain of these behaviors were discussed in Chapter 5 under social play. In this item we are specifically looking at alternating behaviors: that is, going in a certain order, first one and then another; waiting for another child to have a turn; or alternating the use of toys and equipment with other children.

Opportunities for learning and practicing these particular prosocial behaviors occur much more frequently in the early childhood classroom than do occasions for giving. To maintain a smoothly running program, you must help children learn at the outset how to take and wait their turns in a group situation.

Those with brothers and sisters at home may have learned this already, although it is sometimes the inappropriate behavior they learn, such as the biggest or strongest gets the first turn. Research has also shown that authoritarian parents do not necessarily help children learn this prosocial behavior. When parents strictly control their children's actions, the children have less motivation and fewer opportunities to develop moral reasoning and turn-taking skills on their own (Eisenberg, Lennon, and Roth, 1983, p. 854).

To evolve from an egocentric being whose only concern is satisfying his own wants and become someone who understands the wants of others, the young child must learn to see things from another person's perspective, as previously mentioned.

To do this, the child needs the freedom to be able to function on his own in an open environment. His parents can support this development best by helping him understand others' views and by encouraging him to participate in decision making about his own behavior. Following the dictates of authoritarian parents gives the child little opportunity to develop these skills.

Warm, supportive mothering also makes a difference in development of prosocial behaviors in young children. As children move into elementary school, the best support they can have at home is a nonauthoritarian mother who allows and encourages her children to act on their own.

In preschool, however, children must learn to take and wait for turns. You can help them most by setting up the environment so that it speaks to these needs. Arrange activity areas for three, four, or five children at the most, and put signs or symbols for these numbers in every area. Then children can regulate their own numbers during free play. Let children take tags to hang on hooks or pegboards, tickets to put in pockets mounted on the wall, or their pictures covered with clear contact paper to hang in the area where they want to work.

Many centers start the day with a circle time. The teacher lets the class know what activities are available, and the children choose activities by taking tags. If a child finishes playing in her chosen area before free choice time is over, then another child can pick up the tag and take his own turn. This is how children learn about taking turns and waiting their turn. Nevertheless, the teacher must let them do it on their own. Directing individuals into particular areas is the same as the authoritarian parent telling his or her children what to do. If we want children to develop prosocial behaviors, we must not short-circuit the process by trying to do it for them. To learn the necessary social interactions, they must be allowed to experiment with turn-taking on their own.

Giving children this freedom takes forbearance on the part of the preschool staff. It is so much easier for adults to make choices for children. After all, children take so long to make up their minds. But we must remember the purpose of the free choice period in the first place: to allow children to learn how to make their own decisions based on their own interests and needs, and how to deal with the consequences of their choices. Through freedom of choice, children also learn that another child may have the same choice as theirs, and that they may have to wait their turn before their choice is available.

Children also learn by using timing tools such as a kitchen timer or three-minute hourglass when several children want turns using favorite toys or equipment. One child can hold the timer while another uses the toy for three minutes. When it is the next child's turn, the child after her gets to hold the timer. Some children enjoy controlling the timer as much as playing with the toy!

Children can also learn to take turns by "signing up" for a turn. Put a list on a clipboard with a pencil near the activity, and have children sign up (print or scribble their names) one after the other. When their turn is finished, they can cross out their names. Some children whose names are far down the list may need to wait until another day. But then they find they are near the top of the list.

If You Have Not Checked This Item: Some Helpful Ideas

■ Have Children Practice Turn-Taking in Dramatic Play

Set up a particular play area such as a beauty or barber shop and put out two or three chairs for the customers. Then the children will have to wait their turn just as in real life. Or set up a bakery or other facility where people must take numbered tickets to be waited on. Have tickets available for the children to take. Perhaps one child could be the ticket taker.

Set up a traffic light in the classroom for the children to use in their big truck play. The light can be a cardboard milk carton with holes cut out and covered with clear food wrapping paper colored red, yellow, and green. Not only will children learn safety rules, but they also will realize that cars and people must wait their turns before using the road at a street crossing.

■ Bring in a Special Plaything or Activity to Teach Turn-Taking

Introduce a new toy at circle time and have the children help set up the rules for playing with it, such as the number of people who can use the toy at one time and for how long. The children may want to use the kitchen timer you have provided to keep track of the time. One child will surely want to keep the time. The teacher can also help children sign up for turns on a chart.

■ Read a Book

Me First (1992) by Helen Lester (Boston: Houghton Mifflin) is the humorous tale of Pinkerton, a pig who always has to be first in everything he does with the other little pigs in his scout troop. Then one day on a picnic to the beach, he hears a voice asking, "Who would care for a sandwich?" He rushes ahead of the others shouting "Me first!" Suddenly he finds himself in the clutches of a sand witch who demands all kinds of care from him, finally teaching Pinkerton that it does not pay to be selfish.

 COMPLIES WITH REQUESTS WITHOUT A FUSS

Cooperation

A second aspect of cooperation involves complying with requests. This includes following directions, but more especially, it looks at how children cooperate with one another by complying with something another child or the teacher requests of them. For example, a child or the teacher may request another child to help, to wait, to give up something, to take a different role, to give information, or to do something in a certain way.

Complying with requests in a cooperative way is not blind obedience: for example, "Josh, move your truck." Children should know the reason they are being asked to do something. They should be expected to behave in a reasonable way if the request is reasonable: "Josh, Anna Maria needs you to move your truck so she can get her coat out of her cubby."

Nor is cooperative compliance a submission to a demand. Before you decide on checking this item for a child or leaving it blank, be sure it is compliance to a request and not to a demand that you are witnessing: not "Get out of the way, Josh," but "Anna Maria needs you to move your truck," or "It's pickup time, Andy. Please help Jerome pick up the blocks."

Children are more likely to comply with a teacher's request if they are given choices. As Wittmer and Honig (1994) note:

> Toddlers and preschoolers struggling to assert newly emergent autonomy cooperate more easily with caregiver requests if they feel empowered to make choices. Adults can decide on the choices to be offered. (p. 11)

For example, a child who resists helping with block pickup can be given an interesting choice of pushing the blocks over to the shelf with a big "bulldozer" block or loading blocks in the truck and driving them over to the shelf.

Once a child has complied with a request, he can expect to be thanked for doing it. If you are the one who made the request, don't forget to thank the child. When you notice a child complying with another child's request, be sure the requesting child thanks him or her. Cooperative behavior like this implies reciprocal behavior on another's part. You may need to point this out in a pleasant, not correcting manner: "Anna Maria, Josh really moved his truck for you in a hurry. Don't forget to thank him."

If You Have Not Checked This Item: Some Helpful Ideas

■ Model This Behavior Yourself

Make a point of complying with reasonable requests a child makes of you. When you do this, be sure to articulate what you are doing so that other children understand it. For example, you might say aloud as you help pick up blocks, "Andy and Jerome asked me to help them pick up the blocks because they have to leave early today." This should help children understand that you comply with their requests just as you expect them to comply with yours. In addition, it gives them the reason for your response so they will know you may not always help everyone pick up blocks on a daily basis.

If children are demanding things of one another and not getting the desired results, you can also model the behavior that they should use: "Rhonda, why don't you say to Anne, 'Please give me my doll. It's time for me to go home. I'll bring it back tomorrow.'"

■ Read a Book

Carlos and the Squash Plant (1993) by Jan Romero Stevens (Flagstaff, AZ: Northland) tells the story of the Hispanic boy Carlos who helps his father grow vegetables in their garden but hates to take a bath afterward. His mother says if he doesn't wash his ears a squash plant will grow in them—and one day it does! Carlos is so embarrassed that he covers his head with his big straw sombrero and even wears it in the house. Large colorful illustrations show Carlos working, eating, and finally washing—making the squash plant disappear.

HELPS ANOTHER DO A TASK

Caregiving

Along with sharing, this is by far the most common prosocial behavior exhibited in the preschool classroom, possibly because it is much less of a cognitive act. Children simply assist someone in doing a task. They may be asked or they may volunteer to help when they see that a peer or the teacher needs help with something. The children do not need to understand nor intellectualize about what is happening. They do not need to take another person's perspective. They just need to lend a hand, so to speak. Most children have already learned this activity at home, and they soon realize that the early childhood classroom also expects children to help out.

Research shows that this behavior may occur three times more than any other prosocial act. Even so, helping others do a task is not all that frequent in proportion to other behaviors. Seeking help occurs about six times more frequently than giving help among three-year-olds (Moore, 1982, p. 77). But as children grow and develop through

Helping another do a task is one of the common prosocial behaviors exhibited in the preschool classroom.

the early childhood years, helping behavior increases. Whereas slightly more than half of the youngest children assessed in one study (three-year-olds) gave some form of help, 100 percent of children nine and ten years old gave help (Smith, 1982, p. 216).

The youngest preschoolers, nevertheless, may have some problems with helping. They may not know when to help nor how much help to give. Sometimes children overdo their help, becoming bossy and not knowing when to stop. Other times children don't do enough and simply stand around watching before the task is finished. The best way for them to learn the cues for appropriateness in such social behavior is to plunge in and try it. Other children are not shy about telling peers what they are doing wrong.

You, on the other hand, need to set up activities that require children to give assistance. Setting tables for snacks and lunch is one; getting out cots or mats for nap-time, getting out paints and mixing them, filling the water table, feeding the pets, and helping with cleanup are a few of the others. These tasks are multiple learning situations for cognitive concepts as well as learning when and how to help.

Children may have favorite chores as well as chores they try to avoid. Making up a "helpers" chart gives every child a chance at every chore. Let the children help design the chart. It can contain pictures as well as titles for every job. Children can hang their name tags on it daily at circle time or once a week. New jobs can be added from time to time as needed. Use your creativity to invent the jobs. Here are a few you may want to include:

mail carrier: delivers notes to office
zoo keeper: takes care of pets
aquarium attendant: feeds fish
door attendant: opens and closes door
chef: helps prepare snack
waiter/waitress: sets tables
gardener: waters plants

You cannot expect young children to do all the work in the classroom. Picking up the block corner is a case in point. One or two children can easily empty the shelves while building a complicated construction. Putting all the blocks back in proper order during cleanup time may be an overwhelming chore for two. A teacher should get down on the floor with them and lend her assistance, just as the children help her from time to time.

If certain children are not helping at all, you need to engage them in chores. Chores do not need to be drudgery. Children enjoy doing grownup things. Youngsters have no idea that pickup is any less interesting than getting toys out, unless adults make pickup seem less glamorous. In fact, you should make cleanup in your room a fun thing to do.

If You Have Not Checked This Item: Some Helpful Ideas

■ Invite a Helper to Your Class on a Weekly Basis

Anyone engaged in an occupation is a helper. Perhaps a different parent could visit the classroom on a weekly basis to talk to the children about how he or she helps.

One class created a new job on the helpers' chart each week after the helper had visited. Sometimes the children had to stretch their imaginations to create the new job. After a telephone installer had visited the room, they finally decided to add the job "telephone attendant" in which one child would be allowed to answer the classroom phone each day.

■ Use Games for Pickup and Cleanup

Block shelves fill up much easier when they are hungry monsters waiting to be fed by the children, or when children do pickup to music, trying to finish before the song is over. Long blocks can be bulldozers pushing the blocks or toys over to the shelves. Have your children help you think up other pretend games at cleanup time.

■ Read a Book

Herman the Helper (1974) by Robert Kraus (New York: Windmill Books) tells the colorful underwater story of Herman the little octopus who helps his mother, father, brothers and sisters, friends, enemies, and finally himself.

In *Too Many Tamales* (1993) by Gary Soto (New York: Putnam's), Maria helps her mother make tamales for the Christmas party they are having. Maria's mother takes off her diamond ring to knead the dough. Maria puts it on her own thumb and continues to help. Later during the party she remembers the ring, and thinks it must be in the tamales. She enlists her cousins to eat all the tamales carefully looking for the ring before her mother finds out. But the ring ends up on her mother's finger and everyone has to help to make more tamales.

HELPS (CARES FOR) ANOTHER IN NEED

Caregiving

This particular behavior is perhaps the most difficult of the prosocial skills for young children to attain. Helping another in need is an extension of the first item "Shows concern for someone in distress." Whereas showing concern involves "compassion," a psychological support, helping another in need involves "caretaking" or "giving nurturance," a physical act of giving help. The help may consist of giving affection (e.g., a hug, a touch), positive attention (getting help, giving help), reassurance (verbalizing support), or protection (standing by, physical protection).

For young children, giving these things is difficult because the youngsters must first overcome their own anxiety caused by the stressful situation. Then they must have an understanding of how to act. In emergency situations even adults are often confused and have difficulty knowing what to do.

Even very young children have been observed taking action when another child or person is in distress, but the instances are rare compared to other prosocial acts. Toddlers have been seen giving their bottles or cuddly toys to siblings who cry in distress. Giving something to the victim seems to be the main response of young children. They more often seek help than give it, however. In addition, those who seek help in the preschool more often approach adults than peers, although older preschoolers are beginning to turn to their companions for help.

Crying or uttering distressful sounds is supposed to trigger an empathic response in others, according to psychologists. Scientists look to the animal world and note the intricacies of response in many species. Have we humans lost much of this seemingly instinctive concern? We read in the news or see on television the instances of adults ignoring victims who call for help. Much of this inattention seems to be a defensive reaction on the part of people who not only do not want to get involved in the trouble, but also fear they might be victimized themselves.

Can children learn helping? Studies show that children can learn helping behaviors in pretend or symbolic situations, but when the real thing occurs, they still may not respond. Children with nurturing caregivers do give more help and express more sympathy. It seems, then, that modeling behavior does promote prosocial helping (Yarrow, 1973, p. 254).

What kinds of situations calling for help might occur in the classroom? Injury is one. Children or adults may fall and hurt themselves, cut themselves, or burn themselves. Losing something is another situation that requires help. Children may lose mittens, money, or a toy. Accidental damage also necessitates assistance. Children may spill paint on themselves, fall in the mud, or spill milk or other food. They may drop and break a dish, a record, a toy.

How can children help? Depending upon the situation, they could go for help if an adult is not in the immediate vicinity. They could comfort the victim by talking or touching. They could help pick up spilled substances, look for lost items, or give information to help the adult solve the problem.

Children are more likely to give help to others when with someone. Teachers should take advantage of this by involving the children in helping situations whenever possible, rather than doing all the helping themselves. When children are involved on their own, teachers should step back and allow the youngsters to do what they can.

You can also check off this caregiving item if you observe children giving care in pretend situations to their dolls or classroom pets. Does someone put a blanket around her doll saying that she is cold and might catch the flu? Does someone notice that the guinea pig is out of water? If elderly people or babies visit your classroom, watch which children show signs of caring. Does someone get a chair for the guest without being asked?

If You Have Not Checked This Item: Some Helpful Ideas

■ Discuss Helping with the Children

When helping behavior occurs, spend time in small and large groups talking to children about it. Sometimes television events seen by children are good discussions items.

■ When You Model Helping Behavior, Talk About It

You will be helping children all year long. Talk aloud to the other children about what you are doing, and help them find ways to assist you.

■ Read a Book

Who's Going to Take Care of Me? (1990) by Michelle Magorian (New York: Harper) tells the story of little Eric, whose older sister Karin would not be going to day care with him this year because she was going to kindergarten. Who would take care of him? When Eric arrives at day care he discovers that he already knows how to do things for himself, but he spots a little newcomer over in the corner and takes it upon himself to help the new little boy.

Wilfrid Gordon McDonald Partridge (1985) by Mem Fox, (Brooklyn, NY: Kane/Miller) is a little boy who knows all the people in the old folks home next door because he visits them on their front porch. When he hears that one of the residents, Miss Nancy, has lost her memory, he helps her to find it by gathering together just the right collection of things.

Tucking Mommy In (1987) by Morag Loh (New York: Orchard Books) shows two little Asian American girls getting ready for bed with their mother's help, but when their tired mommy falls asleep before their bedtime story is finished, the girls decide it is their turn to tuck Mommy in. So they do.

OBSERVING, RECORDING, AND INTERPRETING PROSOCIAL BEHAVIOR

Sandra is a four-year-old who rarely performs any of the prosocial behaviors on the Checklist unless forced to by the teachers—for example, sharing a toy or waiting for her turn (see Figure 6–1). The teachers have noted that she also seems immature in the area of social skills and plays only by herself, not parallel to the others or with a group. The teachers have concluded that Sandra may not have developed the ability to see things from a perspective other than her own. Therefore, she has little or no empathy for others who need help or who are in distress.

A suggestion to help Sandra develop empathy is to give her two hand puppets: one with a bandage on its arm and the other a helper. You can put the bandaged puppet on your hand. Ask her to find out what happened to the injured puppet. If she likes this kind of play, she may be willing to "branch out" and play "helping puppets" with a second child.

Observe the other children in the classroom for these same prosocial skills. If you find other children who have not performed many of the items on the Checklist, try pairing them with a child who does display these skills, then give the pair a social task to perform together, such as helping you help anyone who needs assistance putting on boots or jackets.

Child Skills Checklist

Name _____ *Sandra* _____ Observer _____ *Angie* _____

Program _____ *Pre-K* _____ Dates _____ *11/5* _____

Directions:

Put a ✔ for items you see the child perform regularly. Put *N* for items where there is no opportunity to observe. Leave all other items blank.

Item	Evidence	Date
4. Prosocial Behavior		
_____ Shows concern for someone in distress	Moved away from Mark when he got hurt	11/5
_____ Can tell how another feels during conflict	Does not answer when asked how other child feels	11/5
_____ Shares something with another	Would not give up her doll to Betty	11/5
_____ Gives something of his/her own to another	She has not done this	
_____ Takes turns without a fuss	Cried when she could not be first on the swing	11/5
_____ Complies with requests without a fuss	Always says "I can't" or "I don't know how" when asked to do something	11/5
_____ Helps another to do a task	Same as above	11/5
_____ Helps (cares for) another in need	Would not help when Mark got hurt	11/5

Figure 6–1 Prosocial behavior observations for Sandra

168

REFERENCES

Beaty, J. J. (1995). *Converting conflicts in preschool.* Ft. Worth, TX: Harcourt Brace.

Damon, W. (1988). *The moral child: Nurturing children's natural moral growth.* New York: Macmillan.

Damon, W. (1983). *Social and personality development.* New York: W. W. Norton.

Eisenberg, N., Lennon, R., & Roth, K. (1983). Prosocial development: A longitudinal study. *Developmental Psychology. 19*(6), 846–855.

Hoffman, M. L. (1982). Development of prosocial motivation: Empathy and guilt. In N. Eisenberg (Ed.), *The development of prosocial behavior.* New York: The Academic Press.

Honig, A. S., & Wittmer, D. A. (1996). Helping children become more prosocial: Ideas for classrooms, families, schools, and communities. *Young Children 51*(2), 62–70.

Hyson, M. C. (1994). *The emotional development of young children: Building an emotion-centered curriculum.* New York: Teachers College Press.

Moore, S. G. (1982). Prosocial behavior in the early years: Parent and peer influences. In B. Spodek (Ed.), *Handbook of research in early childhood education.* New York: The Free Press.

Ramsey, P. G. (1991). *Making friends in school: Promoting peer relationships in early childhood.* New York: Teachers College.

Smith, C. A. (1982). *Promoting social development of young children: strategies and activities.* Palo Alto, CA: Mayfield Publishing Company.

Wittmer, D. S., & Honig, A. S. (1994). Encouraging positive social development in young children. *Young Children. 49*(5) 4–19.

Yarrow, M. R., Scott, P. M., & Waxler, C. Z. (1973). Learning concern for others. *Developmental Psychology, 8*(2), 240–260.

SUGGESTED READINGS

Edwards, C. P. (1986). *Promoting social and moral development in children.* New York: Teachers College Press.

Eisenberg, N. (1992). *The caring child.* Cambridge, MA: Harvard.

Goffin, S. G. (1987). Cooperative behaviors: They need our support. *Young Children, 42*(2), 75–81.

Melson, G. F., & Fogel, A. (1988). "The development of nurturance in young children," *Young Children, 43*(3), 57–65.

Stockdale, D. F., Hegland, S. M., & Chiaromonte, T. (1989). "Helping behaviors: An observational study of preschool children," *Early Childhood Research Quarterly, 4*(4), 533–543.

VIDEOTAPES

Magna Systems, Inc. (1993). *Moral development.* Magna Systems, Inc., 95 West County Line Rd., Barringston, IL, 60010.

National Association for the Education of Young Children (NAEYC). *Discipline: Appropriate guidance of young children.* 1509 16th St. NW, Washington, DC, 20036-1426.

LEARNING ACTIVITIES

1. Use the Child Skills Checklist for prosocial behavior as a screening tool to observe all the children in your classroom. Which ones demonstrate the most prosocial behavior? Do they also have friends in the class? Which children show few prosocial skills? How do these children get along with the other children in general?

2. Choose a child who exhibits few of the prosocial skills. Do a running record of the child on three different days to determine how he or she works and plays with the others. Do an activity with the child to help him or her share, take turns, or help. Record the results.

3. Choose a child who is a good helper and try to involve him or her in getting another child to participate in helping. Discuss the results.

4. Try two of the ideas under "If You Have Not Checked This Item" with a child who shows few prosocial skills. Discuss the results.

5. Read one of the children's books from this chapter with a group of children or do an activity with the group to promote prosocial skills. Discuss the results.

CHAPTER 7

Large Motor Development

LARGE MOTOR CHECKLIST

☐ Walks down steps alternating feet

☐ Runs with control over speed and direction

☐ Jumps up and lands on two feet

☐ Hops on one foot

☐ Throws, catches, and kicks balls

☐ Climbs up and down climbing equipment

☐ Moves legs and feet in rhythm to beat

☐ Moves arms and hands in rhythm to beat

DEVELOPING LARGE MOTOR SKILLS

Physical development for young children involves two important areas of motor coordination: movements controlled by the large or gross muscles and those controlled by the small or fine muscles. This chapter will focus on large motor development, involving movements of the whole body, legs, and arms.

Because motor development is so obvious and visible an aspect of children's growth, we sometimes take it for granted. Of course children will grow bigger, stronger, and able to perform more complicated motor tasks as they increase in age. Of course they will learn to run and jump on their own. Why should we be concerned with motor development in preschool? Pica (1995) has an important answer for child caregivers who hold this point of view:

> Although it is commonly believed children automatically develop motor skills as their bodies develop, maturation only means the child will be able to execute most movement skills at a low performance level. Continuous practice and instruction are required if the child's performance level and movement repertoire are to increase. (p. 2)

Furthermore, there is concern that many youngsters today may be leading much more sedentary lives than children did formerly. The increase in television watching along with the decrease in safe outdoor play areas has cut down tremendously on the motivation and opportunity for young children to run, jump, and move their bodies. Up to half of U.S. children may not be getting enough exercise, according to some studies (Taras, 1992).

In addition, some preschool children obviously need help with large motor skills: the awkward child who seems to trip over his own feet, the child who never can keep up with the others, and the differently abled child who is now included in regular programs. And what about the "accident-prone" child? Is she overly eager or underdeveloped, we may wonder? How can we tell, and can we do anything to help such children?

Although all children develop physically in a predictable sequence of skills that can be observed, there are definitely individual differences. And, yes, there is something we can do to help all children develop large motor skills.

First, we need to become familiar with the entire sequence of normal large motor development. We need to know its origins, patterns, and range for individuals. Then we need to apply this knowledge to the children to determine whether they are developing predictably within the normal range, or whether they may need some special help. Finally, we should assemble a repertory of activities to motivate all the children in our program, including those who may be lagging behind in this development.

Motor Development in Infancy

The infant uses motor skills as tools to explore himself and then the world around him. His initial movements are reflexive or involuntary. He sucks when his mouth touches something. He jumps at a loud noise.

Soon after birth, however, three types of rudimentary movement abilities appear. The nonlocomotor or *stability* skills involve developing control of the head, neck, and trunk, and eventually the ability to sit and stand. *Manipulative* skills involve reaching for, grasping, and releasing. And *locomotor* skills involve creeping, crawling, and eventually walking (Gallahue, 1982, 5–6).

Muscular maturation follows both a predictable sequence and a direction. Large muscle coordination develops before small muscle synchronization. In other words, the infant or young child develops arm movement control before finger control. Development is also cephalo-caudal in direction; that is, it begins at the head and progresses to the feet. Control of the head and upper trunk occurs in the infant before control of the legs and feet. Development also occurs in another direction: from close to the trunk out to the extremities, which is called proximo-distal (Allen & Goetz, 1982, p. 130).

Many of the infant's first movements are random. She lies on her back in a bassinet or crib and kicks with her legs or waves with her arms. Should she happen to strike a mobile or rattle with either her arms or legs, she will usually try to repeat the movement to cause the same interesting sound and touch effect. In repeating the movement over and over, she begins to gain control over her muscles, so that the movement eventually becomes voluntary and controlled.

The rate of development occurs in a predictable sequence and is related closely to the maturation of the central nervous system, the integrating agent. Even though an infant's motor skills cannot develop until the neuromuscular system is ready, a rich environment filled with stimulating sights, sounds, and people motivates the child to initiate and to practice movements.

Are we saying that the environment and the infant's experience with it can improve her motor development? Yes, when the required maturation level has been reached. If there had not been a mobile in the baby's bassinet, she would not have struck it with her arm and then would not have continued to practice this movement. Even if her neuromuscular system was not mature enough for her to control this movement, the mobile's presence might still keep her trying until the proper maturity had developed.

Fraiberg's work with blind infants shows the importance of such environmental factors in the development of motor skills. The blind babies developed trunk control and sitting stability within the same time range as sighted children. Blind babies even could support themselves on hands and knees. But they never learned to creep. They lacked the visual stimuli the sighted babies had to motivate them to move across the floor. Their caregivers had to find other means to stimulate them to attempt locomotion (Fraiberg, 1975).

This is one of several studies that has proved the importance of sensory stimuli, especially sight, sound, and touch, in the development of large motor skills. We also know that caring adults must interact with infants from the beginning: adults must encourage, support, and praise children for accomplishing motor skills, as adults do in all aspects of children's development.

Because such encouragement tends to happen almost automatically in many families, we often think infants and young children develop these skills on their own with little support from adults or the environment. A look at infants and children in institutions where little or no human or material support was offered proves otherwise. Hunt and several other U.S. psychologists visited orphanages in Iran that had an infant-caregiver ratio of 40 to 3 where many of the two-year-olds could not sit up and where many of those in their fourth year could not yet walk alone (Pines, 1979, p. 59). The quality of early child care does indeed make a difference.

The range for mastery of a particular skill varies from one or two months to four to six months in young children. Developmental delays may result when early reflexive movements somehow fail to become integrated into higher-level voluntary movements (Allen & Goetz, 1982, p. 131). Birth defects, physical impairments, certain illnesses or injuries, or neglect may cause this lack of integration. Children whose early movement patterns have not become integrated into voluntary responses either do not learn the higher-level skills or learn to compensate in some atypical manner.

Large motor skills, then, play an important part in the infant's learning, first about himself by moving his body parts, and then about his world as he responds physically to the people and materials around him. His environment plays an important part, as well, in stimulating this development. He gains more and more independence through the movements he is able to master, and when he finally walks, the world is his to explore.

What about the preschool child, the three- to five-year-old? We also need to assess his large motor development to determine how far he has progressed in this predictable growth. The eight items under large motor development on the Child Skills Checklist are neither a complete list of large motor skills, nor a sequence of skills, although one skill may precede the other. Instead, these eight items represent a sample of important motor behaviors that children should have acquired by age five.

It is important to screen all the children in your class at the outset using this or a similar list of skills to identify children needing special help. You and your coworkers can play physical games with the children doing running, jumping, and hopping while another staff member observes and records on a single sheet. At another time walk up and down stairs with children and give children opportunities to move their legs and feet, arms and hands in rhythm as someone observes. Still another time toss various balls to the children for catching, throwing, and kicking practice.

List the children's names on the left side of the sheet. At the top put the eight skills in abbreviated order:

Walks/Runs/Jumps/Hops/Throws&catches/Climbsup,down/Legs&feet/Arms&hands

Observers can check off when they see the children completing each of the skills. Remember, this should not be a test but an observation of natural accomplishments from activities set up in the classroom and playground. Take as many days as necessary to complete these observations. Then you will have an idea of the nature of the large motor skills each child possesses. Setting up developmentally appropriate activities is possible once you have this important information about the children.

 ## WALKS DOWN STEPS ALTERNATING FEET

Three-Year-Olds

Most three-year-olds walk in adult fashion. Their trunk is no longer top-heavy as it was at age two, and they have mastered walking to the extent that they no longer need to watch their feet or balance with their arms. They swing their arms as they walk just like adults. They still may fall occasionally on uneven ground, but they are not so far from the ground that falling hurts too much. Now they can walk upstairs alternating feet unaided, although most three-year-olds put two feet on a step coming down. The balance of some children this age is good enough to allow them to walk a straight line one foot in front of the other.

Although growth occurs in a predictable chronological sequence, it seems to happen in spurts. It seems almost as if the body has to stop and assimilate all the development that has occurred, before going forward again. This "assimilation stop" often happens at the half-year age. Children who walked and ran smoothly at three may seem to have a "relapse" at three-and-a-half. They suddenly act uncertain with their large motor skills and may even seek the hand of an adult as they walk along. This happens especially going up or down stairs. They may have good days when everything about their bodies seems to work well, and bad days when they stumble and fall (Caplan, 1983, p. 177).

Four-Year-Olds

Four-year-olds have control of their bodies and take great pleasure in using them. Children age four walk confidently in many ways: forward, backward, sideways, tiptoeing, or striding along. They are able to walk a circular line for the first time without losing their balance. Most can walk both up and down stairs alternating their feet. Although their skipping is not at all perfected (most can do it only with one foot), some start to roller skate.

Four is an age of great exuberance and expansiveness. If you do not provide enough walking, running, and climbing activities in your center, four-year-olds may make their own. They definitely need an opportunity to practice their large motor skills both inside and outside the classroom.

Five-Year-Olds

Five-year-olds are at the adult stage in walking. This is another period of great growth when children spurt up as much as two or three inches in a year. Much of this growth occurs in the legs, which lengthen more quickly than the other body parts. Boys may be a bit taller and heavier than girls, but they are about a year behind them in physiological development (Caplan, 1983, p. 237).

Children of this age can walk a straight line for about 10 feet without stepping off it. Many can skip with alternating feet now. Even the less active five-year-olds now can walk down stairs alternating feet. Five-year-olds are less expansive and more controlled than four-year-olds in all of their actions, but children age five still love to use their large motor abilities in play.

If You Have Not Checked This Item: Some Helpful Ideas

■ Practice Walking

Studies show that children between the ages of two and six demonstrate observable improvement in basic motor patterns after repeated performance with adult encouragement. Instruction in the movement doesn't seem to help, but practice does (Flinchum, 1975, p. 28).

Play follow-the-leader in the classroom and outside with yourself as the leader who sets the pace. Do all kinds of walking motions and be sure everyone has a chance to copy you before you change to the next movement: march, shuffle, stride, giant-step, tiptoe, bunny hop, skate.

Set up a walking-hopping-sliding trail in your classroom or large motor room with contact footprints stuck to the floor in various patterns of movement with one foot or two.

■ Practice Step Climbing

If your room is at ground level in a building with a second story, make it a practice to take children up and down the stairs every day. If you have no stairs, go for a field trip to a building that has stairs, or get a rocking-boat-steps piece of large motor equipment to practice on. Some playground equipment also has stairs, but ladders are not the same.

■ Play Animal Charades

Have two or three children demonstrate how an animal walks and let the others guess what animal it is. Try elephant, horse, rabbit, kangaroo, snake, and turtle walks.

■ Read a Book

One of the most impressive picture books about walking is surely *Mirandy and Brother Wind* (1988) by Patricia C. McKissack (New York: Alfred A. Knopf). It is an old-time African American story about a young girl, Mirandy, who wants to win her first "cakewalk" and decides to catch Brother Wind to help her. Although long for preschoolers, Jerry Pinkney's elegant full-page illustrations can be "read" to individuals or a small group close to the teacher. If children like the story, they may want to have their own cakewalk.

Many preschool teachers already involve their children in various kinds of walking when they take them on a "bear hunt," walking in place. Now this imaginative experience is available in a lively picture book, *We're Going on a Bear Hunt* (1989) by Michael Rosen and Helen Oxenbury (New York: Margaret K. McElderry Books).

Children also enjoy acting out a story like *The Three Billy Goats Gruff* (1973) as retold by Paul Galdone (New York: Clarion Books). Turn over your "rocking boat" piece of equipment to make it into steps, and have the children billy goats trip-trap over the step "bridge."

Funny Walks (1994) by Judy Hindley (BridgeWater Books) shows people and animals walking in all sorts of ways: hopping, skipping, bounding, slinking, shuffling, scurrying, and marching. Then it invites the listeners to do their own funny walks.

RUNS WITH CONTROL OVER SPEED AND DIRECTION

Running may be the large motor skill you think of when you consider young children. They seem to be perpetual motion machines. This is the principal method of movement for some children. Others run awkwardly and spend much less time doing it than the rest of your children. What should you expect of the three-, four-, and five-year-old children in your program? As with walking, you will need to know the whole range of development for this skill before you can decide where each of your children stands and how you best can help.

Three-Year-Olds

Running is smoother for three-year-olds than it was when they were younger. Their body proportions have grown and changed from a top-heavy appearance. Their legs are now longer and more coordinated in their movements. They have more control over starting and stopping than two-year-olds, but they still have not mastered this skill completely. Since their large motor skills are so much more automatic, they can abandon themselves to the pure enjoyment of running.

Then at about three-and-a-half, many children go through the previously mentioned awkward stage where some of the smoothness of their large motor movements seems to disappear. Teachers need to be aware of these "disequilibrium" times so they can support the child during his "bad days," knowing he will reacquire his smoothness of motion sometime soon.

Such children should not be confused with the truly awkward child. Cratty's studies have found many so-called "awkward" children are boys who seem to show a developmental delay in motor coordination. They exhibit exaggerated awkward behavior. Some of this behavior may be the result of "learned helplessness" obtained possibly from parents who overreact to their every little problem (Cratty, 1982, p. 36). On the other hand, the physical awkwardness of these boys may be more in the eye of the beholder, especially if a teacher compares them with the best-coordinated boys in the class.

A wide range of individual differences exists in physical development as in every other aspect of development. Some children simply will never be highly coordinated. Others may grow up to be professional athletes. The sensitive teacher needs to work with each child, encouraging and supporting him to accomplish all he is capable of. Pressure and ridicule simply have no place in the early childhood classroom. The teacher needs to find interesting motor activities in which the awkward child can succeed and to avoid activities that pit one child against another.

Can awkward children be helped? This seems to depend upon their age and the severity of their problem (Cratty, 1982, p. 37). Providing a wide range of interesting motor activities that are fun to participate in seems the best answer. Three-year-olds are at an ideal age to begin such a program. And because some so-called awkward children are simply beginners in skill development, it is useless to label them as abnormal. Children are children; they are all different in looks, likes, and abilities. Each of them needs your special affection and support as he or she progresses through the sometimes rocky road of physical development.

You need to be aware of these ages and stages as they apply to your children, nevertheless. Take time to visit this year's class next year and you may see some surprises. This year's awkward boy may be the best runner around in another year. The sedentary girl who would never join in may be the leader of the physical activities. A year makes such a difference in the development of young children.

Four-Year-Olds

Expansive four-year-olds are good runners. Their movements are strong, efficient, and speedy. They can start and stop without difficulty, and they like to zoom around corners. They seem to know what their bodies can do and enjoy putting them through their paces. Give them space and time to run.

Some four-year-olds are labeled **hyperactive** because they never seem to stop. Be careful of such labels. Only a doctor can diagnose this condition, formally called **attention-deficit hyperactivity disorder**. Some children are just more active than others, often wearing out parents and teachers in the process. The age of four—with its characteristic exuberance and surplus energy—is the period when parents worry most about hyperactivity. Surely, these parents reason, there is a way to slow down such children. Maybe the doctor will put the child on drugs.

Using drugs to combat so-called hyperactivity is a very serious decision to make for young children in our overmedicated, drug-dependent society. Really active children probably always have been that way, but as four-year-olds, their activity seems exaggerated. You may want more than one medical opinion before deciding what to do. True hyperactivity is sometimes difficult to distinguish from the normal surplus energy of an active four-year-old.

Five-Year-Olds

As mentioned before, five-year-olds seem to spurt up in height, mostly in their legs. They are more mature runners than four-year-olds, and many love to join in games that test their abilities. Their speed and control has increased, and they seldom fall when running across uneven surfaces as four-year-olds sometimes do. Their running games, like the rest of their actions, are usually not as noisy and out-of-bounds as those of four-year-olds.

If You Have Not Checked This Item: Some Helpful Ideas

■ Offer Simple Running Games

Preschool running games should not be competitive. The awkward child may give up trying if he or she is always last. Instead, simple circle games may serve the same purpose. Old classics like "Duck, Duck, Goose" are still favorites of three- and four-year-olds as they walk around the outside of the circle and tap someone who then chases them around to the empty space. No one wins or loses. Games with rules are often too complicated for preschoolers, but they learn to make the right responses in simple games like this and enjoy the running portion.

■ Employ Directed Running

You can make up all kinds of inside and outside running activities. For instance, one child at a time can run to the tree and back until all have had a turn. Make the activity more complicated by having them follow a second direction: Run to the tree, run around it once, and then run back.

■ Have the Children Run to Music

Have children run to music in the large motor area. Have them run fast or slow, loudly or quietly according to the music. Then have them run like animals to music. How would a deer run through the woods?

■ Involve the Children in Running in Place to Chants

Young children need to run. If you do not have the inside space, or the weather outside is bad, have them run and hop in place to a simple chant you have made up:

> *I'm a kangaroo-roo-roo*
> *See me run-run-run*
> *Have some fun-fun-fun*
> *In the sun-sun-sun*

Watch me hop-hop-hop
Never stop-stop-stop
Then I run-run-run
In the sun-sun-sun

■ Try Imaginative Running

Let children pretend to be cowboys or cowgirls riding their horses or jet planes zooming down the runway. Have them pretend to be animals that run such as deer or dogs. Put up pictures of animals that run and have the children imitate them.

■ Read a Book

In *Jonathan and His Mommy* (1992) by Irene Smalls-Hector (Boston: Little Brown), two African American city dwellers take a walk through city streets every day, and that walk turns into a romp of running, zigzagging, reggaeing, and racing. Can your children do the same?

JUMPS UP AND LANDS ON TWO FEET

Jumping is a skill that involves taking off with one or two feet and landing on both feet. Jumping is sometimes confused with leaping, which involves taking off on one foot and landing on the other, or hopping, which is done all on the same foot. The Checklist item mentions landing on two feet so observers will not confuse jumping with leaping or hopping.

The jumping skill has three parts: takeoff, flight, and landing. Teachers can demonstrate each phase so children needing help can practice it correctly. For takeoff, you should bend your knees slightly, crouch your body, and swing your arms forward and upward. For flight, you should continue raising your arms into the air as your body leaves the ground. Land with your feet apart and your body over your feet. Children can practice bending their knees, crouching, and swinging their arms forward. When they feel ready, have them spring up.

Jumping as a large motor skill for preschoolers should be done in place with the child springing up and landing in the same spot at first. Once they are competent jumpers, then they can jump forward landing on both feet, jump from the floor or ground over an obstacle, or jump from a height such as a step or a chair and land on the floor. Some early childhood specialists suggesting having children consider other aspects of jumping:

> Jumping is not only going up and down but discovering the properties of the material jumped in or upon. Will the surface withstand your impact? Will it throw you back, absorb you, tear, rebound, or stretch? Is it different to jump on something hard or soft; into water, sand, hay, or snow? You can jump on something (such as a board), over something (such as a rope or a crack in the sidewalk, or to different heights, or across things (a puddle or a creek). (Olds, 1994, p. 34)

Three-Year-Olds

Some children become quite proficient jumpers by age three, but many do not, and we should not expect them to. They must have developed the strength first, and then must be encouraged to practice the skill. (Most parents do not encourage their children to jump off steps or from furniture!)

Three-year-olds, though, are becoming more long-legged and coordinated. If they are not too heavy, most probably will be able to do some jumping with encouragement and practice. In jumping over an obstacle, most children start by leading with one foot. This is leaping. Springing up with both feet simultaneously in a jump is more difficult, but possible for some children.

Four-Year-Olds

Four-year-olds are much more proficient jumpers, and by age four-and-a-half, most can accomplish any type of jumping: up, down, forward, or over. They may not be able to do a sequence of different actions, though, such as hopping, skipping, and jumping, although they perform some or all of these actions separately. One study showed only 42 percent of preschool children jump well by age three, whereas 72 percent jump well by four-and-a-half (Zaichkowsky, Zaichowsky, & Martineck, 1980, p. 39).

Four-year-olds can jump higher in the air and farther down from higher elevations. The second step from the bottom of the stairs is now their big challenge, one you may want to discourage because of its potential for injury.

Five-Year-Olds

Five-year-olds, as you might expect, are long, high, far jumpers, if they have had practice. Maturity is important as previously noted, but just as necessary is practice of the skill, along with encouragement and compliments from adult caregivers. If children have been ridiculed because of their awkwardness or lack of physical accomplishment in the past, then you may have to spend much of your time helping them improve their self-image.

Some children may not want to try because they have performed so poorly in the past. This may have been due to undeveloped muscular strength and/or coordination, lack of practice, or a half-year "relapse" stage. Now they need to try again to prove to themselves they really do have physical skills. Have them jump over a line on the floor. If they succeed, draw two parallel lines (or use masking tape). As they become successful, let them separate the tape to wider and wider positions. They can do this on their own in a corner of the room if they don't want an audience at first. Most five-year-olds soon will feel secure enough to jump anywhere.

This is the age when rope jumping first appears. Girls may try to make it their exclusive sport, but teachers can be the rope turners so that every class member who wants to participate can have a turn. Again, do not force the awkward child. Before you introduce a jump rope to five-year-olds, be sure to check out the jumping skills of all your children individually, so that no one will be embarrassed in front of peers if he or she tries to jump rope and fails. This failure sometimes happens, and it may prevent a child, especially a boy, from ever putting himself in such an embarrassing situation again, which means he may not participate in group sports in school.

Competition has no place in the early childhood large motor program, as mentioned previously, but neither do total group activities that play up the weaknesses or inabilities of individual children. Total group games such as jump rope seem like such innocent fun, but they are not for the awkward child. It is better to let three children at a time play with a small jump rope than to insist that all children have a turn on a big jump rope, if one of those children will be embarrassed by lack of ability. Observing and recording the large motor abilities of individual children will help you decide what new activities to introduce.

If You Have Not Checked This Item: Some Helpful Ideas

■ Work with Individual Children Who Show Poor Skills

If children are age four and five and still cannot jump, then you should try an activity such jumping over a line. If children are three or younger, you do not need to be so concerned, since jumping may not be well-developed yet. If a child has a physical impairment, she may want to jump but not be able to. Her legs may be in braces, but if her arms are strong, you may be able to place her between two stationary objects like tables or room dividers where she can support herself with her arms and bring her feet up off the ground in a sort of jump if this is appropriate. As Olds (1994) notes:

> In working with differently abled children, the challenge always should be to identify opportunities for action—-find every means possible to maximize the use of capabilities that are strong, and exercise to the fullest extent faculties that are weak. (p. 33)

■ Chair Jumping

Have a "chair jumping day" when individuals or small groups get to jump from one of the small chairs in the room, and you measure their jumps. Keep a record of each child's jumps on a chart or notebook so individuals can see how well they do each week. Do not measure the results against others in the class; otherwise it becomes a competition. Let each child try three jumps, for instance, and have a different child be the measurer for each jumper.

You might want to measure with sticks you have color-coded to certain lengths, a yardstick, or a piece of string you mark off and later measure against a ruler. Whether you want to record in inches, centimeters, or merely red sticks will be up to you and the cognitive developmental level of your children. You need not be absolutely exact with the youngest children. They will be delighted to find they jumped for two red sticks and a blue stick the first time, and three red sticks the second time.

It is good to have a special chair that you cover with contact paper to keep the seat from being scratched. Let the children know that this is the only "jumping chair," and put it away when not in use.

■ Try Concept Jumping

When children are learning the concepts "up," "down," "over," "forward," and "in place," you might try having them act out the motions by jumping. Ask the others to guess what kind of jump a child made. Or let one child call out a concept and another child try to demonstrate it by jumping it.

■ Utilize Jumping Animals

Put pictures of jumping (leaping or hopping) animals on the walls at children's eye level and have them try to imitate the animals (e.g., kangaroo, kangaroo rat, frog, toad, rabbit, deer).

■ Read a Book

Jump, Frog, Jump (1981) by Robert Kalan (New York: Mulberry Books) is a simple cumulative story of a frog in a pond that has to "jump, frog, jump," to catch a fly or escape from a fish, a snake, and a turtle. After reading the book, put contact paper "lily pads" on the floor and have the children jump from one to another.

Moon Jump (1988) by Mustapha Matura (New York: Knopf) shows little East Indian boy Cayal who loves to jump and spends his days and nights jumping on chairs, sofas, the playground, and especially on his parent's bed. One night he jumps so high he lands on the moon where the moon man jumps with him until it is time to jump back home.

No Jumping on the Bed! (1987) by Tedd Arnold (New York: Dial) is the riotous story of Walter who lives up high in an apartment building, and what happens when he disobeys his father and takes one last jump on the bed. Down he goes through apartment after apartment, taking everything with him until he ends up asleep in his own bed.

The Magic Moonberry Jump Ropes (1996) by Dakari Hru (New York: Dial) shows older African American girls trying to get some other children to jump rope with them, but with no luck until Uncle Zambezi comes along with magic moonberry ropes brought back from East Africa. Then their wish for new friends comes true.

HOPS ON ONE FOOT

Hopping is the large motor "bounding" skill in which the child springs off the floor on one foot and lands on the same foot. Jumping uses both feet together, while leaping uses alternating feet to take off and land. A child can hop in place or hop forward for one or more steps. This Checklist item asks you to identify the children in your class who can hop.

Children need balancing skills before they can hop. They also need the leg length and strength to jump first. This means that not many will be truly hopping before three years of age, and maybe not until three-and-a-half. In fact, hopping for most children is not well-developed before the age of four.

You will see large individual differences in this skill as you do in other areas of development, but the largest difference is in gender. Girls four and five years old almost always hop more and better than boys. Hopping is a girl's skill in our society.

Games such as hopscotch and jump rope, which appear among five- and six-year-olds are examples. These games are generally played by girls, not boys. Challenge a boy to play hopscotch and he soon finds that girls his age are much more skilled hoppers, just as girls are better rope jumpers. However, preschool children who play few or no hopping games may have difficulty doing any hopping, whether they are boys or girls.

To help nonhoppers get started, ask them if they can hold one leg off the floor and hop up and down on the other. Have them lean forward slightly in the direction of the hopping leg as they spring up. If they lose their balance, have them try hopping next to a wall. Have them put out one arm to balance themselves against the wall, lift up one foot and try hopping on the other foot. Can they do it? They may need to practice balancing first. How long can they balance on one foot?

Because hopping is more difficult than jumping, children need to practice it frequently but briefly. Their large muscles should be strengthened but not strained.

If You Have Not Checked This Item: Some Helpful Ideas

■ Create a Hopping Trail

Make a hopping-tiptoeing-walking trail in your classroom or large motor room with cutout contact footprints that show hopping steps on one foot; then walking steps with both feet; then hopping on the other foot, tiptoeing, and jumping. Place a hopping trail next to a wall for inexperienced hoppers to balance against with one arm as they hop.

■ Hop to Music

Find a bouncy but slow record and let children try to hop and jump to it. Most four-year-olds will not be able to do more than three or four hops at a time, but the children can switch to jumping if they want.

■ Hop to Drum Beats

Let children make different movements to different drum beats you play. A one-thump beat can mean to walk, a two-thump beat can signify to hop, and a quick-time beat can indicate to run. See if they can follow your rhythm. Don't change your beat too quickly, since most children are really beginners when it comes to moving to rhythm.

■ Read a Book

Hop Jump (1993) by Ellen Stoll Walsh (San Diego: Harcourt Brace) is a simple book about green frogs that do hop-jump movements all day. Blue Betsy frog is bored and tries to twist like the falling leaves. Soon she is leaping and turning. She calls it dancing. The other frogs say there is no room for dancing, but soon they become intrigued, and then everyone is dancing. Can your children do these movements?

Can't Sit Still (1993) by Karen E. Lotz (New York: Dutton) tells a beautifully illustrated story about an African American girl in the city and the many movements she makes in her apartment and on the street during each of the four seasons.

THROWS, CATCHES, AND KICKS BALLS

Many preschool children do not get the opportunity to play with balls until they are older, perhaps when they enter primary school. Although their arm, hand, and leg muscles are not so well-developed and coordinated during the preschool years, your program can encourage this coordination. Children enjoy playing with balls when it involves balls they can handle at their level of accomplishment. Using the smaller, softer balls available these days for indoor play makes this possible.

Throwing and catching are two important upper body large motor skills. Throwing appears first. There are several ways to throw, such as overhand, underhand, and sidearm with two hands or one. Young children seem to go through a general progression, starting with infants who throw small objects overhand but downward, to the two-hand underhand throw, the one-hand underhand throw, and finally the one-hand overhand throw. The size and heaviness of the thrown object also make a difference as to the type of throw (Pica, 1995, p. 116).

Two-year-olds frequently try to throw things such as food or clothing, sometimes in frustration. Their throwing action is more of a jerky, sidearm movement. If they should try to throw a ball, they often stand facing the target, using both forearms

Preschool children need opportunities to throw, catch, and kick balls. A child-size basketball backboard gives them excellent practice in throwing at a target.

together to push a ball forward. The ball often dribbles away, almost accidently. Some youngsters who have the smaller softer indoor balls at home may develop one-hand overhand throws even before preschool. Seeing ballplayers on television and receiving encouragement from adults helps immeasurably. How accurate they eventually become depends on maturity and practice.

Photographic studies made of children throwing reveal four distinct patterns in the development of throwing:

1. Two- and three-year-olds throw mainly with their forearms, using little or no footwork or body rotation.
2. Three-and-a-half-year-olds throw with more body rotation and arm range.
3. Five- and six-year-olds start to throw with a forward step on the same side as their throwing arm.
4. Six-and-a-half-year-olds throw maturely, stepping forward with the opposite foot. (Zaichkowsky, 1980, p. 40)

The children in your classroom should be able to develop throwing skills. Throwing takes practice, not so much instruction as opportunity. Children have to work out how to throw by themselves as their muscles and coordination mature. Give the youngsters many throwing opportunities and they will do the rest.

What can they throw? Let them try inflated beach balls, yarn balls, sponge balls, Nerf balls, foam balls, squeezable balls, squish balls, beanbag balls, grip balls, tactile balls, or Koosh balls. Balls come not only in dozens of materials these days, but also in a huge variety of sizes and shapes, from golf-ball size to giant balls as big as the children. They are made from soft materials to resemble soccer balls, footballs, basketballs, and baseballs, among others.

Where can children throw? Because accuracy is not the point at first, they will need to become familiar with the throwing action itself. Have them throw foam or yarn balls against a wall. When they are ready, have them throw at a large target like a hula hoop hung on the wall or a box standing upright against a wall. A freestanding basketball backboard at preschoolers' height can be used even in the classroom if a foam ball is thrown. Girls and boys alike enjoy throwing balls. But neither will develop this skill to a mature degree without practice.

Evidence shows that practice counts with this large motor skill. Earlier, our society considered boys to be better throwers than girls. "To throw like a girl" was a derogatory comment often made about boys who threw poorly. It describes the throwing stance of stepping forward on the same foot as the throwing arm and throwing from the elbow: the stance of an immature thrower.

Now we know that even grown men in cultures where throwing is not emphasized use the same immature throwing form. On the other hand, modern girls in our own society do not "throw like a girl." Through early childhood programs like yours, both girls and boys can develop this large motor skill.

Because catching a ball is more difficult than throwing, it develops later. In addition to having upper body maturity, children also need eye-hand coordination to track the thrown ball and catch it with their hands. Many of your children may not develop this skill as easily as they did throwing. Most three-and-a-half-year-olds are still at the stage of try-ing to catch by holding their arms straight out in front of their bodies. They will be success-ful only if the ball is large and thrown directly into their arms with little force. Even five-year-olds catch a chest-high ball only 60 to 80 percent of the time (Cratty, 1982, p. 126).

In addition to the necessary practice, this particular skill also requires nervous sys-tem maturity. The child is being asked to respond to moving objects of varying speeds. His response time is much slower than that of an older child or adult. Even when he seems to be ready for the ball to arrive in his hands, he may not be able to bring them together in time.

Preschool girls seem to be more successful than boys in ball catching, perhaps because they have more mature eye-hand coordination. All children need as much practice in catching as in throwing. You, however, need to be aware that they may not succeed as well in catching because they are not ready developmentally.

Some children show fear as the ball approaches them. You may want to start catching practice by throwing soft, colorful objects such as beanbags, yarn balls, beach and foam balls. Better yet, have children begin by catching their own bounced ball. Once they are used to this activity, then you can stand close to them and toss them a large, soft ball. Catching success does not happen in one day or even one week. Let children take their time, but be sure to provide frequent opportunities. Once children have achieved some success, challenge them to catch an object they themselves have tossed up in the air—the hardest challenge of all.

Kicking a ball with the leg and foot is not as easy as it looks for preschoolers. Besides having leg muscle development, children need balancing skills and eye-foot coordination to kick a ball. Kicking for distance and not accuracy is more important for preschoolers (Gallahue, 1993).

Have children start by placing their nonkicking foot next to the ball. Tell them to look at the ball, then kick with their other leg. They can begin by kicking a beach ball any way they want. Once they get the hang of it, have them kick smaller foam balls at a wall. If you have little space for kicking balls, have children kick punchball balloons. If children want to kick harder rubber balls, find a space outside where they will not kick the ball into another child (Sanders, 1992, p. 79).

If You Have Not Checked This Item: Some Helpful Ideas

■ Try Some Kicking Games

Have children take several steps backward from a ball on the ground, then run up and kick the ball. How far can they kick? Another day, put two traffic cones about six feet apart. Have children stay behind a line about six feet back and try kicking a ball between the cones (Sanders, 1992, p. 81).

■ Use Targets for Throwing

Make targets out of cardboard boxes. Paint a simple animal face or clown face on the box. Cut a large hole for the mouth, much larger than the ball or beanbag. Have chil-dren stand behind a line not too far away and try to throw into the hole.

■ Use Pillows for Catching

For children who are having difficulty catching a ball, try throwing a small soft pillow to each one. Stand close enough at first for them to succeed without difficulty. Then step back a little at a time until you are farther away when you throw, and they must track the pillow with their eyes.

■ Read a Book

Harry and Willy and Carrothead (1991) by Judith Caseley (New York: Greenwillow) tells the story of Harry, who was born with no left hand and so wears a prosthesis, along with his friends Willy and Carrothead. The story takes place at school when the boys are five and shows all three engaged in physical activities, especially baseball, where Harry is a great player.

A Story About Courage (1992) by Joel Vecere (Austin, TX: Stech-Vaughn) tells the story of Jarrod, a sixth-grade boy in a wheelchair who tries out for the basketball team and finally finds a position for himself as team manager. Although the story is written about older children, the illustrations are vivid enough to be "read" to the children.

CLIMBS UP AND DOWN CLIMBING EQUIPMENT WITH EASE

Climbing involves use of the arms as well as the legs. It is, in fact, an outgrowth of creeping. Most children begin climbing as soon as they can creep over to an item of furniture and pull themselves up. If they are allowed, they will creep up the stairs. They will try to creep down, too, and soon find out that a backward descent is the only kind that works!

Many three- and four-year-olds enjoy climbing on all sorts of things: jungle gyms, ladders, ladder climbers, dome climbers, slides, rope climbers, trees, rocks, poles, and drainpipes. By the time they are in your program, children this age should be able to climb down as well as up with ease.

Although it takes bravery as well as muscle strength and coordination to be a successful climber, many of your children will be able to accomplish this skill if they have the opportunity. You should consider providing climbing equipment and climbing possibilities both inside and outside your classroom. Safety factors, of course, need to be considered. Since falling is the main concern with climbing, be sure that floor or ground surfaces are cushioned. Padding can be used inside. Sand or wood chips are preferable to grass or hard surfaces outside.

Not all children will attempt to climb. Do not force the reluctant ones. You can encourage them, and help children if they try to climb, but if they refuse, they should not be forced to try. Not all children will want to accomplish climbing skills, which is perfectly acceptable. Children have as much right to their own personal choices and interests as adults. Were you a climber when you were four?

On the other hand, the excitement of accomplishing such a physical feat as climbing to the top of a climber is wonderful to behold. As noted by early childhood specialist Clare Cherry (1976):

If I had room for only one piece of play equipment, my unhesitating choice would be something to climb on. Climbing strengthens muscles, develops postural control, and orients children to varying views of the world. For small children who spend so much time having to look "up" it must be an exhilarating experience to be in places where the view is "down." Few experiences can make a child feel so important as sitting on top of a jungle gym. (p. 53)

For children who indicate they would like to attempt this sort of climbing, you can help them best by standing close enough to catch them if they should falter; to encourage them if they turn to you for help; and congratulate them when they succeed. They may only climb up halfway to start. Then, little by little, they gain courage and expertise enough to complete their climb. You should accept any attempt they make, but not prod them to go all the way when they are not ready.

If You Have Not Checked This Item: Some Helpful Ideas

■ Provide a New Piece of Climbing Equipment

A packing crate (with splintery edges sanded down) is often a tempting piece of homemade climbing equipment that can be used either inside or outside. Ladder steps can be fastened to the outside of the crate if necessary, or children may use a step stool to climb up the crate. Cargo netting is also a fine piece of climbing equipment. Fasten it to a classroom wall with padding underneath or to a horizontal bar outside on the playground.

■ Build a Loft

Lofts not only give preschool children extra space for various new activities, they also provide a new perspective on the activities below. Some lofts use ladders to reach their tops, others use steps or stairs. Some have several means of entrance and exit. Even nonclimbers often learn to manage all the methods of access because being up in the loft is such fun.

■ Have a Multiple-Access Slide

A multiple-access slide is one of the most valuable pieces of large motor equipment you can purchase if your center can afford only one piece of equipment. Children are motivated to learn to climb to get to the platform at the top of the slide. There are usually steps, bars, or ladders to help children reach the top, and the youngsters soon know how to use them all. If you have space inside, an indoor multiple-access slide can serve as a loft as well as a large motor device.

■ Make an Obstacle Course

Use planks, sawhorses, barrels, ladders, and boxes to create an obstacle course for climbing. Rearrange them frequently. Children can climb up, over, and under.

■ Read a Book

So What? (1982) by Miriam Cohen (New York: Dell) is one selection in the well-known "Jim" series that starts with *Will I Have a Friend?* In this story, Jim is out on the playground with his multicultural friends, who are throwing balls, climbing on a climber, shooting baskets, jumping rope, and swinging. Jim hangs upside down on the climber but is afraid to let go with his hands like the other children do. He learns from one of the girls to relax and not be so uptight when things don't go right. Table 7–1 lists the progression of movement skills in children from infancy to age six.

Table 7–1 Large motor skills

Age	Walking	Running	Jumping	Climbing
8 months–1 year	Walks in a wide stance like a waddle			Climbs onto furniture and up stairs as an outgrowth of creeping
1–2 years	Walks in a toddle and uses arms for balance (arms are not swung)	Moves rapidly in a hurried walk, in contact with surface	Uses bouncing step off bottom step of stairs with one foot	Tries climbing up anything climbable
2–3 years	Walks upstairs two feet on a step	Runs stiffly, has difficulty turning corners and stopping quickly	Jumps off bottom step with both feet	Tries climbing to top of equipment, although cannot climb down
3–4 years	Walks with arms swinging; walks upstairs alternating feet; walks downstairs two feet on step	Runs more smoothly, has more control over starting and stopping	Springs up off floor with both feet in some cases, jumps over object leading with one foot	Climbs up and down ladders, jungle gyms, slides, and trees
4–5 years	Walks up and down stairs alternating feet; walks circular line; skips with one foot	Displays strong, speedy running; turns corners, starts and stops easily	Jumps up, down and forward	Climbs up and down ladders, jungle gyms, slides, and trees
5–6 years	Walks as an adult; skips alternating feet	Shows mature running, falls seldom, displays increased speed and control	Jumps long, high, and far; jumps rope	Displays mature climbing in adult manner

MOVES LEGS/FEET IN RHYTHM TO BEAT

Preschool children's acquisition of musical skills crosses several areas of development, including physical, cognitive, language, and creative. But because music itself involves both rhythm and sound (tempo and tone), we will look first at young children's development of rhythm, partly a large motor ability. In Chapter 8 we will consider musical sound, partly a language ability.

All humans are rhythmical beings whether or not we recognize the fact. Rhythm, in fact, is the essence of our life: Witness the beating of our heart and the breathing of our lungs. It is not so surprising to find, therefore, that even infants can make rhythmical responses with their arms, hands, legs, and feet. These claps, kicks, or wavings seem to be triggered by internal stimuli and not by external sounds or motions; although Cratty mentions that in cultures where dance is important, infants too young to stand have been observed picking up the beat of nearby adult dancers with their own bodies and limbs (Cratty, 1986, p. 257).

Nevertheless, the first voluntary rhythmical movements of young children are stimulated by sounds rather than visual cues. As with other physical development, the young child's rhythmic development proceeds in an observable sequence. First to appear are movements of arms/hands and then legs/feet that can follow a regular and rather slow rhythmic beat. Next, the young child's movements are able to replicate an irregular beat. Finally, children can learn to follow sound cues of different intensities. Horizontal movements are acquired before up and down movements of the arms. Rhythmic movements of one leg or one arm appear before the ability to move both limbs rhythmically.

Regardless of development, most young children love to dance and sing. They will make attempts to imitate any rhythmic activity around them. Young children also will follow their own internal rhythms with moving and singing on their own. If we want children to continue the natural development of their musical abilities, then the next move is ours. Adults who notice young children moving rhythmically must compliment them, encourage them to continue their creative movements, and call others' attention to the children's accomplishment.

Children very quickly pick up on the values of adults around them. If the adults show interest in children's dancing, then the youngsters will continue to dance. On the other hand, if adults disregard this action or reprimand children for moving around so much, then children will stop.

You need to provide the stimulus in your program for young children to move rhythmically. That means you must praise children for any impromptu creative moving they do. Then you must schedule creative movement activities in the daily life of your classroom. Be creative yourself and think of the curriculum areas that might include creative movement. An excellent book to follow is *A Moving Experience: Dance for Lovers of Children and the Child Within* (1987) by Teresa Benzwie (Tucson: Zephyr Press).

Creative Movement

An entire class of preschool children can gain tremendously from creative movement and dance activities if the activities are led by a sensitive teacher and held in a creative environment. The teacher can use a drum, tom-tom, tambourine, or simply hand-clapping for the beat, but she must be sensitive enough to pick up the pulse or rhythm of the group, instead of imposing her own rhythm on them. Records or tapes can be used, as well, but again, the teacher needs to rely on the group rhythm, which is usually different—often slower—than that of a record.

The environment should be attractive, orderly, and comfortable. If a gymnasium is used, it should be uncluttered. If the preschool classroom is large enough, clear a space for expansive movements. Preschoolers need to be able to run, leap, and gallop.

The teacher should be the leader—a sensitive and creative leader. If a child does not want to participate, don't make her. You can take her hand and swing it gently to the music. The teacher should be prepared, as well, with a series of simple movement activities for the children to try. Children do not like to be told: "Do whatever you want to do," or "Move any way you want to the music." This only leads to confusion.

Instead, you should lead the children into creative movement activities through the stimulus of a steady, rhythmic beat. They need to master the basic locomotor movements of walking, running, crawling, leaping, and galloping to music or to a beat. Start by beating the tom-tom slowly and having children walk across the floor to the beat. Then increase the tempo of the beat and have them come back across the floor a bit faster. Try other movements, at first slowly and then faster.

They also should master some of the nonlocomotor movements such as swinging, swaying, rocking, bending, and stretching. Continue using a drum or tap on a tambourine to set the beat for movement. Have seated children tap their feet to the beat. Then have them sway or rock or bend while still seated. Change the beat, making it faster or slower, louder or softer. Then have them stand up and make the same move-

Children need to master some of the nonlocomotor movements such as swinging, swaying, rocking, bending, and stretching.

ments as you change the beat. Whatever you do with rhythm, make it fun and do not expect perfection from these developing children of yours.

The short attention span of preschoolers makes it necessary to keep the sessions short (20 minutes) and include a variety of movements and dance activities. Young children like activities that take place on the floor, so be sure to include "snake" and "worm" dances where children can wriggle and crawl. Four-year-olds especially love to run. You will want to include a "jet plane zoom" or a "race car rally" in which children can run to music or a beat.

You could do a follow-the-leader activity in a line where you as leader set the pace. You can march, tramp, slide along, trip along on tiptoes, or walk in cadence, calling out a beat (e.g., "One-two buckle your shoe, three-four shut the door," etc.). Use music as well as a drum to help children move their legs/feet to the beat. Put on a record with a strong beat, and have the children move around the room keeping time. You may want to wind down your session with a slower record. Choose an appropriate tune for a "monster shuffle" or a "dinosaur clump." Children are usually happily exhausted after such a creative movement session.

Researcher Barbara Andress (1991, p. 24) finds that music-related creative movement responses increase among young children in a preschool classroom when three techniques are used: modeling, describing, and suggesting. A respected adult models by moving to music, expressing her own ideas of what she hears. This does not mean the child will imitate the action, but that the youngster will be motivated to move on her own. The adult can, however, encourage a child to move through what is called *tactile modeling*. Using this technique:

> The adult can extend the two index fingers for the child to grip (thus allowing the child to release at any time) and then begin to gently sway or otherwise guide movements to music. (Andress, 1991, p. 26)

For instance, the two can sway side-to-side while singing "Hickory Dickory Dock" or they can face each other and make rowing movements while singing "Row, Row, Row Your Boat."

Describing is also an effective way to promote creative movement. Here the teacher makes statements describing what the child is doing while she is doing it. One statement Andress (1991) used was: "I see Gregory slide his feet with the soft music. Now Gregory is stamping when the music is very loud" (p. 26).

Suggesting is a third technique that teachers can use in combination with the previous two, so long as it is not overdone. In this instance, the teacher suggests movements as she begins to model them: "Let's fly a kite" or "See how my kitty can waltz around" (Andress, 1991, p. 26).

If You Have Not Checked This Item: Some Helpful Ideas

■ Use a Tape Recorder

After tramping, stamping, or tiptoeing, children may want to create some "foot music" of their own. Have them sit while an individual child taps out a rhythm with his or her feet. Record it. Play it back and let the other children try to imitate this rhythm with their own feet.

Children may want to record other rhythms they hear. Have them listen for rhythms in the classroom. Can they hear the bubbling of the aquarium, the dripping of water from a faucet, the clicking of keys in the office down the hall? If you tape such sounds and play them back, children may be able to stand and move their feet to these rhythms.

■ Walk to Music

Play different records or pieces of music with different rhythms, and have your children try to walk around the room keeping time with the beat. Then have them walk to the rhythm of your drum beats or to a clicker. If you do not have a percussion instrument, tap on a glass. Speed up the tempo. Slow it down. Make it syncopated.

■ Use Rock or Rap Music

Rock music and rap are characterized by their strong beat. Bring in several albums or tapes with a beat and let children move/dance to them in the classroom.

■ Move to Chants or Poems

Books with chants and body action rhymes, such as *Move Over, Mother Goose! Finger Plays, Action Verses & Funny Rhymes* (1987) by Ruth I. Dowell (Beltsville, MD: Gryphon House), are wonderful sources of verses with a beat that children can move to. So is a book like *Arroz Con Leche: Popular Songs and Rhymes from Latin America* (1989) by Lulu Delacre (New York: Scholastic).

■ Read a Book

Ayu and the Perfect Moon (1984) by David Cox (London: The Bodley Head), has a little Balinese girl listen to an old woman, Ayu, tell the story of how she danced the Legong dance near the banyan tree in the village square when she was young.

Bravo, Tanya (1992) by Satomi Ichikawa and Patricia Lee Gauch (New York: Philomel) tells how little Tanya and her ballerina bear Barbara go to dancing class where Tanya tries her best but doesn't always dance as well as she does in the meadow by the brook to music only she hears.

MOVES ARMS AND HANDS IN RHYTHM TO BEAT

Most preschool children have participated in hand-clapping activities from infancy. They have imitated mother doing pat-a-cake, and they have imitated others around them who applaud a performance by clapping. Now, in this item, they are asked to perform a musical activity with their hands: moving their arms and hands to a beat.

This can mean clapping or beating out a rhythm with sticks, blocks, or percussion instruments held in the hands.

As discussed in the previous item, rhythm is a natural part of all of us. Our heart goes on beating whether or not we think about it. Our fingers may tap out a rhythm automatically. But can preschool children clap their hands in rhythm to a beat created outside their body? They can if their physical skills have developed normally and they have had practice clapping in rhythm.

The developmental sequence previously mentioned—head-to-foot and trunk-to-extremities—also applies to the physical maturity necessary for children to perform rhythmic movements. In other words, arm control in children occurs before hand control, and hand control occurs before finger control. A second sequence of development begins with control of one arm/hand independent of the other arm/hand (as in waving); next comes the simultaneous use of both arms/hands (as in clapping); and finally comes alternate movements of the two arms/hands (as in drumming).

Although clapping ability appears early in a child's development, the ability to clap with control comes later. Two-year-olds, for instance, enjoy clapping, but usually cannot clap in a pattern without a great deal of help and practice. The concept of clapping in rhythm or clapping out the syllables of a name is beyond most of them.

Three-, four-, and five-year-old children also may have some difficulty at first following a clapping pattern. Yet most of them can learn to clap the syllables of words or names, and enjoy repeating the activity.

Once they have reached this maturity, children need have practice to follow external rhythms. The creative movement activities discussed previously should give the children practice in moving their feet and bodies to rhythm. At the same time they hear you, the teacher providing the beat with your hands. Now it is their turn.

When you sing songs or play records in your classroom, give children practice clapping to the rhythm. Or use familiar folksongs to practice clapping on different beats. For instance, in *Paw Paw Patch*, children can clap on every other beat at first:

WHERE, oh, WHERE is SWEET little SUsy?
WHERE, oh, WHERE is SWEET little SUsy?
WHERE, oh, WHERE is SWEET little SUsy?
WAY down YONder in the PAW paw PATCH.

When children are able to follow this regular rhythm without difficulty, let them try to clap on every beat. Nursery rhymes and jump rope rhymes also are excellent for clapping practice.

Moving the two arms/hands alternately in a vertical motion, such as beating on a drum, indicates more mature development of a child's arm/hand control than does clapping the hands together. Young children enjoy beating on drums, pans, wooden blocks, and almost anything that will make a noise. For beaters they use their hands (fingers, palms, knuckles, fists), drumsticks, mallets, ladles, or anything else they can pound with.

The developmental sequence of drumming with the hands follows that of clapping. But children will have more success in beating a drum in a particular rhythm if they first have had many clapping experiences. When your children demonstrate that they can clap in rhythm, it is time to introduce the drum.

Instruments used in preschool programs fall into the same categories of those used by professionals: sound makers, rhythm, melody, and harmony instruments. Sound makers for young children include pots, pans, glasses, seed pods, stones, and cans with seeds. Rhythm instruments include rhythm sticks, tone blocks, coconut shells, bells, triangles, gongs, cymbals, tambourines, sand blocks, rattles, maracas, and drums, to name a few. Melody instruments include xylophone, marimba, tone bells, tonette, flutophone, and ocarina. Harmony instruments include autoharp, harmonica, guitar, ukelele, banjo, mandolin, accordion, piano, and electric keyboard.

Rhythm instruments such as the drum need to be taken seriously in the preschool: That is, a drum is not a toy but a real instrument, and should be treated as such. Perhaps because teachers do not understand that rhythm instruments are serious instruments used in real bands and orchestras, they allow children to treat these items as toys. Instead, each rhythm instrument should be introduced to children separately, with directions on how to use it properly and limits on using it improperly. In this way children get the most from the experience: They learn how to use the instrument, to appreciate the sound it makes, and to practice the physical skills the instrument affords them.

Unfortunately, rhythm instruments are often used in "rhythm bands" in the preschool classroom, with all of the instruments played at once as the children march around to music. The youngsters, of course, may have fun with such an activity, but it adds little to their enjoyment of music, their skill development, or their appreciation for the instrument they hold. Instead, children tend to bang as loud as they can all at once, creating a cacophony of sound—noise—which drowns out the sounds of the individual instruments, the music, and the rhythm they are supposed to be following.

Drums come in all sizes and shapes. Some are intended to be played with the hands; some played with two drumsticks; some played with one. Commercial drums are usually wooden or plastic with a skin or plastic head over one or both ends. Have several drums and drumsticks available in your classroom. Take time to introduce their use to the children, rather than merely putting the instruments on a shelf. Talk to the children about the drums. Demonstrate what each one sounds like and how it can be played. Let the children try out each drum.

Then have the children sing a song while you clap out the beat. Next, have the children clap the beat themselves as they sing. Finally, let them try beating the drums to accompany the song. They can use drumsticks or their hands. Pass the drums around until everyone has a chance.

Be sure to follow up this drumming activity for several days to give the children practice. You can use different songs, records, or tapes with different rhythms, and a variety of activities. Some children may want to beat the drums while the others march around the room.

If You Have Not Checked This Item: Some Helpful Ideas

■ Try Name Clapping

Focusing on a child's name is the surest way to interest a young egocentric child in almost any activity. At circle time or small group time you can introduce "name clapping": clapping out the syllables in each child's name as the children say the name aloud. Make the activity more interesting by adding other words, such as "hello" or "my name is . . . " Now the children can chant and clap:

Hel-lo-Bob-bie
My-name-is-San-dra
Hel-lo-Ver-on-i-ca

Finally, as the children become more adept, add their last names to this clapping activity:

My-name-is-Mel-is-sa-Brad-ley

■ Use a Tape Recorder

Children may want their own clapped rhythms recorded on the tape recorder and then played back for others in the group to try to imitate. Have each child say his or her name and then clap out a rhythm.

■ Send Drum Messages

Children enjoy sending drumbeat messages. If they have learned to clap out names by syllables, they will be able to send drum messages the same way. Let them try sending their names: ("My-name-is-Ran-dy") with drumbeats. Can the other children guess what they are saying on the drum?

■ Make Your Own Drums

Making drums is an activity for the teacher, not the children, in the preschool. Various types of drums can be made, depending on the material. Use large cans, ice cream containers, oatmeal boxes, round plastic containers, plastic bleach bottles, coffee cans, margarine tubs, or wooden or metal buckets for the body. For the head, use animal parchment (from repair departments of music stores), inner tube rubber, goatskin, heavy plastic, or canvas. Remove one or both ends of the can or container. Cut one or two circular head pieces larger than the container opening. Punch holes around the edge of the drum head material about two inches apart. Soak the parchment or goatskin in water for half an hour. Place the drum head material on either end of the drum body and lace tightly together on sides with cord or rawhide laces. Or place material on the open end and tack to the container.

To make drumsticks, glue small rubber balls on the ends of sticks such as pencils or wooden dowels; or wrap cloth around the ends of wooden ladles; or insert sticks into spools and wrap cloth around the spools.

■ Read a Book

Dancing with the Indians (1991) by Angela Shelf Medearis (New York: Holiday House) tells the fascinating story of African Americans who were rescued by the Seminole Indians during the days of slavery, and whose descendants went every year to Oklahoma to dance with the Indians during their annual powwow. Vivid illustrations portray the Ribbon Dance by the women, the Rainbow Dance, and rattlesnake dancing, as drummers strike the beat. Finally, all are invited to join the Indian Stomp Dance, and they stomp and sway till break of day.

Wood-Hoopoe Willie (1992) by Virginia Kroll (Watertown, MA: Charlesbridge) tells the story of Willie, an African American boy you can always hear coming with his toes tapping or his knuckles rapping. His Grandpa says he must have a wood-hoopoe bird from Africa trapped inside him, one that is always pecking on trees or cackling in rhythm. Then comes the Kwanzaa celebration and the hired drummer has a car accident. Willie saves the day by tapping, patting, and rapping on the African drums while the tambourines shimmy and the gourd rattles shake.

OBSERVING, RECORDING, AND INTERPRETING LARGE MOTOR DEVELOPMENT

It is important at the beginning of the year to screen all of your children using the large motor development section of the Child Skills Checklist. List the name of each child along the left side of a lined sheet of paper. At the top, indicate the eight items of the checklist. Draw vertical lines separating the eight items. Check off the large motor skills you observe for each child. For children who have few checkmarks, you may want to do an in-depth observation on each of the items.

Lionel, whose social play observations appeared in Figure 5–1, was observed for large motor development. Figure 7–1 shows that information.

This observational data gathered for Lionel was helpful to the classroom staff. They could see that Lionel spent more time in sedentary activities. He seemed more at ease sitting and playing than running around engaged in large motor activities. During a parent conference, the teachers learned that Lionel lived in a large apartment building and had little opportunity to run outside and play. However, the staff was also concerned that the program itself offered few large motor experiences for the children. The "N" designation, meaning "no opportunity to observe," was listed for most of the children because the program has neither a playground, gymnasium, nor indoor climbing equipment. Children are taken for walks, weather permitting, and are allowed to run around on the lawn outside the building. But it is obvious that additional large motor activities need to be provided.

Child Skills Checklist

Name _____ Lionel _____   Observer _____ Barb _____

Program ___ Pre-school—K 2 ___   Dates _____ 1/20 _____

Directions:

Put a ✔ for items you see the child perform regularly. Put N for items where there is no opportunity to observe. Leave all other items blank.

Item	Evidence	Dates
5. Large Motor Development		
___ Walks down steps alternating feet	Holds onto rail & puts 2 feet on each step when going downstairs	1/20
___ Runs w/ control over speed & direction	Does not run often	1/20
N Jumps up and lands on two feet		1/20
N Hops on one foot		1/20
N Throws, catches and kicks balls		1/20
___ Climbs up and down climbing equipment with ease	Does not attempt to climb	1/20
✔ Moves legs and feet in rhythm to beat	Taps feet when he beats drum	1/20
✔ Moves arms and hands in rhythm to beat	Claps in time to records	1/20

Figure 7–1   Large motor development observations for Lionel

Because Lionel and many of the other children showed skills and interest in rhythm activities, the classroom team decided to incorporate creative movement and dance activities at one end of the large classroom on a daily basis. As children become accustomed to moving to music and drumbeats, the teachers plan to take the children outside on the lawn for more expansive creative movement exercises.

REFERENCES

Allen, K. E., & Goetz, E. M. (1982). *Early childhood education: Special problems, special solutions.* Rockville, MD: Aspen.

Andress, B. (1991). Preschool children and their movement responses to music. *Young children, 47*(1), 22–27.

Benzwie, T. (1987). *A moving experience: Dance for lovers of children and the child within.* Tucson: Zephyr.

Caplan, T., & Caplan, F.. (1983) *The early childhood years: The 2 to 6 year old.* New York: Putnam.

Cherry, C. (1976). *Creative play for the developing child.* Belmont, CA: Fearon.

Cratty, B. J. (1982). Motor development in early childhood: Critical issues for researchers in the 1980's. In B. Spodeck (Ed.), *Handbook of research in early childhood education.* New York: The Free Press.

Cratty, B. J. (1986). *Perceptual & motor development in infants & children.* Upper Saddle River, NJ: Merrill/Prentice-Hall.

Flinchum, B. M. (1975). *Motor development in early childhood: A guide for movement education with ages 2 to 6.* St. Louis: Mosby.

Fraiberg, S. (1975). Intervention in infancy: A program for blind infants. In B. Z. Friedlander, G. M. Sterritt, & G. E. Kird (Eds.), *Exceptional infant* (Vol. 3). New York: Brunner/Mazel.

Gallahue, D. L. (1982). *Developmental movement experiences for children.* New York: John Wiley & Sons.

Gallahue, D. L. (1993). *Developmental physical education for today's children.* Dubuque, IA: Brown & Benchmark.

Olds, A. R. (1994). From cartwheels to caterpillars: Children's need to move indoors and out. *Child Care Information Exchange.* No. 5, pp. 32–36.

Pica, R. (1995). *Experiences in movement: With music, activities and theory.* Albany, NY: Delmar.

Pines, M. (1979). A head start in the nursery. *Psychology Today. 13*(4), 56–68.

Sanders, S. W. (1992). *Designing preschool movement programs.* Champaign, Il · Human Kinetics.

Tara, H. L. (1992). Physical activity of young children in relation to physical and mental health. In C. M. Hendricks (Ed.), *Young children on the grow: Health, activity, and education in the preschool setting* (pp. 33–42). Washington, DC: Eric Clearinghouse.

Zaichkowsky, L. D., Zaichkowsky, L. B., & Martineck, T. J. (1980). *Growth and development: The child and physical activity.* St. Louis: Mosby.

SUGGESTED READINGS

Beaty, J. J. (1996) *Preschool appropriate practices.* Fort Worth, Texas: Harcourt Brace Jovanovich.

Beaty, J. J. (1996). *Skills for preschool teachers.* Upper Saddle River, NJ: Merrill/Prentice Hall.

Benelli, C., & Yongue, B. (1995). Supporting young children's motor skill development. *Childhood education. 71*(4), 217–220.

Gabbard, C. (1988). Early childhood physical education. *Journal of Physical Education, Recreation and Dance, 59*(7), 65–69.

Kranowitz, C. S. (1994). Kids gotta move: Adapting movement experiences for children with differing abilities. *Child Care Information Exchange,* No. 5, 37–43.

Poest, C. A., Williams, J. R., Witt, D. D., & Atwood, M. E. (1990). Challenge me to move: Large muscle development in young children. *Young Children, 45*(5), 4–10

Rodger, L. (1996). Adding movement throughout the day. *Young children, 51*(3), 4–6.

VIDEOTAPES

Magna Systems, Inc. (1994). *Preschoolers: Physical and cognitive development.* 95 West County Line Rd., Barrington, IL, 60010.

National Association for the Education of Young Children. (1996). *Nurturing growth—child growth and development.* NAEYC, 1509 16th St. NW, Washington, DC, 20036-1426.

State of Indiana. *Structured play: Gross motor activities for everyday (Indiana steps ahead series).* NAEYC, 1509 16th St. NW, Washington, DC, 20036-1426.

LEARNING ACTIVITIES

1. Use the Child Skills Checklist for large motor development as a screening tool to observe all the children in your classroom. Which ones are the most physically accomplished? Which need the most help? What are their ages?

2. Choose a child who seems to need a great deal of help in large motor development. Do a running record on three different days to determine what the child can do physically. Do an activity with the child to promote a skill he or she needs help with. Record the results.

3. How do the girls and boys of the same age in your program compare with one another in each of the large motor Checklist items? How do you explain any differences or similarities? Can you make any inferences or conclusions about gender differences based on your observations?

4. Choose a child who needs help in moving to rhythm. Involve the child using one or more of the rhythm ideas from the text. Discuss the results.

5. Have a staff member involve children in a new large motor game while you observe and record. Discuss your results as compared with the original screening you did. What conclusions can you draw?

CHAPTER 8

Small Motor Development

SMALL MOTOR CHECKLIST

☐ Shows hand preference (which is_____)

☐ Turns with hand easily (knobs, lids, eggbeaters)

☐ Pours liquid into glass without spilling

☐ Unfastens and fastens zippers, buttons, Velcro

☐ Picks up and inserts objects with ease

☐ Uses drawing/writing tools with control

☐ Uses scissors with control

☐ Pounds in nails with control

DEVELOPING SMALL MOTOR SKILLS

Small motor development involves the fine muscles that control the extremities. In the case of young children we are especially concerned with control, coordination, and dexterity in using the hands and fingers. Although this development occurs simultaneously in children along with large motor development, the muscles near the trunk (proximal) mature before the muscles of the extremities (distal), which control the wrists and hands.

Thus it is important for young children to practice use of the large muscles before they become involved in small motor activities to any extent. Delays in developing large motor coordination may very well have a negative effect on the development of small motor skills. But once children can accomplish small motor movements, preschool caregivers should encourage them to engage in all types of manipulative activities so they can learn and then practice the skills needed to use their hands and fingers with control and dexterity.

Reflexes

Surely infants and toddlers use their hands and fingers without much previous experience, you may counter. Why, then, do three-, four-, and five-year-olds have a different situation? The difference is important. It involves voluntary versus involuntary movements. Infants move their arms, hands, and fingers through reflexes, not voluntary movements. The nervous system assimilates these involuntary movements as it matures, allowing children to control their movements voluntarily. As these initial reflexes disappear, children must purposefully learn to replace them by using and controlling their hands and fingers.

A very large number of reflexes are present in the infant. They include the Moro or startle reflex, in which the infant throws out its arms with a jerk and lets out a cry; the rooting reflex, in which the infant turns its head and opens its mouth when touched on the side of the cheek; the sucking reflex, in which the infant sucks if its lips or mouth are touched; the walking reflex, in which the infant makes stepping movements when held in an upright position on a surface; the swimming reflex, in which the infant makes swimming movements when held in the water with its head supported. Many more reflexes exist (Zaichkoswky, Zaichkowsky & Martineck, 1980, p. 37).

The reflex most connected with small motor hand skills is the grasping reflex or palmar grasp in which the baby clamps its fingers around anything put in its palm. This grasp is so strong in the beginning it will support the infant's weight and can be used to lift the baby entirely off the surface on which it is lying. It is difficult, in fact, for the infant to let go. You may have to pry its fingers apart.

Involuntary responses such as this have their origin in the lower brain stem and spinal cord, and eventually come under the control of the higher brain centers of the nervous system as the child matures. This higher part of the brain inhibits these initial reflexes after they have finished their task of aiding the survival of the helpless new-born, and the higher brain center then allows voluntary movements to replace them.

The initial reflexes fade away within their own recognized time table, depending on individual differences of course. Rooting and sucking usually disappear after three months, walking and swimming after five months, and Moro——the last to go——usually leaves after nine months. When such reflexes persist after their allotted time, it may be an indication of brain impairment (Zaichkowsky, Zaichowsky & Martineck, 1980, p. 37).

The grasping reflex lasts until about nine months. Infants cannot start to control hand and finger actions voluntarily before this. Infants may reach for things—but not very accurately—before age six months; letting go is the infants' main problem. Even year-old children may struggle to release an object voluntarily, and some do not gain control of "letting go" before a year and a half.

Readiness

We understand that, like the large motor skills, voluntary small motor skills do not just happen; they must be learned naturally and then practiced by young children. Is there a certain time period when particular skills can be learned best? Again we face the problem of "readiness." When is the child's neuromuscular system mature enough for him to control his movements and perform certain actions? Should we wait until he is ready? Not necessarily. As with large motor skills, we should encourage children to use their small muscles as soon as they can. Because each child's development is different, this time period may differ.

All of us carry within us an inherited biological clock. For some of us, small motor development occurs in textbook fashion, just as the charts for average physical growth indicate. For others, this development happens just a bit behind or ahead of the charts. This staggered individual development will exist in all of the children in your program. Each child has his or her own built-in biological clock. Neither you nor the child knows what time it is for the child except in general terms. Since everyone's development occurs in a particular sequence, the best we can do is to assess the child's development, then provide him or her with appropriate activities, materials, and encouragement.

Is there a "critical moment" then when small motor skills must be learned or it will be too late? Not really, except in broad general terms. The best time to learn a small motor skill seems to be when the skill is changing most rapidly (Zaichkowsky, et al., 1980, p. 36). But because this is not easy to determine, it is best to offer many types of activities for all your children and to help them get involved with activities that offer both success and challenge.

In other words, all of your children are "ready" to begin developing their small motor skills when they enter your program. You do not need to wait. The question is not whether they are "ready," because they are, but whether you are ready to assist them in this important area of development. To do this successfully you will first need to know where each child stands in small motor development, so that you can help them continue in their growth and learning.

You may want to screen them using the eight Small Motor Checklist items. These items are observable behaviors that demonstrate acknowledged small motor skills of young children in the areas of rotation, manipulation, and dexterity, as well as handedness.

SHOWS HAND PREFERENCE (WHICH IS_____)

Many, but not all, of your children will have developed a hand preference by age three. You may want to take note of this preference, but you should not be concerned about it. A great deal of interest and controversy—as well as incomplete understanding—surrounds the development of handedness, or *lateral dominance*, as it is called. Lateral dominance also includes the development of a foot preference and eye preference, which may or may not be the same as the hand preference.

Infants tend to use both hands in the beginning. This behavior is due to reflexive rather than voluntary movements. As the neuromuscular system matures enough for voluntary movements to occur, infants may begin to show a preference for one hand. At first this preference may not be very strong, and because involuntary movements do not disappear all at once, infants may use both hands for many months.

This seems to be the case for one-year-olds. By the age of two years, the child may begin to prefer using one hand over the other. At two-and-a-half, about 58 percent of U.S. children have established a dominant hand, and by age three, about 70 percent have established dominance. Then this percentage does not increase much until eight-and-a-half years. By the age of 11, 94 percent have established a preferred hand and the remaining children are ambidextrous, or have mixed dominance (Zaichowsky et al., 1980, p. 75).

Not all children in the world exhibit the same pattern of development in hand dominance. Hand preference development in Japanese children is similar to that of U.S. children until about age two-and-a-half. But between then and four-and-a-half, development slows considerably. Only 50 percent of Japanese children establish hand dominance by the age of four-and-a-half years (Zaichowsky et al., 1980, p. 75).

This is an important finding, because we know that children develop in the same sequence and within the same timetable around the world. Differences, therefore, must be due to cultural influences: in other words, the child's environment. In the United States we are particularly concerned with handedness, and many parents go out of their way to make sure their children develop right-handedness. They put emphasis on using the right hand by handing things to the right hand and encouraging children to use their right hand to eat, hold, and throw. When the children are successful, the parents praise them and offer positive feedback.

Such practice accompanied by feedback and positive reinforcement is of course the best way to develop any motor skill. In the end, parental influence seems to make little difference, because 90 percent of the human race eventually uses the right hand for small motor activities. More boys, by the way, are left-handed or ambidextrous than girls.

Foot dominance is somehow different from hand dominance. Even infants often show a clear-cut preference for one foot over the other. By the time they are five, 94 percent of children have developed foot dominance.

Our concern over handedness has always centered around children's ability in learning to read and write. Will lefties have more trouble? Will children with mixed dominance have learning problems? Should you try to change a child's hand preference from left to right? The answers are not all that clear. A great deal of controversy exists regarding the relationship between perceptual-motor development and learning disabilities. There is still so much we do not know about human development.

The best advice at the moment, it seems, advocates helping young children develop small motor dexterity, no matter what their hand preference. Children need to succeed. A strong hand preference may help them perform small motor tasks with dexterity. If you know what that preference is for each of your children, you can help them develop it with practice and positive feedback.

If You Have Not Checked This Item: Some Helpful Ideas

■ Do Not Make a Fuss

You may want to know if a child has established handedness, and with which hand, but keep your efforts at a low key. Encourage the child to use whichever hand she prefers, so that she will become more skillful in using it.

TURNS WITH HAND EASILY (KNOBS, LIDS, EGGBEATERS)

Twisting or turning movements—done with the wrist, hand, and fingers by rotating the wrist and/or forearm—take several forms. The child may enclose a doorknob with her hand and try to twist and then pull it to open the door. Depending upon the size and stiffness of the knob and door, she may or may not succeed at first. Or she may not be tall enough to make her small motor skills work effectively. Turning a key in a lock involves this same type of motion.

Another form of small motor rotating involves vertical turning at the wrist or rotating the forearm while the fingers are gripping an implement: a cranking type of movement. Eggbeaters, food mills, and can openers use this motion. Still another type of small motor rotating involves using the fingers to twist a nut onto a bolt, turn a screw into a hole, or twist a lid onto or off of a jar or bottle.

Children at an early age can accomplish this motor skill. Two-and-a-half and three-year-olds, for instance, can turn a doorknob if they can reach it. They love to screw and unscrew lids or tops on jars and bottles. Have parents collect empty plastic bottles and containers of all sizes along with their screw-top lids, and keep the items in a box in the manipulative area of the classroom for the children to practice on.

Small motor control is far from perfect, especially with the younger children; things have a way of slipping out of their fingers from time to time. Thus it is important to use only unbreakable containers such as plastic—never glass—in the classroom.

This same hand-rotating skill is used by three-year-olds and older children as they try to put together a puzzle. Whereas two-year-olds will often try to jam a puzzle piece into place and will give up if it doesn't fit, older children will rotate the piece to try to match the shape of the hole.

Watch and see how your children make puzzles. Obviously perceptual awareness is also at work in this instance, but children first need the small motor rotating skill in order to use their shape recognition ability. Puzzles of differing complexities should be an item on your shelves of manipulative materials. These puzzles offer excellent practice for finger dexterity and eye-hand coordination, as well as the cognitive concepts of matching, shapes, and part-to-whole relationships. Puzzles can help teachers, too. As Maldonado (1996) notes:

> Puzzles provide teachers with a fine observation and assessment tool, allowing teachers to easily observe children. Their concentration, body movement, language, thinking in the form of problem solving, and making choices are accessible to the observer. Teachers should program enough time to sit with each child at a puzzle at least once a month. (pp. 9–10)

Three-year-olds can also use this turning skill to operate an eggbeater, and they love to do it. Be sure to have more than one eggbeater at your water table, since the eggbeater is usually a favorite implement and the focus of many squabbles if only one is available. Children like to try turning food mills and can openers as well, but sometimes youngsters do not have the strength to succeed if the items to be ground or opened are too difficult.

Research has found that objects of differing shapes and those that can be modified are more interesting to children than rigid and unchangeable objects. Novelty is also an important quality in encouraging children to handle and manipulate objects. When the novelty wears off, children are less interested in playing with the items. Teachers should respond to such findings by including a variety of items in the manipulative area, and by changing them from time to time (Cratty, 1986, p. 214).

In addition, teachers should include cooking experiences in the classroom on a daily or weekly basis. Children can help with "cool cooking," that is, food preparation without heat, such as daily snacks. They can scrape carrots and cut celery for dips; mix cream cheese with flavorings; grind peanuts into peanut butter; whip cream into butter. They can also help with "hot cooking" by whipping eggs with eggbeaters for scrambled eggs or grinding cooked apples or cooked pumpkin through a food mill.

More and more teachers are making food preparation a part of their curriculum with the advent of convenient appliances such as hot pots, microwaves, and toaster ovens. It is an activity with special significance for children's development of small motor skills. Or as Cosgrove (1991) points out:

> Many kinds of learning are involved in cooking; motor, sensory, conceptual, and social skills all play an important part in food preparation. All five senses are involved. Stirring, beating, and rolling improve muscle control. Measuring, boiling, and freezing illustrate change. Following directions requires listening. Sharing, cooperation, and good manners encourage social skills. And waiting for someone to say "OK, it's done—let's eat" develops patience. (p. 44)

If You Have Not Checked This Item: Some Helpful Ideas

■ Provide a Collection of Food Utensils for Cooking and Play

Visit a hardware store having a large assortment of food preparation utensils and stock up on all kinds of grinding, squeezing, cranking types of implements. Better still, visit a flea market and buy the same sorts of things second hand. Some of the old-fashioned hand tools of great-grandma's kitchen will make a big hit in your classroom. Keep some of the items in your housekeeping area for pretending, and some near the water table, or on your manipulative shelves for small motor practice. But be sure to let children themselves use these utensils when you do real cooking.

■ Make a Nuts-and-Bolts Board

Fasten bolts of differing sizes to a sanded-down board, and give children a box of nuts to screw onto the bolts. The children will need to use their size-sorting as well as small motor skills.

■ Collect Old Locks and Keys

Have a box of old locks and keys for children to experiment with. The youngsters will need persistence as well as motor skills to match up and make the locks and keys work. But it is an exciting challenge for them.

■ Get a Toy Hopper with a Hand Crank for the Sand Table

Children love to play with sand. Toy stores, toy catalogs, and stores selling beach toys offer sand implements for sifting and grinding that certain children will use for hours. Don't forget to have children wear safety goggles at the sand table.

■ Try a Citrus Reamer

Bring in a citrus reamer that works by hand, and let your children take turns twisting half an orange on it to make their own juice for snack. You may need to help them get started.

■ **Read a Book**

The Best Peanut Butter Sandwich in the Whole World by Bill MacLean (Windsor, Ontario: Black Moss, 1990) shows little Billy assembling the ingredients and then making the best peanut butter sandwich in the whole world. Your children may want to grind peanut butter for their own best sandwiches.

Dumpling Soup by Jama Kim Rattigan (Boston: Little Brown, 1993) tells the story of the little Asian-American girl, Marisa, who helps her Korean grandmother and her aunts to make dumplings for their annual New Year's celebration in Hawaii. They chop and talk and mix and pound, and scrape, scrape, scrape. Be sure to have some real food for your children to prepare after reading this book.

POURS LIQUID INTO GLASS WITHOUT SPILLING

Two-year-olds are able to hold a glass of milk, at first with two hands, and then with one. Most parents are not really concerned that their children do more than this sort of holding. Pouring tends to be an adult activity that mothers do even for their preschool children. Many nursery school teachers and child-care personnel feel the same way. Why should children learn to pour? Won't they just make a mess if they spill? Isn't it much quicker and more efficient if the adults in the classroom do the pouring?

Children should learn to pour not only as a helping activity, but to acquire and practice small motor coordination. Pouring is an excellent authentic activity that children can participate in, and that is both helpful to others and, more importantly, helpful for their own small muscle development. Long ago Maria Montessori, the

Children should learn to pour, not only as a helping activity, but also to practice small motor skills such as eye-hand coordination.

renowned Italian early childhood educator, recognized the value of pouring by including all sorts of pouring activities in her "daily living exercises," which taught children small motor skills such as eye-hand coordination. Today Montessori children still learn by pouring rice before they finally pour liquids successfully from small pitchers.

The size of the pitcher is the key to successful pouring. Put a small pitcher on each of your own children's snack or lunch tables, and let the youngsters help themselves to juice or milk. If they should spill, they can help clean up with a soft sponge, another good small motor exercise.

Allowing children to pour may not be as efficient as having an adult pour the drinks, but you need to think about the purpose of your program. Is it to take care of a group of children, or is it to *help young children develop their own skills* and learn to take care of themselves? Young children take a great deal of pride in being able to do adult-type tasks. Performing these tasks not only makes them feel grown up but also gives them a real sense of self-worth and accomplishment.

There will be accidents. Spills are part of the price our children pay for the complicated task of growing up. Remember the problem of releasing the grip, in which children actually have to learn how to let go because some traces of the palmar grasp reflex may still remain? And if they do not have their minds on what they are doing, they may release their grip without meaning to. Again, make spilling a learning experience, not an embarrassment. They will enjoy squeezing out the cleanup sponge. Three-year-olds may need to use both hands for pouring. But if the pitcher is small enough, four- and five-year-olds can often handle it with one hand.

If You Have Not Checked This Item: Some Helpful Ideas

■ Have Pouring Implements in Your Water Table

Have several sizes and types of plastic pitchers in your water table. Some can be large with lids on the top; some can be small and open at the top. All should have handles. Children can do much of their initial pouring practice here without worrying about spilling.

■ Use Pouring Implements on Your Food Table

Have small plastic or ceramic pitchers that the children can use to serve themselves. You can fill these small-sized containers as they empty. Again, the flea market is a good source for interesting pouring implements such as vinegar cruets and small metal pitchers.

■ Read a Book

Mel's Diner by Marissa Moss (BridgeWater, 1994) tells the story of an African American, Mabel, who helps her mother and father run their diner. She helps set the table in the morning and fills the sugar bowls and napkin holders. After school she comes in with her best friend and sometimes they dance when someone puts a quarter in the juke box.

Sunshine by Jan Ormerod (New York: Lothrop, Lee & Shepard, 1981) is a wordless book showing a little girl getting up by herself, pouring milk on her breakfast cereal, helping her father get her mother's breakfast, brushing her teeth, dressing herself, and finally getting her parents going so they won't be late. Children enjoy seeing a child like themselves behaving so independently. Have them "read" the book to you.

UNFASTENS AND FASTENS ZIPPERS, BUTTONS, VELCRO TABS

Unfastening and fastening zippers, buttons, and Velcro tabs are other self-help skills we want children to accomplish so they can take care of themselves, but also to develop their small motor dexterity. Young children want to do things for themselves. Often they have trouble accomplishing unfastening and fastening tasks because their motor coordination has not developed sufficiently. But just as often their difficulty has to do with lack of practice because the adults around them do everything for them.

It is interesting to note that economically disadvantaged children frequently develop small motor dexterity before middle income children do. Economically disadvantaged children often have more practice. In fact, preschoolers in many large one-parent families are expected to help dress themselves when the working mother has her hands full getting herself ready for work every morning, the baby ready for the sitter, and breakfast ready for everybody before she has to leave.

If mothers and fathers do all the buttoning and fastening of clothing for their preschoolers, the children miss an excellent opportunity for learning how to do it on their own. They may even resist when the preschool teacher encourages them to try, wanting the teacher to perform the same function as their mothers.

Three-year-olds are able to unbutton first—always an easier task—but many can also button large buttons on clothing if given the chance to practice. Most three-year-olds also can fasten regular snaps but may have trouble with the heavy-duty jeans-type snap. Even four-year-olds seldom have the finger strength necessary to make these heavy-duty snaps work.

Four-year-olds should be able to button and unbutton clothing with little difficulty. They can unzip zippers, but often need help getting started with jacket zippers that come apart completely.

Many shoes and articles of clothing are now fastened with Velcro-type fasteners. This seems to be the easiest fastener for children to handle. A Velcro fastener is pulled apart by gripping the end between the thumb and forefinger and pulling; it is fastened merely by pushing one Velcro-covered tab against the Velcro backing. Preschoolers have the strength and coordination to do this with ease.

If You Have Not Checked This Item: Some Helpful Ideas

■ Use Buttoning/Zipping Boards

Make or purchase several boards that will help your children acquire and practice these skills. If you make your own boards, have only one skill practiced on each board: buttoning on one, zipping on another, snaps on another. Then children can practice one of these skills at a time. Have these boards available in the manipulative area of your classroom.

■ Talk with Parents

Talk with parents about the importance of their child's developing small motor coordination. Let them know the kinds of activities their children will be doing in your class. Suggest some of the activities the children could be doing at home, such as self-help skills like dressing themselves—including buttoning, zipping, and snapping clothing—or helping dress younger members of the family.

■ Read a Book

Do Like Kyla by Angela Johnson (New York: Orchard, 1990) tells the story of a little African American girl who copies her big sister Kyla in everything she does. They both get up, stretch, and get dressed, eat breakfast, get dressed for outside with Kyla helping her sister zip up her jacket, and go outside in the snow.

I Love My Baby Sister (Most of the Time) by Elaine Edelman, (New York: Viking, 1984) is a first-person story by a little girl who tells about the things her baby sister can do, as well as the things she does to help her sister, such as showing her how to dress herself. Self-help skills are featured with intriguing illustrations. Your children should be motivated to talk about their own experiences along this line.

PICKS UP AND INSERTS OBJECTS WITH EASE

Manipulative Materials

Picking up and inserting objects is the small motor skill most frequently promoted in the early childhood classroom. This skill involves manipulation of items by gripping them between thumb and fingers and inserting or placing them somewhere else. Using puzzles, pegboards, and stacking toys; lacing, sewing, weaving, stringing beads, and sorting small items call for this skill. Playing with Lego bricks, geoboards, formboards, Bristleboards and many plastic table games also calls for the picking up and inserting skills.

All classrooms should have a permanent space for manipulative activity of this sort with shelves at the children's level equipped with many such materials for easy selection and return. There should be a table in the area next to the shelves as well as floor space for playing with the larger toys.

The selection of materials should cover a wide range of children's abilities, as well. Wooden puzzles, for example, should include simple single pictures with pieces showing an entire part of the picture for beginners, as well as more complicated pictures with many pieces for older or experienced children.

Teachers should plan to check all the manipulative materials at least once a week to be sure all the parts and pieces are there. If some pieces are missing, either replace the piece or remove the material. It does not help beginners to try making puzzles or playing games with pieces missing; many beginners soon give up.

It is not necessary to put out all the manipulative materials that the program owns at once. Add a few new ones to the area every month and remove some of the old ones. Remember that the novelty of materials motivates children to use them. Save some of the more complicated table toys for challenging the experienced children later in the year. If you have a limited supply of materials, consider trading with other programs.

Children's Skills

You will want to know which children visit the manipulative area during your free play period. Use the small motor checklist as a screening device to help you find out. Are children avoiding the area because they are not comfortable with small motor skills? Are boys the ones who avoid the manipulative materials?

Once you identify which individuals avoid manipulative activities, you will be able to sit down at a table with a single child and challenge him or her to make a puzzle with you, stack blocks, or sort shapes into a formboard. If you are keeping file card records of each child, you can add this information to these cards. You or your coworkers may need to spend time every day with children who need extra practice with small motor skills. You may need to encourage these children to complete some of the small motor activities on their own.

It is important for children to succeed in something on their own. Puzzles are well suited to helping children accomplish such a task.

> Through puzzle making, young children experience satisfaction by putting things together where they belong. . . . The child is the problem solver by moving through the dissection of the puzzle, finding strategies to complete it, and evaluating the results. Upon puzzle completion, self-gratification is reached. (Maldonado, 1996, p. 4)

Sometimes your presence at the puzzle table helps a child to stick to her task until it is completed. Let her do it on her own but lend your support through positive comments when she tries several pieces and finally finds the right one.

Gender Differences

Our society seems to encourage girls to engage in small motor activities more than boys. Boys are encouraged to run outside and climb trees or play ball. Girls are given manipulative-type toys for their play. As a result, many girls are more dexterous with their fingers, while boys are more skillful in large motor activities such as running and throwing.

In the end, all children need to be skillful and at ease with both large and small motor activities. Once involved with formal education, both genders will need to handle writing tools and reading activities. Girls who are more skillful with finger dexterity and eye-hand coordination have an edge over boys in writing and reading at present. Is this small motor skill imbalance perhaps the reason more boys than girls have problems in learning to read?

If You Have Not Checked This Item: Some Helpful Ideas

■ Use Bead-Stringing

Put out all kinds of materials for both boys and girls to use in making necklaces. Have macaroni and all sorts of pasta shapes available. The children can color them first by painting. Bring in little sea shells with holes drilled in them (hobby shops do this), as well as acorns and horse chestnuts in the fall, plastic or wooden beads, and any other small items you can find. Save tops from plastic bottles and tops of magic markers; punch holes in them and use them for stringing necklaces and bracelets.

■ Make a Geoboard

Make a one-foot-square wooden board about one-half inch thick and pound in headless nails over the surface of the board in rows one inch apart. Allow the nails to protrude above the surface about an inch. Let the children string colored rubber bands over the tops of the nails, making all kinds of designs. Older children can try to copy design cards you have made, as well.

Make foot-square cardboard cards with dots representing the nails in the exact arrangement as the geoboard. On each card draw the outline of a red square or a blue triangle or a yellow rectangle, and let the children try to copy each shape with similar colored rubber bands on the geoboard. These designs must be simple for three- and four-year-olds, since their copying skills are still at an early level. Kindergarten children will have an easier time copying geoboard designs. If this play becomes a favorite activity, you will want more than one geoboard. Such boards can also be purchased.

■ Make Pegboards

Ask a building supply company for scraps of pegboard it normally would throw away. You can cut the scraps to child-size shapes and sand down the edges. The pegboards do not have to be squares. Triangular pegboards are just as useful and appealing. Get boxes of colored golf tees for pegs and let the children use the tees the same way colored rubber bands are used on the geoboards. You may want to make simple designs on paper or cardboard for the children to copy on their pegboards, as well. Graph paper is helpful if you do not want to spend time measuring spaces.

■ Ask Parents to Help

Have a parent "Board-Making Bee" to help stock your classroom as well as make enough extra boards to take home for their children to play with. You can almost always attract parents or other family members to help your program like this if they know they will be making educational games they can also take home. Besides helping their children both at home and at school, the parents themselves can be learning the importance of small motor activities for their children. Too often adults tend to look upon all children's activities as play, an unimportant entertainment. Parents need to be aware that play is essential to their children's physical, mental, and social development as human beings. Such parent group activities may change parents' outlook.

■ Read a Book

I Need a Lunch Box by Jeannette Caines (New York: Harper, 1988) tells the story of a preschool African American boy who wants a lunch box just like his sister Doris who is going into first grade. When their dad buys pencils, a ruler, and erasers for Doris, the boy thinks of all the items he could put in a lunch box. Then on the day school starts, Mom hands Doris her new lunch box and Dad has a surprise for the boy: just what he wanted.

The Balancing Girl by Berniece Rabe (New York: Dutton, 1981) is the story of Margaret, a girl with physical impairments, who nevertheless is a whiz at manipulating books, blocks, and dominoes. A domino maze, her outstanding creation, not only helps the school carnival succeed, but also reconciles her problems with Tommy, her chief competitor. Be sure to have at least one set of dominoes on hand after reading this story.

USES DRAWING/WRITING TOOLS WITH CONTROL

Preschool programs for two-, three-, and four-year-olds should not be concerned with "teaching" children how to draw pictures or write words. Some of your older children may—and probably will—progress to this stage of development and may be able to do some pictorial drawing and word-writing naturally. Don't expect all your children to reach this more advanced stage. Instead, you should provide children with opportunities to use writing and drawing implements of all kinds to encourage development of their small motor finger strength and dexterity and their eye-hand coordination (see Chapters 11 and 12).

The first time preschoolers use crayons, pencils, or magic markers, they usually hold them in the so-called *power grip*: that is, with all of the fingers clamped fist-like around the implement. This does not give them much control over the marks they will make, since the entire hand, wrist, and arm are involved in the movements rather than the fingers.

As their motor skills develop and they have the chance to practice, they will eventually switch to the *precision grip*: that is, holding the implement between the thumb and fingers.

Young children go through predictable stages in their development of writing skills. Cratty has noted that the earliest stage is a grasp (as mentioned earlier) in which only the pencil touches the page with the arm and hand unsupported in the air. Next, the little finger and elbow side of the hand are rested on the page of paper, but the hand and fingers are moved as one unit. Finally, children learn to use their hand and fingers separately with the hand as an anchor on the paper and the fingers moving the pencil. The final stage, however, may not be reached until between five and seven years of age (Cratty, 1986, p. 224).

Watch and see which of the children are using a mature grip on their writing implement and which still seem to prefer the fist clench. Ask their parents what writing or coloring tools they have at home. Some children may not have had the practice like others, because they have no materials. You may want to send home a few crayons and paper for those who need more drawing and writing practice.

Are your children using these tools with their preferred hand? Check and see. Children often pick up an implement with either hand and start to use it whether or not the hand works well. For those whose handedness you have already identified, you might have them try switching hands if they are crayoning with the nondominant hand.

The stubby fingers of preschoolers sometimes have more success gripping a thick tool, although some youngsters prefer regular pencils and crayons. Felt-tip markers are already thick and easy for them to use. Many preschoolers prefer markers to any other writing/coloring implement. The problem for teachers is reminding the children to keep the markers capped so they don't dry out. Most preschoolers just can't remember. Clemens (1991) offers a clever solution:

> You can make a mound of plaster of Paris, take the caps off your markers, and sink the caps upside-down into the wet plaster, so their open ends are flush with the surface. After the plaster dries, the markers, inserted in their caps, stick out like porcupine quills. Children easily return the markers to the mound when they are not using them. (p. 7)

Easel paintbrushes are thick enough but usually too long for young children to control readily. You may need to cut off a few inches and sand the brushes down. Child-care supply houses have finally gotten the message and are coming out with properly proportioned paintbrushes for preschoolers.

Art and writing skills for preschoolers are discussed more fully in Chapters 11 and 12.

If You Have Not Checked This Item: Some Helpful Ideas

■ Use Coloring Books

Coloring books are quite controversial with preschool program people. There is great concern that these stereotyped pictures will substitute in the classroom for creative art. It seems we have missed the point. Coloring books have little to do with art, but a great deal to do with small motor skills. Coloring books should be kept on the shelves with manipulative materials. Children love to fill in the outline pictures with various colors. At first children merely scribble over them with one color. As they gain control of the crayons, the youngsters work more carefully using different colors. Finally, the children are able to stay within the lines, a very satisfying accomplishment for the child struggling to control the use of his fingers.

Using coloring books, in fact, is an excellent prewriting activity for young children if books contain simple pictures with large spaces. Children can color in the pictures, trying to stay within the lines, or they can trace over the outlines of the pictures with a crayon or magic marker.

■ Have a Writing Center

Place a small table in a quiet area. Have primary pencils, regular pencils, felt-tip markers, ball-point pens, crayons, and notebooks and tablets of various sizes to scribble on. Let the children pretend they are writing.

■ Read a Book

Red Day Green Day by Edith Kunhardt (New York: Greenwillow, 1992) tells the story of Andrew, who goes to kindergarten and needs to bring a color item each time the teacher names a particular color day. Illustrations show the multiethnic children in a colorful classroom busily painting, playing with toys, eating, and sharing the color items they have brought. On the last day, Andrew paints a rainbow to show all the color days at once.

USES SCISSORS WITH CONTROL

Learning to cut with scissors takes a great deal of coordination and practice. Children who have had practice with this activity at home may be way ahead of those who have not, regardless of age. Sometimes the scissors themselves make it difficult for youngsters to learn how to use them. The blunt scissors found in many preschools are often dull and difficult to manipulate even by adults. Try the scissors yourself, and loosen them and sharpen them before giving them to the children. Really good scissors cost money, but it is a worthwhile investment when you consider what fine practice they give children in developing strength in their hands and coordination in their fingers.

You can help children who have not learned to cut in several ways. Show them how to hold the scissors with their favored hand. As with crayons, children sometimes pick up scissors with either hand, but will not have much success if they are trying to use the nondominant hand.

You may also have to model the use of scissors. As Bodrova and Leong (1996) note:

> Sometimes children hold the pencil, paintbrush, or scissors in such a way that it impedes their ability to use the instrument. Teachers may have to model how to hold the instrument because children, although they may have seen adults holding it correctly, often do not focus on the most important attributes of the grip. Describe what you do with your hands in words so that the child can use private speech to guide him. For example, say, "To move the scissors, squeeze, squeeze." (p. 154)

To help children hold the paper they are cutting with the opposite hand, Bodrova and Leong suggest putting a dot on that side of the paper to remind children to hold it with the dot under their thumb. You can then tell them to cut with their thumbs up.

Some teachers start by holding a narrow strip of paper stretched taut between two hands for the child to cut in two. Once a child can do this cutting without difficulty, get another child to hold the paper and let each take a turn holding and cutting. Give them a task of cutting all the yellow strips into small pieces.

On another day, show the child how to hold the strip of paper in her own hand and cut with the other hand. She needs to keep her scissors in her dominant hand. Let her practice on different kinds of paper, including construction paper, typing paper, and pages from magazines. Finally, draw a line on a sheet of paper and let the child practice cutting along a line. Be sure to have at least one pair of left-handed scissors.

Most four-year-olds can cut along a straight line without difficulty, but many have trouble turning corners and following a curved line. Children need practice of all kinds in cutting. Whenever you are preparing art materials for the children to use, especially cutouts which need to be pasted, try to involve the children in helping to do the cutting.

If You Have Not Checked This Time: Some Helpful Ideas

■ Use Wrapping Paper Ribbons

Let children practice cutting wrapping paper ribbons into confetti. Ribbons have more body than ordinary paper and so cut easier. Someone may need to hold the ribbon while the other cuts. Save the confetti for a celebration.

■ Read a Book

Paper Boats by Rabindranath Tagore (Honesdale, PA: Boyds Mills Press, 1992) is a delightful story of a boy from India who cuts out paper boats, writes his name and the name of his village on them, and sets them afloat. Simply and beautifully presented with lines by the Indian poet Tagore and unique full-page illustrations that are paper cutouts themselves, this story seems almost three-dimensional. Let children sit close to see Bochak's cutouts. Can they then cut out their own simple paper boats and set them afloat in the water table?

POUNDS IN NAILS WITH CONTROL

Holding a nail and pounding it with a hammer held in the opposite hand is the most complicated small motor skill thus far discussed. Many children will not be able to do it well until they are older and more coordinated. Even adults often have difficulty. Try it yourself and find out.

Handedness makes a difference. So does arm and wrist strength. The small toy hammers in play sets should not be used. They are not heavy or strong enough to have much effect other than frustrating the pounder. A small adult hammer is better.

Both boys and girls should be encouraged to pound. It is an excellent activity to develop small motor strength and coordination. If you do not have a carpenter's bench in your room, you can set up a woodworking area by hanging tools on the wall from a pegboard and using a tree stump as a pounding surface. Slices can also be cut from a stump and placed on a table for pounding. Nails go into tree stumps easier than into boards. Place a towel under each stump slice to absorb the noise. Leithead (1996) suggests that when the top of the stump is completely covered with nails, it can be sliced off, making a clean surface for new pounding (p. 12).

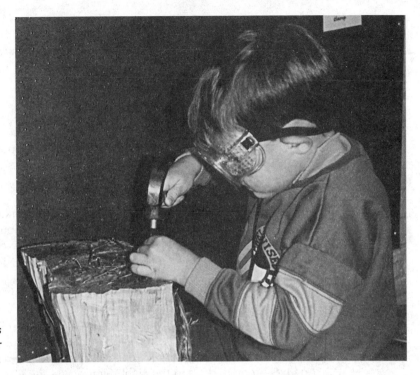

Pounding nails into stumps is another excellent small motor activity that children love to do.

Leithead has observed that children's first hammering of nails into stumps is random. As they master the skill, they begin to make designs, sometimes their own initials. She notes other uses for pounding:

> The hammering center usually has two stumps and two hammers of different weights. Children can experiment scientifically, predicting which hammer will be the most efficient and then testing their predictions by counting the number of blows each hammer takes to sink a nail. (1996, p. 12)

To get children interested in this or any activity area in your classroom, simply go into the area yourself and begin pounding something. Pounding always attracts attention, and soon children will want to do the same thing the teacher is doing. Again you should check to make sure they are holding the hammer in their favored hand. You can control for the safety factor by limiting the number of hammers or tree stumps available for pounding. Also be sure the pounders wear safety goggles.

If You Have Not Checked This Item: Some Helpful Ideas

■ Use Soft Materials

Do not start your pounding activities with wood. Children need to acquire the skill before they will be able to drive a nail through wood easily. Start with a softer material such as fiberboard, ceiling tiles, or styrofoam.

■ Use Large-Headed Nails

Children should use large-headed nails at first. Most tacks are too short for the pounder to hold, but roofing nails or upholstering tacks are large enough and long enough to work well.

■ Read a Book

Hammers, Nails, Planks, and Paint by Thomas Campbell Jackson (New York: Scholastic, 1994) is the illustrated story of how a house is built showing all of the people involved from the architect and surveyor to the carpenters, plumbers, electricians, bricklayers, and painters.

How a House Is Built by Gail Gibbons (New York: Holiday House, 1990) tells the same house-building story but with more details, along with pictures of various kinds of houses and a lineup of all of the construction workers involved. A great deal of pounding with hammers is shown.

OBSERVING, RECORDING, AND INTERPRETING SMALL MOTOR DEVELOPMENT

As you did with the large motor checklist items, you should also screen your entire class on the eight small motor checklist items. Make a similar chart with the children's names on one side, and the eight items across the top. Check off the accomplishments for all your children based on your observations. Then at a glance you can see by the blanks which of the children may need special help to accomplish small motor skills.

Observe each of these children who need special help separately during the free choice period, recording their actions in a running record. Later you can transfer this information onto the entire Checklist for an individual by checking off items and writing in evidence. Finally, you should make an individualized Learning Prescription for each child needing special help. The activities you choose to help the child in "Areas Needing Strengthening" should be based on his or her "Areas of Strength and Confidence." For example, Figure 8–1 shows the small motor checklist for Lionel, the new boy discussed at the ends of Chapters 5 and 7.

Using the information gained on the social play checklist and the large motor checklist, the staff put together the learning prescription for Lionel shown in Figure 8–2.

Because Lionel shows the ability to make puzzles and to fasten and unfasten zippers and buttons, the staff thought he could use his small motor skills to work with another child in a class project. He likes art activities such as using playdough and finger painting, but does not use paintbrushes, writing tools, or scissors. Could this be because he is left-handed?

The staff says that they will provide him with left-handed scissors and give him support in the activity of cutting out pictures of cars for the class scrapbook. They have not had a woodworking bench, but Lionel says he has helped his grandfather pound nails. Perhaps he and other children could pound together simple rhythm instruments from wood, paint them, and then use them in a rhythm activity (Lionel excels in rhythm). Using things Lionel likes to do and is good at doing may help him get involved with the other children.

Child Skills Checklist

Name _Lionel_   **Observer** _Barb_

Program _Preschool – K2_   **Dates** _1/20_

Directions:

Put a ✔ for items you see the child perform regularly. Put *N* for items where there is no opportunity to observe. Leave all other items blank.

Item	Evidence	Date
6. Small Motor Development		
✓ Shows hand preference (which is _left_)	Uses left hand to eat, turn things	1/20
✓ Turns with hand easily (knobs, lids, eggbeaters)	Plays with eggbeater at water table easily	1/20
✓ Pours liquid into glass without spilling	Pours own milk at lunch	1/20
✓ Unfastens/fastens zippers, buttons, Velcro tabs	Dresses & undresses self with ease	1/20
✓ Picks up and inserts objects with ease	Makes puzzles with ease	1/20
____ Uses drawing/writing tools with control	Does not use paintbrushes or writing tools	1/20
____ Uses scissors with control	Does not use scissors	1/20
N Pounds in nails with control	Woodworking not available	1/20

Figure 8–1   Small motor development observations for Lionel

Learning Prescription

Name _Lionel_   Age _3_   Date _1/20_

Areas of Strength and Confidence

1. _Does manipulative activities well by self_
2. _Performs or participates in music and rhythm activities_
3. _Has good small motor coordination_

Areas Needing Strengthening

1. _Needs to develop large motor skills_
2. _Needs to learn to play with others_
3. _Needs to develop small motor skills of writing, drawing, cutting_

Activities to Help

1. _Bring in pair of left-handed scissors and have Lionel cut out pictures of cars from magazine to make a car scrapbook with one of the other boys._
2. _Bring in hammer, nails, and tree stump; ask Lionel to help another child with pounding nails to make rhythm instrument shaker._
3. _Have Lionel and other children paint the rhythm instruments they make._

Figure 8–2   Learning prescription for Lionel

REFERENCES

Bodrova, E., & Leong, D. J. (1996). *Tools of the mind: A Vygotskian approach to early childhood education.* Upper Saddle River, NJ: Merrill/Prentice Hall.

Clemens, S. G. (1991). Art in the classroom: Making every day special. *Young Children, 46*(2) 4–11.

Cosgrove, M. S. (1991). Cooking in the classroom: The doorway to nutrition. *Young Children, 46*(3), 43–46.

Cratty, B. J. (1986). *Perceptual & motor development in infants and children.* Upper Saddle River, NJ: Merrill/Prentice-Hall.

Leithead, M. (1996). Happy hammering . . . A hammering activity center with built-in success. *Young Children, 51*(3), 12.

Maldonado, N. S. (1996). Puzzles: A pathetically neglected, commonly available resource. *Young Children, 51*(4), 4–10.

Zaichkowsky, L. D., Zaichowsky, L. B., & Martineck, T. J. (1980). *Growth and development: The child and physical activity.* St. Louis: Mosby.

SUGGESTED READINGS

Beaty, J. J. (1996). *Skills for preschool teachers.* Upper Saddle River, NJ: Merrill/Prentice Hall.

Dunn, M. L. (1979). *Pre-scissors skills.* Tucson, AZ: Communication Skill Builders.

Paul, A. (1975). *Kids cooking without a stove: A cookbook for young children.* Garden City, NY: Doubleday.

Schickedanz, J., Schickedanz, D. I., & Forsythe, P. D.. (1982). *Toward understanding children.* Boston: Little, Brown.

Thompson, D. (1981). *Easy woodstuff for kids.* Beltsville, MD: Gryphon House.

Wortham, S. C. (1994). *Early childhood curriculum: Developmental bases for learning and teaching.* Upper Saddle River, NJ: Merrill/Prentice Hall.

LEARNING ACTIVITIES

1. Use the Child Skills Checklist section on small motor development as a screening tool to observe all the children in your classroom. Pay special attention to which hand each seems to favor. Also note which ones spend time in small motor activities and which do not.

2. Compare the Checklist results for the children in your classroom in both large and small motor development. Do you see any relationships?

3. Choose a child who seems to need a great deal of help with small motor skills. Do a running record of him or her on three different days concentrating on small motor skills. Do a learning activity with him based on the results.

4. How do the girls and boys of the same age compare with one another in small motor skills? What conclusions can you make based on your observations?

5. Put out a new small motor activity for the children to use. Observe and record the results. What conclusions can you draw?

CHAPTER 9

Cognitive Development: Classification, Number, Time, and Space

COGNITIVE DEVELOPMENT CHECKLIST

☐ Identifies objects by shape

☐ Identifies objects by color

☐ Identifies objects by size

☐ Sorts objects by likenesses

☐ Puts events in sequence; objects in series

☐ Counts how many are present

☐ Knows what happens today

☐ Can build a block enclosure

DEVELOPING COGNITIVE CONCEPTS

Cognitive development of preschool children is concerned with how their thinking abilities evolve. We are only beginning to understand how this takes place. The work of researchers like Swiss psychologist Jean Piaget in his investigation of how knowledge is created (see Table 9–1) has given us new insights into how children think as well as how their thinking evolves. The theories of Russian psychologist Lev Vygotsky have helped us apply this information to the classroom. Work with computer models of children's thinking have added even more understanding of how the brain works and of its unimagined complexity.

One of the surprising findings resulting from this research is the fact that young children's thinking is not the same as that of adults. Piaget's Stages of Cognitive Development in Table 9–1 shows how children below the age of seven think in concrete terms and have not yet developed the abstract thinking of older children and adults. But perhaps the most startling finding to those unfamiliar with this research is: *Children create their own knowledge.*

Using the physical and mental tools they are born with, children interact with their environment to make sense of it, and in so doing, they construct their own mental concepts of their world. The brain seems to be conditioned to take in information about objects and their relationship to one another. What do things look, feel, taste, sound, and smell like? What can they do? How are they like one another? How are they different? What happens if you touch, push, or throw them?

As children manipulate the objects in their environment, they learn to make different responses to different objects. The new knowledge that they gain is assimilated into their previous knowledge, thus helping their thinking patterns evolve. To Piaget, children's cognitive development comes from maturation, their interactions with their environment, and their spontaneous discoveries about it.

Piaget puts the knowledge that children are constructing into three categories:

Table 9–1 Piaget's stages of cognitive development

Sensorimotor Stage (Birth to age 2)

Child thinks in visual patterns (schemata).
Child uses senses to explore objects (i.e., looks, listens, smells, tastes, and manipulates).
Child learns to recall physical features of an object.
Child associates objects with actions and events but does not use objects to symbolize actions and events (e.g., rolls a ball but does not use ball as a pretend car).
Child develops object permanence (comes to realize an object is still there even when out of sight).

Preoperational Stage (Age 2–7)

Child acquires symbolic thought (uses mental images and words to represent actions and events not present).
Child uses objects to symbolize actions and events (e.g., pretends a block is a car).
Child learns to anticipate effect of one action on another (e.g., realizes pouring milk from pitcher to glass will make level of milk decrease in pitcher as it rises in glass).
Child is deceived by appearances (e.g., believes a tall, thin container holding a cup of water contains more than a short, wide container holding a cup of water).
Child is concerned with final products (focuses on the way things look at a particular moment, "figurative knowledge," and not on changes of things or how things got that way, "operational knowledge"), and he cannot seem to reverse his thinking.

Concrete-Operational Stage (Age 7–11)

Child's thoughts can deal with changes of things and how they got that way.
Child is able to reverse her thinking (has ability to see in her mind how things looked before and after a change took place).
Child has gone beyond how things look at a particular moment and begins to understand how things relate to one another (e.g., knows that the number 2 can be larger than 1, yet, at the same time, smaller than 3).

Formal-Operational Stage (Age 11 +)

Child begins to think about thinking.
Child thinks in abstract terms without needing concrete objects.
Child can hypothesize about things.

Note: Some information adapted from *The child's construction of knowledge: Piaget for teaching children* (pp. 69–93) by G. E. Forman and D. S. Kuschner, 1983, Washington, DC: NAEYC.

Physical knowledge
> Children learn about objects in their environment by physically manipulating them. They begin constructing the mental concepts of shape, size, and color about these objects.

Logico-mathematical knowledge
> Children construct relationships about the objects such as alike and different, more and less, which ones go together, how many, how much.

Social knowledge
> Children learn rules for behavior and knowledge about people's actions through their involvement with people.

As they interact with the objects and people in their environment, young children acquire physical knowledge and logico-mathematical knowledge simultaneously. According to Charlesworth, "as the physical characteristics of objects are learned, logico-mathematical categories are constructed to organize information" (1996, p. 6) Thus cognitive concepts are formed:

> Early childhood is a period when children actively engage in acquiring basic concepts. Concepts are the building blocks of knowledge; they allow people to organize and categorize information. (Charlesworth, 1996, p. 1)

While Vygotsky's theories support many of Piaget's findings, Vygotsky believed that after age two culture and cultural signs are necessary to expand children's thinking (Charlesworth, 1996, p. 7). In other words, cognitive development does not come from the child alone but from the adults and mature peers around him, as well as from mental tools (Vygotsky called them "signs") that the child develops such as speech, and later writing and numbering.

While Piaget emphasized children as explorers and discoverers, constructing their knowledge independently, Vygotsky developed the concept of the zone of proximal development or *ZPD*, defined as

> the area between where the child is now in mental development and where she might go with assistance from an adult or more mature child. (Charlesworth, 1996, p. 7)

To gain cultural knowledge, the child needs assistance or scaffolding, which is provided by more mature learners. To Vygotsky, good teaching involves presenting material that is a little ahead of the child's development. Teachers know they have identified a child's ZPD when the child responds with enthusiasm to the activities the teacher provides.

Both Piaget's and Vygotsky's points of view are incorporated into quality early childhood programs today by giving children opportunities to explore and discover on their own as well as to interact with adults who support their efforts and challenge them in making new discoveries.

Whether children acquire all of their knowledge independently or with the help of adults and mature peers around them, modern researchers agree with the basic findings of these two child development pioneers: that thinking is information processing. Today an information-processing approach is being used to study children's thinking from infancy on. Researchers in the field employ computer programs on error analysis to reveal children's conceptual understanding, eye-movement analysis to reveal how children process visual information, and chronometric methods to study children's reaction times (Siegler, 1986, pp. 5, 102).

USING PLAY

Both Piaget and Vygotsky agree that children create their own knowledge through exploratory play. They do it by playing around with things, people, and ideas. Most people think of play as something recreational, something we do for enjoyment, and something rather inconsequential. For adults, this definition of play may be true, but for infants and young children, play is a way of trying out and finding out about the world around them. Children fool around with toys, their clothing, their hands and feet, sounds, words, and other people. Youngsters use their senses of taste, touch, sound, sight, and smell in a playful manner with anything and everything they can get their hands on, in order to find out what an object is, what it feels like, what it sounds like, what you can do with it. The fact is that child's play is practice in learning to think.

From the time he is born, the human infant pursues such information with a single-minded determination. At first, everything goes into the mouth. Then the infant bangs objects against the side of the crib to see what they sound like, to see what they will do, or to find out what will happen. The toddler has an extra advantage. He has expanded his field of exploration by learning to walk. Suddenly the world's objects are his to touch, pick up, shake, throw, taste, and take apart. He uses his senses to "play" with his world and to find out what it is about. And as soon as he can talk, he plays with words and word sounds as well.

All the information extracted through this playful exploration of the environment is filed away in predetermined patterns in the brain, to be used to direct or adjust the child's behavior as he continues to respond to the stimuli around him. We now know that this knowledge is organized by the brain in predictable patterns from a very early age.

STAGES OF EXPLORATORY PLAY

Exploratory play itself occurs in predictable, observable patterns as young children grow and develop. All children seem to go through three definite stages of play every time they explore the possibilities of a new object or activity on their own. To make such stages easy to recognize and remember we call them "the 3-Ms": manipulation, mastery, and meaning. Children progress through these developmental stages by being allowed to explore new objects and activities on their own. If we make children do things our way, we are short-circuiting their learning process. Our guidance should come after children have a chance to try out things on their own (Beaty, 1996, pp. 78–80).

When children of any age first begin to explore a new object, they play around with it, turning it upside down or inside out, or using it in ways it was never meant to be used. For example, when children first use unit blocks they often fill containers or trucks with them and then dump them out. Building with the blocks comes later, after children have become acquainted with the possibilities of blocks through *manipulation*. With paints, children start by messing around with the brushes and paints, perhaps filling a page with color and then covering it with another color. They are manipulating the medium. With a computer, children often start by "piano-playing" the keys, that is, pressing all the keys instead of pressing one and waiting for something to happen on the screen. Children need this manipulation experience to discover how things work.

Once they are familiar with the medium, they quickly go on to the next stage of exploratory play: *mastery*. To master the use of a material or activity, young children need to try it out over and over, much to the distraction of many adults. Repetition is the hallmark of the mastery stage, almost as if children were setting up a natural practice session for themselves. With blocks they build endless roads or walls or towers. With paints they often repeat a scribble or line on page after page. With the computer they call up their favorite screen again and again. You yourself are probably witness to the story-reading mastery phase when children want the same story repeated endlessly.

After they have satisfied this urge to master the material, many children go on to a new exploratory stage in which they put their own *meaning* into the activity. With blocks they construct buildings. With paints they create pictures. With computer programs they may add their own twist such as playing an invented "I stopped you!" game with a partner. With familiar stories they often rename characters or change the plot. Not all preschoolers reach this meaning stage, but many do if they have been encouraged to develop naturally through exploratory play.

CLASSIFICATION

The basic process that children use to develop their reasoning abilities is classification, the method of placing objects that are alike in the same class. For the brain to classify, children first need to be able to tell what things look like: their shape, color, size, and other attributes. Then they must be able to tell which objects are alike according to particular attributes and which ones are different. Complex mental and physical abilities come into play as children develop classification skills: language and vocabulary; identification of shapes, colors and sizes; and visual perception in identifying likeness and difference. How do children learn these complex skills?

> Children learn classification and other mathematical structures the same way that they learn about the rest of the world—by manipulating actual objects and constructing new knowledge after reflecting on their physical and mental actions. (Micklo, 1995, pp. 24–28)

They do this through exploratory play with particular materials. Your support is necessary in providing them with such materials and encouraging their interaction.

ASSESSING DEVELOPMENT

How have your children fared in constructing their own knowledge? They need to have built up mental representations of objects: ways to differentiate things by their appearance or by their sound, ways of telling how things are alike or different, and ways to decide how things fit together as a part of a sequence or a series. These are the types of patterns or concepts the brain forms in organizing the data it takes in.

You will need to assess each of your children by observing their ability to accomplish the eight Checklist items at the head of this chapter. The first four items refer to classification concepts the child needs to know; next is a seriation concept involving sequences and series; the counting item involves children's number sense, including one-to-one correspondence; next comes their time sense, and finally their use of space. Once you have made your assessment, you should plan activities or playful exploration periods for children to continue developing their thinking skills.

 # IDENTIFIES OBJECTS BY SHAPE

Development of thinking begins with the infant's seeing, hearing, and feeling things in her environment: her mother's face, her bottle, or mother's breast. Her brain takes in these important visual perceptions and stores them in particular schemes or patterns that are mental representations for the objects and events she experiences. Her brain seems to be conditioned to pay attention to certain things in her environment and ignore the rest.

Research has shown, for instance, that an infant looks longer at the human face than at anything else around her (Schickedanz, 1982, p. 152). The infant seems, in fact, to prefer visual stimuli that have a contour configuration. She is beginning her construction of knowledge.

The first aspect of this knowledge is called "figurative knowing" because it deals with shapes and configurations, as well as the patterns of movements, tastes, smells, and so on (Saunders and Bingham-Newman, 1984, p. 117). The infant will have to recognize these objects and shapes again and again. He will need to respond to his caregivers, his bottle, his rattle, and other environmental objects appropriately. Perceptual recognition, then, is the earliest form of the infant's store of knowledge. As early as three months old, infants can perceive an object's shape as being constant (Siegler, 1986, p. 150).

The first Checklist item on shape is concerned with refinement of the child's perceptual recognition. To think, reason, and problem-solve, the child needs to know and discriminate among basic shapes of things. We start with geometric shapes because the concept of shape is one of the first concepts to emerge in the child's cognitive development. He needs to distinguish among a circle, a square, a rectangle and a triangle—not to do math problems, but to be able to categorize and distinguish mentally among the objects in his environment.

Adults are often surprised to learn that some young children view all enclosed figures as being similar. In other words, these youngsters think a circle and a square are the same! How can that be? Researchers say that these children are operating geometrically in the *topological* domain, which views

> . . . circles and squares as being equivalent figures, both figures having closed boundaries. Children have difficulty differentiating one figure from the other until they begin to be aware of features of the boundaries of the figures themselves. At this time, work with shapes should begin. (Richardson, Goodman, Hartman, & LePique, 1980, p. 67)

Topology studies geometric properties of objects. In topology, the boundaries of objects do not change when the object is bent or stretched (like a rubber band) because no tearing occurs. In other words, in topology a circle or a triangle is the same as a square, because one can be transformed into the other without tearing the boundary. This seems to be a function of the brain's right hemisphere. Adults who have strokes that damage their left hemispheres also have this trouble distinguishing basic shapes. Furthermore, we know the brain's right hemisphere and its functions are important in children's early development.

> Until age 2, infants and toddlers function primarily as though they had only a right hemisphere, and they respond better to those functions processed by the right hemisphere than to those processed by the left. (Cherry, Godwin, & Staples, 1989, p. 11)

But now it is time for them to change. Young children who have difficulty distinguishing one shape as being different from another need to learn the special features of a shape that distinguish it from a similar shape. They need to learn to see the objects in their environment from a linear rather than a topological point of view.

This learning takes place not just by a teacher telling the child, "This is a square," "This is a circle," but more effectively by the child's hands-on playing or exploring with all of his senses about what makes a particular object a circle or what makes another shape a square.

Children in this preoperational stage of development (see Table 9–1) learn best from three-dimensional objects first, and then from pictorial representations, before finally recognizing more abstract symbols. Seeing pictures of the various shapes is helpful, but it is too abstract as the only method for young children to learn. Youngsters first need hands-on activities with concrete materials.

Your program should provide the children with many such experiences. Since the children learn these classification skills through the senses, you should give the youngsters all kinds of sensory play opportunities. Play with dough, for instance, allows children to make dough balls, which the youngsters flatten into circles with their hands or roll flat with a rolling pin and cut into circular cookies. Sensory learning involves taste, touch, smell, and sight in this instance. Clay and playdough provide similar experiences.

Block building is an excellent medium for creating circles, squares, rectangles, and triangles. In the beginning you will need to name the shapes the children are making. They probably already know "circle" and perhaps "square," but "rectangle" and "triangle" are interesting new grown-up words. Can the children build a triangle, one of the most difficult shapes for youngsters? Their triangles may be rather rounded in the beginning, because corners are hard for the children to deal with. Put masking tape on the floor in the shapes of circles, squares, rectangles, and triangles and let children try to build these shapes with their blocks.

The diagonal line is the last to appear in children's cognitive learning. This is why triangles and diamonds are very difficult for children to make.

If You Have Not Checked This Item: Some Helpful Ideas

■ Start with One Shape at a Time

Children need to focus their attention on one concept before expanding it to include other aspects. The circle is good to begin with because children are used to the roundness or ovalness of the human face. They need to experience examples of all kinds of circles. Let the youngsters find out how many circles they can discover in the classroom. Did they find the wheels on toy vehicles, the casters on the doll bed or office chair, the clock, or the mark on the table made by a wet glass?

Bring in a collection of things that contain some circular shapes, and let each child try to sort out the circles. Include items such as bottle tops, coasters, jar lids, and rings. Then have the children try sorting blindfolded. Can they sort circles by feel alone? If some children are frightened by having a blindfold tied over their eyes, let them shut their eyes or hold a hand over them.

■ Give Children Enough Time to Explore

How long should they concentrate on this shape before including a second shape in their explorations? It depends on your children and their interest. Be sure every child has a chance to have enough sensory involvement with circles so that he or she can internalize it. The internalization may take several weeks, depending on the age and experience of your children. If one child needs more time to work with circles before she truly understands the concept, be sure that you provide this time for her.

Time is an important aspect of young children's learning. Most early childhood programs in the United States are not geared to this crucial element. In Europe it is different. For example, the acclaimed preschools of Reggio Amelia in northern Italy give individual children as much time as they need to complete their activities. In addition, children have the opportunity to use the same materials over and over again until they have gained some control over them and have internalized the concepts involved. We remember this stage of learning as mastery, one of the 3 Ms. As a result, the children get deeply involved in their work/play and produce "astounding" (in the eyes of visitors) arts and crafts products.

> Time is used differently in Reggio preschools than in preschools in the United States. Experiences and themes last months, as opposed to the one- or two-week units typical in the United States. And children are never expected to move on to something new until they have exhausted their own ideas fully. Often, in Reggio, children were observed painting at easels for an entire morning or working with clay for hours. (Seefeldt, 1995, p. 42)

As teachers and early childhood specialists from both countries realize, it is not the product that is important, but the process the child goes through to produce the art. Because this process is treated so seriously and given so much time in the Reggio preschools, the children's products are extraordinary.

Whether U.S. teachers will change their point of view about time is questionable, because time is treated differently in this country. Many Europeans tend to be more relaxed about time than their U.S. counterparts. Perhaps what U.S. preschools need to stress instead is that children's experiences need to be repeated over and over for them to learn from the process.

■ Have Children Make Their Own Circles

Use circle-making activities that involve molding clay, shaping dough, finger painting, cutting out circles, cutting out jack-o'-lantern tops, stamping circular shapes on paper, and tracing around circular objects. When the children finally have a strong sense of what a circle is, introduce the square as the next shape.

■ Read a Book

Tatum's Favorite Shape by Dorothy Thole (New York: Scholastic, 1977) is the story of little Tatum, an African American boy who has trouble in school keeping the different shapes straight until his mother plays a shape-finding game with him at home.

■ Use a Computer Program

Preschool children can learn to use a computer with ease, and love to do so. *Learning Shapes* (Houston: Access Unlimited, 1988) is one of the simplest matching programs using four basic shapes. Children must find the shapes hidden within colorful scenes in *Inside Outside Shapes* (Fairfield, CT: Queue, 1986) and *Stickybear Shapes* (Hilton Head, SC: Optimum Resource, 1983). In *Shape Starship* (Big Springs, TX: Gamco Industries, 1986), children move a pointer to one of four choices matching objects of the same shape and size with objects of different color; objects of the same color and shape but different size; and objects with similar shapes.

IDENTIFIES OBJECTS BY COLOR

Another way the brain classifies things is by color. Research shows that infants as young as four to six months old begin discriminating colors. Most children recognize red, green, yellow, and blue along with black and white first before they recognize secondary colors such as violet, pink, and brown (Richardson et al., 1980, p. 123). Children develop color perception shortly after shape recognition, although they seem to talk about colors first. Adults make more reference to color than shape, and children quickly pick up this fact.

Your children may, in fact, be able to name many colors just as they name numbers, without truly knowing what the name means. Naming colors is a function of language development in which children must link a visual image with a recalled name. Just because a child tells you the name "red" does not mean that she can identify the color. Ask the child the color of her shirt. Ask the youngster to find something red in the classroom.

Color, like shape, is an aspect of visual perception that the child's brain uses to help her classify objects and discriminate their differences. Although the child sees colors from the beginning, she now needs to put names to the different ones.

Again, concentrating on a single color at first and then adding other colors is best. While basic colors are usually easier for children to recognize, you must take advantage of seasonal and holiday colors as well. Orange should certainly be a part of your classroom during the fall Halloween season, and pink as well as red for Valentine's Day.

Allow children to play with colors as they do with blocks. Give them things like poker chips or golf tees and let the children see if they can find all the reds. Some children will be able to sort all of the items by color, but don't expect everyone to be so accurate at first. Let the children experiment with the look and texture of "redness" in all of its shades as they mix it with white paint. Give the children plenty of time to experience one color before you focus on another.

As your group begins its investigation of other colors, you can add colors one by one to the easel. Have colored lotto cards, colored plastic blocks, and many other table games featuring colors. Be sure to bring in many different items of the color you are exploring. If you have bilingual children, be sure everyone learns color names in both languages.

Differently abled children can learn color concepts along with all of the other youngsters. Set up your activities to allow children with physical and mental impairments to participate. If you keep concept games in the manipulative area, be sure the shelves are low enough for everyone to reach.

If You Have Not Checked This Item: Some Helpful Ideas

■ Let Children Mix Colors

Let children have the fun of mixing colors. Put out squeeze bottles of food coloring, spoons for stirring, and plastic cups or muffin tins full of water. You may want to use only one or two colors at first, or you may want to let children discover how mixing blue and yellow together makes green, since this is such a dramatic change. At another time, use cups of predissolved colors, medicine droppers, and muffin tin cups full of clear water.

Children can play with mixing colors in many ways. The youngsters can finger paint with the color you are focusing on. When the children add a new color to their repertory, add the same one to the finger paint table. Have them mix the old and new colors together to see what happens.

■ Cut or Tear Colored Paper

Colored construction paper can be used in many ways. When children have learned two or three colors, let them cut up or tear pieces of construction paper in these colors for a sorting activity or for making collages. Do not confuse children by combining shape and color activities when they are first learning color or shape concepts.

■ Play Concept Games

Children love to play any game that focuses on them. A game that asks them to identify the color of their clothing makes an excellent transition between activities: "The boy with the blue and white sneakers may go to lunch; the girl with the red and white shirt may go next; all the children with brown pants may go."

■ Do a Color Dance

Bring in filmy, see-through cloths of three different colors: red, blue, and yellow. Have a child hold each color as they dance or sway to music. Turn the lights off and have a spotlight (projector or strong flashlight) shine through the colors. What happens when blue and yellow dance together? Read children the book *Color Dance* by Ann Jonas (New York: Greenwill, 1989) to see what other secondary colors they can make with the cloths.

■ Read a Book

Many picture books feature colors. One of the most simple yet dramatic is Leo Lionni's classic *Little Blue and Little Yellow* (New York: Mulberry, 1959), in which a little blue circle and little yellow circle want to play together but are not allowed to by their families. When the two circles finally do come together, a dramatic change takes place: They, of course, become green.

Early childhood specialist Sue McCord has added a most effective activity for demonstrating the blue-yellow change: She reads the story at naptime with the room darkened and two flashlights covered with blue and yellow cellophane playing on the ceiling as the children watch from their cots. The yellow circle and blue circle on the ceiling turn just as green as paint when they finally come together.

Who Said Red? by Mary Serfozo (New York: Macmillan, 1988) shows a girl and boy in the country discussing the colors red, green, blue, and yellow as they explore objects of these particular colors.

Kente Colors by Debbi Chocolate (New York: Walker, 1996) shows in bold colors and rhymthic verse the special colors of Kente cloth from West Africa. Each featured color is spread across large double page illustrations framed with a border of the cloth itself. Emerald green, indigo blue, yellow Kente for pineapples, sunset red, mud pie brown, crown gold, and silver and black on dancers' backs fill the pages with dazzling hues.

Planting a Rainbow by Lois Ehlert (San Diego: Harcourt, 1988) illustrates in brilliant colors how a garden full of red, orange, yellow, blue, and purple flowers and green ferns is planted in the spring and grows into a rainbow garden.

■ Use a Computer Program

Color and Shapes (Lansing, MI: Hartley Courseware, 1984) contains four simple activities based on matching colors and shapes. *Color Find* (Hays, KS: ECS, 1985) is a simple drill and practice program with nine colors to match. *Mickey's Colors and Shapes* (Buffalo, NY: Walt Disney Software, 1990) has three activities involving Mickey Mouse juggling, completing a scene, and finding hidden animals by identifying colors and shapes.

 # IDENTIFIES OBJECTS BY SIZE

As the young child constructs his own knowledge by interacting with the objects and people in his environment, his brain seems to pay special attention to the relationships between things. Size is one of those relationships. Is it big? Is it small? Is it bigger or smaller than something else? The property of size, like the properties of shape and color, is an essential understanding the child needs to make sense of his world.

Early in life the infant develops **size constancy**, the ability to see the size of an object as constant no matter if it is close or far away. By the time they are in preschool, children need to be able to compare objects that look the same but are of different sizes. These various orders of size are often thought of in terms of opposites: big-little, large-small, tall-short, long-short, wide-narrow, thick-thin, and deep-shallow. Once again language plays a part because the child has to link a visual image with a recalled descriptive word. Direct comparison of objects based on one of the above opposites seems to be the best way for young children to learn size.

Comparisons

Comparing one object with another is one of the best ways to investigate the properties of something new or different. This is, in fact, how the brain works. It focuses on, takes in, and evaluates data about the new object on the basis of what the brain has previously processed about a similar object. Information-processing researchers mention three functions that the brain must complete to process new perceptions:

1. attending
2. identifying
3. locating

> **Attending** involves determining what in a situation is worthy of detailed processing. **Identifying** involves establishing what a perceptual pattern is by relating the pattern to entries already in memory. **Locating** involves determining how far away an object is, and in what direction. (Siegler, 1986, p. 135)

When you are first using comparisons with your children that focus on the concept of size, be sure to use objects that are alike in all of their properties except size. This is not the time to use different-colored or -shaped items. Instead, try using two similar items, one large and one small. Then talk to the children about how the objects are alike and how they are different.

Using Opposites

Making a direct comparison of two objects that are similar in every aspect except size is one of the best methods for helping children learn the concept of size. Use things such as two apples (a big and little one), two cups, two blocks, two books, or two dolls. Be sure to talk in positive terms ("This one is big. This one is little"), rather than in negative terms ("This one is not big"), which may only confuse the child. Also be sure the children are comparing the two objects themselves, and not their position in space. Some children look at two similar objects and say that the closest one is biggest because it looks bigger than a more distant object. This tends to happen when children's size constancy is poorly developed or when you are asking them to compare pictures of objects rather than the real three-dimensional objects themselves.

Use the size opposites *big* and *small* in all sorts of comparisons in your classroom before you move on to another aspect of size such as tall and short. Be sure that you yourself use the words for size opposites whenever you can in the classroom: "Look, Kenya has built a tall building and Rhonda has made a short one." "Can someone bring me a large block from the shelf?" "Can you find a small one, too?" "Who can find a thick pencil? Who can find a thin one?" A pretend shoe store in the dramatic play area is a fine opportunity to feature size concepts.

If You Have Not Checked This Item: Some Helpful Ideas

■ Play Size Transition Games

When you are waiting with the children for lunch to be served, for the bus to come, or for something special to happen, it is a good idea to have a repertory of brief transition games, finger plays, or stories to tell. This time provides an excellent opportunity for concept games such as: "The girl wearing the shirt with wide stripes may stand up." "The boy wearing the T-shirt with narrow stripes may stand up." Or play a guessing game with your fingers. Hold your hands behind your back and ask the children to guess which hand has a big finger held up and which has a little finger held up. Then show them. Can one of your children then be the leader of this game?

■ Read a Book

New Shoes for Silvia by Johanna Hurwitz (New York: Morrow, 1993) is a warm family story about Silvia in Guatemala receiving a present of new red shoes from her aunt in the United States. Each member of the family makes a wonderful comment about the shoes as Silvia tries them on, but then they each agree: The shoes are too big. Silvia makes the best of it by using them for doll beds, a two-car train, two ox carts working in the fields, and containers for her shell collection while she waits for her feet to grow . . . which they finally do.

■ Use a Computer Program

Many opposites programs are extremely simple to operate by pressing the left or right arrow key. Each key controls one of the two opposites (e.g., little and big). A colorful animated sound graphic grows or shrinks with the press of a key in *Stickybear Opposites* (Hilton Head, SC: Optimum Resource, 1986) and *City Country Opposites* (Heightstown, NJ: McGraw-Hill Media, 1986).

SORTS OBJECTS BY LIKENESSES

Once they have begun to notice the similar properties of objects, children can begin to separate or classify them, a necessary ability in cognitive development for the brain to sort out and process the wealth of incoming data obtained through sensory activities. Sorting objects and materials gives children practice in this skill and involves identifying the similarities of objects as well as understanding their relationships. The more we learn about young children's development of thinking abilities, the more we realize that thinking is concerned primarily with information processing and retrieval.

Once children begin to notice the similar properties of objects, they can sort and classify according to attributes.

Piaget and other researchers have noted that children progress through a sequence of sorting skills, and that each skill is more complex than the previous one. The earliest sorting skill to appear is simple classification, which many two- and most three-year-olds can do. Children doing simple classification can sort or group objects that actually belong together in the real world. For example, they can group together all the toy animals that live on the farm in one set and all the fish and creatures that live in the ocean in another set, if the youngsters have had the appropriate experiences concerning such animals. This activity is not quite true classification, because it is based on associations between the animals and their homes rather than the animals' likenesses or differences.

Another type of simple classification in which young children place things that "belong together" into a group involves putting all of the toy trucks, cars, and motorcycles together in a group because "you can drive them," or putting the proper hats on all the dolls, or putting all the blocks together because they make a house.

Less verbal children seem to do as well in simple classification tasks as verbal children (Richardson et al., 1980, p. 181). These simple classification tasks do involve real classification skills. To perform them, children need to understand the rule for sorting and follow it with consistency. In addition, the youngsters must discriminate likenesses and differences based on function or some other rule to place objects in the correct group. The main difference between this kind of sorting and real classification is that simple classification is based on something other than appearances only, and the groups formed are not true classes.

A more mature type of classification that many three-year-olds and most four- and five-year-olds can do involves classifying objects into separate sets based on a common characteristic like color, for instance. You can ask the children to place all the red blocks in one set and all the blue blocks in another.

The problem most young children have in doing this kind of sorting involves consistency. They have difficulty keeping in mind the rule upon which the sorting is based. Often, they will start sorting objects on the basis of color but will switch in the middle of the task to some other property, like shape, and may even switch again before they are finished.

Children need to practice with all kinds of sorting games, activities, and collections—and the youngsters love this practice. Give a child a box of mixed buttons and let him sort it any way he or she chooses. Talk with the child afterward, and ask how he decided on which buttons to put in each pile. Look around your classroom for other objects to sort, such as dress-up clothing, blocks, and eating utensils. By age five, children with experience can sort objects into intersecting sets based on more than one characteristic: color as well as size, for instance.

Collections

Once children are familiar with various size, shape, and color categories through their own explorations and the games you have played with them in identifying and naming objects, let them try to apply their skill to collections with more than one attribute. Children enjoy playing with collections of natural objects just to discover what they feel like, see what they look like, and explore how they can play with them. A collection of shells, acorns, or rocks can be kept in plastic containers on the shelves of the manipulative/math area for children to bring to a table in the area and play with. They need to find out how the items are alike. Bottle caps, felt-tip marker caps, keys, and buttons also make fine collections for sorting.

In case you wonder if such play is actually important, here is what preschool math specialists have to say:

> Collections encourage children to become more flexible in their thinking. There is no predetermined, correct way to sort the objects. The goal is for children to find a variety of ways to group the materials. . . . Collections can help children take another person's perspective. As they discuss or argue about how to group the items in a collection, they become aware that different people view the same objects in different ways. (Moomaw and Hieronymous, 1995, p. 56)

If You Have Not Checked This Item: Some Helpful Ideas

■ Sort Blocks During Cleanup

Have children help sort a certain size of the unit blocks during cleanup before putting them back on the shelves. This activity will give you an indication of who can and cannot sort objects based on likenesses. Make the activity a game, though, and not a task.

■ Play with Lotto Cards

Make or purchase simple lotto cards that the children can match. You can mount different-colored construction paper onto cardboard, cover it with clear self-adhesive paper, and cut it into playing card size. Have at least four cards for each color. Mix the cards up, and let the children try to sort them out.

Get several duplicate catalogs from companies, such as car dealers, and cut up the catalogs, mounting four similar car pictures on each set of four cards.

■ Invent Collection Sorting Games

Take a shoe box, three empty margarine tubs with a hole cut in the top of them, and a collection of three kinds of objects. You can use three varieties of beans, three sizes of paper clips, or any other similar collection. Let the child dump the collection into the top of the shoe box and sort it piece by piece into the margarine cups. This activity provides good small motor practice in picking up small objects, as well.

■ Read a Book

Is Your Mama a Llama? by Deborah Guarino (New York: Scholastic, 1989) is a rhymed story about little Lloyd llama, who goes from one animal to another asking each if his mother is a llama, and hearing in return descriptions of each mother before the page turns to show the mother.

■ Use a Computer Program

Several computer games have players sort items into classes. *Animal Photo Fun* (Allen, TX: DLM, 1985) has six games in which children match animals with their habitats. Children use a joystick to move Grover to one of four environments in *Sesame Street Grover's Animal Adventures* (New York: Hi Tech Expressions, 1985). Then they place different animals in their proper location in the sky, land, or water. In *Dinosaurs* (Mill Valley, CA: Advanced Ideas, 1984), children classify six dinosaurs by what they eat and where they live. Be sure to have plastic animal and dinosaur figures for children to play with when these programs are in use.

PUTS EVENTS IN A SEQUENCE; OBJECTS IN A SERIES

In observing children to determine their cognitive development, we have been concentrating thus far on the classification aspects of what is known as "logico-mathematical knowledge." Children display three aspects of this knowledge:

1. *classification abilities:* the ability to understand particular characteristics or properties of objects and the ability to group things into classes with common properties
2. *seriation abilities:* the ability to understand "more than" or "less than," and the ability to arrange things systematically in a sequence or a series based on a particular rule or order
3. *number abilities:* the ability to understand the meaning and use of numbers, and the ability to apply them in counting and ordering (Saunders & Bingham-Newman, 1984, p. 120)

The next Checklist item involves seriation abilities in children. To arrange events in a sequence, the child first has to recognize their properties and relationships. How are they alike? How different? What is the common thread that connects them? Then the child must understand order: that something comes first, something happens next, something occurs last. His practice in sorting items by likenesses should help him note both properties and relationships among events as well.

Just as the young child often changes the rule he is using as he sorts a number of things, he also displays inconsistency in arranging events in a sequence. It is as if his immature mind cannot hold for long the rule upon which the sequencing is based. Or, perhaps, as Siegler (1986) notes:

> Children's performance on relatively unstructured tasks, such as sorting, may reflect what they find interesting rather than what they know. (p. 267)

Cards with action pictures frequently are used in sequence games. The cards show sequences of an action from beginning to end, with one part of the sequence on each card. For example, one set of cards may have pictures of a pencil lying on a desk, rolling off the desk, falling through the air, hitting the floor, and lying on the floor.

Three- and four-year-olds often arrange only the first and last cards correctly. Another card set may show a baseball being thrown, going straight through the air, being hit by a bat, looping through the air, and being caught by a person with a baseball glove.

Such sequence cards really are not appropriate for preschoolers, since games with rules are beyond many of them at their developmental level, and since many of the cards depict events that are unclear and difficult even for adults to arrange. Some preschoolers will be able to arrange three easily understood sequence cards in their proper order. Kindergartners, with their increased maturity, are more successful. When asked to tell about a series of events in the order they occur, many young children can do it correctly if the events are familiar. But if the sequence is too long and complicated, the best most preschoolers can do is to identify the correct beginning and ending.

Ask your children to relate their favorite stories, ones you are familiar with. Do the youngsters get the plot sequence correct? Ask them to tell you what they would do in a fast food restaurant to get something to eat. Did they include all the essential steps? Can they act out a sequence like this in their dramatic play? Real and concrete activities are more meaningful to children than abstract ones.

Seriation tasks also ask us to observe children to see if they can arrange objects in a series from the smallest to the largest or vice versa. Children's previous activities with opposites should prepare them for identifying extreme differences among objects.

Young children can usually arrange items in a series if they are provided with cues. Montessori-size cylinders, for instance, can be arranged in a board containing a series of graded holes. Children try to fit the cylinders from small to large in the increasingly larger holes. They match the size of each cylinder with the size of each hole by experimenting to see which cylinders do fit or do not fit. Once they have learned the concept, many children can line up the cylinders in the proper order without cues from the board.

Stacking blocks, boxes, and rings work on the same principle of arranging items in a series, usually from the largest to the smallest. Even toddlers soon learn that the smallest ring will not go down all the way on the stacking column. Instead, they have to put the largest ring on first. Then, if one ring is left over, they will need to start over again to find their mistake. Russian matreshka dolls, a classic folk art, are a series of hollow wooden dolls, each smaller than the next, that fit inside one another. The point is that children play these learning games on their own, and thus come to discover the concept of sequencing through their own play.

It is true, though, that three- and four-year-olds have difficulty forming a consistent series from a large number of items when no cues exist, just as they have trouble sorting large collections or arranging a large number of action cards into the proper sequence. Although young children are able to compare two items on the basis of size, as soon as several other graded items are added, the youngsters have difficulty arranging the items in the proper order.

Most preschoolers understand the concept of bigger and smaller, but when this concept is applied to a series, the complexity of the many comparisons seems to confuse some youngsters. How can an object that is bigger than one item also be smaller than the item that precedes it?

You may find that you have not checked this particular Checklist item for any but the most mature children. This finding is to be expected with three- and four-year-olds. Five-year-olds, on the other hand, usually are more successful. You may decide to add a number of new series games and activities to your manipulative or science/math areas to promote this skill. Be sure the new materials provide enough cues for your children to succeed. Most of all, be sure these activities are fun to do.

If You Have Not Checked This Item: Some Helpful Ideas

■ Make Cards from Photos You Take

Children learn best from their own actions. Take a series of three photos of the child herself performing an action: For instance, pouring flour into a bowl, kneading it with her hands, and playing with the Playdough; or starting a block house, completing the house, and taking it down. Cover the photos with clear adhesive paper for protection and put the sets in envelopes for all the children to play with. If youngsters understand number sequence, you can number the pictures on the back for the children to check on their accuracy.

■ Use an Illustrated Recipe Chart in Cooking

Use a large chart with each step in the cooking process numbered and illustrated. You can use drawn outlines of measuring cups and spoons, or actual three-dimensional plastic utensils mounted on cardboard. Discuss each step with the children as they do it. Ask them which comes next, and so forth.

You may discover that some of the preschoolers' problems with sequencing can be explained by their incomplete understanding of a particular process. For instance, children who had completed all of the steps in the recipe chart for making a birthday cake and were ready to put it in the oven were asked: "What should we do next?" Some said "eat it," while others thought that candles should be put on it, but nobody understood that the next step was to bake it.

■ Make a Pictorial Daily Schedule

Draw or paste pictures to illustrate the time blocks of your daily schedule in the order of their occurrence. Display this pictorial schedule prominently, and discuss it with the children whenever the need arises, using questions such as: "What do we do first today?" "What comes next?"

■ Arrange Children

Have groups of three children at a time arrange themselves from shortest to tallest on three boxes of graduated sizes. Let them tell who is tallest. Then let them shift around on the boxes. Now who is tallest? Give everyone a chance to be tallest. To arrange children without the graduated boxes may make the truly shortest child feel bad, since children have gotten the idea from us that tallest is best.

■ Read a Book

The traditional classic stories of *Goldilocks and the Three Bears, The Three Little Pigs,* and *The Three Billy Goats Gruff* all feature a graduated series of characters from the smallest to the biggest along with their graduated series of furniture, cereal bowls, houses, and even noises. Children love these stories and will want to join in on the repetitious dialog or sounds as you read or tell the stories. The youngsters may also want to act out the stories as well.

You can cut out the pictures of the three characters from extra paperback copies of each of these books. Then you can mount the cutouts on sandpaper, and use them with your flannelboard activities. Can your children arrange the characters in proper order from smallest to biggest? Children need this physical activity to develop such abstract concepts.

■ Read a Wordless Book

All wordless books are illustrated in a sequence of events from first to last. You can "read" them to children. Children can tell them to you. If children have trouble understanding them, ask "What comes next?" or "And then what happened?" A current favorite is the bizarre wordless book *Tuesday,* by David Wiesner (New York: Clarion, 1991), in which frogs on lily pads take off from the pond on a Tuesday night, and sail through the air to the town, causing quite a commotion. The only text shown is the time written on blank white pages opposite the blue-black pages of floating frogs.

COUNTS HOW MANY ARE PRESENT

Learning the concept of number is important for young humans to accomplish. They will be dealing most of their lives with numbers involving size, distance, amounts, time, temperature, costs, money, and measurement. In their mind's quest to create its own knowledge, the children will be going through a predetermined sequence of development, internalizing the information gained from their sensory interactions with the world around them.

Even two-year-olds display a rudimentary knowledge of numbers when they hold up two fingers to show you their age and count aloud "one-two." For most, this counting is more of a parroting response than a true understanding of "two years." However, some two-year-olds can count by rote to 10, and many three- and four-year-olds are able to count by rote to 20 (Siegler, 1986, p. 279).

Again, this rote counting does not mean the children understand the concept of number at first. Often, in fact, children do not get the sequence correct in their counting or leave out a number or two. These mix-ups and omissions are understandable, since the children are performing a memory task at first, not a concept task. Their counting is really chanting as in a nursery rhyme. You will find if you ask them that many children do not know the meaning of each word. In fact, their chanting of numbers seems more like one long word instead of 10 separate ones: "onetwothree-fourfivesixseveneightnineten."

Nevertheless, chanting numbers like this is important in the cognitive development of the child. Cognitive development proceeds from the general to the specific. Children first chant a line of numbers and then begin to understand specific number names from the line. Listen to the children as they chant. Are they getting the number names right and in the right order? Chant along with them to help them hear the correct pronunciation.

This type of counting is due in part to the children's limited language experience. To understand the meaning of each number word, the child must form a mental image of it. You cannot expect this mental image formation in many two-year-olds. By age three, some children will have formed mental images of certain numbers because of their sensory experience with these numbers in their environment. It is therefore important for parents and other adults to use numbers frequently in the children's everyday living, and to involve children in the use of numbers with activities such as chanting, measuring, weighing, counting out items, counting out money, and playing games involving the counting of moves.

With infants and toddlers, the chanting of numbers and the singing of number rhymes such as "one-two, buckle my shoe" are important preludes to the understanding of number concepts. But before children of any age can be expected to know the meaning of each number, they must first accomplish several of the developmental skills mentioned earlier.

Children will need to be able to place objects in a series and understand that the objects are more or less than one another. The youngsters will need to know the answers to questions such "which group has the most?" And, of course, they will need to know the names of the numbers. Some of these skills are just developing in the preschool classroom, but many children will not fully grasp the concepts of seriation and number much before the age of seven or second grade (Cowan, 1978, p. 181).

For children who can count to 10 or 20, but have no real understanding of numbers or of what counting really means, try having them count to 7 or to 13. The children will have to slow down and think about what they are doing. They may not be able to stop at a number other than 10 or 20 at first. Play games with individuals or small groups, asking each to count to a number other than 10 that you will call out. Make such games exciting. Children who have not learned to count will soon be picking up this skill to play the game.

Be sure bilingual children learn to count along with you. They can also count in their native language for the others to hear and even learn. Make counting by rote fun for all, but be sure to do it often. Familiarity with numbers can only happen for preschoolers if the numbers and number games are repeated frequently.

Next, children must master simple one-to-one correspondence for them to develop number sense. This is what we are asking them to do when they count objects. Learning that a number stands for an object is their next step in the sequence

*In developing number sense, chil-
dren learn that numbers stand for
objects, and they must learn to
count objects.*

of learning number concepts. At first many youngsters try to rush through their counting without actually including all of the objects. The children seem more concerned
with saying all of the numbers than with making sure each number represents an
object. They eventually come to learn that the key principles governing counting are:

1. The number names must be matched one-to-one with the objects being counted.
2. The order of the number names matters, but the order in which the objects being
   counted are touched does not matter. (Resnick, 1989, p. 163)

Preschool children learn these principles not by being taught, but by being
involved playfully in hands-on counting. As with learning shapes and colors, concrete
objects should be used first, pictures later, and finally number symbols. From such
activities children teach themselves:

1. number names
2. number names in order
3. one-to-one correspondence

Children become familiar with the names and the task by repeating them many times
in many forms. Through repetition and trial-and-error, they finally get it right.

Most adults are not aware of the importance of learning to count. Cognitive scientists, on the other hand, believe that:

Figuring out how to count is evidently a key ingredient in developing an understanding of number. In the skill of counting, the transition from novice to expert often occurs during early childhood. (Price, 1989, p. 55)

Thus, it is important that children count or hear you counting every day in the classroom, and that you provide youngsters with many opportunities for doing so on their own. Start with fewer items than 20 in the beginning, just as you did with number chanting. Then the children will learn to stop before they get to 20. Also have the children touch each item as they count. If they skip one, have them try again. Or have them hand you an item as they count it. But be sure it is fun or interesting for them, and not a task involving right or wrong.

Learning to sort also is good preparation for counting things. Putting a cup with a saucer or a hat on a doll helps them understand one-to-one correspondence. Now they must apply their learning to numbers. They learn by their sensory actions that the number "one" represents the first object, that "two" represents the second, and so on. This learning is a first step. But counting in a progression still is not the same as understanding one-to-one correspondence.

Children may be able to count a row of 10 or even 20 children, and still may not be able to choose four of them. Give them practice. Once they are able to count up to 10 objects in a progression, the youngsters can practice picking out a particular number of items, such as three dolls, five blocks, or seven dominoes. Phrase your questions or directions to give the children practice with both activities. "How many red markers are there?" asks them to count in a progression. "Bring me four napkins," takes them one step further in their development of number concepts.

It is also important that children count *on their own* in all sorts of unsupervised everyday activities. Cognitive scientists point out that:

Only in this way is enough practice likely to be generated to produce a real effect on the rate of number-concept development . . . Preschool programs can foster number-concept development mainly by providing many occasions and requests for quantification and by eventually tying these requests to situations of comparison, combination, and increase or decrease of quantities. (Resnick, 1989, p.164)

Put out small collections of items in margarine tubs on the tables of your manipulative area, and have children count them. They can do it on their own and record their number on the tape recorder if you have it set up for them. Have "Count Me" signs hanging around the room on objects like your fish aquarium, your painting easel paints, and the hats in your dramatic play area. What other things would the children like to count on their own? Ask them. If they want you to check on their accuracy, you will have to count these things, too, a good modeling behavior.

Using Marks, Picture Symbols, Number Symbols to Record

To support children's number activities, you or your children can record their counting. You should not use number symbols at first, but simple marks to represent the numbers. For example, keep an attendance chart with all the children's names and mark a symbol for each child present. Then the children can count the marks. Have children keep track with marks on a pad or punches on a card with a paper punch of how many times they feed the guinea pig or water the plants, or of how many cars pass by the building. Then have them count the number of marks or punch holes to get the total.

Use shape symbols, stick figures, or picture symbols for numbers, too. Put signs in each activity area with a particular number of stick figures or peel-off picture symbols to represent the number of children allowed in the area at once. Have a certain number of hooks on the wall with tags on them for use in each area. Have children take the tags while in the areas. Check from time to time with the children in the area, having them count how many participants are in the area and whether this is the proper number.

Use charts and bar graphs at appropriate times to record numbers. Hang a calendar chart near the guinea pig's cage and record the number of carrots he eats every day by drawing carrot symbols. Record how tall each child's seeds grow every week by posting a chart with the child's name and having him or her measure the height with a ruler. Help children record the height after their names. Or use a bar graph that can be colored in up to the height the plant has grown.

Later in the year when the children have shown that they understand one-to-one correspondence, you may want to use real number symbols along with the picture symbols. Numbers alone are often too abstract for many of the children at the beginning of the year.

If You Have Not Checked This Item: Some Helpful Ideas

■ Have Children Count One Another

Any activity is more meaningful to a young child if it involves her and her peers directly. Have children help you take attendance in the morning by going around and counting how many children are present. Have the counting children touch each child. Give the counters help if they need it with numbers above 10.

■ Have Many Counting Materials

Fill your manipulative or math area with counting materials or games. Use egg cartons for children to fill the sections with items and count how many there are. Use buttons, shells, dominoes, spools, paper clips, and macaroni as items to fill the sections.

■ Do a Follow-the-Leader Counting Walk

Walk around the room with three or four children doing a follow-the-leader touch-and-count walk. Do it out loud the first time and then silently once children know how. For example, after touching three items silently yourself, stop quickly and ask "how many did we touch?" Congratulate the ones who get it right, and continue your walk. When all the children have caught on, let one of them be the leader.

■ Have Children Set the Table

Let the children set the table for meals and snacks. They may need eight spoons and eight forks for each table, along with eight plates, cups, and napkins. Can they do it? This real task is an especially powerful activity for teaching one-to-one correspondence.

■ Read a Book

Counting books are as popular as ABC books these days. Here are a few: *One Smiling Grandma* by Ann Marie Linden (New York: Dial, 1992) is a simple rhyming Caribbean counting book showing large double-page pictures of an island girl counting from 1 to 10 her grandma, birds, fish, shells, market ladies, and steel drums.

Moving from One to Ten by Shari Halpern (New York: Macmillan, 1993) takes David, his two angry cats, three worried sisters, and six tired people on a long ride across the country to their new house.

In *Joe Can Count* by Jan Ormerod (New York: Mulberry, 1986), a little African American boy counts with his fingers from 1 to 10 the objects he imagines as he stands facing the reader on each page. Then he counts 10 real puppies and one chooses him for its very own.

Fish Eyes: A Book You Can Count On by Lois Ehlert (San Diego: Harcourt Brace, 1990) is a long, narrow book perfect in shape for the colorful fish within. Against a dark blue background, from 1 to 10 jumping, smiling, flipping, darting fish with see-through holes for eyes flash across the pages.

How Many, How Many, How Many by Rick Walton (Cambridge, MA: Candlewick, 1993) is a problem-solving adventure for children as they are asked to count things like how many jump over the candlestick, how many bears are coming home, how many legs ants walk on, and how many numbers are on a phone.

■ Use a Computer Program

Preschool children can learn to use a computer with ease, and love to do so. Because counting activities are especially well-suited to computer programs, many computer math games for preschoolers include counting. Children will need to be able to find and use the number symbols 1 through 9 on the computer keyboard to work many of these programs. For children who have taught themselves to use the letter keys, this should present no problem. Show them the top row of the keyboard where the numbers are, and let them learn to use the programs on their own. Be sure you have a color monitor.

Mickey's Runaway Zoo: Fun with Numbers (Walt Disney, 1990) contains a simple counting activity from one to nine in which children press one of the partially hidden numerals and that number of animals moves a zoo wagon.

Millie's Math House (Edmark, 1992), one of the highest rated math programs, has Millie the talking cow inviting children to match shapes to build a mouse house, count jellybeans for a cookie machine, match shoes to feet, and find sets on a cash register.

Charlie Brown's 1-2-3 (Queue, Inc., 1985) shows a Peanuts scene when children press a number key, but then they must count out the number of objects with the space bar or number keys to animate the scene.

Number Farm (DLM, 1984) contains six interesting games with various counting experiences including counting the number of sounds made by things on the farm.

KNOWS WHAT HAPPENS TODAY

Understanding Time

Time is the next cognitive concept we need to look for in young children. Three-, four-, and five-year-olds are only at the beginning of their temporal understanding. We need to provide them with simple activities involving time, but we cannot expect them to develop a mature understanding of so abstract a concept during the preschool years.

Time comprehension for young children has a number of different aspects: (1) the ability to understand what comes *before* and what comes *after*; (2) the ability to describe past events; (3) the ability to anticipate and plan for future events; (4) the ability to describe the order or sequence of things; (5) the ability to understand the passage of time and how it is measured (with clocks, calendars); and (6) the understanding of units of time (seconds, minutes, hours, days, weeks, months, years, centuries).

The child's ability to arrange things in a sequence or series based on a particular order as discussed earlier begins the learning process. This knowledge that events may occur in a particular order with something happening first, something next, and something last generally precedes a child's understanding of time intervals.

Because young children are still egocentric, looking at everything exclusively from their own point of view, they do not perceive time as adults do. To young children, time occurs because they are there. For example, "snack time" and "nap time" do not happen unless they participate. They learn to understand the movement of the hands on the clock only very superficially: that two hands pointing straight up means lunch time. Calendars likewise have little meaning for young children, although they can repeat the names of the days of the week.

Time is a very abstract concept. It is not something you can see. Even adults realize that the passage of time seems uneven in different circumstances. If we are occupied, time goes quickly, but if we are bored, it seems to drag. For young children the present moment is the most important. Children's comprehension of past and future is limited to periods of time close to the present.

Time is one of the basic organizing dimensions of the child's experience, and as such time needs to be considered an important part of the child's cognitive development. Although the young child will not develop a mature perception of time while in your classroom, you need to be aware of each child's present development in this area to provide activities and support for the continued growth of the time concept.

Using the Daily Schedule

Since children learn best from things and events that involve them directly, using the daily schedule to help them understand the concept of time is a good place to begin. First, you must have a daily schedule that is clear and consistent. The activity periods can be of various lengths as long as they follow one another in the same order daily. A brief transition activity between each period helps children understand that the next period is about to begin.

A full day's program might consist of:

A.M.	P.M.
arrival	naptime
morning circle	free choice
free choice	snack
snack	afternoon circle
outdoor play	departure
toilet	
story	
lunch	

If you follow this same schedule consistently day after day, children not only feel secure about what will happen, but they also come to an understanding about the sequence of things. The abilities to represent mentally and to remember the order of events are essential ingredients in the young child's development of the concept of time. Even if your morning free choice period varies in length from day to day, the children will still know that it comes after morning circle and is followed by snack time.

The morning circle time is essential in bringing about awareness of this sequence, in helping children make choices and plan for future activities, and in giving them an awareness of time in general. The Checklist observer should attend the morning circle to hear which children give appropriate answers to the teachers' questions about the activities to follow and which children do not seem to understand time intervals.

Although many teachers do calendar activities at this time as well, they need to be aware of children's superficial understanding of calendars and clocks. We really cannot expect children to understand these abstract concepts much before age seven.

But four-year-olds are aware of established sequences and become upset if things are not done in the regular order. If one of your periods is to be omitted, this should be made clear at circle time. On the other hand, activity periods can vary in length without anyone seeming to notice. Teachers who have had to shorten their day by several hours report that the children hardly notice the difference so long as the activities follow one another in regular sequence.

Giving children advance notice that a period is coming to a close is another method for helping them understand the passage of time. "Five more minutes before cleanup time," may not have the same meaning for young children as it does for adults, since children still do not really understand "minutes." But youngsters do know that this signal means that the free choice period is almost over and that they must soon help to clean up.

Having some kind of transition between each activity period also helps a child to order the day mentally. When everyone has finally arrived and it is time for morning circle, you can give a transition signal by playing a chord on the piano, or singing a transition song such as:

(Tune: "Happy Birthday!")
Good morning to you,
Good morning to you,
Good morning everybody,
Good morning to you.

Come sit in our group,
Come sit in our group,
Good morning everybody,
Come sit in our group.

When circle time is finished, you can play a concept game as a transition to send the children to their activities: "All the children with red on may go to their activity area." Free Choice period usually ends with cleanup. When children are finished with that, they go to the snack table on their own. The transition from snack to outdoor play could be a song that will send them to get their outdoor clothes on:

(Tune: "The Farmer in the Dell")
We're waiting to go out,
We're waiting to go out,
Jill and Joe and Rodney too,
Get ready to go out.

We're waiting to go out,
We're waiting to go out,
All the girls at table one,
Get ready to go out.

When they come in from outdoor play, the youngsters already know that they go to the bathroom and wash their hands after hanging up their coats. From the bathroom they generally go over to the library corner, where one of the teachers will be waiting with a book to read. The transition activity to lunch can involve something from the story you have just read: One Smiling Grandma is looking for two boys and one girl to go to lunch.

Activities such as these help children establish a meaningful order to the day. This order is more than an explanation in words, for the children themselves must interact with their environment to construct mentally the concept of daily time sequences.

A brief afternoon circle time is important to help children internalize these activities and to help you realize their understanding of the things they have been doing. Now is the time to discuss what the children liked best about the day. Ask things like

"What did you make today that you can tell us about?" "What did you choose to do during free choice in the morning?"

Just as the morning circle asked them to look at the daily schedule and make plans for the future, so the afternoon circle asks them to look back at the past and think about what they accomplished. Checklist observers need to be present at this group meeting, as well, to determine who really understands the daily schedule and can remember past events.

If You Have Not Checked This Item: Some Helpful Ideas

■ Play a Time Game

Since children learn best by playing, and especially by playing something that involves themselves, you might play a time game with them that involves children pretending to be your various activity periods. For instance, you could have one child represent each of the morning periods: arrival, morning circle, free choice, snack, outdoor play, storytime, and lunch. Put a sign on each child. The sign could have both words and a symbol: a handshake for arrival, a circle for morning circle, blocks for free choice, a glass of juice for snack, a swing for outdoor play, a book for story-time, a plate for lunch. Then let the children arrange themselves in a line in the order in which the periods occur. To get the children started, ask which child should come first? Which one next? Do the same for afternoon activities.

■ Play Before and After Games

Make up brief transition questions that you ask the children while they are waiting for something else to happen: for example, you could ask them "Does lunch come before nap or after nap?" "Does snack come before outdoor play or after outdoor play?" Have them make up similar questions of their own.

CAN BUILD A BLOCK ENCLOSURE

Understanding Space

Space, like time, is another of the basic organizing dimensions of the young child's experience. Like the other basic dimensions, it has several aspects: enclosure, position, closeness, distance between things, location, order, shapes and sizes, including body parts and body space. The concept of space answers the question "where?" about things. It is one of the three dimensions, along with number and time, that eventually merge to make up the basis for logical thought (Osborn & Osborn, 1983, p. 115).

Also like time, space is an abstract concept that young children cannot represent mentally until they experience "enclosure." As with the other knowledge they create, the idea of space comes from their sensory exploration of things. Children see and perceive objects as being close to or far away from other things.

"Space" is an abstract concept that young children may not be able to represent mentally until they experience "enclosure," for example, by building a block enclosure.

In the beginning, the infant's only experience with space involves the nearness of objects. When the object is out of sight, it is literally out of mind for him until he develops so-called **object permanence** at about eight months. Before that time he will not continue to search for an object that is out of his range of vision or one that has been hidden. He acts as though the object he cannot see is no longer there, as if it has disappeared completely and no longer exists.

With experience and maturity he comes to understand that objects in his environment are still there even though out of his sight. Yet even with object permanence, most young children cannot perceive objects from any point of view other than their own. Nor can most children imagine how an object will look if its position in their space is changed.

Because space is not perceived readily by a youngster unless it is enclosed, Checklist observers are asked first to look for this aspect of space perception in assessing a child's cognitive development in this dimension.

Using Block Building

One of the most effective activities for developing cognitive concepts about space involves playing with "unit blocks," those deceptively simple and plain wooden units, half units, double units, quadruple units, cylinders, curves, triangles, ramps, pillars, floorboards, and switches that were invented before World War I by Carolyn Pratt for use by her children in the experimental City and Country School in New York City (Winsor, 1974, p. 3).

Unit blocks are found today in almost every nursery school, preschool, and in many kindergartens throughout the country. Children learn to sort and categorize during cleanup by putting the blocks back on the shelves having the correct cutout block shape as mentioned earlier. The block center is a favorite area for children's play during free choice period. The youngsters build houses and farms and towers and hospitals and anything else their imagination can invent. Adults rarely think of block building as a primary activity for children to develop such an abstract cognitive concept as space.

Adults often have trouble thinking this way because they often have trouble keeping in mind how children learn: (1) by constructing their own knowledge through sensory interactions with things in their environment, and (2) through free play with such materials. Abstract concepts can come to life in children's minds when such versatile yet defined playthings as unit blocks represent these concepts.

Harriet Johnson, another pioneer early childhood specialist who worked with Carolyn Pratt and later founded the nursery school that still later became the demonstration school for the Bank Street College of Education, spent years observing children's use of building blocks. She eventually published her findings in the 1933 classic study "The Art of Block Building" (Johnson, 1974, pp. 9–24). She found that children go through predictable stages in learning to use blocks based on their maturity and experience, when they are given the freedom to use blocks naturally without adult interference. Sound familiar? Her observational data give strong support to much current research on child development.

Her block-building stages serve us well today in our observation of children's cognitive development. What better way to determine if children understand spatial concepts and relationships than by watching how the youngsters use unit blocks? If the first understanding that children can grasp about space comes only when they can enclose it, then their block creations offer a fine way to witness whether they have mastered this concept.

The children Johnson worked with ranged from two to six years in age, and varied in their experience with blocks. She found that the older children with no experience still progressed through the same stages as the younger ones, but with greater speed. An amended version of her stages include:

1. carrying, filling, dumping
2. stacking and lining
3. bridging
4. enclosures
5. patterns
6. representation

Two-year-olds as well as older children with no block-building experience begin by massing the blocks together, carrying them around, filling up containers (or toy trucks) with them, and dumping them out—over and over—but not building. This manipulative action is typical of the novice child's approach to most new activities: getting the feel of the blocks, the heft of them, the way you can move them around, but not using them for their purpose (which he has not figured out yet), then repeating the activity. It is a pattern the child will use throughout his natural development of block-building skills if he is given the freedom to proceed on his own.

Somewhere between the ages of two and three, real building begins. The first real building stage is either stacking blocks into a tower or lining them up in a row. Some children do one activity first, some do the other. Some combine the tower and the row. Some learn to straighten their blocks neatly so that their towers will not fall. Others pay little attention to either vertical or horizontal alignment. Once they have mastered this first attempt, they tend to repeat it again and again before moving on to the next stage (Johnson, 1974, pp. 11–12).

Eventually the children are faced with the problem of bridging, or using a horizontal block to span the space between two upright parallel vertical blocks. If the youngsters are working without the help of a teacher or peers (and they should be), it may take a great deal of time to resolve this building problem. The children's concepts of size and distance are still somewhat hazy at this age, and they often make many trials and errors before they can get the right size block. The other solution to the bridging problem, of course, is to move the two upright blocks closer together so that the horizontal bridging block will fit. Some children discover one solution but never the other.

Even when peers at higher levels are building nearby, the novice builder usually does not try to copy their methods. Block building, like art, is a very personal and satisfying expression of a child's individual creativity. What someone else is doing matters very little. For that reason, teachers should not interfere with children's block building. The youngsters truly will learn cognitive concepts only by struggling with building problems on their own and finding their own solutions. Once children have learned to bridge, this skill is incorporated into their own personal building style, to be used over and over.

The next stage for children to master is enclosures. Adults find it difficult to understand why children have trouble making an enclosure. A child will start out correctly by making two walls joined at a corner to enclose the corral for her toy horse, but somehow be unable to turn the next corner for the third wall, and thus the wall goes on and on. She seems to know what she wants to do, but is unable to do it. It is frustrating indeed, something like the adult standing before the bathroom mirror trying to cut her own hair. The child needs your support but not your help in arriving at her own solution, her own understanding of space and how to manipulate the objects in it.

Many three- and even four-year-olds make incomplete enclosures for a long time before they perceive how to close the gap. Their enclosures tend to have some rounded corners, as well, for children still have difficulty at this age either constructing or drawing a square as noted earlier. Once they have mastered the problem of completing an enclosure, they incorporate this into their block-building repertoire.

A few children begin naming their enclosures when they start to build, but most youngsters do this after they have finished the enclosures. It may be a "garage for their car" or "house for their doll" or "house for the guinea pig." This building may not have been in their minds as they started to build, but they know adults want them to name things, so these names sound reasonable.

Whether the name is reasonable depends upon whether the toy car, doll, or guinea pig fits into the building. You will have an additional opportunity to observe the children's conception of space and size when you see whether the object fits its enclosure. Often it does not. Children sometimes try to force a toy car into a block building without seeming to realize that the car is too big and will not fit. Why can't children see that it does not fit, we wonder? Their mental structures still are not refined enough to handle such details. Children need more practice as well as maturity. Playing with unit blocks on their own will help correct these deficiencies.

With skill in towers, rows, bridging, and enclosures, children are ready to build in patterns—decorative, repetitive, often geometric—building either horizontally or vertically and incorporating the entire repertory of building they have developed over the years. Four- and five-year-olds use the same building styles they began with at ages two and three, but in a more sophisticated, complex manner. You thought block building was simple children's play? Now that you know it is neither simple nor play as adults know it, perhaps you will want to record with a camera the children's stages of building over the year or two they are with you.

The final stage, as with art, is representative building. Children start by building a structure and then giving it a name such as school, playground, house, store, fire station. Eventually they learn to name the building first and then build it according to their own inner design. Most early efforts at representation do not look much like the building they name. But practiced builders eventually are able to represent a wide range of structures. Their play now becomes less solitary or parallel and more of a group effort as discussed in Chapter 5. Once children have mastered the skill of building with unit blocks, they are usually ready to contribute to another child's building or invite other children to help them. At this point they often want their structures to remain standing at the end of the period so they can play with them later. You may have to enlarge your block-building area if you have many such skilled builders.

Keep magazine pictures of houses, stores, bridges, roads, barns, and office buildings mounted in your block-building area at the child's eye level. Where can you mount pictures when block shelves are in the way? Pull the shelves away from the walls and use them as room dividers for your building area. Then you can mount pictures on the walls. Take photos of completed buildings and their creators, and mount the photos attractively in the same area to motivate further building.

If You Have Not Checked This Item: Some Helpful Ideas

■ Have a Special Building Day

If boys tend to dominate the block-building area, have a special building day for all the children wearing red (or blue or sneakers or some other distinctive feature that will include girls). If one child never seems to build, perhaps you could choose the feature from that child's clothing to identify a group that will then help him or her get interested.

■ Build Things Seen on a Field Trip

Take your camera along on your next field trip and snap photos of structures that children might want to represent in blocks when they return to the center: highways, bridges, towers, office buildings, stores, barns, and houses. Mount the pictures in the block area and watch what happens.

■ Supply Pictures to Motivate Building

Make photocopies of illustrations from a book that features buildings, and mount the copies in the block area to motivate building. The children will not copy the buildings in the pictures as adults view them, but from their own inner view of what buildings in the pictures look like.

■ Read a Book

Block City by Robert Louis Stevenson (New York: Dutton, 1988) is a modern version of Stevenson's classic poem "Block City" from *A Child's Garden of Verses*. The beginning pages show, in large colorful drawings, a little boy building a block city to represent a Medieval city in a storybook. Then follows pictures of the Medieval city coming to life as the boy falls asleep. Finally the boy awakens and knocks down his block city.

Up Goes the Skyscraper! by Gail Gibbons (New York: Macmillan, 1986) is a tall nonfiction picture book showing how a skyscraper is constructed.

OBSERVING, RECORDING, AND INTERPRETING COGNITIVE DEVELOPMENT

Sheila, the girl who was observed Chapter 2, was found to have many items checked on this section of the checklist as shown in Figure 9–1. When the classroom staff reviewed Sheila's entire checklist, they were not surprised to see her results in cognitive development. Sheila had already seemed to them to be a bright child with exceptional language and art skills, but she seemed to have difficulty gaining access to group play. She preferred to play by herself, although often parallel to others. In fact, one of the staff members predicted that every one of the items for Sheila under cognitive development would be checked. The prediction was almost correct. Sheila does not play with blocks, probably because of a personal preference and not because she could not handle them.

It is important for staff members to look at the total picture when they observe and record a child's development, and to confer with others about the results. Not every child will accomplish every item in a section, although a girl like Sheila probably could have. All of us have personal preferences—even preschool children.

Child Skills Checklist

Name _____Sheila — Age 3_____ Observer _____Connie R_____

Program _____HeadStart_____ Dates _____10 – 22_____

Directions:

Put a ✔ for items you see the child perform regularly. Put N for items where there is no opportunity to observe. Leave all other items blank.

Item	Evidence	Dates
7. Cognitive Development: **Classification, Number, Time and Space**		
✔ Identifies objects by shape	Can draw and distinguish circles, squares, triangles	10/22
✔ Identifies objects by color	Names all the colors she uses	10/22
✔ Identifies objects by size	Plays size matching games with ease	10/22
✔ Sorts objects by likenesses	Likes to arrange animal figures in proper sets	10/22
✔ Puts events in a sequence; objects in a series	Can follow a recipe chart with understanding	10/22
✔ Counts how many are present	Can count all the children in the class with accuracy	10/22
✔ Knows what happens today	Is first to note when it's time for next activity	10/22
___ Can build a block enclosure	Never plays with blocks	10/22

Figure 9–1 Cognitive development observations for Sheila

REFERENCES

Beaty, J. J. (1996). *Preschool appropriate practices.* Ft. Worth, TX: Harcourt Brace.

Charlesworth, R. (1996). *Experiences in math for young children* (3rd ed.). Albany, NY: Delmar.

Cherry, C., Godwin, D., & Staples, J. (1989). *Is the left brain always right?* Belmont, CA: David S. Lake.

Cowan, P. A. (1978). *Piaget with feeling.* Ft. Worth, TX: Harcourt Brace.

Forman, G. E., & Kuschner, D. S. (1983). *The child's construction of knowledge: Piaget for teaching children.* Washington, DC: NAEYC.

Johnson, H. M. (1974). The art of block building. In Elisabeth S. Hirsch (Ed.), *The block book.* Washington, DC: NAEYC.

Micklo, S. J. (1995). Developing young children's classification and logical thinking skills. *Childhood Education, 72*(1), 24–28.

Moomaw, S., & Hieronymus, B. (1995). *More than counting: Whole math activities for preschool and kindergarten.* St. Paul, MN: Redleaf Press.

Osborn, J. D., & Osborn, D. K. (1983). *Cognition in early childhood.* Athens, GA: Education Associates.

Price, G. G. (1989). Mathematics in early childhood. *Young Children, 44*(4), 53–57.

Resnick, L. B. (1989). Developing mathematical knowledge. *American Psychologist, 44*(2), 162–169.

Richardson, L. I., Goodman, K. L., Hartman, N. N., & LePique, H. C. (1980). *A mathematics activity curriculum for early childhood and special education.* New York: Macmillan

Saunders, R., & Bingham-Newman, A. M. (1984). *Piagetian perspective for preschools: A thinking book for teachers.* Upper Saddle River, NJ: Merrill/Prentice Hall.

Schickedanz, J. A., Schickedanz, D. I., & Forsythe, P. D. (1982). *Toward understanding children.* Boston: Little, Brown.

Seefeldt, C. (1995). Art—A serious work. *Young Children, 50*(3), 39–45.

Siegler, R. S. (1986). *Children's thinking.* Upper Saddle River, NJ: Merrill/Prentice Hall.

Winsor, C. B. (1974). Blocks as a material for learning through play—The contribution of Caroline Pratt. In E. S. Hirsch (Ed.), *The block book.* Washington, DC: NAEYC.

SUGGESTED READINGS

Bee, H. (1989). *The developing child* (5th ed.). New York: Harper.

Berk, L. E., & Winsler, A. (1995). *Scaffolding children's learning: Vygotsky and early childhood education.* Washington, DC: NAEYC.

Bodrova, E., & Leong, D. J. (1996). *Tools of the mind: The Vygotskian approach to early childhood education.* Upper Saddle River, NJ: Merrill/Prentice Hall.

Cherry, C. (1972). *Creative art for the developing child.* Belmont, CA: Fearon.

Gardner, H. (1983). *Frames of mind: The theory of multiple intelligences.* New York: Basic.

Hohmann, C., Carmody, B., & McCabe-Branz, C. (1995). *High/Scope buyer's guide to children's software.* Ypsilanti, MI: High/Scope Press.

Schultz, K. A., Colarusso, R. P., & Strawderman, V. W. (1989). *Mathematics for every young child.* Upper Saddle River, NJ: Merrill/Prentice Hall.

VIDEOTAPES

Magna Systems, Inc. (1994). *Preschoolers: Physical and cognitive development.* 95 West County Line Rd., Barrington, IL 60010.

National Association for the Education of Young Children. *The adventure begins: Preschool and technology.* NAEYC, 1509 16th St. NW, Washington, DC, 20036-1426.

National Association for the Education of Young Children. *Block play: Constructing realities.* NAEYC, 1509 16th St. NW, Washington, DC, 20036-1426.

LEARNING ACTIVITIES

1. Use the Child Skills Checklist cognitive development section as a screening tool to observe all the children in your classroom. For which of your children did you check most of the items? How did these children do on other areas of the Checklist, for example, in small motor development?

2. Choose a child for whom there are few checks under cognitive development. Observe him or her on three different days, making a running record to help you get a more detailed picture of his cognitive skills. Plan an activity to help this child and record the results when you use it.

3. What are the ages of the children who had the most checks on the Checklist? What are the ages of the children with the least checks? What are the children's backgrounds? Can you make any inferences about cognitive development based on this information?

4. Choose a child who needs practice in discriminating likenesses and differences and set up activities for him or her to practice this skill, or play some appropriate games with the child. Record the results.

5. Read one of the children's books or use a computer program from this chapter with a child you have identified as needing help in a particular area. Plan an activity together based on the book or program. Discuss the results.

CHAPTER 10

Spoken Language

Spoken Language Checklist

☐ Listens but does not speak

☐ Gives single-word answers

☐ Gives short-phrase responses

☐ Does chanting and singing

☐ Takes part in conversations

☐ Speaks in expanded sentences

☐ Asks questions

☐ Can tell a story

DEVELOPING SPOKEN LANGUAGE

Spoken language is one of the important skills that makes us human beings. We assume, without much thought, that our children will learn to speak the native tongue before they enter public school. Language acquisition cannot be all that difficult, we decide, otherwise how could a little child do it? After all, the child does not have to be taught; language acquisition just seems to happen. It is nothing to get excited about, we think, unless it does not happen on schedule.

As a matter of fact, the acquisition of a native language is one of the greatest developmental accomplishments and mysteries we may ever encounter involving the young child. It is a great accomplishment because the child starts from scratch with no spoken language at birth and acquires an entire native tongue by age six; sometimes the child acquires more than one language if he is in a bilingual family. The acquisition of this complex skill is a great mystery because we are still not exactly sure how it takes place.

True, we may not show concern while all goes well, but we should learn all we can about the kinds of things that help or hinder the acquisition process to smooth the way. The years from age two to five are especially crucial in this process. That is when the child's vocabulary suddenly expands from 250 words to 2,000, and he teaches himself the rules of putting words together properly to speak in complex sentences. During these years the child is often in an early childhood program; thus, the language environment you provide can have a significant effect on his progress.

To support your children's language development, you must know at the outset how accomplished they already are as speakers. A good way to start is to use an observation screening device such as the eight Child Skills Checklist items under spoken language to assess each of your children at the beginning of the year. Then follow up with written or tape-recorded language samples of each child's speech.

265

Stages of Language Acquisition

Language acquisition begins at birth. A child's first language is crying and cooing, an infant's first communication sounds. Mothers, fathers, and caregivers soon learn what such sounds mean and can respond properly. Crying in its many forms may mean "I'm hungry," "I'm wet," "I'm sleepy," "I'm uncomfortable," or "Don't leave me." Cooing may mean "I'm content," "I'm happy," or "So good to see you."

Adults' responses to these first communication sounds is important because infants see that their vocalizations have had an effect on those around them. They will then make the same sound when they want that same effect. Adults should talk to youngsters each time they respond to their sounds. "I hear you crying, Lori, and it sounds to me like you're hungry." As adults use the same words over and over, infants continue their own similar communication sounds. By the time they are toddlers, youngsters will be saying "hungie" when they want something to eat, because they have heard that word used by adults in association with feeding.

Infants and toddlers continue their sound-making because it is fun for them. Certain sounds give them great pleasure, especially when adults respond with a similar sound of their own. This playing around with sounds is the manipulation stage of exploratory learning discussed in Chapter 9. Children apply the same three Ms in learning to speak as they do in learning to play with blocks, paint, use the computer, and every new learning situation they experience. Just as they did with cognitive concepts, they are constructing their own language.

Next comes a "one word" stage where toddlers use only one word to express several things. Often the first word is "mama," and the youngster will use it to mean: "Where are you, Mama?" or "Mama, pick me up," or "Mama, I'm glad to see you!" or "Don't leave me, Mama!" The happy or anxious sound of the word conveys as much meaning as the word itself.

> The specific words that children learn and the meanings that they construct for these words will depend on their experiences, interests, and the language that surrounds them. Some children begin by labeling things (learning many nouns); others use words that prompt social interactions (greetings, or words that influence the behavior of others). (Davidson, 1996, p. 84)

As toddlers acquire more names of objects and action words, they say these single words over and over, not necessarily because they are demanding something, but because they are in the **mastery stage** of language acquisition. Repetition is the name of the game.

Next, they begin putting words together into short phrases that stand for sentences: "Mommy, hungie." ("Mommy, I'm hungry.) "Go car." ("I want to go in the car.") "All done now." ("I'm all finished eating.") They often put their own meaning into such phrases: "Jeremy TV," which the adult has to figure out. ("Jeremy turned on the TV when he wasn't supposed to!") This compressed form of speech is often called "telegraphic speech" because only important words are used, as in a telegram.

All children everywhere acquire the language they hear spoken in their homes in this manner during their early childhood years. If they hear a second language spoken consistently in the home, they will acquire this language, as well.

Preschool Stages of Language Production

By the time children enter preschool around the age of three, most have progressed beyond telegraphic speech to expanded sentences. However, you may not discover exactly where each youngster stands at the outset because another set of circumstances has come into play. When young children who are still at the beginning stages of language learning leave the comfortable home environment where they are used to the people around them, and come into the strange, new environment of the preschool, they may stop speaking altogether at first.

Preschool teachers and assistants must understand that young speakers, no matter what their language and how fluent they are at home, may progress through several stages of language production before they become fluent speakers in the classroom. Although these stages are often applied to second-language acquisition, they can help teachers of all children aged three to five adjust to the new situation and progress in their language development (see Figure 10–1).

Some children are fluent speakers from the start and have no need to progress through these stages. Others are fluent at home but silent at preschool until they become acclimated to the new situation. How long this takes depends upon each child's development. Non-English-speaking children may take longer to progress through the stages as they acquire a new language.

Figure 10–1   Stages of language production in preschool

Adapted from Ramsey, 1987, pp. 157–158.

Preproduction Stage

When children first enter a strange, new language environment they often respond by being silent. Children who are learning English as a second language often concentrate on what is being said rather than trying to say anything.

Transition to Production

When children have settled in and become more comfortable they often begin speaking by giving single-word answers to questions.

Early Production

Children may respond to questions and activities in short phrases. They may be able to engage in simple conversations and even do chants and singing.

Expansion of Production

Children speak in expanded sentences, ask questions, tell stories, and carry on extensive conversations.

LISTENS BUT DOES NOT SPEAK

Preproduction Stage

For many English-speaking children, this first Checklist item refers more to the child's emotional adjustment to the classroom than to his or her speaking abilities. As previously noted, a child must feel at ease in the strangeness of the classroom environment and among her peers to speak at all. The so-called nonverbal child is frequently one who lacks confidence to speak outside the confines of the home. The child may have a shy nature or may come from a family that uses little verbal communication; or the child may have a physical disability, such as a hearing impairment, that has interfered with language development.

Spend time assessing a nonverbal child using the entire Child Skills Checklist. The areas of self-identity, emotional development, and social play are especially important. Does the child have trouble separating from her parents when she comes to the center? Can she do things for herself with any confidence? Does she seem happy? Does she play by herself or with others?

Set up a meeting with her parents and discuss the Checklist results with them. If the results point toward some type of impairment, the parents will want to have the child tested further by a specialist. If the parents indicate that the child talks fluently at home, then the nonverbal child may be demonstrating her feelings of insecurity in a strange new environment rather than a language problem.

Your principal task with the shy or uncommunicative child will be to help her feel comfortable in the classroom. Using pressure to get her to talk before she is at ease may well produce the opposite results. You and your coworkers will need to take special pains to accept the child as she is and to try to make her welcome in the classroom. You can invite her to join appropriate activities, but if she refuses, then you need to honor her reluctance. It often takes a great deal of patience and forbearance on the part of an early childhood classroom staff to allow the shy child to become at ease in her own good time.

If the nonverbal child seems to feel comfortable with one other child, then you may be able to have that child involve her with the others. On the other hand, sometimes the only solution is to leave the nonverbal child alone. If your environment is a warm and happy one, she eventually should want to participate.

Help the non-English-speaking child feel comfortable, too. Can someone on the staff speak his language? If a number of children in the classroom speak this same language, say Spanish, be sure to provide this language during the day. Bring in a Spanish speaker if none of the staff speaks Spanish. Perhaps a family member can visit or a high school or college student who wishes to practice the language. Language tapes and songs are available and should be used to help all the children learn new words through games and fun.

Provide a Stress-Free Environment

The environment must be stress-free. For many children, speaking among a group of peers is a new and untried experience. To help them feel at ease about speaking, you need to help them feel at ease about themselves by accepting them as they are. Show you accept them with smiles, hugs, and words of welcome and encouragement. Show you are happy to see them every day and want them to participate. Take time when they leave to say you were happy to have them in the class and look forward to seeing them tomorrow.

In addition, you need to accept everyone's language, no matter how poorly pronounced or how ungrammatical it is, and whether it is English, a dialect of English, or another language altogether. Language is a very personal thing. It reflects not only the different children's stages of development, but also their families' language. You must be especially careful not to correct a child's language. Telling him he is saying a word wrong or using the wrong word is a personal put-down for himself and his family. He will learn the correct form himself when the time is right by hearing you say the word and by practicing it with his peers. Nonverbal children watch closely and listen carefully to how you deal with other speakers in the classroom.

You and your coworkers can serve as good language models for everyone, helping and supporting them in classroom activities, but taking care not to correct their speech. Modern linguists now realize that it is pointless for adults to try to correct a preschooler's speech by making him repeat words according to an adult standard that he is not yet ready to use. Correcting, in fact, is a negative response that tends to reinforce the unwanted behavior and make the child think there is something wrong with him personally. Instead of improving a child's language, correcting often makes the child avoid speaking at all in the presence of the corrector.

Occasionally a child who has been pronouncing words normally will slip back into baby talk or stop talking altogether. She may also display other behaviors such as thumb sucking and wetting. Since this tends to be an indication of stress or an emotional upset, you will want to talk with the parents about the pressures in her life that may be affecting her adversely, causing the temporary language regression. Is there a new baby in the family? A new father or mother? A death or a divorce? Someone in the hospital? Someone out of work? A move? Young children feel these emotional upheavals in their families as severely as adults. Sometimes the first indication of such stress for a child is her slipping back to earlier speech patterns.

But because they are in a group of other child speakers, most young children will quickly revert back to the speech patterns and word pronunciations they hear around them, once the stress is relieved. Their brains are programmed to do such copying at this stage of their lives. Even non-English-speaking children will soon join the mainstream of language with continued exposure to mainstream speakers. The common mispronunciations of preschoolers should be overlooked rather than corrected. As soon as the development of their vocal apparatus allows them to, they will be pronouncing English words just like everyone else.

You can keep your classroom as free from stressful situations for the young child as possible. She should not be put on the spot and forced to perform verbally, creatively, or in any other way. Offer her opportunities and encouragement, but do not force the shy or unsure or bilingual child to speak.

If You Have Not Checked This Item: Some Helpful Ideas

■ Use a Prop for Security

Many young children feel more secure when they have something in their hands, especially something soft and cuddly with the quality of a security blanket. You might want to keep several stuffed animals for children to choose from and hold when feeling out of sorts, or when first coming to the classroom and not yet feeling comfortable. Your "nonverbal child" may even end up talking to her animal. It may be the beginning of her verbal integration into the classroom.

■ Use a Puppet

Almost every child likes the idea of putting a puppet on his hand. Have a box of various kinds of puppets and let the nonverbal child choose a different one every day if he wants. Preschool children tend to play with puppets as if the puppets are a part of themselves rather than a separate toy like a doll. Because puppets have mouths, children often first experiment by trying to bite someone with the puppet, in fun, of course. Later the youngsters get the idea of having the puppet speak with their mouth, perhaps in a whisper or in a different tone from their own voice. Shy children are often more willing to have a puppet speak for them than they are to speak for themselves. You might find yourself able to talk with a shy child's puppet through a puppet you put on your own hand.

Puppets can be played with alone, but they often lead naturally to involvement with other children. Thus, puppets are an excellent transition material to help the shy child integrate himself painlessly into the activities of the classroom.

■ Read a Book

Louie by Ezra Jack Keats (New York: Scholastic, 1975) tells the story of inner city boy Louie who has never been heard to speak a word. When he attends a neighborhood puppet show, he becomes entranced with the doll puppet Gussie, and says his first word: "Hello."

Chatterbox Jamie by Nancy Evans Cooney (New York: Putnam's, 1993) tells the story of Jamie, who talks up a storm at home but when he first goes to nursery school, can't bring himself to say a word. Days pass before he finally gets up the courage to tell about his own baby sister when Kristen's mother brings her baby to school.

GIVES SINGLE-WORD ANSWERS

Transition to Production

As teachers observe nonverbal children in the class, they may decide when the time is right to find out who will respond to a simple question that can be answered with one word such as "yes"/"no" or "here"/"there." If a child does respond, then teachers can expand these one-word questions to a small group that includes the nonverbal child.

Playing question-and-answer games with several children may help the nonverbal or bilingual child feel confident enough to try her own skill at answering. "What do you see on the top shelf that is blue?" or "What is Alex wearing on his feet today?" or "What is this we are having for a snack?" These games should be fun and not a test of right or wrong answers. Accept any answers the children give without a fuss.

Play follow-the-leader language games with a few children at a time, including the nonverbal child, having them march around the room behind you and name out loud any item you touch. The nonverbal or bilingual child will hear what the others say and may eventually join in. If children like this game, do it every day, touching more than one item at a time. Children love challenges, so think of other variants of this game you can play with them. How about a "Guess-What-I-Touched" game? Have the children cover their eyes while you go over to a shelf and touch something.

Have a Spanish speaker (or other language speaker) play the same simple games with the children, a small group at a time. Everyone can learn to name the items in Spanish as well as English. Once the nonverbal children join in the answering, you know they will soon be on their way to speaking more fully.

If You Have Not Checked This Item: Some Helpful Ideas

■ Help the Child Succeed at Something

All children need to experience success at this stage of their development. If they are having trouble speaking, then help them be successful at something else. Perhaps they can finger paint or model with clay or playdough. Such art activities are also therapeutic for children under stress.

■ Make Name Cards for Items Children Name

Children who can give only single-word answers may also be able to name items in the room from your follow-the-leader games. Have anyone interested go around the room with you one at a time while you write down each object they can name. Tape this name card to the object. This is not so much a reading activity as a motivation for speaking.

■ Have a Feelie Bag

Put several familiar objects from the classroom in a bag and ask each child from one of the small groups to put his hand inside, feel the object without taking it out, and try to guess what it is. Encourage everyone to try to name an object. Afterward, have children collect three or four objects themselves from the classroom shelves and make their own feelie bags to use with other children. Make sure nonverbal children and second-language speakers are in the group and have the opportunity to try their skill in guessing and saying the names of the objects if they want to.

■ **Read a Book**

The Dancer; La Bailarina by Fred Burstein (New York: Bradbury, 1993) takes a little Hispanic girl and her daddy through the streets of the city from home to her ballet class in 22 words, three on each page, saying the same thing in English, Spanish, and Japanese. She says "hello," "good-bye" and "thank you" phonetically in each of these languages, as well as commenting on the flowers and fish that she sees.

Table+Chair+Bear: A Book in Many Languages by Jane Feder (New York: Ticknor & Fields, 1995) shows a single object such as a bear, a chair, a mirror, or a tricycle on each page with the name of the object listed in 12 languages at the side in English, Korean, French, Arabic, Vietnamese, Japanese, Portuguese, Lao, Spanish, Chinese, Tagalog, Cambodian, and Navajo.

 GIVES SHORT-PHRASE RESPONSES

Early Production

As young children become more used to the classroom, they will begin to respond to your questions and comments in short phrases. When second-language speakers pick up enough English from the other children around them they, too, will respond in short phrases and incomplete sentences. When your English speakers learn enough of a second language you have introduced into the classroom, they should be able to repeat short phrases in that language, as well.

Some of the children mentioned above may already be fluent in English, but hesitant in speaking in the classroom because they are away from the comfort of their homes. When their comfort level in preschool is high enough, they will join in talking with the others, first with short phrases, then sentences.

Second-language speakers will pick up English quickly if this is the language spoken around them. They learn it not by being drilled in new words but by hearing the language spoken around them and trying it out as they join the other children in games and activities. They, too, may be hesitant at first in using these new words. You must accept any responses they give to your questions and comments, whether in English, their home language, or in gestures.

They may not pronounce the English words the same as the other children do at first, but they should see by your actions that you accept whatever they say. You can repeat their response to see if you got it right, if this seems appropriate. This gives them yet another chance to hear English responses without being corrected by the teacher.

Be sure language is spoken throughout the classroom throughout the day, not in children's shouting or noisy roughhousing, but in busy voices engaged in stimulating activities. As Ramsey (1987) notes:

> Sensory experiences also provide opportunities for children to hear and say a lot of descriptive words in a memorable context. Sliding down a slide or fire pole, feeling concealed objects, looking at pictures of familiar and unfamiliar objects, smelling different

substances, and moving one's body in unusual ways often prompt children to use descriptive and creative language. (p. 157)

If You Have Not Checked This Item: Some Helpful Ideas

■ Help the Child to Feel Accepted

Children want to talk like the others around them. Their mispronouncing of words may make them feel out of place, whether they are second-language speakers, dialect speakers, or nonfluent English speakers with articulation problems. You need to show by your actions and words that you accept the child as she is, that you are happy to have her in the class, and that you will support and encourage her in all her endeavors. Preschool-age children have the ability to pick up mainstream English pronunciation quickly when they are surrounded by English speakers. Your acceptance of the way they speak their home language and the way they pronounce English words is an important first step toward their success in language production.

■ Read a Book

My Kokum Called Today by Iris Loewen (Winnipeg, Manitoba, Canada: Pemmican Publications, 1993) is a wonderful story told in first person by a modern Cree Indian girl living in a big city with her mom, who gets a phone call from her "kokum" (grandmother) inviting them back to the Indian Reserve for a round dance. Although only a few words in Cree are used, child listeners will soon be saying "astum" meaning "come here," or "bannock" for biscuit, and perhaps be envious of the laughter and love expressed by the Cree people as they dance, sing, work, and play together.

In *Seya's Song* by Ron Hirschi (Seattle: Sasquatch Books, 1992) a S'Klallum Indian girl remembers the time when her grandmother ("seya") spoke to her in S'Klallum words. As this modern girl walks along a path down to the sea, she seems to hear these words once again. For every object she sees there is a S'Klallum word in parenthesis. (Children are often surprised to learn that the word for grandmother is different among different Indian nations.)

DOES CHANTING AND SINGING

Early Production

Just as they play with blocks, toys, and each other, children also play with words. Youngsters make up nonsense words, repeat word sounds, mix up words, say things backwards, make up chants, and repeat rhyming words. Most people pay little attention to this activity, as it seems so inconsequential. What we have not seemed to realize is that through this playful activity, children are once more at work creating their own knowledge. This time the content is language rather than cognitive concepts, and this time the child is manipulating the medium (words) with his voice rather than his hands or body. Once again he is structuring his experiences by finding out what words do and what he can do with them. Play is once more the vehicle because of the pleasure it gives him.

All children play with words, especially in the early stages of language development, but of course there are great individual differences in the amount of language play you will witness among your children. We do know that children who are involved in rhyming activities at an early age carry over this interest in poetry into adult life, and that children who have had early experience with nursery rhymes are more successful later in reading than children who have not (Caplan and Caplan, 1983, p. 41). It behooves us, then, to observe children's language play and provide encouragement and support for all youngsters to become more involved with chanting and singing.

Although mothers often promote language play with their infants by playing word and action games with them such as pattycake and peekaboo, much language play is solitary. Children carry on monologues in which they manipulate sounds, patterns, and meanings of words. These three areas have, in fact, been identified by specialists as common types of word play (Schwartz, 1981, pp. 16–26).

Infants from 6 to 18 months often "talk" to themselves before going to sleep, repeating rhythmic and rhyming sounds. The infants sound almost as if they are really talking, only with nonsense words. With older children, sound play contains more meaningful words, consonants, and blends. The children often repeat these words in nonsensical fashion: "Ham, bam, lamb, sam, wham, wham, wham."

Pattern play is a common form of play that involves manipulating the structure of the language. The child begins with a pattern and then substitutes a new word each time he says it: "Bobby go out; Mommy go out; Daddy go out; doggie go out" or "Bite it; write it; light it; sight it; night it; fight it."

Meaning play is not as common among younger children, but it is really more interesting. Here the child interchanges real with nonsensical meanings or makes up words or meanings. An interesting example Schwartz (1981) found was children doing water play with floating and sinking objects, and telling the objects to "sink-up," meaning "float" or "sink-down" (pp. 19–20).

Piaget describes much of the talk of three- to five-year-olds as egocentric. It is as if much of their speaking is not directed to anyone in particular, but produced for their own pleasure. Some children go around muttering to themselves most of the day, especially when they are involved in an interesting activity. The muttering seems to disappear by the time they enter public school, but it may become inner speech instead (Caplan & Caplan, p. 41).

Are any of the children in your class engaged in word play? They will be if you sponsor or promote it. Do finger plays and body action chants with the children during circle time or for transitions between activities. Singing of all kinds stimulates interest in rhyming words and word play.

Children who are not speaking in the classroom or who are speaking only one or two words can sing. Strangely enough, singing, which is controlled by the right hemisphere of the brain, can occur even when speaking, which is controlled by the left hemisphere, is limited. In addition, children who do not speak English can sing in

English. They may not understand the words, but they can sing or chant them along with the other children. Even shy, nonverbal children often join in singing before they have the courage to speak in the classroom.

With this information in mind, you should be filling your program with songs and chants. Children who get caught up in the joy of music will join in. Other children may hesitate at first, but may soon find the musical activities you provide to be so contagious they cannot resist. Do not force any child to participate. Invite everyone, and have such a good time yourself, no one will want to be left out!

To teach children songs and chants, you need to repeat them over and over with the children every day. Sing morning greeting songs, transition songs, finger plays at circle time, singing games in the large motor area, songs for seasonal holidays, songs for rainy days, sunny days, snowy days, songs about animals, and especially songs and chants about the children themselves.

Use nursery rhyme favorites of your own and make up words to familiar tunes, using the children's names whenever possible, and you will soon create an interested group of young singers. Records are fine for occasional use, but give your children a language boost by helping them learn their own words to songs and chants. You need not be a good singer yourself. The children will never know the difference. If you cannot sing, then chant with the children in unison or in a monotone, and clap your hands. For example:

(Tune: "Are You Sleeping?")
Where is Carmela?
Where is Carmela?
Here she is!
Here she is!
Very nice to see you,
Very nice to see you,
Come and play,
Come and play.

Other tunes you can use with your own words include:

"Here We Go 'Round the Mulberry Bush"
"Lazy Mary, Will You Get Up"
"Row, Row, Row Your Boat"
"Sing a Song of Sixpence"
"This Old Man"
"Twinkle, Twinkle Little Star"

Learn folksongs from different cultures through records, songbooks, the children themselves and their family members. Invite family members to visit the class and sing songs in their home language. English-speaking children can sing along, too, just as second-language children can sing your songs with English words. All it takes is repetition. Sing the songs and chants over and over. Children are geared to enjoy such repetition anyway. Remember the mastery stage of exploratory play?

Chants are rhyming verses spoken in unison rather than sung to a tune. Many chants, especially jump rope rhymes, are just like children's early sound, pattern, and meaning play. Perhaps that's why children enjoy them so. Children enjoy the sounds and rhythms of chanting as much as they do singing. As Buchoff (1994) notes:

> Chanting promotes successful language experiences for all children regardless of background or talent. It is useful for children who speak nonstandard English, as well as children who are learning English as a second language. (p. 26)

Like singing, you can chant verses from books or make up your own. Peppy, rhyming verses are best like those from jump rope rhymes and nonsense poetry. Pick out a verse from *Anna Banana, 101 Jump-Rope Rhymes* by Joanna Cole (New York: William Morrow, 1989) and try it out with the children. Have them repeat it with you over and over, making motions if they want, or clapping their hands. Do this on a daily basis and soon they will have memorized all the chants you share with them. Whether children understand the words makes no difference. Anyone who can speak can chant:

> *California oranges,*
> *Fifty cents a pack,*
> *Come on, Lashandra,*
> *Tap me on the back.*

Have the children themselves create their own chants. Soon everyone will want to join in. As Buchoff (1994) notes:

> Chanting is a worthwhile and exciting activity with creative opportunities limited only by the imagination of the teacher and the children. It makes hearing and using our language fun. And that is just what learning should be! (p. 27)

Still another language opportunity using music is singing games. Singing games ask for the children to listen to the words of the song and then follow the actions called for. Many singing games are on records. Some are concept games such as "This Is a Song About Colors," in which each child represents a particular color. The song asks each color to stand up or sit down at various times. The teacher should play the record first so the children can hear the directions before acting them out. After repeating this singing game many times, children will be able to sing and act out the song even without the record.

Traditional singing games can be sung and acted out without records:

> "Do the Hokey Pokey"
> "Go in and out the Windows"
> "London Bridge Is Falling Down"
> "The Farmer in the Dell"
> "Ring Around the Rosy"
> "The Grand Old Duke of York"

"Here We Go Looby Loo"
"Where, Oh Where Is Sweet Little Susy"
"Pass the Shoe from Me to You"

Children learn to follow the directions by repeating the games over and over. Some children do not understand the words they hear, but merely follow the other children around. Imitation like this is another effective language learning method for young children. Let children make up their own motions if they want, as some may be too complicated for preschoolers. Make it fun for all, but do not force any child to participate. Nonparticipants can listen and learn.

If You Have Not Checked This Item: Some Helpful Ideas

■ Make Up Your Own Singing Game

Have the children make up new words to a singing game they already know, and then act it out. For instance, instead of "The Farmer in the Dell," they could sing "The Keeper in the Zoo," and then act out the zoo animals that the keeper takes in descending size.

■ Read a Book

Teddy Bear, Teddy Bear, illustrated by Michael Hague (New York: Morrow, 1993), is a brightly illustrated book showing a teddy bear acting out verses of the classic action rhyme:

Teddy bear, teddy bear,
Turn around,
Teddy bear, teddy bear,
Touch the ground.

The Lady with the Alligator Purse adapted by Nadine Bernard Westcott (Boston: Little Brown, 1988) is another traditional jump rope rhyme acted out in nonsensical verses by Miss Lucy, Tiny Tim, and The Lady with the Alligator Purse, who saves the day by ordering pizza.

TAKES PART IN CONVERSATIONS

Early Production

Some children still in the early production stage of classroom language production may be able to engage in simple conversations with other children or with you. As soon as they are able to converse with ease, their speaking ability will show even greater improvement from practice with their peers, some of whom may speak at a

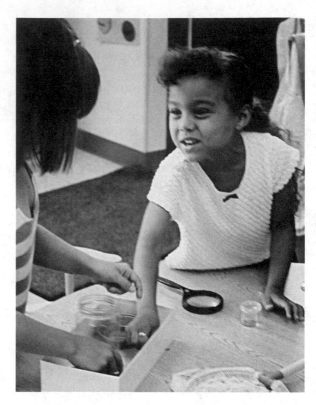

As soon as children are able to converse with ease, their speaking ability will show great improvement as they practice with their peers.

bit higher level. Children improve in speaking most rapidly when in the presence of speakers whose abilities are a bit higher than their own.

For this reason it is important to have mixed age groups in preschool programs. The younger children learn language skills from the older ones. The older children have an excellent opportunity to practice their skills with someone a bit younger. Even children seem to be able to adapt their language level intuitively to less mature speakers, thus enabling younger children to improve their speech.

Just as the infant is predisposed to acquire his own language in a particular manner, he also seems to bring with him in life a preprogrammed way to extract and learn the rules of conversation naturally. Researchers have noted that infants as young as 10 weeks are beginning to learn behaviors necessary for later conversation (Holzman, 1983, p. 3). For instance, to converse speakers must listen to what someone says, speak one at a time, and then pause for the other speaker to have a turn.

Another interesting finding is that mothers seem to treat their baby's gestures, cries, coos, smiles, and babbling as meaningful contributions to a real conversation. An infant's arm may reach out toward her rattle. The mother responds by picking up and giving the rattle to the child, at the same time conducting the following conservation: "Oh, you want your rattle. Here it is. Here's your rattle." Baby takes the rattle and shakes it. Mother replies. "Yes, your rattle. Your nice rattle." Baby pauses to hear mother say this, shakes the rattle, and smiles. Then the baby pauses to hear the mother again respond. "Oh, you like your rattle. Shake your rattle." The baby shakes the rattle, and pauses once more for the mother's response. The mother smiles and nods head in approval. "Shake, shake, shake," and so forth. Thus the rules for conversation are learned long before the child can speak.

We may wonder: Who is reinforcing whom? The mother starts the conversation, but the baby listens and replies with her physical response, which makes the mother say the next thing, and the baby responds again. It takes two to have a conversation. Children learn this from infancy, unless there is no one to talk to or no one who will listen. Parents who do not talk to their children during this preverbal period of development make a great mistake. We need to address children in their native language from the moment they are born if we want to motivate them to become fluent speakers themselves.

You have undoubtedly heard that one of the best things caregivers of preschoolers can do is read to their children. This is true. But an even greater contribution to their development is to converse with children, to listen and respond to them in conversational speech. Because many mothers intuitively treat preverbal youngsters as real contributors to conversations, the youngsters eventually become such. You can do the same with children in your classroom.

> When parents or teachers respond quickly and with enthusiasm to children's verbalizations, they enhance language. Displaying interest, physical warmth, and encouragement when children speak are a part of this responsive style; rich verbal responses to children's utterances are especially important. . . . Children come to recognize the power and importance of language when they see the impact it has on parents and teachers. (Trawick-Smith, 1994, p. 12)

Take time to have a personal conversation with each child in the class at least once during the day. Talk about things that are personally meaningful to the child, such as some activity she is engaged in at the moment. If you miss any of the children, start with them the next day. If they do not respond to your conversation, fill in for them as best you can. But always leave room for the child to do her part when she is ready.

If You Have Not Checked This Item: Some Helpful Ideas

■ Converse in Small Groups

Spend time every day in conversations with small groups of children. One of the best times is at snack or lunch. Be sure an adult sits at each of the children's tables and helps carry on a conversation. Talk normally about anything that interests you or the children. You do not have to be the "teacher" who is teaching them the names of the fruits on the juice can. Instead, relax and enjoy your snack or meal with the children. Say the kinds of things you would at your own meal table at home. "Whew, isn't it hot today? I think summer is coming early." "What's that you say, Jamal, you like summertime best of all?" "Me too. I love to swim and picnic." "You like to do that too, Marisa?" "Yes, you are lucky to live next to the park." Children who do not take part in this group conversation nevertheless listen to and learn from it.

■ Encourage Dramatic Play

Children's own conversations often take place in dramatic play situations. Puppets and dolls stimulate conversations, even imaginary ones. Bring in props to encourage imaginative play in the housekeeping area, the block-building area, and the water or sand table. Take props outside to encourage dramatic play there, too.

■ Read a Book

Anna Maria's Blanket by Joanne Barkan (New York: Barron's, 1990) is an imaginary tale about a little girl's blanket that gets upset and talks back to her because she is going to nursery school and plans to leave the blanket behind. The story is one long conversation between Anna Maria and her blanket. Colorful, realistic illustrations show Anna Maria playing with and caring for her doll and stuffed animal toys. She finally resolves the situation by showing the blanket how to be a babysitter when she is away.

Yo! Yes? by Chris Raschka (New York: Orchard, 1993) tells the simple story of two boy strangers, a black child and a white one, who meet on a city street and have a simple conversation with one or two huge words on each page. When they finally agree to become friends, they say "Yo!" on one page, "Yes!" on another and then both together on the same page, "Yow!"

SPEAKS IN EXPANDED SENTENCES

Expansion of Production

Young children ages three, four, and five are just at the age when their speaking develops most rapidly. From the simple phrases they spoke earlier, now they are suddenly able to expand the subjects and predicates of their sentences into longer, more complex thoughts. While their early communications included gestures—"Want more," they might have said as toddlers while pointing at a pitcher of milk—they now speak complete, expanded sentences, such as "I want some more milk," with no necessity for gestures.

How did this expanded language come about? Linguists are searching for answers by starting with infants and audiotaping their utterances, videotaping their interactions with their caregivers, and comparing infants' development with deaf children, children from other cultures, and children from a variety of backgrounds.

We know that soon after an infant walks, he talks. We also know that all human infants are predisposed to acquire their native language. Their brains are programmed to sort and store the information that will later be used in producing speech. Human infants give their attention to human voices, listening and then responding, at first in babbles, but as soon as possible in word sounds. Then sometime between a year and a half and two years of age, the infants realize that everything has a name. Immediately their vocabulary starts expanding as they begin to absorb the words for everything they see and touch.

This is the crucial time for meaningful caregiver intervention. The parent or caregiver can name objects and actions. The children listen and try to imitate. The caregivers will listen to the children and respond; all of this interaction takes place in the natural give-and-take manner of parents playing with their children.

This is also the crucial time for an enriched physical environment and the child's freedom to explore it. To learn names for things, the youngsters need to see them, feel them, hear them, try them out. Young children will want to see the doggie, pet the doggie, and laugh at the doggie's funny antics with a rubber bone. Young children learn words by interacting with the things that are represented by words in their environment. The more things the child interacts with, the more words the child will have the occasion to learn, as long as support, encouragement, and good language models are also at hand.

Young children do not learn word meanings by having someone teach the meanings, but rather they induce the meanings on the basis of hearing the words used in life experiences. Not only are young children predisposed to learn language this way, but adults and older children also seemed predisposed to "teach" children language this way. Observers watching mother-infant interactions soon picked up this behavior. The language behavior of the infant seemed to elicit the particular language behavior from the mother that was most appropriate to the infant's level of development. As the infant's ability improved, the mother's level of response expanded (Holzman, 1983, p. 87). Even more surprising is the fact that anyone playing with an infant seems able to adapt intuitively to the infant's language level, even other children.

Studies with four-year-old boys who had no younger brothers or sisters showed that the boys were able to adjust their language to a two-year-old with good language ability and another two-year-old with poorer skills, in explaining how a toy worked. The boys listened to the toddlers' responses to their own instructions and made adjustments intuitively (Holzman, 1983, pp. 107–108). This result may very well indicate that not only are infants born with the method for acquiring their native language, but also that the speakers around them are endowed with a similar skill for helping them acquire it.

By around age two, children are able to use the proper word order consistently in their primitive sentences. As they suddenly blossom into pretend play at this time, a parallel expansion seems to occur in their language. Their sentences grow longer and more complex, and their vocabularies increase (McCormick & Schiefelbusch, 1984, p. 72). Once they have absorbed the basic rules for forming sentences, they are on their way, for they then will no longer need to rely exclusively on imitating the language around them. Instead they will be able to produce sentences they have never heard. For most children, this mastery has occurred by age 4.

Obviously, it is important for children to be involved with competent speakers of the native language. If youngsters do not hear the language used or do not engage with someone in speaking it during these crucial years, they may have difficulty acquiring it.

You need to know which children in your class are speaking in the expanded sentences that most three-, four-, and five-year-old children should be able to use. Some who are not speaking in sentences may be shy or ill-at-ease children who have the ability but not the confidence to speak in the classroom. Others may come from homes where language is not used so extensively. Still others may come from homes where English is not spoken. For these and all of your children, you will want to provide rich language opportunities that allow the youngsters to hear sentences spoken and to respond.

For children learning English as a second language, it was once believed that their parents should learn English and use it with them at home rather than their native language. That is no longer true today. As Ramsey (1987) notes:

> Current research suggests that it is better for parents to continue to speak to their children in their home language. . . . The more skilled children are in their home languages, the more able they are to learn a second language. (p. 159)

Today we are coming to recognize the value of home languages that are different from English, and are finally beginning to promote rather than discourage their use by children and their parents. The National Association for the Education of Young Children (1996) has recently issued a position statement responding to linguistic and cultural differences in early childhood education that includes some of the following recommendations:

1. Recognize that all children are cognitively, linguistically and emotionally connected to the language and culture of their home.
2. Acknowledge that children can demonstrate their knowledge and capabilities in many ways.
3. Understand that without comprehensible input, second-language learning can be difficult.
4. Actively involve parents and families in the early learning program and setting.
5. Recognize that children can and will acquire the use of English even when their home language is used and respected.
6. Support and preserve home language usage. (pp. 4–12)

If Spanish is the first or second language for many of the children in your program, be sure to provide opportunities for all the children to be exposed to the language in a natural manner. Have a Spanish hour when nothing but Spanish is spoken. Read books and sing songs in Spanish. Do number games and dramatic play in Spanish. Children love to hear and say new words. Have their favorite chants and songs translated into Spanish, or get new ones from the book *Arroz con Leche: Popular Songs and Rhymes from Latin America* by Lulu Delacre (New York: Scholastic, 1989). If you do not speak Spanish, invite a speaker from a nearby high school, college, or the children's families.

> A second language is truly a gift that everyone should feel good about receiving; both the Hispanic children whose language you have recognized, and the non-Hispanic children who have learned to say and understand simple phrases in the new language. (Beaty, 1996, p. 135)

But what if your program includes numbers of children who speak many different languages? Inner-city early childhood programs are becoming more language-diverse than ever these days. How can you accommodate such diversity? Ramsey (1987) describes a program attended by children of foreign students representing 15 different languages. The program rose to the occasion by requesting the parents to help them make a book with simple sentences in all 15 languages that the teachers often needed, such as

> "Your mother will be here soon" or "Do you need to go to the bathroom?" The parents and their children then enjoyed coaching the teachers. This activity also gave the foreign families, who were having to experience daily their lack of expertise in English, the opportunity to be the experts. (p. 160)

If You Have Not Checked This Item: Some Helpful Ideas

■ Provide Dramatic Play Opportunities

Children's imaginative play is one of the best preschool activities to motivate and promote language growth in young children. Youngsters take on roles in which they must produce dialog. Even the shy, nonverbal child will learn by listening to the others. Be sure to schedule enough time for children to become involved in this pretending type of play. Take a role yourself to help the shy child join the others. Once he is involved, you should withdraw.

■ Go on Field Trips

Children need many real experiences with their world to process and use information in thinking and speaking. Give the youngsters many new things to think and talk about by going on field trips. These out-of-class experiences do not have to be elaborate or to distant locations. Have one adult take three children down to the corner store to buy something. Take a small group on a walk around the block to see how many different sounds they can hear. Be sure to take a tape recorder along to play back and discuss later. Go on a field trip to a tree every week in the spring or fall to see how it changes. You may want to take along a camera to record the experience and to motivate talk about it back in the classroom. Be sure to use new vocabulary words to label the new things and ideas the children have experienced. Also label them in a second language if this is appropriate. Then use them over and over with the children.

Listen to children's own interests. Have they ever really explored the building they are in? Do they know where the heat is produced? Young children are fascinated by things like furnaces, which adults take for granted. Take the children to see such things, and then listen to the sentences they produce.

■ Read a Book

Abuela by Arthur Dorros (New York: Dutton, 1991) tells the story of a little Hispanic girl from New York City, Rosalba, and her grandma "Abuela" who came from Puerto Rico. Your children may be excited to learn yet another word for "grandma." This grandma takes care of Rosalba while her parents are at work. They go by bus to the park, where they feed the pigeons. Since Abuela speaks mostly Spanish, the pages are interlaced with single words and simple sentences in Spanish that Rosalba explains to the readers. Then they take off (in their imaginations) to soar above the city, out to the airport, and even above the Statue of Liberty. A wonderful Rosalba doll can be purchased with the book to give your children yet another experience in recreating this bilingual adventure.

ASKS QUESTIONS

Expansion of Production

This language skill is another good indication that your children's command of language is developing normally. Most children are able to ask questions as adults do by about age four. Before that, they go through a predictable sequence in learning to ask questions just as they do in other areas of development.

Children usually do not learn to ask questions until they have learned to answer them when you ask them something. Between a year and a half and two years of age, when they are putting a few words together to form primitive sentences, they also ask their first questions, if caregivers have been asking them questions first. The word order of these first questions is the same as a statement but with a rising intonation at the end: "Jamie drink milk?" meaning "May Jamie have a drink of milk?" or "Should Jamie drink his milk?"

Next, they begin to learn the use of the "wh" words at the beginning of questions, words like *what, where,* and *who*: "Where Mama going?" or "Where going?" meaning "Where is Mama going?" This type of question becomes quite popular because the adult generally responds, and suddenly the child realizes he has stumbled onto another way of controlling an adult: asking a question that the adult will answer. This is not always true with mere statements. Since he delights in adults' attention and their responses to things that he originates, he will often burst into a period of questioning. It is not only that he wants to know the answer, but also that he wants an adult's attention.

The next stage in learning to ask questions comes as he expands his sentences to include auxiliary verbs such as *can* and *will*. These questions, though, are often expressed in inverted order; for example, "Where Daddy will go?" instead of "Where will Daddy go?"

The final stage is the expanded question in proper word order, which most children are able to ask at around four years: "Can I go with you?" "What are you doing?" "Why doesn't the light go on?"

If you discover through your observation that certain children have not yet attained this level, what will you do? Will you sit down with them and teach them how to ask a question correctly? If you have been reading this text carefully, you know the answer is "no." Young children do not develop language skills by being taught formally. How do they learn? They learn language just as they learn to develop their perceptual skills: They teach themselves word order by hearing the language forms spoken around them and by practicing language themselves when their physical and mental development have progressed to the point at which they can do so.

If You Have Not Checked This Item: Some Helpful Ideas

■ Ask Questions Yourself

When you understand that children do not ask questions until they have learned to answer them, then you will include your own asking of questions in your activities with the children. Circle time is a good time for everyone to hear the English word order of questions, and to volunteer to answer the inquiries if so inclined. Even the children who are not at the point of answering questions in front of a group will learn by listening.

■ Ask Children to Help You Gather Answers to Questions

You can ask a child to ask three or four other children for some information you need. For example, if you are planning a field trip, you might ask several children to go around asking others if their mothers would like to come along. This may not be the most accurate way to gather this information, but it is excellent practice in questioning skills, and you can always check the accuracy of the information with the parents later.

■ Read a Book

Mama, Do You Love Me? by Barbara M. Joosse (San Francisco: Chronicle Books, 1991) is the highly acclaimed story of the little Inuit (Eskimo) girl Dear One who asks her mother this question over and over, upping the ante each time. Her mother replies in a kind of folk poetry that captivates young children listeners. "How long?" "Till the stars turn to fish in the sky, and the puffin howls at the moon." Vivid illustrations show a puffin howling, ptarmigan eggs breaking, lemmings in mukluks, and Dear One turning into a musk ox, walrus, and polar bear. But still the mother's love holds firm, and the two dance together at last in bright dresses against the white Arctic background. A Dear One doll also accompanies this book, making it possible for your children to be the little Inuit questioner herself as they re-create this story.

 CAN TELL A STORY

Expansion of Production

Children whose speaking has become fluent in all the other Checklist items are often competent and confident enough to tell full-blown stories about themselves or those around them to individuals, to small groups, and sometimes to the total group. Not every child will be able or willing to perform such a linguistic feat, but some are.

If your book center shelves are stocked with good books that you read to the children, some of them will develop the ability to tell these stories themselves.

Before children can tell such stories, though, they must first have experienced hearing many stories told and read to them. If the reading and telling of stories holds a prominent place in your program, and if your book center shelves are stocked with some of the fine books mentioned in this text, then you should have some child storytellers.

Are you a storyteller? If you want your children to participate in storytelling themselves, then they need an adult model to imitate. Don't believe you are too shy to tell stories. Anyone can do it. After all, what is a story? An anecdote, an experience, an adventure, a fable, a tale. Not every story comes from a book. Did you tell the children what happened to you on the way home from the center yesterday? That's a story. Did you tell them what your pet cat did when the neighbor's dog got into the yard? That's another story. All of life that is happening around you and the children can be woven into story after story.

What happened when the children went on a field trip to the pet store, or museum, or zoo? What about the little kitten in the cow barn at the farm you all visited? How did that pesky squirrel finally reach the birdseed you put up so high in your bird feeder? All of these incidents make fine oral stories. Keep your senses alert for such daily storytelling possibilities and you will soon have a long list.

Begin telling the children some of these interesting anecdotes at circle time, and they will quickly respond with stories of their own. Maybe something about the new baby, or their pet iguana, or the trick their brother played last night, or the trip they are going to take during the summer. When other children see how interested you are about such stories, they will want to contribute, too.

You may want to write down the stories children tell about the field trip they went on or an incident from their lives. Use a big pad of newsprint so everyone can see what you write as the child dictates. Be sure to reread this story aloud over and over in the days to follow. Remember how important repetition is for children's early learning. Children can dictate stories into a cassette recorder, too, and play them back whenever they want.

> Research indicates that children must experience many types of dramatic play and story-telling to reach optimal language and literacy development. The responsibility for story-telling was once restricted to the teacher's domain. Renewed attention on developmentally appropriate practices, however, has shifted the responsibility to include the child. Children are now being asked to tell their own stories, including original make-believe versions and retelling of old favorites. Teachers are exploring ways to incorporate children's experiential background when guiding children to verbalize stories. (Soundy & Genisio, 1994, p. 20)

If You Have Not Checked This Item: Some Helpful Ideas

■ Tell Group Stories

Keep your senses alert for a good story theme about something that happens in the classroom or on the playground. Afterwards, gather the group together and talk about it: what happened when the storm came and the electricity went off; where they think the ambulance was going so quickly with its siren blaring; how Ross felt when he finally had the courage to swing hand over hand across the monkey bar.

Different children can tell their versions of these incidents. Be sure you accept every version. Can anyone make up an imaginary version of the incident? Bring in one of the storybook dolls such as Dear One from *Mama, Do You Love Me?* or Rosalba from *Abuela.*

How do the children think they would relate the episode? Can anyone do it? What about one of the animals from the block center? Or how about one of the plastic dinosaurs? What would he have to say?

■ Do Tape-Recorded Stories

You could start a story on the tape and ask interested children to finish it. You might start something like: "As I was coming to school today, I heard a very strange noise. It sounded a little like a train. It sounded like it was coming around the corner. I felt like running away, but I didn't. Instead, I. . . . "

You can pass the tape recorder around a small group and have each child in the group add to the story. Afterwards, play it for all to hear. Later children may want to start their own stories and pass the recorder around.

■ Read a Book

Cloudy with a Chance of Meatballs by Judi Barrett (New York: Atheneum, 1978) is a hilarious tall tale of a world in which food falls from the sky. The story might motivate your children to make up their own tall tales about food. What kind of food would fall in their stories? What would happen to it?

Isla by Arthur Dorros (New York: Dutton, 1995) contains familiar characters for children who have heard the story of *Abuela* the Hispanic grandma and her granddaughter Rosalba. In this new adventure, Abuela tells Rosalba a story about *la isla*, the island where she grew up, Puerto Rico. Then they fly there together in their imagination and visit friends, relatives, forests, towns, cities, beaches, and the harbor.

Can your children tell any stories they have heard from their own grandparents or others? You might invite a family member to come in and tell such a story to the group. If the relative speaks a language different from English, ask someone to come along who will translate. Encourage the telling of stories in languages other than English. When you read *Isla*, be sure to point out the Spanish words that Abuela uses.

Native Americans consider storytellers to be important members of their communities. The boy narrator of the story *Knots on a Counting Rope* by B. Martin and J. Archambault (New York: Holt, 1987) is blind, but loves to hear his grandfather tell him the story of his birth and of how he got his proud name "Boy-Strength-of-Blue-Horses." When the boy finally rides his horse across the finish line in the exciting tribal day horse race, his grandfather is able to paint a vivid word picture for the boy about his perilous ride. Then he can tie a wonderful new knot in his storytelling counting rope.

OBSERVING, RECORDING, AND INTERPRETING SPOKEN LANGUAGE

The language Checklist results for Sheila were much like the teachers in her classroom had predicted (see Figure 10–2). Every item was checked except "Takes part in conversations." Although Sheila spoke to other children, it was rarely in the form of conversation, but more often a command or a complaint. Because Sheila showed evidence of "Speaks in expanded sentences," the staff members believed Sheila eventually would join in with other children in classroom activities, including conversation. In fact, Sheila's language skill could be used to help her become involved with the others. The teachers made plans for Sheila to tell several other children, one at a time, how to use one of the computer programs that the class had recently acquired.

Child Skills Checklist

Name _____Sheila — Age 3_____ Observer _____Connie R_____

Program _____HeadStart_____ Dates _____10 - 22_____

Directions:

Put a ✔ for items you see the child perform regularly. Put *N* for items where there is no opportunity to observe. Leave all other items blank.

Item	Evidence	Dates
8. Spoken Language		
_N_ Listens but does not speak	She is beyond this level	10/22
_N_ Gives single word answers	She is beyond this level	10/22
_N_ Gives short-phrase responses	She is beyond this level	10/22
✔ Does chanting and singing	Yes; likes to repeat rhyming verses- "see you later, alligator"	10/22
____ Takes part in conversations	speaks to others but does not converse	10/22
✔ Speaks in expanded sentences	"she ate my orange crayon so I can't finish my pumpkin"	10/22
✔ Asks questions	yes	10/22
✔ Can tell a story	Yes; she tells long anecdotes to teachers, not children	10/22

Figure 10–2   Spoken language observations for Sheila

REFERENCES

Beaty, J. J. (1997). *Building bridges with multicultural picture books: For children 3–5.* Upper Saddle River, NJ: Merrill/Prentice Hall.

Buchoff, R. (1994). Joyful voices: Facilitating language growth through the rhymthic response to chanting. *Young Children, 49*(4), 26–30.

Caplan, T., & Caplan, F. (1983). *The early childhood years: The 2 to 6 Year Old.* New York: Putnam.

Davidson, J. (1996). *Emergent literacy and dramatic play in early education.* Albany, NY: Delmar.

Holzman, M. (1983). *The language of children.* Upper Saddle River, NJ: Merrill/Prentice Hall.

McCormick, L., & Schiefelbusch, R. L. (1984). *Early language intervention.* Upper Saddle River, NJ: Merrill/Prentice Hall.

NAEYC. (1996). NAEYC position statement: Responding to linguistic and cultural diversity—recommendations for effective early childhood education. *Young Children, 51*(2), 4–12.

Ramsey, P. G. (1987). *Teaching and learning in a diverse world: Multicultural education for young children.* New York: Teachers College Press.

Schwartz, J. I. (1981). Children's experiments with language. *Young Children, 36*(5), 16–26.

Soundy, C. S., & Genisio, M. H. (1994). Asking young children to tell the story. *Childhood Education, 71*(1), 20–23.

Trawick-Smith, J. (1994). Authentic dialogue with children: A sociolinguistic perspective on language learning. *Dimensions of Early Childhood, 22*(4), 9–15.

SUGGESTED READINGS

Alvarado, C. (1996). Working with children whose home language is other than English: The teacher's role. *Child Care Information Exchange, #*107 (Jan/Feb), 48–55.

Barrera, R. M. (1996). What's all the fuss? A frank conversation about the needs of bilingual children. *Child Care Information Exchange, #*107 (Jan/Feb), 44–47.

Barton, B., & Booth, D. (1990). *Stories in the classroom: Storytelling, reading aloud and roleplaying with children.* Portsmouth, NH: Heinemann.

Cobb, J., & Rusher, A. (1996). "Grand conversations" with multicultural books. *Dimensions of Early Childhood, 24*(3), 5–10.

Genishi, C., & Dyson, A. H. (1996). Ways of talking: Respecting differences. *Child Care Information Exchange, #*110, 43–46.

Honig, A. S. (1995). Singing with infants and toddlers. *Young children, 50*(5), 72–78.

Neuman, S. B., & Roskos, K. A. (1993). *Language and literacy in the early years: An integrated approach.* Ft. Worth, TX: Harcourt Brace.

Torgerson, L. (1996). Starting with stories: Building a sense of community. *Child Care Information Exchange, #*109 (May/June), 55–58.

Wolf, D. P. (1996). Children's conversations: Why are they important? *Child Care Information Exchange, #*110, 40–42.

VIDEOTAPES

Goldman, B. D., Roberts, J. E., & Nychka, H. *SMALLTALK: Creating conversations with young children* (six-tape set). Child Development Media, Inc., 5632 Van Nuys Blvd., Van Nuys, CA, 91401.

INREAL, *Language in action: Developmentally appropriate practices for supporting young children's construction of language in a social context.* Child Development Media, Inc., 5632 Van Nuys Blvd., Van Nuys, CA, 91401.

LEARNING ACTIVITIES

1. Use the Child Skills Checklist spoken language section as a screening tool to observe all the children in your classroom. Which children seem to need help in more than one of the items? How do these children fare in the various areas of cognitive development?

2. Choose a child who seems to be having difficulty with spoken language and observe him or her on three different days doing a running record of language activities. Compare the results with the Checklist results. How do you interpret the evidence you have collected? Are any pieces of evidence still missing about this child's language performance?

3. Choose a child whom you have screened as needing help in several of the Checklist items, and carry out one or more of the activities listed. Record the results.

4. Teach the children a chant or singing game. How did the children perform whom you noted as needing help in this area? What can you do to help if necessary?

5. Do a tape recorder activity with a small group of children. Have them tape record their own words and then play them back. They may want to tell about themselves, tell a story, or say a verse.

CHAPTER 11

Prewriting and Prereading Skills

PREWRITING AND PREREADING CHECKLIST

- [ ] Pretends to write with pictures and scribbles
- [ ] Makes horizontal lines of writing scribbles
- [ ] Includes letter-like forms in writing
- [ ] Makes some letters, prints name or initial
- [ ] Holds book right-side up; turns pages left to right
- [ ] Pretends to read using pictures to tell story
- [ ] Retells stories from books with increasing accuracy
- [ ] Shows awareness that print in books tells the story

DEVELOPING PREWRITING AND PREREADING SKILLS

Why should a chapter on children's writing and reading skills be included in a book on observing the development of preschool children? Surely learning to write and to read has little to do with child development, does it? Teaching children to write and read should come later when children are in first grade, shouldn't it? The answers to these questions are quite different today than they would have been as recently as 15 or 20 years ago.

Today research shows more clearly how writing and reading can be developed naturally by children, how children make sense of their world through playful exploration, and how children's brains take in this information and extract rules from it to help the children use it. Such research has changed our minds forever about the way children develop and how we can best support their growth.

We know now that writing and reading are outgrowths of the same communication urge that drives children to express themselves orally and even pictorially. We also know that given the proper tools and support, all children everywhere go through the same sequence of stages in teaching themselves to write and to read. It is true that learning to write and to read are as much a natural part of a child's development as learning to talk. Child development specialists are finally coming to realize that "learning to write is largely an act of discovery," as one specialist puts it (Temple, Nathan, & Burris, 1993, p. 2).

The term used currently to describe children's natural development of writing and reading skills is **emergent literacy**. Scholars studying child development have this to say about it:

> In both oral and written language systems, children construct personally meaningful rule systems based on their developing understandings of oral and written language surrounding them in their daily life experiences (Schrader & Hoffman, 1987, p. 9).

From these personal rule systems, children teach themselves to talk (as discussed in Chapter 10) and also to write and read, as we will discuss here.

Thus, writing and reading join language, thinking, emotional, social, and motor skills as other aspects of development that children can arrive at on their own by playfully experimenting with the materials in their environment.

This does not mean, however, that writing and reading development always occur naturally in all children. Many youngsters come from families with few toys, let alone books for reading or the tools for writing. Furthermore, most parents are unaware that their children can develop these skills naturally. Children need their parents' support to progress in this natural development. They need the tools to write with, the print materials in their environment, and encouragement to try them out on their own. In addition, children need to practice prewriting and prereading skills over time, just as they do running or speaking.

Without tools to write with at home, preschoolers can do little more than make marks on steamy windows or scratches in the dirt. Without books to look at, preschoolers have little motivation to try reading. Without parents' modeling their own reading and writing, children have no reason to think this is something they should do. Without parent expectations that they should experiment with writing and reading on their own, children may never try it.

On the other hand, this does not mean teachers should sit down with preschool children and formally teach them how to write and read, any more than they should formally teach them how to walk and talk. Cognitive psychologists worry that preschool teachers, who are in a critical position for nurturing in young children the "roots of literacy," may not know how to do it.

> When teachers are unfamiliar with current knowledge about the natural development of literacy in young children, they impose skill-oriented expectations and tasks on these youngsters—copying and tracing standard adult print, for example. Such activities not only are stressful for three-, four-, and five-year-old children, but they do not afford children the opportunity to use their self-constructed knowledge in meaningful ways (Schrader & Hoffman, 1987, p. 13).

Instead, we should be filling the children's environment with examples of written language and books; we should serve as models by doing a great deal of writing and reading ourselves in the presence of the children; and we should provide them with the tools and encouragement to attempt writing and reading on their own.

Although the natural development of writing and reading occur simultaneously in children, this chapter discusses writing first and then reading.

Do any of your children pretend to write, perhaps at the easel, by scribbling letter-like symbols? Do any of them insist on writing their own name on their art products? Assess all the children in your classroom by using the first four items of the prewriting and prereading checklist. Then set up a writing table or a writing area complete with a variety of writing tools, and watch what happens.

PRETENDS TO WRITE WITH PICTURES AND SCRIBBLES

Young children's first natural attempts to write are usually scribbles. Isn't this drawing, you may wonder? Initial scribbling is also done at the outset in art, you may point out.

True, children do not at first distinguish between drawing and writing. At an easel, they may be scribbling a picture or scribbling their own idea of writing, or both together. But if easel painting is new to them, they are probably doing neither painting nor writing. Instead, they may be just trying out the brush and paint; in other words, manipulating the medium, the first stage of the "3-M's" playful exploration process.

You can ask them what they are doing, but often they are just playing around with the painting tools without any particular product in mind. Both drawing and writing are a fascinating process for young children when they start. They are not planning to produce a picture or a written message. This tends to be an adult's objective. Preschool children may be just learning to control the brush and paint: quite a lengthy process for some children who have had no practice at home with painting or writing tools. Remember that self-directed exploratory learning takes time for preschool children. Give them plenty of time and encouragement to experiment.

At the flat surface of a writing table, the same process is at work, but the tools seem to make a difference. Children recognize that pens and pencils are used for writing. Crayons and felt markers may be used for drawing or for writing. Children often combine the two in their initial attempts. Once again they may be manipulating the medium, but some will be experimenting with early writing that includes pictures.

> Out of scribble, around ages 3 to 6, children begin to figure out that these marks on paper can be signs of meaning. They now attempt to discover strategies for conveying an idea, a thought, or something they like to others. And like reading at this age, their notions of print and pictures overlap; just like a picture is seen as conveying a narrative, so is a picture in writing thought of as symbolizing text. (Neuman and Roskos, 1993, p. 41)

Children's early attempts at writing vary greatly according to what discoveries they have made about the writing they see done around them at home, in school, on television, in stores, and restaurants. In dramatic play, they may make a scribble on a pad while "taking an order" at the pretend restaurant. In the classroom writing center, they may cover a page with swirls, lines, and circles that start in the middle and go around the outside. The lines may include a head with arms and legs protruding or an oval with "rabbit ears" as they write a letter to a friend about their pet. On the signup sheet for a turn at the computer they may print one wiggly letter-like symbol that represents their name, or they may make another head with arms and legs to represent themselves.

Ferreiro and Teberosky in their now-classic book *Literacy Before Schooling* (1982) note:

> In children's own first spontaneously produced graphic representations, drawing and writing are undifferentiated. Gradually some lines acquire forms like drawings, while others evolve towards imitations of the most salient characteristics of written language. (p. 52)

Although drawing and writing both represent things symbolically, the two are quite different. Drawing maintains a similarity to the object it represents, whereas writing does not. Writing is an entirely different system having its own rules, whereas drawing does not. Young children are unaware of the difference initially and thus use both pictures and scribbles interchangeably in their early writing.

As children make new discoveries about print through their own explorations and their involvement with picture books, they construct their own ideas about writing. At some point children seem to recognize that writing is different from drawing, and their scribbles take a somewhat different form. Children as young as three years may recognize the difference between writing scribbles and drawing scribbles. In fact, some children do drawing scribbles on one part of an easel paper and writing scribbles that "tell about the picture" on another part (Vukelich & Golden, 1984, p. 4).

The two kinds of scribbles often look completely different. Writing scribbles may be smaller and done in a horizontal linear manner across the top or bottom of the page, something like a line of writing. But not always. Individual differences in writing scribbles vary greatly, with some squeezed together at one side of the drawing and others just a circle or line in a corner. The children who make such writing scribbles seem to understand that writing is something that can be read, and they sometimes pretend to read their scribbled writing. This is one of the first steps in the natural acquisition of writing.

If You Have Not Checked This Item: Some Helpful Ideas

■ Set up a Writing Center

If our goal is to encourage children to explore writing on their own, then we must provide a setting for this to occur. A writing center can be just as exciting for children as a block center. Most programs put a table in their writing center with writing supplies on a nearby shelf. Some centers report that a more enticing piece of equipment is a real child-size writing desk, perhaps the rolltop variety or the type used in children's bedrooms. Drawers can be filled with the tools of writing: pads, tablets, paper, envelopes, cards, stickers, tape, rulers, rubber stamps and stamp pads, paper clips, paper punches, erasers, pencils, pens, and markers. Or keep these items in plastic containers on nearby shelves. Another desk or table can hold a typewriter or computer (or both). A stand-up chalkboard or small individual boards encourage scribbling and writing with chalk, as well. On the wall should be a bulletin board for displaying children's scribbled messages.

■ Fill Room with Environmental Print

What written symbols and signs do you notice in your home environment or on the way to the classroom? Books, magazines, newspapers, catalogs, phone books, ads on TV, posters, cereal boxes, food containers, T-shirts, letters, computer keys, computer programs, street signs, traffic signs, gas station signs, fast food restaurant logos, store signs, billboards, all kinds of advertising, and on and on. This is what we mean by *environmental print*. All these symbols and signs can be featured in the classroom as well. Each of the learning centers can have its own signs and labels. Put out old magazines and catalogs and have children cut out pictures of favorite signs to be pasted in a sign scrapbook.

■ Read a Book

Good Morning Franny, Good Night Franny by Emily Hearn (Toronto, Canada: The Women's Press, 1984) is the story of two city girls: Franny, who propels herself swiftly down the city streets in her wheelchair; and Ting, the Chinese girl from the variety store whom she befriends. Franny helps Ting to learn English, writing their names and the words "good morning" and "good night" in Ting's scrapbook. One day when Franny wheels down to Kim's store, it is empty and Kim has gone. Sadly she wheels herself out to the park where they had played, and there on the sidewalk at the park entrance are written in chalk the words "good morning Franny." At the exit she also finds words on the sidewalk: "good night Franny."

MAKES HORIZONTAL LINES OF WRITING SCRIBBLES

Once children's scribbles have become horizontal lines instead of circular or aimless meanderings, they are indicating they understand writing is something different from drawing. Still their first scribbled lines do not resemble letters or words at all. Temple (1993) notes how different learning to write actually is from what logic tells us it ought to be:

> Learning to write, it would seem, is nothing other than learning to make letters and to combine them into words. But studies of writing development have suggested that young children learn to write through a process that is quite the opposite. Rather than learning to write by mastering first the parts (letters) and then building up to the whole (written lines), it appears that children attend first to the whole and only much later to the parts. (p. 19)

Young children, in fact, seem to have extracted through their own observations only the broad general features of the writing system: that it is arranged in rows across a page and that it consists of a series of loops, tall sticks, and connected lines that are repeated. Only later will children differentiate the finer features of the system: separate words and letters.

Where have they acquired even this much knowledge of written language so early in life? Look around you. They, like all of us, are surrounded by written material: in newspapers and magazines, in television advertising, on the labels on food products, on soft drink bottles, in letters in the mail, in the stories read to them, on store signs, on greeting cards, on car bumper stickers, and on T-shirts. The printed word is everywhere. This is the writing referred to previously as *environmental print*.

Some families, of course, encourage their children to print their own names at an early age, and may even take time to write out the creative stories that their young children tell them. Some children have older brothers or sisters who bring written material home from school. Some children come from homes with computers. These children see family members engaged in writing or reading and try to become involved themselves.

Observe to discover which of your children do pretend writing, this first step in the writing process; which ones have progressed beyond this beginning; and which have not yet started.

As young children create their own knowledge about writing, they will be extracting certain information from the writing around them that Marie Clay, the New Zealand literacy specialist, calls principles and concepts:

1. *Recurring principle:* Writing uses the same shapes again and again.
2. *Generative principle:* Writing consists of a limited number of letters from which you can generate a limitless amount of writing.
3. *Sign concept:* Print stands for something besides itself, but does not look like the object it stands for.
4. *Flexibility principle:* The same letter form may be written in different ways, but the direction the letter faces is the same.
5. *Page-arrangement principle:* English is usually written in lines of print from left to right and top to bottom on a page. (Adapted from Clay, 1975; Temple, 1993; Davidson, 1996)

Can you tell which of these principles the children who scribble in horizontal lines have extracted? Probably 1 and 2, and possibly 4. As they repeat lines of loops, sticks, crosses, or circles across the page in their imitation of writing, children are exhibiting the recurring principle of writing: "that writing consists of the same moves repeated over and over" (Temple, 1993, p. 2). Horizontal lines of scribbles like this are not always produced from left to right or top to bottom. Children sometimes start at the bottom or the middle of the page and they may even write one line from the left and one from the right.

At the same time, youngsters are also displaying the *mastery* stage of "3-M's" exploratory play. They will fill pages with lines of scribbled "writing" like this, and it gives them great satisfaction. After playing around with this new skill during the manipulation stage, children now repeat this scribbled writing over and over in order to master it. At the easel or at the writing table or desk you will see certain children hard at work filling their papers with these horizontal lines, just as if they were writing a letter or a story.

Be sure it is the children who are in charge of this natural emergence of literacy. You should not be the one to set goals for their writing. Instead, observe where each child stands in her own developmental sequence, put out new materials to keep her interested, and comment favorably about what she is doing. "Latoya, you have certainly worked hard this morning filling so many pages with writing. Would you like to put it up on the writing center bulletin board?"

If some children show no interest in becoming involved with prewriting activities like this, do not pressure them to try. You can invite them to experiment with using markers or chalk or whatever materials you put out daily. They may hear you comment on the writing that other children have done. Then it is up to them, not you, to decide to try it for themselves.

Voluntary and not enforced participation in writing activities should be the rule in your program. Some children need to develop better eye-hand coordination before they engage in flat surface writing. They might learn more from painting at the easel or playing with the utensils you have put out at the water or sand tables instead. If the youngsters can build a tall block tower without its toppling over, can drive a nail straight into a piece of wood, or can use a pair of scissors with ease, then their eye-hand coordination is probably developed enough for them to use a writing implement.

If You Have Not Checked This Item: Some Helpful Ideas

■ Put out a Variety of Writing Materials

Most children will not try to become involved in writing if there is no sign of writing in their environment. If you do not have a special writing center, set up a writing table or desk with different implements, and you will soon have a group of budding writers.

For paper it is best to use unlined sheets. Children will be placing their scribbles all over the page at first, and lined paper may inhibit this free form exploration of how writing works. For them to progress to horizontal scribbles, they need blank sheets of paper. Use typing paper or stationery as well as tablets and pads of different sizes and colors.

For writing tools, you will want to include a variety, and change them every week or so. We sometimes think of pencils first, but research with beginning writers shows that pencils are the most difficult of all writing implements for young children to manipulate effectively (Lamme, 1979, p. 22). Children themselves choose colored felt-tip markers as their favorites. You should also include colored chalk and a small chalkboard, crayons, and a few pencils, in addition to the markers. It is not necessary to have only the large primary-size pencils. Some preschoolers have great difficulty handling these thick pencils and prefer to use regular pencils. Put out a variety of writing tools, and children will find out on their own what works best for them.

■ Use Sand or Salt Trays or Finger Painting

Put out small trays of sand or salt in your writing area so children can practice "writing" with their fingers. It is easy to "erase" this writing simply by shaking the tray. Finger painting on tabletops or paper also gives the children practice doing linear mock writing with their fingers.

■ Be a Writing Model Yourself

Do a lot of writing in the presence of the children. If they see writing is important to you, they will want to do it, too. If you are doing Checklist recording or running records in their presence, children will often want to use your pen and paper to do some pretend writing themselves, as mentioned earlier. Don't give up your writing tools, but instead, be sure you have a well-equipped writing center from which they can get their own recording notebook. Serving as a writing model will almost always stimulate certain of your children to try their own hand at writing.

INCLUDES LETTER-LIKE FORMS IN WRITING

Just as an infant's babbling finally begins to take the sound of real talking, so a child's first linear scribblings eventually begin to look like real writing. For many children, the lines of their scribbles become somewhat jagged and then finally take on features of real letters such as straight, curved, or intersecting lines, although no real letters are formed (Schickedanz, 1982, p. 243). Children may paint such letters on easel paper or scribble them on flat paper at writing tables. When this scribbling takes the form of horizontal lines containing letter-like forms, linguists call it **linear mock writing** (Temple, Nathan, & Burris, 1993, p. 29). This advanced scribbling happens as a natural developmental sequence when children have the freedom and opportunity to experiment with writing on their own. Teaching, in fact, has little or no effect at this point.

We recognize that children extract the elements of writing from their environment and play around with these elements using writing tools and paper. Once again youngsters are manipulating and then mastering the medium (writing) until they have learned how to handle it, what it can do, and what they are able do with it.

They practice lines of mock writing over and over just as they did their first horizontal scribbling. But as it begins to look more like conventional writing, some children believe that it must have meaning. If this is writing, they reason, then someone who knows how to read should be able to read it. Often they will take a piece of mock writing to an adult and ask her to read it. How should you respond? Be honest about it. "Oh, Sharon, your writing is beginning to look almost real. Can you tell me what it says?" Some children really have a story in mind when they do their mock writing, and they will be able to tell it to you. Others think that their "words" must speak only to someone who can read.

Researchers, however, see something very important when they analyze children's mock writing:

> Though mock letters clearly are not alphabet letters, they do reveal progress in children's development from scribbling to writing. DeFord (1980) carefully analyzed mock letter forms and found that they reveal the following concepts of letter form: symmetry, uniformity of size and shape, inner complexity, left-to-right directionality, linearity, and appropriate placement. (Hayes, 1990, p. 62)

Observe to see which of your children are at this stage in their experimental writing. What can you do to help them progress further?

If You Have Not Checked This Item: Some Helpful Ideas

■ Encourage Children to Write Messages

Children who are at the meaning stage in their exploratory writing can write messages in mock writing to other children, to their parents, or to you. Have youngsters write notes to their parents inviting them to visit the classroom, or write a block corner sign asking other children to leave their buildings standing. If you want (or if the children ask), you can write the real words under the scribble writing. This is not necessary, though. Many children know what their scribbled messages say, and they can convey the meaning to the message recipients. Specialists who are studying young children's emergent literacy call these early writing attempts *personal script*, while mature writing is known as *conventional script*. By using these terms, you can avoid telling children their writing is "not real" or is "nothing but scribbles."

■ Put up Personal Mailboxes

If there is a reason to produce writing, then many children will show an interest. Have children help make personal mailboxes by painting empty cereal or shoe boxes you have collected and opening them at one end. Have them put their name (scribbled or printed) on each box, and stack the boxes on a shelf in the writing center. Don't forget to put up your own box and those of your coworkers. Then you can begin by writing brief messages to the children. Encourage them to answer your notes and to write scribbled messages to one another, to be placed in their mailboxes.

■ Take a Field Trip to the Post Office

Taking a field trip to the post office makes a great deal more sense when children are engaged in prewriting activities such as those previously mentioned. Then, when they return to the classroom, they can set up their own pretend post office in the dramatic play area with paper, envelopes, stamps, stampers and stamp pads, and the personal mailboxes the children have made. Ask the post office for the mail kit it has available for classrooms.

■ Have a Class Mailbox

Put your written communications to children or their parents in a class mailbox. You can have a child take the mail out every day and (with your help) distribute it. You should plan on writing one note to each child on a weekly basis. It should be simple and nice: "Roberto, I love your new sneakers!" or "Sandy, thanks for helping Cheryl today." When the note is delivered to the child or to her mailbox, one of the adults in the class can help him or her read it. This modeling behavior on your part should stimulate children to want to write notes to classmates or answer your notes on their own.

■ Read a Book

The Postman by Rosalinda Kightley (New York: Macmillan, 1987) includes simple, colorful pictures with a rhyming line of text at the bottom of each page telling where the postman is delivering mail.

The Post Office Book: Mail and How It Moves by Gail Gibbons (New York: Harper, 1982) is an illustrated nonfiction book for young children about the process of how mail is sorted and delivered.

A Letter to Amy by Ezra Jack Keats (New York: Harper, 1968) tells the story of Peter, an African American character in many of Keats' books, who writes a birthday invitation to his friend Amy and takes it outside in the rain to mail. The wind blows the letter out of his hands and he ends up knocking down Amy in his struggle to retrieve it.

Like Me and You by Raffi (New York, Crown, 1994) is a Raffi song put into book form showing a child from a different country on every page either receiving or writing a letter.

MAKES SOME LETTERS, PRINTS NAME OR INITIAL

Just as the one-year-old begins to say word-like sounds that parents recognize as words, the preschooler begins to write word-like forms by making letter-like scribbles. When adults see this, they often point it out: "Oh, Hilary, you made an *l* in your writing, see!" "Yes, you did it again. Do you know that you have an *l* in your name?" Many children have been taught to print the letters of their names. This is different. Scribbles evolve more as cursive writing. But as the child realizes that her scribbles are being recognized by adults as real letters, she tries to make real letters by printing them.

Although adults often intervene at this point, children still learn alphabet letters on their own by being surrounded by letters and hearing them used. This is the way it should be. The youngsters' own names are often the first source. Children may learn to say the letters in their names soon after they recognize their name sign on their cubby. Many children are then able to identify those particular letters wherever they see them.

Reciting or chanting the ABCs is not the same. Just as children can chant the numbers from 1 to 10, but not understand what any of the numbers mean, so preschoolers often chant the alphabet without the slightest idea of what they are saying. Programs like "Sesame Street" can help children learn the letter names, and some youngsters may have learned letters from this technique, although watching television is a passive method.

Preschoolers begin to write word-like forms naturally by making letter-like scribbles when appropriate materials and support are available.

Other children may have learned alphabet letters from a personal computer at home or in the classroom. A number of software programs feature alphabet games for children two to six years of age. Using the computer keyboard also helps children learn alphabet letters. In many ways, computer programs are superior to television as a learning tool because they actively and playfully involve children in their own learning. Computers should be used playfully with young children, rather than in formal lessons. Children should be free to use a classroom computer during free choice time the same way they use blocks or dolls or the water table.

Also be sure to have alphabet games on the shelves of your manipulative area; alphabet letters mounted on the wall at children's eye level; alphabet books in the book area; and wooden, plastic, sandpaper, or magnetic alphabet letters available for the children to play with. Play alphabet games with the youngsters, but do not teach the alphabet formally. You will find that if you have filled the children's environment with letters, children will teach themselves the alphabet letters they need to know. Formal teaching, even of the alphabet, is not appropriate during the preschool years because this is not how young children learn.

In recognizing letters, children progress through a particular sequence just as they do in learning to make speech sounds naturally. The first distinctive feature children seem to recognize is whether the line that makes the letter is straight or curved. Letters that are round such as *O* and *C* are recognized first. Then letters with curved lines such as *P* and *S* are noted. Next, curved letters with intersections such as *B* and *R* are distinguished from curved letters without intersections like *S* and *J*. Letters with diagonal lines such as *K* and *X* are among the last to be recognized (Schickedanz, 1982, p. 311). This pattern follows the one noted in Chapter 9, that young children have difficulty distinguishing shapes with diagonal lines.

As children begin to print letters, their first attempts are usually flawed. Youngsters make the same mistakes in writing letters that they do in recognizing letters: that is, they often overlook the letter's distinguishing features. Development of children's written language, just as their other aspects of development, progresses from the general to the particular. Until they are able to perceive the finer distinctions in letters, they will have difficulty making letters that are accurate in all the details.

Let the children practice on their own. Pointing out errors is not really productive, just as it was not in their development of spoken language. In time their errors will become less frequent as the children refine their perception of individual letters and gain control over their writing tools.

One of the children's problems in printing letters correctly has to do with the letters' orientation in space. Children are often able to get the features of the letters accurate, but not the orientation of the letters. Children reverse some letters, and some they even write upside down. Occasionally their letters are facing the right direction, but just as often their printing may be a complete mirror image of the real thing.

Part of the answer may lie in the fact that children have already learned that an object's orientation—that is, the direction it faces—makes no difference in identifying the object. For instance, a cup is a cup no matter whether the handle is pointing toward a person or away from her. A flashlight may be lying horizontally or standing on end, but it is still a flashlight. Objects, in other words, do not change their identity because they face a different direction.

But letters do. Letters made with the same features are completely different depending on the direction they face and whether their vertical lines are at the top or bottom. If children's brains have not extracted these orientation rules for distinguishing letters, they are sure to have trouble identifying and printing such letters as *d, b, p,* and *q.* All four of these letters are made with the same curved and straight lines. Yet it may take some years for children to get their orientation straight. Children often reverse letters even into the elementary grades. As Schickedanz (1986) notes:

> In much of children's early writing, vertical and horizontal placement are mixed . . . orientation of letters themselves is not consistent. Sometimes letters are reversed; sometimes they are placed upside-down. These characteristics, plus a tendency to write in any direction—left to right, right to left, top to bottom, bottom to top—are all related. Until children understand that space can be organized in terms of coordinates, they do not select any consistent direction in which to place their writing. (1986, p. 84)

One of the problems in children's playing with three-dimensional alphabet letters is the fact that they can be reversed or turned upside down. If you have such letters in your writing area, be sure to have real alphabet letters mounted on the nearby wall at children's eye level so that the youngsters can easily see the letter's proper orientation. Magnetic letters are better than letter blocks or plastic letters in this respect. At least the magnetic letters cannot be turned around backwards when placed on a metal backing.

Another detail children sometimes overlook when they first print letters is whether the letters are open or closed: the difference between *O* and *C*, for example. This visual discrimination problem may have to do with children's perception of space and their difficulty in making enclosures as discussed in Chapter 9. The youngsters, in fact, may not really see this detail at first.

With practice and maturity, children resolve these problems themselves unless they have a learning impairment. It is not up to you to correct them. They are progressing as they should through the fascinating task of creating their own knowledge about letters and words. Your best strategy as a teacher is to fill the environment with words, letters, and occasions to write, as well as to support and encourage the children's own attempts at writing. But do not formally teach them.

If You Have Not Checked This Item: Some Helpful Ideas

■ Have Children Sign up for Turns

Children can use their mock writing to sign up for turns to use the computer, to play with blocks, to paint at the easel, or to ride a wheeled vehicle. Put small clipboards or sign-up sheets at the entrances to your activity areas, next to the computer or easels, or wherever children need to take turns in the classroom. Tie a pencil to the clipboards and tell the children to put their names under each other's. Have them cross off their names after they have finished their turns, so that the next person can have a turn. Some children can already print their name or initials. If other children say they cannot write their names, tell them to try. Tell them to use their personal script just as they do at the writing table. They will remember which personal scribble is theirs when it is time for their turn. It is important that children understand that you consider their scribbles as real writing. Then they will continue in their developmental sequence on their own.

■ Make Alphabet Letters Personal

Children always learn in a more meaningful way if the subject is somehow connected to them. Help children recognize the first letter in their own first name by playing games with it. You can have letter cards on yarn necklaces that the youngsters can wear. Let the children find their own letters. Then let the youngsters see if they can find any other child with a letter like theirs. Be sure to have enough similar letters, and make them big enough so everyone can see them easily.

■ Have Alphabet Cards

Let children play with alphabet cards having a picture of an object on them. That will allow youngsters to see the letter in the proper orientation. The object on the card will also give them a clue to the name of the letter. It is best to have cards showing both upper- and lowercase letters. Then children will see that each letter can be written in two different ways. It is not helpful for children to use only capital letters, since they will need to write in lowercase in the elementary grades.

■ Have a Typewriter

Bring in a manual typewriter for the children to experiment with. Children love to play with letters and words that they can type. Let the youngsters teach themselves how to use it. They will need to investigate the keyboard to find each letter they want, and then learn to press one key at a time to print their letters.

■ Use Computer Alphabet Games

Computer alphabet programs are good introductory programs for young children who need to learn to locate letters on the computer keyboard. Be sure the programs are simple, colorful games, not lessons, in which pressing a single letter key brings up an appropriate animated graphic on the color monitor screen. Of the many alphabet programs on the market, these are some of the more popular simple ones:

Alphabet Fun: Big and Little Letters (Mahwah, NJ: Troll, 1991)
Animal Alphabet and Other Things (Fairfield, CT: Queue, 1986)
Donald's Alphabet Chase (Buffalo, NY: Walt Disney Software, 1990)
Fun with Letters and Words (Evanston, IL: Westcott Software, 1987)
Mickey's ABC's (Buffalo, NY: Walt Disney Software, 1990)
The New Talking Stickybear Alphabet (Hilton Head, SC: Optimum Resource, 1988)

■ Read an Appropriate Alphabet Book

There are many good alphabet books on the market, but you need to review any you plan to use with your children to see if they are age-appropriate. Some alphabet books are for very young children. Looking at the simplicity of the pictures may help you determine the age level. If there are pictures of children in the book, are the children in the book the age of yours?

Some alphabet books are too sophisticated for young children. These books often display the talent of the artist rather than helping children recognize letters. Other alphabet books are confusing to young children because of the unfamiliar objects used as illustrations. Alphabet books are most effective if they:

1. use both upper and lower case letters
2. have simple illustrations that children can recognize
3. use illustrations with only one common name (not *cat/kitten* or *rabbit/bunny*, for instance)
4. use words starting with a single consonant (*cow, sail, ball*) rather than a blend (such as *church, ship,* or *brown*, for instance)
5. have a theme, a simple story, or rhyming verses

Two examples of appropriate alphabet books are: *Eating the Alphabet: Fruits & Vegetables from A to Z* by Lois Ehlert (San Diego: Harcourt Brace, 1989) and *The Icky Bug Alphabet Book* by Jerry Pallotta (Watertown, MA: Charlesbridge, 1986). These books are more effective if read to one or two children at a time rather than a group. The children need to sit close to the teacher to identify the objects being named and see the shapes of the letters. Have the books on your bookshelves so children can look at them on their own. Chall's extensive study on learning to read in the United States found that children's early ability to identify letters was an important predictor of reading achievement in first and second grades (1967, p. 141).

■ Serve Alphabet Soup

Serve alphabet soup for lunch and see if the children can identify any of the letters.

■ Have Fun with Pretzels

Have pretzels for snack sometime and see what letters your children can make by breaking off pieces before eating the pretzels.

HOLDS BOOK RIGHT-SIDE UP; TURNS PAGES LEFT TO RIGHT

Children need many early experiences with books before they finally learn to read independently. It is especially important for you to make sure they have all kinds of book experiences both in the classroom and in the home. Many programs purchase duplicates of books in the classroom for a home lending library. Children sign out for a book each day and return it in the morning. This also gives families the chance to read to their children the same books the youngsters are using in the classroom. Young children need to have their favorites read again and again for them to develop a strong affinity for books and reading. As Clay (1991) notes:

> The most valuable preschool preparation for school learning is to love books, and to know that there is a world of interesting ideas in them. (p. 29)

In the classroom it is important for an adult to read to a small group or the total group *on a daily basis*. In addition, staff members should look for opportunities to read books to individuals during the day. Finally, books need to be available in an enticing book center full of book posters, puppets, and book character dolls and stuffed animals, where children can look at the books on their own and play with book extension activities.

But surely, you may exclaim, a preschool child will know how to hold a book, which side is up, and which way to turn to the pages. Not necessarily. The youngest children or those with no previous book handling experience may not know how to hold the books or turn the pages. Do not show them how. Let them find out for themselves just as you do with their painting or scribbling.

Observe how each of the children handles books. If you see a child who does not hold the book right-side up, you don't need to correct him. Instead, ask him to pick out a book he would like you to read for him. You might then ask him how you should hold the book. If he still does not have a clue, then say you'd like to look at the pictures together with him. Can he help you hold the book so that both of you can see the pictures? Be sure to follow up with this child and books in the days to come.

Even though a child may have seen you reading books many times, he still may not know how to hold a book if he has not had the experience. Take special care to observe which children play in the book center and which ones do not. Invite children who do not show an interest in books to choose a book for you to read to them alone. Most children enjoy having the teacher pay special attention to them. And you remember that one of your most important tasks is to bring together children and books in happy and satisfying ways.

This means that you and your coworkers must serve as good book-reading models. Note in your daily plans who will be the book readers for a particular day. Ask the readers to choose books they especially like, and to tell the children why they like them. Have them plan a book extension activity to use after they have read the books they like. For instance, for some of the books discussed in this text they might do the following:

> *Abuela*: Have a child fly a Rosalba doll around the classroom and come back and tell you what she saw.
> *Mama Do You Love Me?*: Give a child a Dear One doll and have her ask you some of the same questions as Dear One did in the story.
> *Bet You Can't*: Bring in a basket and have the child fill it with blocks and carry it over to the block shelf.

Eat Up, Gemma: Bring some plastic food items into the book center and ask the child how he would try to get Gemma to eat them.

Children need such hands-on experience with books—the more the better. We need to find all sorts of ways to get books off the shelves and into children's hands. As Gottschall (1995) notes:

> When children can easily see the pictures and print, they also gradually gain the prereading skills that they will need for primary school: they learn how to hold a book; that you read from left to right and from top to bottom; that stories have a beginning, a middle, and an end; and that printed words stay the same and can be read again and again. (pp. 30–31)

If You Have Not Checked This Item: Some Helpful Ideas

■ Use Big Books

Although they are more expensive than regular size books, a few big books fill a useful role in preschool programs. They can help young children understand how a book works, for instance. Use big books when reading to a group. Put the big book on an easel so children can see the pictures and text, and you can turn the pages easily. At the same time, have one or two small copies of the same book that the younger listeners can hold. Have them turn the page when you do. Big books available from The Book Vine for Children, 3980 Albany Street, McHenry, IL, 60050 include:

> *Eating the Alphabet* (Ehlert)
> *Goodnight Moon* (Brown)
> *Planting a Rainbow* (Ehlert)
> *Who Said Red?* (Ehlert)
> *Hattie and the Fox* (Fox)
> *The Rainbow Fish* (Pfister)
> *Mama, Do You Love Me?* (Joosse)

■ Put Books in Every Center of the Classroom

Sometimes we categorize things so distinctly that we overlook other possibilities. That seems to be especially true with our use of picture books in the classroom. We usually keep them on the shelves of the book center, and they seldom find their way into other areas of the classroom. If we want children to become involved with books in a hands-on way, we need to consider keeping some books in the other curriculum areas. Perhaps a large cloth or plastic pocket hanging from a shelf in each area can contain a picture book suitable for that area. An adult can read the book to children playing in the area, and children can look at it on their own. Some suggestions include:

Block center
> *Building a Bridge* (Begaye)
> *Tar Beach* (Ringgold)
> *This Is My House* (Dorros)

Dramatic play
The Leaving Morning (Johnson)
If I Ran the Family (Johnson & Johnson)
Feast for 10 (Falwell)

Science center
Planting a Rainbow (Ehlert)
Gilberto and the Wind (Ets)
Hey! Get Off Our Train (Burningham)

Manipulative/math center
Joe Can Count (Ormerod)
Moving from One to Ten (Halpern)
How Many, How Many, How Many (Walton)

Writing center
A Day at the Beach (Lee)
The Day of Ahmed's Secret (Heide & Gilliland)
A Letter to Amy (Keats)

Art center
Paper Boats (Tagore)
A Color of His Own (Lionni)
Who Said Red? (Serfozo)

Music center
My Mama Sings (Peterson)
Dancing With the Indians (Medearis)
Max Found Two Sticks (Pinkney)

Large motor center
Color Dance (Jonas)
Jonathan and His Mommy (Smalls-Hector)
No Jumping on the Bed (Arnold)

PRETENDS TO READ USING PICTURES TO TELL STORY

As children become more familiar with picture books, they begin looking through them on their own, at first flipping through and missing some of the pages, but later turning each page separately and looking at it intently. As certain books become their favorites, they go through them again and again. They will also ask an adult to read them over and over.

Now it's their turn to read. Children who have handled books and enjoyed hearing them read aloud take just as much pleasure in pretending to read these books themselves, especially to an adult reader. As Elster (1994) notes:

As children learn about books and reading, they often pretend to "read" favorite stories by using the pictures to tell the story.

"Pretend reading" of favorite books is an activity familiar to many parents and teachers of young children. During pretend reading—also called emergent reading or reenactment—children practice reading-like behaviors that build their confidence in themselves as readers. (p. 27)

Because they do not yet read words, young children recreate the story aloud mainly from the pictures. Their story may not include all the pictures in the book at first, but rather the ones that make the biggest impression on them. Children may also include some real words from the story if they remember them from hearing the story repeated. Other extraneous information may also find its way into their story, especially if the adult reader has discussed the illustrations with them. Thus the story they are pretending to read often comes out quite different from the book version. But children read it along in their own way, turning the pages and saying the words just as if they appear in the book that way.

The illustrations in picture books often carry information that is not in the text. When picture content becomes a focus of discussion during read-alouds, children who do emergent readings are likely to link up their attention to pictures and their memory of discussions. (Elster, 1994, p. 29)

It is not up to you as a teacher to correct the child's pretend reading of a story. Instead, you should accept it just as you do his pretend writing with pictures and scribbles. This emergent reading is an early stage of a child's learning to read, a wonderful display of his interest and attention to the way a book works and how a story goes. Whether it is accurate is beside the point. Your role is to congratulate the child on his reading and invite him to do more of it.

You will find that the more reading you do for individual children and small groups, the more you can expect the children to do "pretend reading" for you. If none of the children in your program has offered to do such pretend reading, it may mean that you have never asked them to do it. Or it may mean they are not that familiar with the books because the stories have not been repeated enough. Remember the "3-M's"—manipulation, mastery, and meaning—and be sure to reread favorite books over and over to help children master the stories. As Elster (1994) notes in his research on Head Start children's emergent reading:

> Children are more likely to choose books and engage in emergent readings with books that are familiar to them. (p. 30)

Using book audio- or videotapes is not the same. Children need to see and hear real books read by a live person sitting close to them and talking about the story afterwards. Then they need to do follow-up extension activities of their favorite books by using puppets or doll characters or acting out the story as a character themselves (Beaty, 1994, 1997). How will you know which books are their favorites? Listen to the children when you have finished reading. Does anyone say "Read it again, teacher"? That will give you a clue.

If You Have Not Checked This Item: Some Helpful Ideas

■ Read a Favorite Book

Often a favorite book is one that

1. is written about an experience children can relate to
2. has an interesting-looking character with a funny name
3. has simple illustrations in bright primary colors
4. has a brief text with a line or two on a page
5. uses repetition, rhyming words, or distinctive expressions
6. has an exciting or funny story line or cumulative incidents and is easily remembered

Several of the following books by Helen Lester have become favorites of preschool children for all of these reasons:

> *It Wasn't My Fault* (Boston: Houghton Mifflin, 1985) tells the hilarious tale of Murdley Gurdson, who bumbles through life, and it's always his fault. When a strange bird lays an egg on his head, his luck finally changes—or does it?

Listen Buddy (Boston: Houghton Mifflin, 1995) is the tale of Buddy the bunny rabbit, who never listens until he meets up with the Scruffy Varmint.

Me First (Boston: Houghton Mifflin, 1992) tells the story of Pinkerton pig, who always has to be first until he answers yes to the question "Who would care for a sandwich?" and the sandwich turns out to be a sand witch who needs lots of care.

A Porcupine Named Fluffy (Boston: Houghton Mifflin, 1986) is a sad little porcupine whom everyone laughs at because of his name until he meets a rhinoceros named "Hippo."

Tacky the Penguin (Boston: Houghton Mifflin, 1988) tells the tale of the oddball penguin whose goofy antics chase away the horrible hunters and save the day for his friends.

Any or all of these books can easily become favorites if you read them often enough and have the children get involved in re-creating the humorous incidents. Their bright, funny illustrations mark them as books children will remember and be able to retell in pretend reading.

RETELLS STORIES FROM BOOKS WITH INCREASING ACCURACY

At the same time young children are pretending to write and beginning to identify letters, they are also involved in the natural emergence of reading skills. They are asking parents and teachers to read them stories and scribbling their own stories in mock writing. They are drawing their own primitive illustrations, scribbling mock stories about them, and "reading" them back to the teacher. To children, reading and writing are all the same thing. You write something and you read it back; you read something and you write about it. And it is very exciting to "read" your own "writing"!

Nevertheless, until recently most educators somehow never made the connection that writing and reading emerge naturally and develop simultaneously in preschool children. Even teachers who noted that many more "early readers" were entering kindergarten these days still believed that writing was different. Maybe some children could develop reading on their own, but surely children had to be taught to write, didn't they?

Perhaps it is because writing and reading have always been taught as distinct subjects in primary school that educators in the past never looked closely at what was actually happening with younger children. Now, however, the evidence is in. Studies over two decades by child development specialists in the United States, Argentina, New Zealand, and elsewhere agree that:

The young child's reading and writing abilities mutually reinforce each other, developing concurrently and interrelatedly rather than sequentially. . . . Furthermore, reading and writing have intimate connections with oral language. Truly, the child develops as a speaker/reader/writer with each role supporting the other. (Teale, 1986, pp. 3–5)

Child development specialist Judith A. Schickedanz in her book *More Than the ABCs: The Early Stages of Reading and Writing* suggests several sequential stages in young children's natural development of reading based on her research with preschool children. The first two of these stages are converted here into Checklist items:

1. retells stories from books with increasing accuracy
2. shows awareness that print in books tells story
3. attempts to match telling of story with print in books
4. wants to know what particular print says

Next time a child asks you to read a story, have her choose a favorite tale, one she has heard before. After you have finished, tell her it is now her turn, that she should tell the story to you. She can turn the pages if she wants and "read" the story to you. Make it fun, so that she will want to repeat the activity again and again. This means, of course, you will need to spend much of your reading time on a one-to-one basis with individuals rather than reading to a whole group. Most teachers find this very rewarding, and so do children.

Schickedanz notes that the child's accuracy in retelling book stories is influenced by four factors:

1. characteristics of the child's language
2. structure of the book
3. familiarity with the book
4. past experience with books in general (pp. 51–52)

Children tell the story in their own language, at their own developmental level, with the same articulation they use when they speak. If they speak a dialect, they will retell the story in this dialect. If they are learning English as a second language, they will retell the story the way they speak English rather than the way the story is written in the book. The more times the child hears the story, the more accurate her retelling will become.

The book's structure also influences the accuracy of the child's story retelling. Research has found that the best beginning books for helping children learn to read are predictable books, those that "contain selections with repetitive structures which enable children to anticipate the next word, line, or episode" (Bridge, 1986, p. 82). If children are familiar with a story and can anticipate what comes next, they will have a much easier time retelling the story themselves.

If the child is familiar with the book you are reading, and is familiar with books in general, then she can follow the story more easily if she knows what's coming. If the book is written in a predictable pattern, then it is also easier for the child to remember the story line and to recall what comes next. The following books contain patterns that make them excellent predictable books to use with preschoolers and kindergarten children:

Caps for Sale (Esphyr Slobodkina, Scholastic, 1968)

If You Give a Mouse a Cookie (Laura Numeroff, Harper, 1985)
Nine-in-One, Grr! Grr!, (Blia Xiong, Children's Book Press, 1989)
Stone Soup (Ann McGovern, Scholastic, 1968)
The Three Bears (Paul Galdone, Scholastic, 1972)
The Three Billy Goats Gruff (Paul Galdone, Clarion, 1973)
We're Going on a Bear Hunt (Michale Rosen, McElderry, 1989)
Bringing the Rain to Kapiti Plain (Verna Aardema, Dial, 1981)
This Old Man (Carol Jones, Houghton Mifflin, 1990)
The Very Hungry Caterpillar (Eric Carle, Scholastic, 1981)
The Wheels on the Bus (Maryann Kovalski, Little, Brown, 1987)
Brown Bear, Brown Bear, What Do You See? (Bill Martin, Holt, 1967)

Through listening to stories like these read over and over, young children begin to develop a *story schema* or sense of story: a mental model of the basic elements of a story. From this mental model children develop expectations for the setting, the characters, the order of incidents, and how the story will end (Neuman & Roskos, 1993, pp. 36–37). Neuman and Roskos continue:

> This sense of story comes about by hearing stories, and by being read to on a regular basis. Perhaps no other finding in research is as well documented as the simple fact that reading regularly to young children significantly influences their understanding of what reading is all about as well as their later proficiency in reading. (p. 37)

Do you read daily to the children in your class? It will be evident by the number of children who are able to retell the stories from your books with accuracy.

If You Have Not Checked This Item: Some Helpful Ideas

■ Read Predictable Books

In *The Three Billy Goats Gruff,* children who know the story remember the size of the goats, where they were going, how they went across the bridge ("trip, trap, trip, trap") what the troll said to each goat ("Who's that tripping across my bridge?"), and many more details. They can tell it almost by heart. If they want to tell you the story by pretending to read as they turn the pages, let them. Also ask them to tell the story afterwards without looking at the book. You try it first and let them correct you if you leave out anything.

Children who are not as familiar with books and reading may still agree to tell you the story, but theirs may be a story created by them as they look at the pictures. Your acceptance of any story they tell is important. As they progress in their experience with stories and books, their retelling will become more accurate. On the other hand, some children who know stories very well may after a time become reluctant to retell them. Schickedanz (1986) points out that "a decrease in a child's willingness to tell a story may indicate an increase in the child's understanding about the exactness and stability of the story that is printed in a book. Reluctance, in this case, indicates progress, not regression" (p. 56).

SHOWS AWARENESS THAT PRINT IN BOOKS TELLS THE STORY

The next developmental step in prereading skills involves print awareness. If you are reading to children on a one-to-one basis, they already may have indicated something about their print awareness or lack of it. At first children believe that the pictures in the book tell the story. They may not pay any attention to the text. Even when they do, they may not understand that it is the print and not the pictures that the reader is reading.

Some children are so unaware of the purpose of print that they may cover it unintentionally with their hands if they are holding the book. Others may understand that the reader needs to read the print, but they may also think the reader still needs the pictures to know what the words say (Schickedanz, 1986, p. 57).

Researchers have discovered a sequence most children go through in sorting out print from pictures in a picture book:

1. At first the text and the picture are not differentiated.
2. Then the children expect the text to be a label for the picture.
3. At the third stage the text is expected to provide cues with which to confirm predictions based on the picture. (Clay, 1991, p. 32)

Books that contain both print with pictures and wordless pages with pictures often confuse youngsters who are just beginning to be aware of print. *Where the Wild Things Are* by Maurice Sendak (New York: Harper, 1963) has text on every page except for six pages in the center of the book that depict the wild things having their wild rumpus. Some unaware children insist that the reader read the words for these textless pages.

Do You Want to Be My Friend? by Eric Carle (New York: Crowell, 1971) has a mouse asking a horse's tail the title question, and then going through a series of wordless pages with animals seen from their tail ends, to the conclusion of the book where another mouse answers "yes." Unaware children may feel that you are skipping pages if you do not read something for every wordless page.

The wordless books on the market today also require that you or the children make up the words for the story to go along with the pictures. Using such wordless or partially wordless books with preschool children may help clarify for you the listener's level of print awareness, although they may still be confusing for some children.

As children pretend to read you their favorite stories, some of them use the same narrative style and almost the exact words as the book itself. Are they really reading? If you cover the print as they read you will discover that most have memorized the words after hearing the book read many times. But eventually these same children, without being taught, will come to notice the print and realize that the print, not the pictures, tells the story in the book.

You can determine who these children are by asking them where you should look in the book when you read it to them. By now, some of these youngsters may try to match the telling of the story with the print in the books, and some may even want to know what a particular print says. In the final stage prior to reading they will actually begin to read the words. This is how literacy finally emerges naturally when interested adults bring experimenting children together with appropriate books.

Not all children in preschool will arrive at this stage. Individual development, personal interests, and home background have a great deal to do with children's accomplishments. Your role is to fill your program with exciting books, extension activities, opportunities for reading, and time for children to explore to their heart's content. Then reading to individual children and listening to them read to you may be one of the most satisfying activities any of you engage in.

If You Have Not Checked This Item: Some Helpful Ideas

■ Make Newsprint Stories

Bring a newsprint pad into the book area and have children dictate stories to you that you write on the pad. Can they read them back? Another day paste an interesting picture on the newsprint and have children dictate a story about the people or animals in the picture. Mount these stories around the room and read them with individuals from time to time.

■ Have Children Dictate Stories for Wordless Books

Children can dictate words for the wordless pages of the books previously mentioned. You can write them down and read them back when the books are in use. Wordless books about children like themselves can be the motivation for your children to dictate stories to go along with the wordless pages for books like

> *Sunshine* (Jan Ormerod, New York: Lothrop, Lee & Shepard, 1981)
> *Moonlight* (Jan Ormerod, NY: Puffin Books, 1982)
> *A Boy, a Dog and a Frog* (Mercer Mayer, NY: Dial, 1967)
> *Tuesday* (David Wiesner, NY: Clarion, 1991)
> *Oink Oink* (Arthur Geisert, Boston: Houghton Mifflin, 1993)

■ Fill the Environment with Print

As mentioned earlier in the chapter, you need to fill the classroom with print: charts, place cards, books, magazines, newspapers, telephone directory, labeled food containers, and signs of all kinds. Have the children help you make the signs. Ask them what should be labeled in the classroom and then spell the words aloud as you print them on the signs: aquarium, door, table, chair, telephone, dramatic play area, and so forth. Then have them help mount the signs on the appropriate objects.

OBSERVING, RECORDING, AND INTERPRETING PREWRITING AND PREREADING DEVELOPMENT

Although young children develop prewriting and prereading skills at the same time and in much the same manner that they develop spoken language, we realize that the same emphasis has not been placed on the natural development of preschool writing and reading by many adults around them. Therefore, there may be children who can produce mock writing and letters, but who have not practiced it. There may be some children who are aware of print and try to read it, but have not been noticed. If you screen your entire class using the Child Skills Checklist items on writing and reading skills, you may find certain children who exhibit some of these skills.

After observing the four-year-old boy Jeremey previously referred to, the teacher was able to complete the following Checklist section shown in Figure 11–1.

Child Skills Checklist

Name _Jeremey— Age 4_   **Observer** _Betsy_

Program _Pre – K_   **Dates** _5/5_

Directions:
Put a ✔ for items you see the child perform regularly. Put *N* for items where there is no opportunity to observe. Leave all other items blank.

Item	Evidence	Dates
9. Prewriting and Prereading Skills		
_N_ Pretends to write with pictures and scribbles	He no longer scribbles but tries to write real words	5/5
_N_ Makes horizontal lines of writing scribbles	same as above	5/5
_N_ Includes letter-like forms in writing	same as above	5/5
✔ Makes some letters, prints name or initial	Prints his name copies other words	5/5
✔ Holds book right-side-up; turns pages left to right	Yes- likes to look at books	5/5
✔ Pretends to read using pictures to tell story	Likes to repeat stories in books	5/5
✔ Retells stories from books with increasing accuracy	Can tell story without book	5/5
✔ Shows awareness that print in books tells the story	Points to word and asks if it says " ___ "	5/5

Figure 11–1   Prewriting and prereading observations for Jeremey

Jeremey's accomplishments as recorded on the Checklist helped this teacher understand that Jeremey was showing real progress in his prewriting and prereading skills. She had not realized how far along he had progressed. She decided to work on a one-to-one basis with him using predictable books. After Jeremey heard the story repeated, perhaps he could retell it. If he really liked the story, she would ask him if he knew what particular print said certain words. She also decided to encourage him to "write a story" about what he was building in the block area.

This teacher also decided that now was the time to expand her writing table to an entirely new and separate classroom writing area with an old rolltop desk, many writing tools and paper, a small table with a manual typewriter, and magnetic alphabet letters. Who knows which other children would emerge with self-taught knowledge of letters and words!

REFERENCES

Beaty, J. J. (1997). *Building bridges with multicultural picture books: For children 3–5.* Upper Saddle River, NJ: Merrill/Prentice Hall.

Beaty, J. J. (1994). *Picture book storytelling: Literature activities for young children.* Ft. Worth, TX: Harcourt Brace.

Bridge, C. A. (1986). Predictable books for beginning readers and writers (pp. 81–96). In M. R. Sampson, *The pursuit of literacy: Early reading and writing.* Dubuque, IA: Kendall/Hunt.

Chall, J. (1967). *Learning to read: The great debate.* New York: McGraw-Hill.

Clay, M. M. (1991). *Becoming literate.* Portsmouth, NH: Heinemann.

Davidson, J. (1996). *Emergent literacy and dramatic play in early education.* Albany, NY: Delmar.

Elster, C. A. (1994). "I guess they do listen": Young children's emergent readings after adult read-alouds. *Young Children, 49*(3), 27–31.

Ferreiro, E., & Teberosky, A. (1982). *Literacy before schooling.* Portsmouth, NH: Heinemann.

Gottschall, S. M. (1995). Hug-a-book: A program to nurture a young child's love of books and reading. *Young Children, 50*(4), 29–35.

Hayes, A. H. (1990). From scribbling to writing: Smoothing the way. *Young Children, 45*(3), 62–68.

Lamme, L. L. (1979). Handwriting in an early childhood curriculum. *Young Children, 35*(1), 20–27.

Neuman, S. B., & Roskos, K. A. (1993). *Language and literacy learning in the early years.* Ft. Worth, TX: Harcourt Brace.

Schickedanz, J. A. (1982). The acquisition of written language in young children, in Bernard Spokek (Ed.), *Handbook of research in early childhood education.* New York: The Free Press.

Schickedanz, J. A. (1986). *More than the ABCs: The early stages of reading and writing.* Washington, DC: National Association for the Education of Young Children.

Schrader, C. T., & Hoffman, S. (1987). Encouraging children's early writing efforts. *Day Care and Early Education, 15*(2), 9–13.

Teale, W. H. (1986). Written language development during the preschool and kindergarten years. In Michael R. Sampson, *The pursuit of early reading and writing* (pp. 81–95). Dubuque, IA: Kendall/Hunt.

Temple, C. A., Nathan, R. G., & Burris, N. A. (1993). *The beginnings of writing.* Boston: Allyn and Bacon.

Vukelich, C. & Golden, J. (1984). Early writing: Development and teaching strategies. *Young Children, 39*(2), 3–8.

SUGGESTED READINGS

Cashion, M., & Eagan, R. (1989). Developmental considerations in learning to read. *Day Care and Early Education, 16*(3), 10–12.

Dyson, A. H. (1990). Symbol makers, symbol weavers: How children link play, pictures, and print. *Young Children, 45*(2), 50–57.

Roskos, K. A., & Neuman, S. B. (1994). Of scribbles, schemas, and storybooks: Using literacy albums to document young children's literacy growth. *Young Children, 49*(2), 78–85.

Waring-Chaffee, M. B. (1994). "RDRNT . . . HRIKM" Investigations in children's emergence as readers and writers. *Young Children, 49*(6), 52–55.

VIDEOTAPES

Holguin, Roxanna. *Early book stages.* Child Development Media, Inc., 5632 Van Nuys Blvd., Van Nuys, CA 91401.

LEARNING ACTIVITIES

1. Use the Child Skills Checklist section on prewriting and prereading skills as a screening tool to observe all the children in your classroom. Compare the children who have checks at the higher levels of prewriting skills with their results in spoken language. Can you draw any conclusions?

2. Set up a writing area with paper and writing tools and make a running record of how children use it on three different days.

3. Observe and make a running record of children using a typewriter or computer on three different days. How do they go about teaching themselves how to use the instrument or programs? Are they using trial and error to teach themselves? Do they learn from their errors? How?

4. Have a child select a favorite book for you to read; afterward, ask the child to tell you the story page by page.

5. Read a well-known predictable book to an individual child. Does he show any awareness of the print? Can he retell the story?

CHAPTER 12

Art Skills

Art Skills Checklist

- ☐ Makes random marks on paper
- ☐ Makes controlled scribbles
- ☐ Makes basic shapes
- ☐ Combines circles/squares with crossed lines
- ☐ Makes suns
- ☐ Draws person as sun-face with arms and legs
- ☐ Draws animals, trees, flowers
- ☐ Draws objects together in a picture

DEVELOPING ART SKILLS

This chapter on the development of children's art skills and the following chapter on the development of imagination focus on the growth of creativity in young children. Too often creativity is not included in discussions of the major aspects of children's development—emotional, social, physical, cognitive, and language. Yet it is as notable a drive in the development of the young human being as thinking or speaking.

The unfolding of a young child's creative urge is a joy to behold for most sensitive early childhood caregivers. To help foster and not suppress such development is just as important here as it is for speaking, writing, and thinking skills. Yet somehow we equate creativity with special talent that not everyone displays; therefore we downplay or ignore the development of creativity as more of a frill than a necessity for getting along in life.

In downplaying or ignoring creativity we deprive the developing human of a basic aspect of his or her expressional capacities. Every child, surprising as it may seem, has the potential to become an artist, a musician, a writer, or an inventor, if his interests carry him in that direction, and if his caregivers and teachers support rather than control his urge. The fact that few people become artists is evidence of society's low priority for creativity and high priority for conformity.

Creativity connotes originality and novelty. To create, one brings into existence a new form. Creative people have original ideas, do things in new and different ways, see things from unique and novel perspectives. Creative people do not imitate, they do not follow the crowd. In a word, they are nonconformists.

Who are they? Artists, inventors, poets, writers, actors, musicians, interior decorators, chefs, architects, clothing designers, to name a few—and young children. They are all people who follow their own bent, and who use their ingenuity to design something new. Young children are naturally creative because everything they do, make, or say is completely new to them. They explore, experiment, put things together, take things apart, and manipulate things in ways no adult would ever think of, because the youngsters don't know any better.

Children come into the world uninhibited and with an entirely fresh point of view, their own. They continue to follow its bent until "they learn better," until they learn how society expects them to behave. Only youngsters with strong enough psyches or strong enough outside support to resist society's inhibitions become the artists or creators whom we value as adults.

Could the children in your classroom become such creative adults? If their natural-born creativity is supported and valued by the adults around them, and if it has an opportunity to blossom and grow, then children have the chance to escape the smothering pressure to conform and can enrich their own lives and those of others with the products of their talent.

This chapter on creative development deals with representational drawing, not only because such art is an important part of most early childhood programs, but also because many early childhood caregivers need help in restructuring their art programs. Too many activities in such programs suppress rather than support creativity. As De la Roche (1996) notes:

> Must all snowflakes and shamrocks and turkeys be the same shape? Do they have to be prepackaged and regular to be lovely enough to be hung up in the window? Is regularity and sameness what we want from preschool, kindergarten and first-grade children? Snowflakes are not regular. (p. 82)

The chapter could just as well deal with the development of science skills, which also depend on children's natural exploratory bent. Yet science at the preschool level has somehow escaped the controlled approach that many teachers take with art. It seems good for children to explore plants and animals in all sorts of ways. But somehow many teachers seem to feel that drawings should be done only in the manner prescribed by adults, because of course "adults know better."

This traditional point of view needs to be challenged. We need to step back and take a good look at the development of creativity. When does creativity appear in human beings? What are its characteristics? What can we do to help it grow? How can we keep from suppressing it?

This chapter looks at an eight-step developmental sequence in drawing skills that appear in all children in the same order. Even visually impaired children exhibit the beginning steps of the sequence until the youngsters' lack of visual feedback discourages them from continuing. You will note this sequence is similar to the steps children take in developing physical skills, cognitive skills, and especially writing skills with early scribbling.

It is obvious that the brain is programmed to accomplish all kinds of development in this order, from the general to the specific, as youngsters have the opportunity and materials to interact with their environment in a playful manner (manipulating, mastering, and creating meaning), and thus discovering what it and they are able to do. The same creativity emerges naturally in all aspects of art, from making collages to modeling clay, but this chapter will focus on the natural emergence of representational drawing skills as an example.

MAKES RANDOM MARKS ON PAPER

During their first year of life, children really do not draw. If they have access to a crayon, they are more apt to put it in their mouths than to put a mark on a paper. Around the age of 13 months, according to Piaget, children's first scribbling begins (Lasky & Mukerji, 1980, p. 9). The first marks they make are usually random. These marks have more to do with movement, in fact, than with art. The toddler is often surprised to find that a crayon, a pencil, or a paint brush will make marks. Youngsters are often captivated by watching the lines that their movements can make on a surface. The surface is not always paper, much to their caregiver's dismay. Children will mark on walls, tabletops, or anything else that will take a mark.

We need to be careful about scolding the child for her mistake. She was only investigating the properties of a strange new implement; she had no idea she was damaging anything. We want her to understand that the exploring and the marking were all right to do, but not on the walls and table. Harsh punishment at this stage may abort the budding creator's continued exploration of art. Have her help you clean off the marks with a child-size sponge, give her a tablet to mark on and put a newspaper under it to control slips.

This first stage of art skill development is purely mechanical and manipulative. The child is gaining control over the art tool, whether it is a crayon, paintbrush, pencil, felt-tip marker, or chalk. The child makes random marks without using eye control. Visually impaired children make the same kind of random marks. The urge to express oneself through drawing seems to be inborn, because young children with no art materials will make marks anyway on frosty windows or in the dirt. Writing scribbles also begin like this but eventually veer off in a different direction.

Older children in your program who have had no access to art materials (or those who have been suppressed in their attempts at home) still go through these same Checklist stages (also shown in Figure 12–1). However, their progression through the stages occurs more rapidly. It takes older children far less time to learn how to handle art materials through spontaneous exploratory play. As art specialist Nancy R. Smith (1993) describes so vividly:

> Children begin painting basically the same way whether they are as young as 1½ or as old as three. When they begin, their thoughts are focused primarily on motoric and kinesthetic sensations. The arm and body dance around and above the paper in repetitious and reflexlike movements. But the traces left by their gestures—dots, dashes, zigzags, and circular webs—are striking to the eye and begin the child's education in graphic language. (p. 6)

You will note that in all of these early art experiences, young children are once again teaching themselves through playful exploration of the medium with the "3-M's" of manipulation, mastery, and meaning. The end results that appear on their papers are not art products, not paintings as such, but the footprints of the process of emerging art skills.

1. *SCRIBBLE*
   UNCONTROLLED
   Marks made on paper for enjoyment. Child has little control of eye and hand movement. No pattern.

   CONTROLLED
   Control of eye and hand. Repeated design.

   NAMED SCRIBBLE
   Child tells you what s/he has drawn. May not be recognizable to adult.

2. *SHAPE AND DESIGN*
   Child makes shapes such as circles, squares, ovals, triangles.

   Child's muscle control is increasing and s/he is able to place shapes and designs wherever s/he wants.

3. *MANDALA*
   Child usually divides circle or square with lines.

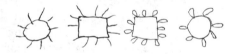

   SUNS
   Formed from ovals, square or circle with short lines extending from the shape. The extending lines take many variations.

4. *RADIALS*
   Lines that radiate from a single point. Can be part of a mandala.

5. *HUMANS*
   Child uses SUN design and develops a face by adding human features. . . a "sun face".

   Child elongates several lines of the SUN design to create arms and legs.

6. *PICTORIALS*
   Child combines ALL stages to make recognizable design or objects.

Figure 12–1 Stages of art development

Source: Beaty, J. (1996). *Skills for preschool teachers*. Upper Saddle River, NJ: Merrill/Prentice Hall.
Reprinted with permission of B. Helm.

If You Have Not Checked This Item: Some Helpful Ideas

■ Have Art Materials Available Daily

Creativity blooms only when children have the freedom to try things on their own. Have paints available at one or two easels all the time. Have colored chalk and a small chalkboard, sets of watercolor felt-tip pens, sets of primary crayons, soft pencils, and various kinds of drawing paper available on low shelves next to art tables. Let children select and use their own materials in a spontaneous manner.

■ Make Only Positive Comments on Children's Art Efforts

Beginning drawers will often produce art that is smudgy and uninteresting from an adult point of view. Refrain from negative comments. You realize that the children are not trying to draw a picture at first, but only to manipulate the medium. Your comments should reflect this: "You really worked hard in art this morning, Jeff. I'm glad you enjoy it so much."

MAKES CONTROLLED SCRIBBLES

From about two years of age on through three and four, and sometimes later depending on the child, an individual will mark on paper in a scribbling manner. At first the scribbles may be endless lines done in a rhythmic, manipulative manner. Eventually the child will use eye control as well as hand/arm movement to make her scribbles and direct their placement on the paper. One scribble often is placed on top of another until the paper is a hodgepodge of lines and circles. Painters may cover their painted scribbles with layers and layers of paint before they are finished.

The result of this effort has little meaning to the child at first, for she is not trying to create something, but merely experimenting by moving colors around on a paper. The process, not the product, is important to her. Adults, however, think of art mainly in terms of creating a product. Their response to scribbling is often either to dismiss it as unimportant and worthless, or to ask children to tell them what they have drawn. Once children learn that adults expect this sort of information, the youngsters often begin naming their scribbles. This behavior does not mean that they really had something in mind when they began moving the brush or crayon around on the paper. Our comments should focus on their efforts in the process of drawing, not on the "imperfect" products they first create.

Scribbling is hardly worthless. It is the first step in the self-taught process of learning to draw. In many respects scribbling is the equivalent of babbling as the child learns to speak. We support children in their babbling and congratulate them when they finally make sounds that seem to be words. Think what might happen to their language development if we forced them to stop making such worthless sounds, just as some adults force children to stop wasting their time making "worthless" scribbles.

Children work hard at scribbling. Only they know when a scribbled "drawing" is finished—actually, the *process* is finished. Some youngsters go over and over the lines they have made, almost as if they are practicing the way to make a straight or curved line. We understand these children have progressed to the "mastery" stage of exploratory art. Their early products seem to show a greater proportion of vertical lines, especially in easel paintings (Smith, 1982, p. 301). But many children are able to make multiple horizontal, diagonal, and curved lines as well. Back and forth the youngsters work, sometimes changing their hand direction when they get tired and sometimes even changing hands. While two-year-olds place one scribble on top of another, three- and four-year-olds frequently put a single scribble on one paper (Kellogg, 1970, p. 18).

Rhoda Kellogg, the art specialist who collected and analyzed thousands of children's drawings from around the world, identified 20 scribbles that children make. Not all children make all 20 scribbles that they are capable of producing. Individuals tend to concentrate on a few favorites and repeat them in many variations. The fact that all children everywhere produce some of the same 20 scribbles spontaneously— and no others—seems to indicate, though, that this early form of art must be inborn in the human species.

Kellogg (1970) considers these scribbles to be "the building blocks of art" (p. 15). The individual's scribble "vocabulary" most easily can be read in his finger painting. He will draw his "designs" with one or more fingers, and then "erase" them before starting over. Because they do not pile up one on top of the other as with opaque paint or crayons, it is easier to see which of the 20 basic scribbles he favors.

It is not necessary for the early childhood teacher to identify a child's scribbles, but he or she needs to understand the importance of scribbles in the sequence of art skills development. Many children continue to revert to scribbles even when they have progressed beyond them to shape drawings. This is a perfectly natural progression. All child development tends to occur in a spiral rather than a straight line. We can expect children to slip back even while they are progressing forward.

How long can you expect children to go through this scribbling stage? It depends upon the individual child and her development and experience. Time undoubtedly will be different for each of your children, because, as Seefeldt (1995) notes:

> Preschoolers who have been deprived of a period of messing around with art materials, as too many in the United States who have been expected to produce an adult-pleasing product as toddlers, will require a great deal of time to mess around with art materials before they can use them to express ideas or feelings. (p. 42)

If You Have Not Checked This Item: Some Helpful Ideas

■ Provide Controllable Materials

Beginners will not be able to progress much beyond scribbling unless they can control the materials. Be sure to provide fat, kindergarten-size crayons for children to grip well. Children can use thin crayons, too, but sometimes the youngsters bear down so hard they break them. Mix your tempera paints with just enough water to make them creamy but not drippy. Add cornstarch or flour to thicken them if they are too thin. Buy short stubby easel paintbrushes that young children can manipulate easily. If you already have the long kind, cut off the ends of long easel paintbrushes so youngsters can handle them better. Wrap ends of colored chalk with masking tape to help gripping and control smearing.

In the beginning, provide easel painters with contrasting colors rather than complementary colors to prevent muddy results. Children have more control when they start with only two contrasting colors instead of several different kinds. Avoid putting red and green together, yellow and purple together, or blue and orange together. Haskell (1979) recommends any of the following combinations instead:

1. yellow with blue or red or green or brown
2. orange with green or purple or brown or red
3. white with blue or red or green or purple (p. 74)

■ Be Nondirective

Allow children to explore and experiment with paint and chalk, finger paint and crayons, and felt-tip markers and pencils completely on their own. Put the materials out for their use during free play, or have materials invitingly placed on low shelves near art tables for the youngsters' own selection.

■ Read a Book

Mouse Paint by Ellen Stoll Walsh (San Diego: Harcourt Brace, 1989) is a small book telling a simple but captivating story of three little white mice who hide from the cat on a white page. One day when the cat is sleeping, they find three jars of paint—red, yellow, and blue—and have a wonderful time dancing in paint puddles with the colors, first one by one and then mixing them up.

MAKES BASIC SHAPES

As children's physical and mental development progress and they are able to control the brush and paint more easily, their scribbles begin to take on the configuration of shapes. Kellogg (1970, p. 45) has identified six basic shapes in children's early art: rectangle (including square), oval (including circle), triangle, Greek cross (+), diagonal cross (×), and odd shape (a catchall). These shapes do not necessarily appear separately but rather mixed up with other scribbles or with one another.

If children have had the freedom to experiment with art as toddlers, they usually begin to make basic shapes spontaneously by age three. Children's perceptual and memory skills help them to form, store, and retrieve concepts about shapes quite early if they have had appropriate experiences (see Chapter 9). The particular shapes a child favors seem to evolve from his own scribbles. Attempts at making ovals and circles usually appear early. This form seems innately appealing to young humans everywhere, perhaps because of their preferred attention to the oval human face.

Children progress through natural stages in learning to draw: Random marks, controlled scribbles, and basic shapes are early stages.

Circular movements in their scribbling eventually lead them to form an oval. Then the youngsters often repeat it, going around and around over the same shape. Visual discrimination of the shape and muscle control of the brush or crayon finally allow them to form the shape by itself instead of intertwined within a mass of scribbles. Memory comes into play as well, allowing the children to retrieve the oval from their repertoire of marks and to repeat it another day.

In this manner the child's capacity to draw shapes seems to emerge from his capacity to control the lines he makes in his scribbling. In other words, he makes one of the basic shapes because he remembers it from creating it spontaneously in his scribbling, not because he is copying the shape from his environment. As he experiments, he stumbles onto new ways to make new shapes. But certain ones seem more appealing, and individual children return to them again and again.

Three- and four-year-olds first create rectangles by drawing a set of parallel vertical lines and then later adding horizontal lines at the top and bottom, rather than drawing a continuous line for a perimeter (Smith, 1982, p. 301). We understand why when we remember the problem children first have trying to make an enclosure with blocks (see Chapter 9). Thus we see why it is important to give them many opportunities and much time to practice. The children are teaching themselves to draw, just as they did to build with blocks, walk, talk, think, speak, write, and read.

If You Have Not Checked This Item: Some Helpful Ideas

■ Provide Materials Children Can Use on Their Own

Easels always should be available. They are one of the best motivators for spontaneous drawing that you can have available. Children soon find out that all they need to paint is to put on a painting smock and go to the easel. There is no need to get out paints, for they are already mixed and waiting. There is no need to ask for help or direction from the teacher. If an easel is free during free choice time, they can go over to it and paint.

For children who are experienced easel painters, it is always good to challenge them with a new activity. Perhaps they would like to try flat table painting with paints in a muffin tin. Or you might make a table easel with two sections of cardboard taped together to form an inverted "V" over a table. Paper can be fastened to it with masking tape. Paint can be mixed and waiting in muffin tins or jars taped to the table so they will not tip over.

Remember that children are still in the exploratory stage and should not be expected to paint a picture. If they want your comments, you can talk to them about the colors, lines, and shapes they have created. They may want the paper displayed on the wall. If not, label it with their names and dates and add it to their portfolios (see Chapter 14).

COMBINES CIRCLES/SQUARES WITH CROSSED LINES

The next step in the sequence of children's self-taught art skills involves combining two of the shapes they have made. Kellogg has observed and written a great deal about this behavior. The Greek cross (+) and the diagonal cross (×) are favorite shapes. These are often combined with an oval or rectangle to make what is sometimes called a "mandala." Mandalas don't necessarily stand alone on a sheet of paper but are usually repeated by children in a balanced way. Groups of these shapes or others form the bulk of art for many three and four-year-old children.

Pictorial drawing eventually evolves out of particular combinations of shapes. One of the first representations to occur in children's art is the human being. This representation seems to evolve naturally from the child's first experiments with an oval shape combined with a cross inside it (the mandala), which then leads to an oval with lines radiating from its rim (the sun), which finally evolves into an oval with two lines for arms, two for legs, and small circles inside the large head/body oval for eyes (the human).

From mandalas to suns to humans is the natural sequence much of children's spontaneous art follows. Watch for this development in the children in your program. Talk to parents about the spontaneous way art skills develop in children if youngsters have freedom to explore on their own. Both you and the parents may want to save children's scribbling and early shape drawings to see if you can identify the sequence of their development. Be sure to date the art.

*Next, children combine shapes
naturally, such as a circle and a
cross, making a shape called a
"manadala."*

Because the mandala is a key part of this sequence, it is treated as a separate Checklist item for observers to look for. The circle with the cross inside is a symbol found throughout the world. In some Asian religions it is the symbol of the cosmos. Obviously young children are producing it spontaneously without any notion of its symbolic meaning. But there must be an inborn appeal for such a shape for it to appear as a natural sequence in children's art. Kellogg (1970) believes its overall balance makes it so appealing to the human species (p. 68).

Children's early scribblings show many examples of crossed lines as well as ovals and rectangles. It seems only natural that children eventually would experiment by trying to put the two together. Many scribbles show early attempts at placing a cross over a circle, possibly because children make many scribbles this way: one on top of the other. As children gain control of their drawing tool and remember how to make the shapes they like, a shape like the mandala emerges naturally. If this shape is appealing to them, then they will repeat it endlessly.

Perhaps this method reveals how early humans came to include the mandala in their repertoire of symbols. Circles and squares with crosses inside them are found throughout the world in the rock writing petroglyphs and pictographs of ancient cultures.

Not all children make mandalas, but most do. These basic shape combinations are never really lost once they have become a part of a person's art vocabulary. Take a look at the doodles adults make in a nonthinking, spontaneous fashion. You yourself still may draw the mandalas you first discovered as a child!

If You Have Not Checked This Item: Some Helpful Ideas

■ Provide Variety in Your Art Materials

Not all children may enjoy painting at an easel. You should include other possibilities as often as possible. Finger painting is one. It can be done on a smooth paper, a tabletop, or a cookie sheet. Paper finger paintings can be hung to dry and are thus preserved if the child wants to save them. Tabletop finger paintings can also be preserved before cleaning the table by pressing a paper onto them and rubbing the back of the paper.

Finger paint itself can be made from liquid starch that is poured onto paper with powder paint shaken into it; from wallpaper paste mixed with water and poster paint to the proper consistency; or with soap powder mixed with a little water and paint powder. Soap powder can also be whipped until stiff and used as white paint against colored construction paper.

MAKES SUNS

A combination of an oval with lines radiating from its rim is often the next step in the child's natural sequence of drawing a pictorial representation. We call this shape combination a "sun" because it looks like the symbol adults use to represent the sun. Children do not call their sun-shape a sun unless adults or more experienced peers first give it the name. The youngsters are not drawing a sun, but merely experimenting with shapes. If this combination appeals to them they will repeat it many times. When they finally do begin to draw pictorially they sometimes call this figure a "spider."

Although this figure seems quite simple to draw, the sun does not appear spontaneously in children's drawings at first. Two-year-olds can make curved and straight lines, but they rarely produce suns before age three (Kellogg, 1970, p. 74).

The sun figure may well emerge from the children's experiments with the mandala figure. Most of children's early attempts at sun figures include some kind of marks in the center of the figures—either lines, dots, or ovals. Once the children have begun to make a sun with a clear center, they have progressed beyond the mandala to something new. These early suns with center marks are not forgotten, however. When children begin to draw "sun-faces," their first humans, they include the center marks for eyes, nose, and mouth.

We see sun figures in primitive rock art as well. Early civilizations must have followed the same sequence in their progression of artistic representation.

If You Have Not Checked This Item: Some Helpful Ideas

■ Draw with Chalk

Colored chalk is very appealing to children if they can grip it and control its tendency to smear. Wrap the upper end with foil or masking tape to make gripping easier. Soft, thick chalk is best. The regular size breaks too easily with the pressure some children apply. Chalk should be used dry at first for children to become used to its properties. Then you can wet either the paper or the chalk for a richer effect. Use either a water-sugar solution (four parts warm water to one part sugar) or use liquid starch, and apply it to the paper for children to draw on with dry chalk. Or use the liquid as a dip for children to wet the chalk but draw on a dry surface. Many children like the rhythm of dipping and drawing (Haskell, 1979, p. 45). Dry chalk marks on wet paper can also be smeared around to create different effects. Draw on brown paper grocery bags for still a different effect.

■ Draw with Felt-Tip Pens

Water-soluble felt-tip pens are always favorites with children. They seem able to control them more easily than paintbrushes or crayons. The pens' thick size and smooth marking ability make them especially well-suited to preschool art. Some marking pens have brush-tip rather than felt-tip points. These have the spreading capacity of water-color paint. It is not necessary or even desirable to give each child an entire set of pens of all colors. Give the youngsters only a few colors at a time until they express the need for more.

■ Keep Art Activities Spontaneous

Do not use pictures, figure drawings, or models for your children to copy. This is not how spontaneous art develops. Even children who have reached the pictorial stage do not need to copy. You will find that they draw what they know rather than what they see.

■ Read a Book

My Crayons Talk by Patricia Hubbard (New York: Holt, 1996) tells the sprightly story of a little girl with people-size crayons that say things to her. For example, her purple shouts "Yum, bubble gum." Brown, blue, yellow, gold, silver, red, green, orange, black, white, and pink crayons all have other exciting or funny things to say on every double-page spread.

 ## DRAWS PERSON AS SUN-FACE WITH ARMS AND LEGS

One of the first pictorial figures that the young child draws naturally is a person. He draws it as one large head/body oval with two lines coming out of the bottom for legs, a line from either side for arms (sometimes these are omitted), circles or dots inside the head circle for eyes and sometimes a nose and mouth. It looks like the sun he has been drawing, only with two side "rays" for arms, two longer bottom "rays" for legs, and sometimes short top "rays" for hair. All children everywhere seem to draw their first humans in this spontaneous manner. They are known in the art world as "tadpole" people because of the resemblance.

To adults unfamiliar with the child's sequence of development, these are strange humans indeed: all head and no body, with arms and legs attached to the head. Surely children age three and four can see that a person's arms and legs are attached to the body and not the head, you may say. Adult concepts about art, however, have little in common with what is happening with the beginning child artist.

All along adults have looked at the products of children's art (the drawings or paintings) as the most important thing, when to the young child, the process is more important. Children are not drawing a picture at first but developing a skill. Their efforts progress through an observable sequence of development from general to specific, from holistic to detailed drawings.

Production of a human is the transition to pictorial drawing for most young children. The method they apply is the same one they used for making shapes and symbols. They draw *what they know how to make, and not what they see.* Out of their practice with mandalas and suns comes this sun-face human with a few of the "sun's rays" for arms and legs. They do not draw stick figures until much later, and then only by copying what adults or older children are drawing. Stick figures do not emerge naturally but seem to be an adult invention.

It is not surprising, in fact, that children's first humans are all face. We remember that even infants attend to this image most frequently. The human brain seems programmed to take in details about faces. This, after all, is the most important part of the human being.

As children first create their circle humans, they do not always repeat their drawings exactly. All children make armless humans at one time or another, even though the youngsters may have drawn arm lines earlier. This behavior does not indicate the children are regressing or are cognitively immature. It may appear only because the proportion of two parallel legs to a head is more appealing alone than with arms sticking out at the sides. Children rarely draw legless humans (Kellogg, 1970, p. 101). The behavior may result from the brain's tendency to overgeneralize in early categories. Later details will be more discriminating.

Without many examples of a single child's drawings, it is risky to try to determine where he or she stands in this developmental sequence. Schools or psychologists who try to evaluate a child's maturity on the basis of only one drawing of a person (such as the Draw-a-Person Test) are basing their findings on extremely sketchy information. Kellogg (1970) found that one-third of 2,500 public school children who were asked to "draw a man" each day for five days drew such different humans that their scores on the Draw-a-Man Test varied as much as 50 percent (p. 191).

As children have more practice drawing their early people, they often add hair or hats, hands or fingers, feet or toes. The additions may be lines, circles, or scribbles. Children may identify their persons as being themselves or someone else. The actual size of the person named in the drawing is usually not considered by young children. Instead, they often draw the most important person in the picture as the biggest.

Eventually children will add a body to their head drawings. They often do this by drawing two extremely long legs and putting a horizontal line part way up between them. You may remember that this is the common method they used earlier to draw rectangles. Youngsters often will draw a belly button in the middle of the body. By this time they frequently are drawing other pictorial representations, as well. These representations, as you will note, are also based on the children's previous experience, showing once again how development proceeds in a continuous sequence from the general to the specific, so long as children have the freedom to learn naturally.

If You Have Not Checked This Item: Some Helpful Ideas

■ Record Children's Stories About Their Drawings

Some children verbalize a great deal about their drawings. Others do not. You should take your lead from the child. If he or she likes to tell you stories about the people in the drawings, you may want to record these. Children may want to have their stories displayed along with their art on the classroom walls. On the other hand, they may want to make a scrapbook of their art or to take their art home. If children do not want to talk about their art products, then you can support them best by comments like: "You surely used many colors in your drawing today, Sheila. Which ones do you like best?"

Keep in mind that much early children's art is not pictorial, so there really are no stories to tell about it, unless, of course, adults press children to make up something. Brenda S. Engel (1996) also notes:

> Essentially all expressive forms contain their own meaning; they do not have to be interpreted through another medium. Visual work, for example, does not have to be explained through words, just as words do not have to be explained through pictures. (p. 75)

■ Talk with Children About Their Art Through Observations

Engel (1966) believes that instead of trying to elicit stories about children's artwork or making evaluative comments, teachers should first observe several aspects of the work and then, when it seems appropriate, talk with the child about these aspects (p. 75). Such aspects could include its medium, shapes, colors, design, scenes, or purpose. Then the teacher could mention to the child artist what she sees in the drawing/painting, and hope that the child might respond.

For example, she might say: "Ricardo, it looks to me as if you started your painting with a lot of red paint and then covered part of it with yellow. Then you have a row of figures down at the bottom in still a different color. Did you paint them first or last? They really give your picture a balanced look." It is then up to the child to respond or not in any way he chooses.

DRAWS ANIMALS, TREES, FLOWERS

Animals

Once children have discovered the way to draw a person, they will often begin drawing animals as well. Youngsters' first animals are hard to distinguish from humans. It is obvious the animals are based on the same practiced form: a head with eyes, nose, and mouth, a body with arms sticking out from the sides and legs coming out the bottom. Often the animal is facing front like a person and seems to be standing on two legs. We know the drawing is an animal instead of a person because of the two ears sticking up straight from the top of the head. Sometimes these are pointed like cat ears or circular like mouse ears. These are transition animals.

Eventually the young artist will find a way to make his animal horizontal with an elongated body parallel to the bottom of the paper, four legs in a row from the bottom of the body, a head at one end, and often a tail at the other end. The features of the face are still positioned in a frontal pose and not a profile even though the animal is positioned with its side showing. Most animal head profiles do not appear in children's drawings until around age five years or later.

In fact, many children do not draw animals until they go to kindergarten. This behavior—or lack of it—may be due to their progress in their own developmental sequence, but drawing animals also reflects the kindergarten curriculum. Often kindergarten teachers give children outline animals to copy that may, in fact, short-circuit the youngsters' spontaneous development.

Kellogg (1970) argues that many teachers believe a child's self-taught system differs too widely from adult drawing, and therefore the child needs to be taken by the hand and taught how to draw "correctly" (p. 114). Children sometimes abandon art in elementary school because of insufficient teacher approval for their natural art.

Trees, Flowers

The first trees are also transitional drawings based on the human figures children have taught themselves to draw. They look like armless humans with two long legs for the trunk and a circular head for the treetop, which often contains small circles or dots that may be leaves, but look more like fruit. The trees are not drawn to size. They may be similar in height to the humans in the picture or even smaller. A few four-year-olds may draw trees, but most children are five before they begin these drawings.

As children have practice and freedom to draw, more details evolve on trees. The tops of some trees resemble the sun with the rays as branches and balls at the ends of the branches as leaves. Other children make branches coming out from the trunk like arms on a human. The first flowers are also based on a familiar model: a sun with a stem.

The children in your classroom may not have advanced to this level. In this case, you should leave the Checklist item blank. Given the freedom to develop art skills spontaneously, children will make their own progress as individuals. It is not your role to push the youngsters ahead, but to provide materials, time, and support so the children may make their own progress according to their own biological timetables.

Children who are able to draw representational objects with crayons or felt-tip markers may not be able to do this same level of drawing with a paintbrush and paint if they have not used paint before. It is important to realize children must go through the same developmental stages of manipulation, mastery, and meaning with each new medium they encounter. As Smith (1993) notes:

> Experimentation with paint usually begins when children enter preschool or kindergarten. Often they have already been drawing with crayons and pencils for some time and can produce lines and shapes in these media readily. Nevertheless, consistent with the laws of development, they must begin at the beginning in paint, with rhythmic, motoric actions. . . . They are not lagging behind, but simply building up the necessary knowledge in the paint itself. (p. 18)

If You Have Not Checked This Item: Some Helpful Ideas

■ Add New Art Activities

Your children may want to try drawing with liquid glue from a plastic squeeze bottle. They may want to draw with a pencil or other marker first and then follow the lines with glue. Or they can try the glue without guidelines. Because glue is transparent when it dries, you may want to add food coloring to the bottles. This liquid glue is a much more free-flowing medium; children will need to play with it for awhile to see how it works and how to control it just as they did the first time they used paint. They will need to squeeze and move the bottle at the same time, a trick of coordination that may be difficult for some. Don't expect pictorial designs from glue drawing.

■ Read a Book

Planting a Rainbow by Lois Ehlert (San Diego: Harcourt Brace, 1988) tells a simple story in large, bold type of a little girl and her mother who plant bulbs and seeds for flowers that grow in rainbow colors. Brilliant flower cutouts against a white background, with color-coded pages of flowers in the center of the book, clearly display the shapes and color categories of the blooms. Be sure you use this book for reading only, and not as a model from which children would be expected to draw their flowers. Young children's art does not evolve from copying models.

The Very Busy Spider by Eric Carle (New York: Philomel, 1984) is another simple book with a large colorful barnyard animal against a white background on every other page who tries to entice the spider to play its game. But the spider doesn't answer because she is too busy spinning her web on the opposite pages.

Coyote: A Trickster Tale from the American Southwest by Gerald McDermott (San Diego: Harcourt Brace, 1994) tells a traditional folktale of Coyote, who wants to sing, dance, and fly like the crows. But when the crows teach him how to do this, all he does is brag and boast, so they have to teach him another more severe lesson. Soon he falls to the ground and ends up covered with dust just like he looks today. The large stylized illustrations show a blue coyote against an orange desert background.

COMBINES OBJECTS TOGETHER IN A PICTURE

A few of the children in your classroom may begin doing pictorial drawings at three and a few more at age four. Do not expect all youngsters to do so. Let them progress through their own sequences of development at their own individual rates. Those who do draw pictorially will be using the previously discussed repertoire of figures they have developed. Their drawings will be representations and not reproductions, for the young child draws what he knows, not what he sees.

This principle is especially apparent in children's spontaneous drawings at age six, when many youngsters go through a stage of so-called X-ray drawings that show both the inside and outside of objects at the same time. The children's drawings depict things as the youngsters know them, rather than just what they can see. People are shown inside houses without walls as in a cutaway drawing, for example.

The children in your classroom probably will not have reached this stage; nor will they have developed a baseline in their drawings much before age five. Objects are still free-floating on their art papers just as their first spontaneous letters are (see Chapter 11). This different perspective used by young children is sometimes used by adult artists as well.

Children also interpret their pictorial drawings differently from adults. Youngsters often do not start out to draw a particular thing. Instead they describe their art more by the way it turns out than by what they had in mind. The way it turns out may have more to do with the materials they are using than anything else. Runny paint in easel drawings may remind the youngsters of smoke, rain, or fire, for instance, so they draw a picture of a rain or a fire.

On the other hand, some children purposefully draw a picture of the post office that the class visited on a field trip. The picture will look, of course, just like the building shape they have learned to do spontaneously, and not at all like the post office itself. Children first draw buildings by combining mostly rectangular shapes in various ways and not by looking at buildings. The drawing often has a door in the middle and at least two square windows above it. Roofs may be flat or pointed and often have a chimney with smoke coming out. The drawing catches the essence of the building, not the reality. Some four-year-olds also draw cars and trucks, as well as boats and planes. Often it is hard to tell the difference between early cars and trucks.

Once children have a repertoire of figures that the adults around them seem to accept, they will begin to put the figures together into scenes. The size and color of their objects will not be realistic. The more important the object or person, the larger the child will make it. Colors will have little relation to the object being depicted. They depend more upon the particular brush the child happens to pick up, or a color the child happens to favor at the moment. Objects will be free-floating, as mentioned, and not anchored to a baseline. But the effect will be balanced and pleasing, nevertheless.

Children who verbalize about their art may tell you things about their drawings that have little to do with what your eyes seem to show you. The youngsters must be speaking about an inner vision of their world, you decide. You are right, of course. And from inner visions come creative ideas, you remember. Let's support this beginning urge toward creativity in all children by giving it the freedom to grow spontaneously.

If You Have Not Checked This Item: Some Helpful Ideas

■ **Encourage Children to Draw About Field Trips**

Not all your children can or want to draw pictorially. But for those who do, you can suggest they draw a picture about a trip you have taken together. Children find it satisfying to be able to represent things they know about. They can tell about the things in words, have you write down their words, or record their words on tape. But it is also good to make a drawing or build a block structure about new things they have encountered. Their products help you as a teacher to find out what is important to them and how they conceptualize the new ideas they have gained.

■ **Have Children Draw About Things in Their Repertoire**

If you know children can draw people, houses, trees, and animals, they may want to draw a picture of their house and family. Those who want to can have you write down their story about the drawing.

OBSERVING, RECORDING, AND INTERPRETING ART SKILLS

Screen all your children using the eight items of the Child Skills Checklist under art skills. Write their names on the left side of a chart you make and list the eight Checklist items at the top of the chart with a word to represent each one (see Figure 12–2). If you find that most of your three- and four-year-olds have not progressed beyond the random marks or scribbles stages, then ask yourself if your program has allowed the children the opportunity, the freedom, and the time to pursue art on their own.

Is the children's art truly their own, or have teachers intervened to help them draw a house or animal "correctly"? As Gellens (1996) notes:

> Children's art must reflect the child. Art must be the child's own work from beginning to end. A teacher's hands should never touch the artwork . . . The art activity must meet the child's developmental level and offer a risk-free environment where the child can create. It must help the child move from one level to the next in a pressure free atmosphere that is fun and exciting. It must be totally child produced. (p. 7)

Do you have at least one easel in the classroom set up and ready to use? Do you have an art area where children can get their own supplies and do their own work without teacher directions? Give children this opportunity and freedom to explore and experiment with art on their own. Then do a second screening using the eight Checklist items to see if more checkmarks have appeared under art skills.

Figure 12–2 Screening for art skills

Date: ___10 / 22___

	Marks	Scribbles	Shapes	Combines	Suns	Humans	Animals	Pictures	
Randy	✓	✓							
Ellen	—	—	✓	✓	✓				
Jackie	—	—	✓	—	✓	✓			
Ron	✓								
Billy J.	✓	✓							
Jeff									
Sheila	—	—	—	—	✓	✓	✓	✓	
Josh	✓	✓							
Karyn	✓	✓	✓						
Rebecca	✓	✓	✓						
Lamar	✓								
David	✓	✓							
Michelle	—	—	✓	✓					
Billy S.	✓	✓							
Lionel	✓								

REFERENCES

De la Roche, E. (1996). Snowflakes: Developing meaningful art experiences for young children. *Young Children, 51*(2), 82–83.

Engel, B. S. (1996). Learning to look: Appreciating child art. *Young Children, 51*(3), 74–79.

Gellens, S. (1996). Children's art must be child produced. *Children Our Concern, 21*(1), 7–9.

Haskell, L. L. (1979). *Art in the early childhood years.* Upper Saddle River, NJ: Merrill/Prentice Hall.

Kellogg, R. (1970). *Analyzing children's art.* Palo Alto: National Press Books.

Lasky, L., & Mukerji, R.. (1980). *Art: Basic for young children.* Washington, DC: National Association for the Education of Young Children.

Seefeldt, C. (1995). Art—A serious work. *Young Children, 50*(3), 39–45.

Smith, N. R. (1993). *Experience & art.* New York: Teachers College Press.

Smith, N. R. (1982). The visual arts in early childhood education: Development and the creation of meaning. In B. Spodek, *Handbook of research in early childhood education.* New York: The Free Press.

SUGGESTED READINGS

Beaty, J. J. (1996). *Skills for preschool teachers.* Upper Saddle River, NJ: Merrill/Prentice Hall.

Edwards, C., Gandini, L., & Forman, G. (1995). *The hundred languages of children: The Reggio Emilia approach to early childhood education.* Norwood, NJ: Ablex.

Edwards, L. C. (1990). *Affective development and the creative arts: A process approach to early child-hood education.* Upper Saddle River, NJ: Merrill/Prentice Hall

Isenberg, J. P., & Jalongo, M. R. (1993). *Creative expression and play in the early childhood curriculum.* Upper Saddle River, NJ: Merrill/Prentice Hall.

Spodek, B. (1996). Educationally appropriate art activities for young children. *Child Care Information Exchange,* #108, 40–42.

LEARNING ACTIVITIES

1. Use the Child Skills Checklist for art skills as a screening tool to observe all the children in your classroom. For children with checks at the higher levels in the sequence of art skill development, compare their scores in cognitive development, especially in "Identifies objects by shape" and "Identifies objects by color." Can you draw any conclusions from this comparison?

2. Based on your screening survey, choose one or two children who have not shown much interest or development in art, and try to involve them in an art activity. Use one of the other Checklist areas in which they have shown interest and skills as the basis for the art activity. Record the results.

3. Set up your art area so children can use it without adult help or direction. Make a running record of what happens in this area before you have changed the setup and afterward.

4. Carry out one of the suggested art activities from the chapter with a group of children who show interest. Compare their results with their Checklist standing in art skills. What can you conclude from this?

5. Save all the art products of one of your children over a six-month period. Be sure to date them. How do they compare with the sequence of art skill development discussed here?

CHAPTER 13

Imagination

IMAGINATION CHECKLIST

- ☐ Pretends an action without taking a role
- ☐ Assigns roles or takes assigned roles
- ☐ Takes on characteristics and actions related to role
- ☐ Needs particular props to do pretend play
- ☐ Can pretend with imaginary objects
- ☐ Uses language for creating and sustaining plot
- ☐ Uses exciting, danger-packed themes
- ☐ Uses elaborate themes, ideas, details

DEVELOPING IMAGINATION

A second important aspect of creativity in young children is their development of imagination. For young children, imagination is the ability to pretend or make believe, to take a role other than their own, to create fanciful situations, or to act out a fantasy of their making. It is an activity that most children seem to engage in during play a great deal of time before the age of seven. It is a type of play that many adults fail to see as significant in the development of the child, because they do not understand it. But early childhood professionals have come to recognize imagination as one of the most effective means for promoting the development of the young child's intellectual skills, social skills, language, and most especially, creativity (Smilansky, 1968, p. 12).

One of the basic tools for creating is imagining, the ability to see a picture in our mind's eye. This ability allows us to tap into memories of the past and reform them as possibilities for the present or future. Children's make-believe relies heavily on this capacity to draw on such internal images and to create new ones. The Singers, who have done extensive research and writing on children's imaginative play, believe that imagining is essential to the development of intellectual and language skills as well. Children remember ideas and words they have actually experienced because the youngsters can associate the ideas with pictures in their minds (Singer & Singer, 1977, p. 6). This association reveals why children need to have many real experiences. Otherwise, they have few images stored in their brains to draw on.

A number of adults who have been identified as creative report that they engaged in a great deal of daydreaming and fantasy play as children (Singer, 1973, p. 228). This finding is not surprising when we realize that imaginative play relies heavily on the young child's creative skills. She must utilize previous experiences in new and different ways. She extracts the essence of a familiar experience such as getting ready for bed, and applies it creatively to a pretend activity such as putting to bed her doll, who doesn't want to go. Or she may take the role of the doll herself as well as that of the frustrated mother who is losing her patience with the stubborn dollie.

343

The child experiments with the situation, playing it this way one time and that way another. If a peer joins in, then there is another point of view to reckon with. If the original player strays too far from her role, she may lose it to a player with more definite ideas on how a mother should act. Or she may switch to a different role herself and try on yet another set of characteristics. She learns to recall fragments of past experiences and combine them in novel ways, adding original dialog, fresh nuances to her characterizations, and new directions to her plots. No playwright ever had better practice.

In addition to being her own creative playwright, she is also the actor, the director, the audience for other actors, and an interactor with others, whether she plays her role or steps out of it to make "aside" comments on progress of the spontaneous play. Just as with every other aspect of her development, she is developing her own creativity when she has the freedom and time to participate in imaginative play. As the Singers (1990) note:

> We assume that early imaginative play is a precursor of later fanciful thought, and we propose that such play has particular adaptive features. When children engage in symbolic games they are practicing mental skills that will later stand them in good stead, just as practice in walking, balancing, or swimming aids in the development of motor skills. (p. 22)

This time the knowledge children create is about real life and the other actors in it: how they behave; how they respond to stressful situations; how they carry out their work roles; how they speak; how they interact with one another. Adult observers of imaginative play find that most of the make-believe play of children centers around "the social problems of adults with whom children have close contacts" (Smilansky, 1968, p. 21). Common themes include the family and home; doctors and hospitals; work and professions; school; and dramatizations of escape, rescue, and superheroes.

Playing at life is not the inconsequential activity many adults seem to think it is. Children who have had extensive practice with imaginative play are often those who are most successful in life as adults. Many children from low-income homes who have not been allowed or encouraged to engage in such play may be at a disadvantage as adults, for they have missed an important grounding in social, intellectual, and creative skills.

Chapter 5 discusses imaginative play as it applies to the development of children's social skills in solitary, parallel, and group play. This chapter will look at the same phenomenon in relation to the development of creativity in young children. To discover where the children in your classroom stand in the sequence of their development, assess each child using the eight items of the Child Skills Checklist as you observe children pretending in the dramatic play area, at the water table, in the block area, at the wood bench, with science materials, at the painting easels, or on the playground.

You will find young children pretend about everything they do, both alone and with others. Tap into this rich vein of creativity in young children yourself, and you may see life and the world from a completely new and fresh perspective: the *what if* point of view. This *what if* perspective is the true magic of childhood, the belief that children can make life anything they want it to be.

Adults know from the hard facts of reality that life cannot be changed so easily— or can it? What if we also believed we could really make life anything we wanted it to be? Does believing make it so? Children act as if this idea were true. Is there a way we can help them develop into adults who will actually be able to make their adult lives come out the way they want them to be? Is there a way we can preserve the child in ourselves so we can do the same? Take a hard look at the developmental sequence in imaginative play that follows to see what you need to do to keep this spark alive in children and to rekindle its essence in your own life.

PRETENDS AN ACTION WITHOUT TAKING A ROLE

This Checklist item describes one of the earliest of the imaginative play behaviors in young children. Incredibly enough, it appears as early as one year (Smilanksy, 1968 p. 10). By 18 months, infants may go through the imaginary routine of feeding themselves with an empty spoon and cup, and even saying "Yummy!" The Singers (1977) believe this tendency to play or replay past events through imagery is one of the basic capacities of the human brain (p. 3). At first the pretend actions involve only the child himself; later they may involve toys, dolls, and eventually people. The youngsters do not take a role in this play. They are themselves. The only pretending is the action. As Davidson (1996) notes:

> When children first begin pretending, they will engage in single acts of symbolic play, as in the case of a child pretending to drink from a toy glass. Often very young children will pretend with regard to action, without necessarily taking on another role. The child may care for the baby by rocking it, without pretending to be a mother or a father. (p. 32)

By two years of age, most children spend a great deal of time at home or in a toddler program replaying fragments of everyday experience if given the chance. Pieces of familiar routines are repeated with little change or little effort to expand them into a longer sequence. The toddler will put the baby to bed by putting the doll in the cradle, covering it, and saying "Night-night." Then the toddler will pick up the doll and begin the routine all over again. Once a particular routine is established with a two-year-old, it seems to become quite rigid, almost like a ritual (Segal & Adcock, 1981, p. 92).

Words are not all that important in the pretending of two-year-olds, however. The youngsters use them sparingly, mainly to accompany actions or for sound effects. Once these youngsters get an idea for pretend play, they try to put it into action immediately. They do not set the stage with words, or search for appropriate props.

Props may be used, though, if they are available. Two-year-olds use props realistically, for the most part. Dishes are used realistically for eating, and not as a pretend steering wheel or a flying saucer. Because these youngsters are also impulsive in their behavior, props can influence the type of pretend play they engage in. A toy broom can inspire them to sweep, for instance, even though they had no previous plans for cleaning.

The first imaginative play of youngsters mainly concerns chores and routines, such as eating, going to bed, caring for the baby, talking on the phone, turning on television, shopping, visiting grandma, driving the car, and getting gas for the car. Two-year-olds are very serious about it, and take offense if adults make fun of their sometimes comical modes of pretending.

Doll play is also a frequent activity for both boys and girls of this age. Dolls are usually undressed, laid in a box or bed, and covered completely over with a piece of cloth in a very ritualized routine (Caplan & Caplan, 1983, p. 143). These children are not pretending to be mother or anyone other than themselves because they have not yet developed perspective-taking, that is, the ability to see something from another point of view.

The play of two-year-olds is frequently solitary and rarely involves more than one other player. They and their agemates have not yet developed the social skills for coming together in a common endeavor. When two children this age play together, one usually imitates the other. However, others will join in if they see one child doing something, and sometimes a wild melee ensues. The pretend play of children this young is brief at best, and it may disintegrate suddenly into running and squealing if other children are around.

Young three-year-olds who have not done much imaginative play may start in this manner in your center: pretending by playing a familiar home-centered routine, but not taking on a role. They may eventually expand their early single actions into a string of actions composing an episode. For example, they may put the baby doll to bed, get out the dishes, set the table, pick up the baby, and sit down to eat.

As they become more experienced players by interacting with others around them, they are often assigned a role by a more mature player. Whether they can actually play this role depends on their perspective-taking ability: whether they can see things from a different perspective than their own. Some children merely watch what the others are doing. Some continue with their own pretend actions, but with little recognition of a role as such. Others imitate their play partners and little by little learn how to play a spontaneous pretend role.

As with stages of social play, children seem to progress from watching others to solitary imaginative play, to parallel play, and eventually to cooperative play. As an observer, you may see this progression more easily with children who play with pretend objects such as dolls, figures of people and animals, or cars and trucks. They may be playing in the block area, house area, manipulative area, or sand table. In the dramatic play area itself, where children are playing roles in a spontaneous drama, it is sometimes difficult to recognize who has a role and who is playing the same theme in the same space but without a role.

If You Have Not Checked This Item: Some Helpful Ideas

■ Have Appropriate Props Available

Knowing that the youngest children pretend mainly about familiar household routines, you should have eating, cleaning, and sleeping props available in your dramatic play area. Put out all kinds of baby dolls and their beds as well.

■ Read a Book with an Accompanying Doll Character

Children identify closely with the characters in the books they like, both human and animal characters. Be sure to have dolls or puppets that look like characters from some of your books. As children's literature specialist Barbara Z. Kiefer (1995) notes:

I found that picture books inspired imaginative experiences for children. Their language in response to picture books allowed them to participate in the imaginary world created by the author and artist or to create their own images. Younger children often "chose" a character that they wanted to be as they read or looked through a book. (pp. 29–30)

After reading a book having a doll character, be sure to put both book and doll together in the book area or the doll area to encourage children to pretend with them. The most immature pretenders in your class may still not be ready to "be" a character from a favorite book, but they may like to pretend with dolls or stuffed animals that represent characters they like. One of the best and most reasonable sources for books and book character dolls and animals is

Demco's Kids & Things
P.O. Box 7488
Madison, WI 53707-7488

Be sure to write for their catalog. Favorite books and dolls available from Demco include

Baby Rattlesnake (baby rattlesnake puppet)
Cleversticks (Chinese boy puppet)
Curious George (Curious George monkey puppet)
If You Give a Mouse a Cookie (mouse doll and cookie)
If You Give a Moose a Muffin (moose hand puppet and muffin)
Mama Do You Love Me? (Inuit girl doll character)
Whistle for Willie (African American Peter doll character)

ASSIGNS ROLES OR TAKES ASSIGNED ROLES

Three-year-olds usually find it is more fun when several children play together. You will have checked on this previously in your observations concerning social play. This item signals the beginning of peer play for most children. Pretend episodes usually do not last long in the beginning because most children of this age are not yet flexible when it comes to differences of opinions. This inflexibility sometimes shows up when it comes to who will play what role.

Many three-year-olds try to control imaginative play by assigning the roles. The dominant child takes the role he or she wants and assigns the others, who may or may not agree. Most children this age want their own role. As their creativity blossoms through this type of play, their solutions to role assignment problems are often highly creative and something an adult would not have thought of. Listen to your children to see how they resolve such problems.

The role of mother is a favorite one for girls of this age. What would you do when four girls playing together want to be the mother and no one will give in? After a few minutes of discussion—or rather argument—when it became clear that Janie (who spoke up first about being the mother) would not change, nor would the other three, then a different solution needed to be found. The girls accepted the fact that the household could only have one mother, but they could not accept that they would have to be sisters or babies or grandmothers. Suddenly one of the girls said, "We'll all be other mothers who are visiting Janie this morning," and they were.

Three-year-olds who are playing pretend roles at home often will act the same way in assigning roles, even to adults. "I'll be the mother and you be the baby," is a role reversal commonly proposed by a child to her mother. Go along with the role reversal if you are the adult, and you will enjoy observing how your child plays your role as mother.

Here is a typical role assignment situation played by three-year-olds and recorded in a running record:

> Sherry is in the play grocery store holding a box of cereal. She hands box to child playing role of cashier. Walks back to grocery shelves. Picks up box and puts it in grocery cart. "Here's our groceries, Mother," she says to Ann who is standing nearby. Picks up bag filled with groceries and carries it to play house. Walks back to grocery store. "I'm gonna be mother," she says loudly to herself. "Mother, it's time to go home," she says to Ann. Ann gives no response but pays for her groceries. "There are no more groceries. We have to leave now," says Sherry. Still gets no response from Ann. "I'm the mother and you're the grandmother. I'm not a little kid," she says to Ann. No response. They walk to house together. She puts her bag down and helps Ann with hers. "We have to unload everything now." They start to unpack all the groceries. "Oh, no, daughter," she says to Ann, "When it's cleanup time we have to pick all this up." Both girls laugh.

Since Ann was originally the director of this play episode and Sherry had evidently agreed to the role of daughter by taking it, it is interesting to see what strategies Sherry now uses to get out of an unwanted role. First she states loudly but to herself that she is going to be the mother. Since she receives no response, she retains her daughter role at first, but then states outright to Ann that she is the mother and Ann can be the grandmother. Sherry still gets no response. Silence does not signify consent among young children. Silence may only mean that the challenged child does not want to engage in an argument, not that she agrees to give up her role. Sherry tries calling Ann "daughter," but Ann refuses to get involved verbally, so the role problem is still unresolved before cleanup time ends the play.

Another imaginative play episode previously recorded in Figure 1–3 shows older three- and four-year-olds engaged in the type of role assignment problem being discussed here:

> Katy is playing by herself with plastic blocks, making guns; she walks into other room.
>
> K: "Lisa, would you play with me? I'm tired of playing by myself."

They walk into other room to slide and climbing area.

K: "I am Wonder Woman."

L: "So am I."

K: "No, there is only one Wonder Woman. You are Robin."

L: "Robin needs a Batman because Batman and Robin are friends."

All this takes place under slides and climber. Lisa shoots block gun that Katy has given her. Katy falls on floor.

L (to teacher): "We're playing Superfriends and Wonder Woman keeps falling down."

Katy opens eyes, gets up and says:

K: "Let's get out our Batmobile and go help the world." *She runs to other room and back making noises like a car.*

L: "Wonder Woman is died. She fell out of the car." *She falls down.*

K: "It's only a game. Wake up, Lisa. You be Wonder Woman. I'll be. . . . "

L: "Let's play house now."

Katy begins sliding down slide.

K: "We have a lot of Superfriends to do." *(She says this while sliding.)* "Robin is coming after you!" *(She shouts to Lisa, running from slide and into other room.) Lisa has gone into housekeeping area and says to Katy:*

L: "Katy, here is your doll's dress." *(Lost yesterday.) John joins the girls.*

L: "I'm Wonder Woman."

K: "I'm Robin."

J: "I'm Batman. Where is the Batmobile?"

K: "It's in here."

They run into the other room and Katy points under the slide platform, telling John what the Batmobile can do. Then they all run into the other room and back again.

K: "John, we are not playing Superfriends any more."

This typical pretending episode illustrates perfectly the kind of role assignment and switching so characteristic of children this age. It is obvious from the children's easy agreements that they have played together before and therefore accept certain conditions. Katy is the director here and assigns the roles. She takes the role of Wonder Woman and assigns Lisa the role of Robin. Lisa really does not agree (we soon see), but she accepts her assignment. She probably has gone through this with Katy before and knows that if she plays along without making a fuss, her turn will come. It comes quite soon, in fact, when she notes that Katy seems to have abandoned the Wonder Woman role by suddenly getting out the Batmobile and "going to help the world."

Here Lisa announces that she is Wonder Woman and has fallen out of the car and died. Katy agrees to Lisa's new role by saying: "It's only a game. Wake up, Lisa.

You be Wonder Woman." When John joins the game and takes the role of Batman, the girls do not object at first. But obviously they know how to get rid of unwanted players by announcing: "John, we are not playing Superfriends any more."

(The teacher later told the observer that she allows superhero play as long as it does not get out of bounds. She does not allow gun play and did not realize that was happening or she would have intervened.)

Observe to discover what other creative ploys your children use to get peers to take role assignments or to get out of assigned roles they don't want and into ones they really want. Other strategies used to resolve play conflicts in a positive manner are discussed in Chapter 5.

If your children are engaged in this kind of dramatic play, you will probably be checking this item. If you leave it blank, it means either that the child is not playing because he has not reached this level of group imaginative play, or that he does not assign roles or accept assignments. If this is the case, he has probably not reached the group play level, because children who play together like this soon come to an understanding about role assignments.

If You Have Not Checked This Item: Some Helpful Ideas

■ Be a Model for Pretend Play

It is not up to you to force a child into group play. Such play should be totally spontaneous. But you can certainly help a shy child become involved with a group by taking a role yourself and inviting the child to take a role and come along with you into the play group. Davidson (1996) suggests other ways the teacher can help support pretending:

> If a child is pretending to cook, the adult can ask about what is cooking, showing that this act of pretending is valued. If a child needs help taking on or expanding a role, adults can model pretending. If an adult picks up a play phone and talks, often a child will then imitate by picking up the other phone and answering. (p. 33)

On the other hand, teachers need to restrain themselves from entering pretend play too vigorously. After all, this is the children's spontaneous creation and should remain so. Teachers can help in many ways to get onlookers involved or to keep the play going on an even keel, but then they should extract themselves unobtrusively as players. As Berk (1994) notes:

> Adults walk a fine line in making effective contributions to children's pretense. The power of adult-child play to foster development is undermined by communication that is too overpowering or one sided. (p. 36)

■ Read a Book

A Lion for Lewis by Rosemary Wells (New York: Dial, 1982) is the story of dress-up play in the attic by two five-year-olds and three-year-old Lewis, who always gets assigned to play the inferior roles and never a main character. He is baby to the older children's mother and father, sick child to their doctor and nurse, and maid to their king and princess. Lewis eventually gets his way, however, much in the manner of real children, by finding something better that the older children really respect: in Lewis's case, a lion suit into which he climbs to turn the play upside down. It is the same kind of creative solution that real children use when their peers block them.

Developing creativity, as you can see, means much more than becoming an artist or writer. Perhaps the most valuable lesson children learn from imaginative play, in fact, is how to develop creative solutions to life's sticky interpersonal problems. What an exceptionally strong inducement that is for the promoting of imaginative play in early childhood!

When You Were Little and I Was Big by Priscilla Galloway (Toronto: Annick, 1984) is a role-reversal story about a little girl who makes believe she is big and her mother is little. The illustrations show the girl looking like the big mummy, only wearing her same red overalls and striped shirt, while the mummy appears little. The girl narrates the story and tells her mother what she would do in each one of several everyday situations, just like her mother has already done with her.

TAKES ON CHARACTERISTICS AND ACTIONS OF ROLE

Four-year-olds have more experience than three-year-olds when it comes to creating a role in their pretend play. Because they desperately want to participate in the adult world, four-year-olds try out all sorts of adult roles: mother at work, father at work, doctor, nurse, bus driver, astronaut, waiter, fast-food cook, gas station attendant, mail carrier, firefighter, truck driver, train conductor, or crane operator. In addition, four-year-olds play their roles with many more realistic details. They select props more carefully, dress up more elaborately, and carry out the role with more appropriate dialog and actions.

If you listen carefully to four-year-olds when you are observing them doing imaginative play, you will be able to learn a great deal about their understanding of the people and situations in their world. In addition, you may gain quite a respect for their use of creativity in developing their roles. Even the mundane roles of mother, father, brother, and baby are played with new twists and novel solutions to problems. Dialogue is expanded, and the players even express emotions quite eloquently where appropriate.

Language is used more than ever before to set the scene and create the mood. Because the players are beginning to make greater distinctions between real and pretend, they often make aside-like comments about things that are not real, just pretend, so that you, their peers, and even they themselves understand what is real and what is pretend.

Four-year-olds are also more flexible about taking different roles. Children who would not take a bad guy's role at age three may play it to the hilt with great gusto at age four.

Observe your children carefully as they pretend in the dramatic play area, in the block corner, at the water table, and on the playground. Are they playing roles with greater realism than before, using expanded dialog, showing more emotion, and almost becoming the character? If so, you should mark this item on the checklist.

If You Have Not Checked This Item: Some Helpful Ideas

■ Have Many Sets of Flannelboard Characters

Children can use cutout characters from their favorite storybooks to play with on a flannelboard. Obtain an extra paperback copy of the book, cut out the characters (away from the children), and mount them on cardboard with sandpaper or Velcro backing. Keep the characters in a manila envelope with an uncut copy of the book inside. Then children can look at pictures from the story when they play. The youngsters can act out scenes from the book if they want, or they can have the characters participate in brand-new adventures. This activity is good practice in role playing with characters the children already know. A child can play by herself or with another child. More than two children at the same flannelboard is a bit crowded. Keep more than one flannelboard in the book area if you want this to be a popular activity. Flannelboards can be made by mounting flannel or felt to a piece of cardboard folded in two and hinged at the top so that it stands easily on a table. Some favorite storybooks in paperback from which you may want to cut out characters are:

> *Will I Have a Friend?* (Miriam Cohen, New York: Collier, 1967)
> *Corduroy* (Don Freeman, New York: Viking, 1968)
> *Whistle for Willie* (Ezra Jack Keats, New York: Puffin, 1977)
> *Where the Wild Things Are* (Maurice Sendak, New York: Scholastic, 1963)
> *Strega Nona* (Tomie dePaola, Upper Saddle River, NJ: Merrill/Prentice Hall, 1975)
> *The Three Billy Goats Gruff* (Paul Galdone, New York: Clarion Books, 1973)

NEEDS PARTICULAR PROPS TO DO PRETEND PLAY

Play researcher Sara Smilansky (1968) discusses three types of pretending that occur in dramatic play: pretending with regard to a role, pretending with regard to an object, and pretending with regard to an action. Teachers can support children's pretend play by providing representational props, toys, and dress-up clothes. The youngest children and those just learning to do pretend play need more realistic props. As Gowen (1995) describes:

> Representational toys are toys that strongly represent real objects and beings, such as dolls, toy vehicles, dishes, cooking utensils, stoves, telephones, and doctor's kits. . . . These toys prompt children to pretend to engage in the activities of others, to do the things they see adults do. (p. 78)

If three-year-olds have had a chance to pretend when they were two, then they gradually develop new skills and interests in their imaginative play. The fragments of familiar routines that occupied the children earlier become more extended and less rigid as the youngsters mature. Three-year-olds begin to think a bit about the pretending they are about to do, rather than acting on a sudden impulse. This forethought often leads them to preplan the play by finding or gathering certain realistic props. In fact, some three-year-olds cannot proceed with play until they find the right prop.

Teachers can support children's pretend play by providing appropriate props, toys, and dress-up clothes.

The rigidity many three-year-olds express in their ritualistic manner of pretending thus often carries over in their insistence on particular props to play. Three-year-olds may believe they need a particular hat, costume, doll, or steering wheel to carry out a role. Many times the object is the basis for the play, but not so much on impulse as with two-year-olds. Three-year-olds very much enjoy dressing up and playing a role, and they have a much broader concept of how to do it.

Props may very well serve the children as an instrument for getting out of themselves. Because three-year-olds are still strongly self-centered, they may need a prop to break away from their own point of view. Just as shy children can lose themselves in speaking through a hand puppet or from behind a mask, three-year-olds may need the extra impetus of an object outside themselves to get them started in pretending to be someone else.

Family activities are a large part of three-year-olds' pretend play in preschool programs. Play researcher Fergus P. Hughes (1991) notes:

> There are clear indications that threes, unlike twos, begin to identify strongly with adults—to become increasingly interested in what adults do and to imagine themselves doing the same things. Perhaps as a result, threes become interested in dramatic play, in which they have an opportunity to act out adult roles for themselves. (p. 74)

Doll play, hospital play, and pretending to be a community helper are common themes. Three-year-olds also enjoy driving cars and trains, flying jet planes, and being firefighters. They can carry these themes out in dramatic play, block building, table block games, clay creations, the water table, and the woodworking bench, as well as with puppets and toy telephones—anywhere and everywhere children gather.

It is up to you and your coworkers to provide the props that support pretend play in these areas. Bring in a set of jet planes and figures of people, place them in the sand table with posters of planes mounted on the wall nearby, and see what happens. Be sure to provide safety goggles to keep sand out of eyes. Some astute child is sure to point out that pilots of some kinds of planes wear goggles, and soon you may have several goggled "pilots" zooming around the classroom with their planes!

After a trip to the zoo or animal farm, bring in toy animals to the block center along with figures of people, toy trees, cars, and perhaps a little train to carry people around the block center zoo that the children may build. It is important to provide appropriate props for children to pretend with in various learning centers of the classroom after such a trip. Playing with such props is not just a matter of fun, but it helps young children to symbolize in a concrete way the more abstract ideas gained from the trip. Classroom staff can encourage children to remember what they saw on the field trip and build their own miniature trip site, or pretend to be one of the people they met at the site.

Young children learn best through concrete, hands-on activities. The props you provide for imaginative play can help them create spontaneous dramas about any topic of current interest. As Gowen (1995) notes:

> Props relevant to the children's culture and community can enrich the children's efforts to construct and express their understanding of significant events and roles in their lives. (p. 78)

For example, one morning Ricardo's grandmother visited his preschool and helped the children prepare tamales for lunch. Afterward the teacher put out a plastic set of Mexican food in the housekeeping area for the children to pretend with. She also read them the book *Too Many Tamales* by Gary Soto (New York: Putnam's, 1993).

For days thereafter a number of the children spontaneously acted out the tamale preparation, but with their own unique twist. Since the Mexican food set included only plastic tacos, the children invented their own tamales by using plastic egg rolls from a Chinese food set and wrapping them with paper for corn husks! Then they hid a toy ring in the wrapping for someone to try and find, just as in the storybook (Beaty, 1997, p. 159).

Not every child will be interested in pretending in this manner, just as not every child will like a particular book. Do not force or even urge youngsters to participate who show no interest. Read the story, put out the materials, and let those who want to engage in playing with them. As Gowan reminds us: "As always, the rule in promoting development through play is to follow the child's lead" (1995, p. 78).

If You Have Not Checked This Item: Some Helpful Ideas

■ Have a Variety of Props Available

In the large motor area, have large wooden riding trucks, wagons, and a wheelbarrow, as well as large hollow blocks and floorboards for building child-size structures.

Put out a full-length mirror in the dress-up area. Include costume jewelry, scarves, handbags, wallets, belts, vests, shoes, aprons, all kinds of hats, doctor's equipment, goggles, binoculars, badges, umbrella, and canes. An assortment of men's and women's clothes in teenage size is often easier for young children to handle than adult-size clothing.

Think of the learning centers in your classroom as areas for children's imaginative play to take place. What props can you put in the block area after a field trip to a construction site, for instance? What about construction vehicles and workers, string for wires, straws for pipes, and popsicle sticks for lumber? Think about filling other centers with such accessories: sand table, water table, woodworking area, clay table, writing center, and of course, the dramatic play area.

■ Take Many Field Trips

For children to become involved in spontaneous dramatic play activities, they must have firsthand knowledge about them. Ask children where they have gone with their parents. If many have gone on picnics, put out picnic props in the dramatic play area. If many children have not experienced a picnic, plan a picnic field trip to a nearby park . . . or even to the playground outside. Afterwards put out the props.

Take field trips to nearby sites of interest to the children such as barber/beauty shop, farm, fast-food restaurant, laundromat, farmer's market, flower shop, pet store, repair shop, gas station, shoe store, fire station, or doctor's clinic. Then put out dress-up props in the dramatic play center and miniature figures in the block area for children to pretend with. A book that lists props for these and many other trips is *Resources for Dramatic Play* by Lois Brokering (Carthage, IL: Fearon Teacher Aids, 1989).

■ Read a Book

For descriptions of multicultural picture books you can read to your children and afterward put out dolls or puppets for them to pretend with, read *Building Bridges with Multicultural Picture Books* by Janice J. Beaty (Upper Saddle River, NJ: Merrill/Prentice Hall, 1997). Some examples of favorite books for which doll characters are available include

> *Abuela* (Arthur Dorros, New York: Dutton, 1991; Hispanic girl)
> *Amazing Grace* (Mary Hoffman, New York: Dial, 1991; African American girl)
> *At the Crossroads* (Rachel Isadora, New York: Greenwillow, 1991; African boy)
> *Carlos and the Squash Plant* (Jan Stevens, Flagstaff, AZ: Northland, 1993; Hispanic boy)
> *Cleversticks* (Bernard Ashley, New York: Crown, 1991; Chinese boy)
> *The Legend of the Bluebonnet* (Tomie DePaola, New York: Putnam, 1983; Native American girl)
> *Mama, Do You Love Me?* (Barbara Joose, San Francisco: Chronicle, 1991; Native Alaskan girl)
> *One of Three* (Angela Johnson, New York: Orchard, 1991; African American girl)

Rise and Shine, Mariko-chan! (Chiyoko Tomioka, New York: Scholastic, 1991; Japanese girl)

Tar Beach (Faith Ringgold, New York: Crown, 1991; African American girl)

CAN PRETEND WITH IMAGINARY OBJECTS

Children go through a succession of levels in pretending with objects just as they do with roles. Beginners seem to need highly realistic objects for their pretend play: a toy telephone for a real telephone; a plastic apple for a real apple; a toy car for a real car. As they mature and become more experienced pretenders, children are able to use less representational props: a cylinder block for a telephone; a ball for an apple; a unit block for a car. This is called object substitution.

The most highly imaginative children are able to make an even greater leap in substitution of objects. They can pretend without any concrete object at all. They can call on an imaginary telephone grasped just so in their hand. An imaginary apple is held somewhat differently with their fingers curled around empty space. An imaginary car can speed along the floor with their hand directing its movements and their voice making sound effects.

Observe your children in the dramatic play area to see how they use objects in their pretending. Often children pay for their groceries with imaginary money, although they may carry a real purse. They may ride around the room on an imaginary motorcycle, but wear a real cycle helmet, or eat pretend food in the housekeeping area, but use real toy forks and spoons. As Gowen (1995) notes:

> The inclusion of imaginary elements in play indicates that the child can entertain these ideas without them being tied to concrete objects and real beings. As the child's representational abilities develop, she can imagine objects and beings and more readily symbolize them with words alone. (pp. 79–80)

Not all children arrive at this stage of using imaginary objects rather than real ones. It is often children with more experience or better use of language who use less representational toys or imaginary ones. Does this mean a teacher should not include so many realistic props in the dramatic play or block centers? Davidson (1996) notes:

> There is some research that shows that less realistic props are preferable for older children, since the props do not put a limit on the direction of the play. Although more open-ended props can be provided for older children, it is important to remember that more realistic props may be needed by less skilled older players. (pp. 33–34)

However, many toy companies carry the realism too far, making toys that move by themselves, make their own sounds, and have lights that go on and off. You will not find such toys in most preschools, and with good reason. Children's own imaginations are not challenged if the toy does everything and all a youngster can do is to turn it on and watch it perform. Such toys tend not to hold children's interest for more than a few days, while toys that children must interact with never lose their appeal. Martha B. Bronson in her book *The Right Stuff for Children Birth to 8: Selecting Play Materials to Support Development* (Washington, DC: NAEYC, 1995) says this about toys for preschoolers:

> Fantasy play is at its height during this age period. Children of both genders use dolls that represent fantasy characters (family members, robots, police, etc.). To promote creative imaginative play, these dolls should be generic rather than detailed and specific. (p. 88)

Bronson also favors giving children materials to construct their own play scenes rather than purchasing prefabricated scenes such as a house, school, garage, airport, or farm. Unit blocks and building bricks "require more flexibility and creativity on the part of the child and support more variety in play" (Bronson, 1995, p. 88). Although preschool children enjoy realistic equipment, they are capable of creating their own settings from very simple materials.

Nevertheless, children will often choose a representational toy rather than a substitute object. Although it is important to have representational toys for everyone, having too many can discourage the development of imagination. Learning centers where imaginative play takes place should also include open-ended materials that children can use to create their own imaginary objects and settings: styrofoam, tissue tubes, empty boxes of all sizes, pipe cleaners, feathers, plastic bottles of all sizes, cardboard cartons, and other throw-away items that seem appropriate.

There is one other interesting form of object substitution you should look for in your observations of children's pretending with objects. When children play with toy people, animals, and dolls, pretending they can move and talk, they are doing what is called *active agent* object substitution. At first children play with toy figures as passive recipients of the play. They may feed them or dress them or ride them around in a vehicle. When the toy becomes an active agent, the child walks it around as if it were alive, and also talks for it. Gowen (1995) notes:

> An especially sophisticated form of active-agent play occurs when children have two or more toy beings interact with one another. For example, the child hops one toy person into the toy car and says in a low voice, "I'm going to work now," then turns another toy person around and says in a high voice, "Okay, I'll see you later." (p. 80)

If you want your children to become involved in this highly imaginative play, be sure to provide appropriate materials: figures of people and animals, especially ones that can stand by themselves, as well as vehicles that can carry the figures.

If You Have Not Checked This Item: Some Helpful Ideas

■ Model the Desired Behavior

Some children need to see an adult pretending in order to get the idea of what to do themselves. One study showed that the most highly skilled preschool pretenders had mothers who pretended with their children at age one (Berk, 1994, p. 36). Be sure you occasionally join the children in their pretending. You need to remember that it is their play, and you should only be a visitor. Better than taking a role may be to make an appropriate comment when you see them doing imaginative play. "Oh, Reggie, I bet those animals really like those pens you are building for them." Or, "Here's a cracker for your doll, Samantha. Do you think she's hungry?"

■ Read a Book

Galimoto by Karen Lynn Williams (New York: Mulberry, 1990) tells the story of an African boy, Kondi, who is determined to find enough wire to build himself a *galimoto*, a push toy car with a long steering wheel. After a series of narrow escapes he finally assembles his galimoto into a pickup truck, although he thinks he may remake it into an ambulance, airplane, or helicopter tomorrow.

USES LANGUAGE FOR CREATING AND SUSTAINING THE PLOT

While two-year-olds do most of their pretending without much language, three-, four-, and five-year-olds depend upon language to set the scene and sustain the action. If they are playing by themselves, they often will talk to themselves about what is happening. They also will speak for the characters—all of them. If the youngsters are playing with other children, they often use a great deal of dialogue to carry out their ideas. This behavior promotes their improved use of language and dialogue with others. In addition, it provides yet another opportunity for them to express creativity in the fresh and novel way they use words.

Words direct what the children do, the way the youngsters act, who the characters are, the unfolding of the plot, and the way the children resolve conflict. Children involved in pretending who do not have the language skills of the more advanced players are able to listen and eventually imitate the advanced players' use of language. Everyone involved gets excellent practice in improving speaking skills, trying out new words, and using familiar language in new ways.

For some children, a new experience is the use of language to express feelings. The characters in these spontaneous make-believe situations need to express how they feel about what is happening to them. Many children have trouble putting their feelings into words. Younger children prefer to "act out" rather than speak out. This type of imaginative play gives them the opportunity to learn how to express feelings.

The youngsters, in fact, are projecting their feelings by expressing what a character feels. Even if the character is a doll, a puppet, or an inanimate figure of a person or an animal, the children have yet another opportunity to speak. Children three and four years old are often more comfortable expressing the feelings of toy people than their own. The youngsters like to take their dolls or stuffed animals to the doctor's office, to listen to these pretend people express their fears, and to comfort them. In

Three- and four-year-old children depend on language to set the scene and sustain the plot of their pretend play.

doing so, the children sort out their own impressions about the situation and try out their own sometimes novel ideas for resolving problems.

Smilansky (1968) has found three main functions of language in this sort of dramatic play: imitating adult speech, imagining the make-believe situation (mainly dialog), and managing the play. In this regard, language serves to explain, command, and direct the action (p. 27).

If you listen carefully to the actors in imaginative play, you will note they carry out all three of these functions. They definitely imitate adult speech. You can practically hear yourself speaking if you are the parent or the teacher of any of these children. Children also bring imagery to life in the characterizations they express through dialogue. Finally, someone in the group, usually the self-assigned director, is forever stepping outside her role to explain or reaffirm what is going on.

If inner imagery allows the child to pretend in the first place, then talking aloud allows him to expand the meaning of what he visualizes. He not only hears himself speaking, but he also receives feedback from others' reactions. This feedback helps him revise and refine ideas and word use. Until he arrives at the point where he can create and sustain the action of pretend situations through language, he will miss the value of using his imagination in this manner. Eventually he must use mainly language and not just imagining in thinking. Thus imaginative play serves as a sort of transitional activity for the preschool child to learn spoken words for his internal images.

Creative adults, especially writers, need to be able to express their imagery in words like this. Mental pictures are not enough. Many writers admit to experiencing rich fantasy lives as children. Having a variety of opportunities for pretending in the preschool setting may help your children to become such creative adults.

If You Have Not Checked This Item: Some Helpful Ideas

■ Use Hand Puppets

Have a variety of hand puppets available for the children: animals, characters from books, community helpers, adults, and children figures. A puppet theater made from a cardboard carton can help motivate the children's use of puppets as play actors. You may need to put on a puppet show yourself to set the stage, so to speak, for your children's dramas. Younger children tend to use puppets as an extension of their arms, using the puppet's mouth for pretend biting rather than for speaking, as mentioned previously. Your modeling behavior can show the children a better way to use puppets.

It is not necessary to have a puppet theater in the beginning, but your more advanced pretenders may expand their repertoire of imaginative play if a puppet theater is available. Make puppets or purchase them from toy stores, children's book stores, science museum shops, nature stores, store kitchen departments where they are sold as pot holders, or educational supply catalogues such as Demco's Kids & Things (P.O. Box 7488, Madison, WI 53707-7488).

USES EXCITING, DANGER-PACKED THEMES

Most four-year-olds do everything in a more exuberant out-of-bounds manner than three-year-olds, including pretending. Four-year-olds are more noisy, active, and aware of things outside themselves. They are fascinated with matters of life and death, and they begin to use such themes more often in their imaginative play. Superheroes and other television characters show up in their pretending. Bad guys are captured. Good guys are rewarded. People get shot and killed.

Adults look askance and blame television. They think that TV watching surely must be bad for young children. By the age of four, children are viewing an average of four hours of television a day. Surely this viewing must affect their pretending and imaginations. Research by children's play specialists, the Singers, however, resulted in findings contrary to what they had expected. They found no relationship of statistical significance between watching television and imaginary play. Pretending neither increased nor decreased as a result of watching television.

The strongest correlation the Singers found was between the amount of television watched and overt aggression in the classroom. How true, nursery school teachers agree, without perhaps realizing that four-year-olds have always exhibited aggression in their play. The real reason for the increased aggression could well be that sitting and watching television for long periods does not allow young children to discharge their pent-up energy and aggressive feelings as does normal active play (Segal & Adcock, 1981, p. 138).

Four-year-olds are extremely active and must have daily opportunities to discharge this pent-up energy. It is only natural for this energy to take the form of powerful superhero character roles from the television programs the children watch. Ask adults who were raised before the days of television what form their wildest pretending took, and you will hear tales of cowboys and Indians, cops and robbers, or war play.

The argument against allowing superhero play talks about the television cartoons children see that show superheroes controlling others through threat, force, and violence. Many teachers describe superhero play in their classrooms as being characterized by "disjointed bursts of activity which deteriorated rapidly into too-rough, too-loud play" (Pena, French, & Holmes, 1987, p. 11). In addition, "From our observations, it appears that superhero play may not be able to sustain itself and be reasonably free of adult intervention" (Pena et al., p. 13).

What should a teacher do who has a strong belief in the value of fantasy play, but does not believe the amount of adult intervention required to keep superhero play from bursting out-of-bounds is worth the effort? Should superhero play be banned from the classroom entirely? No, say many teachers. There are ways to extract important learnings from this powerful play activity that seems to have so many youngsters in its grip:

> Star Wars hero Luke Skywalker learned from his mentor that the Force contained both Good and Evil. Luke had to learn to control the Evil in order to realize the Good. Superhero play is much like the Force; and like Luke Skywalker, we must learn to control the negative aspects of superhero fantasy play in order for children to realize its many benefits. (Johnston, 1987, p.16)

One of the more creative suggestions is to scale down the most violent play: that is, to turn it into a table-top activity. Most of the television characters are available in a variety of sizes from dolls to matchbox-scale figures, just right for table-top play. "By allowing this activity *only* while sitting at a table, running and crashing bodies cease to be a problem. The benefits of superhero play are not diminished simply because children are seated while they play" (Johnston, 1987, p. 17). Pretending, after all, can take place anywhere. Again, teachers must control the types of characters brought into the classroom. Use of guns, swords, and other weapons should not be allowed.

Group play comes into its own when children reach age four. When they first get together, however, it often degenerates like superhero play into a wild sort of activity without plot or dialog, almost a regression from children's previous role playing. This wildness seems to be a natural progression in their learning to get along with one another. The establishment and recognition of dominance is dealt with in such rough-and tumble play. Children also develop coping skills as they focus on the sometimes aggressive actions and reactions of peers. Out of these interactions comes a sense of common group purpose that sets the stage for the more organized play to follow.

Teachers can help, not by preventing wild play, but by redirecting its energy into the exciting, danger-packed themes that four-year-olds favor. Doctor play, always a favorite, can involve taking sick or injured patients to the hospital in an ambulance with a loud siren. One teacher found her children needed help organizing and elaborating on their ambulance plot. Some of the children were running around the room making loud siren noises. The teacher suggested they build an ambulance out of large hollow blocks. Now what could they do? This time, the teacher decided to play a role herself. A running record of an observation of four-year-old Jessica includes the following:

> *Jessica runs to climber, climbs up and sits on top. Teacher, who is trying to involve children in dramatic play, suggests they use the climber as their hospital. They are building an ambulance out of large blocks. Jessica climbs down & begins stacking blocks one on top of the other. She sits and watches others finish by taping paper plates colored yellow on front to use as headlights. She picks up plate and tapes it to rear of ambulance.*
>
> *Jessica runs to table to get felt-tip marker. "I want the yellow marker. Lots of yellow." She gets marker. "What am I gonna write on? I want to color something. I'll color the wheels black." Jessica drops yellow marker and picks up black one. She colors in back paper plate wheel with marker. "I want to color something yellow." Teacher suggests steering wheel. She does it.*
>
> *Jessica runs and climbs into block ambulance. "I'm the driver." She uses her plate as steering wheel. "I wanna be the patient." Jessica gets up and lies down in middle of ambulance. She gets carried to "the hospital" by teacher and other children. She lies by the climber and pretends to be sick, moaning and groaning. Other children leave, but she stays.*
>
> *Then she gets up and runs to table where teacher is helping children to make doctor bags. Teacher asks her what name she wants on her bag. She answers, "I want to be a nurse, not a doctor." Teacher asks what tools a nurse uses. She answers, "Nurses help, they don't use tools. Doctors use tools." Teacher asks, "What does your mother use when you are sick?" She answers, "I don't know."*
>
> *Jessica takes bag and runs back to ambulance with bag on arm, smiling. She yells, "Lisa, lay down, you're the patient." Jessica sits in front seat and drives ambulance using paper plate steering wheel. She hops up again and runs to teacher, asking her to be the doctor. She jumps up and down, urging the teacher to hurry. "Hurry, we're ready," she repeats. Teacher comes and helps carry Lisa to hospital.*

The teacher noted that more children participated in this particular role play than any others she had witnessed. An ambulance had gone by on the street outside earlier in the morning, siren blaring, and the children who saw it were excited but alarmed. This event prompted their building of the block ambulance. But the teacher's own participation in the play certainly stimulated the extra number of children to become involved. The teacher's idea for extending the play by helping the children make doctor bags added immensely to the drama. The running record, however, caught four-year-old Jessica just as she normally acted, always on the run.

Jessica's stereotyped answers about doctors is also typical of this age. Gender roles seem to become more rigid, with girls insisting on playing the mother, waitress, or teacher, while boys often want to play father, driver, policeman, or superhero. Same-gender groups form about this time, with girls' play becoming more relaxed and verbal, and boys' play faster paced and more aggressive (Segal & Adcock, 1981, p. 101).

Block play, for instance, may get out of hand with four-year-olds. It sometimes disintegrates into throwing when adults are not around, or even when they are. Try to change the violent direction of the block play by giving players a new task involving excitement or mystery: "Where is the mysterious tunnel I saw on the floor this morning, boys? What, you didn't see it? I'm surprised. I thought you had x-ray vision. I could see it right through the rug. You don't believe me? Well, maybe if you make your own tunnel, you'll be able to see the mystery tunnel, too. Jeff, you and Lennie know how to build tunnels. Maybe you could make a mystery tunnel at one end of the rug, and Jesse and Tyrone could make a tunnel at the other end. If the tunnels come together in the middle, you'd all be able to run your cars through one long tunnel. What do you think?"

If you observe that individual children who are four years old have not started playing with exciting, danger-packed themes, it may be that they are less mature than the others. How do they compare with other four-year-olds in motor skills, for instance? Obviously, it is not appropriate to push such children into something they are not interested in. Provide them with many opportunities to engage in play themes of their own interests. You will know what some of these are from your observations and conversations with such youngsters.

If You Have Not Checked This Item: Some Helpful Ideas

■ Read a Book

White Dynamite and Curly Kidd by Bill Martin Jr. and John Archambault (New York: Holt, 1986) bolts the reader through the heart-stopping ride of Curly Kidd on White Dynamite, meanest bull at the rodeo. Young Lucky Kidd clings precariously to the rails while describing Dad's furious ride in rodeo-talk: "Rackin'! Crackin'! The bull's sky trackin' . . . " But it is the bucking, swirling realistic illustrations, flinging dirt every which way, that create the most excitement—especially the discovery on the last page that, surprise, Lucky Kidd is a girl!

Put out sticks for horses after you read this book. But you may want to draw a chalk circle on the floor for a rodeo ring to keep your riders contained.

Amazing Grace by Mary Hoffmann (New York: Dial, 1991) describes the exciting imaginative play of African American Grace who dresses up and pretends to be Joan of Arc, Anansi the Spider, a peg-leg pirate, Hiawatha, and Mowgli in the backyard jungle. Put out a box of fancy dress-up clothes after this reading.

Abiyoyo by Pete Seeger (New York: Macmillan, 1986) is a South African folktale about a boy who annoys everyone by playing his ukelele, which makes people dance, and his magician father, who angers everyone by making things disappear with his magic wand ZOOP! They are put out of town where they live until the monster Abiyoyo who eats people makes his appearance. The boy's playing makes the monster dance till he falls down, and his father's magic wand zoops the monster out of existence. They return as heroes.

Children can make their own magic wands from sticks and ukeleles from shoeboxes if they want to reenact this story.

USES ELABORATE THEMES, IDEAS, DETAILS

The themes that four-year-olds use in their pretending are many of the same ones they used at age three, only much expanded. The youngsters still enjoy playing house. Both boys and girls play with dolls and take roles in the housekeeping corner. Doll Play now includes dressing as well as undressing, but the central action usually involves putting the doll to bed. Many girls of this age prefer playing with little girl dolls rather than baby dolls. Play with dollhouses, however, is still too detailed to hold the interest of most four-year-olds. They like the dolls more than the houses. Even block structures are not played with as much as they will be played with at age five. At age four, the pretending takes place during the process of building, rather than with the finished product afterwards.

Doctor play is at its peak at age four, and it will seldom be as popular again. All kinds of themes involving community helpers are used, especially after a visit by a community helper or a field trip to a work site. Superheroes are popular, as we have seen, especially television characters. Monsters sometimes appear, but they are still a bit too scary for four-year-olds to handle.

The pretend play of older four- and five-year-olds is characterized by the elaborate nature of the drama, no matter whether the theme is a common one or an invented adventure. Five-year-olds add all kinds of details through their dialog, dress-up, props, and imaginations. Their play gets so involved, in fact, that it even carries over from one day to the next. The players remember where they left off the day before and can start right in again.

There is much more talk during pretend play, as well, because five-year-olds have a better command of the language. With their improved language skills, they clarify ideas and talk out problems. Concerns about sickness, accidents, and death are dealt with more realistically in the imaginative play of five-year-olds. Although the youngsters like to use props, those with a high level of fantasy can pretend without props.

Boys and girls begin playing more in groups of the same gender by this time. The structure changes the nature of the play somewhat, with girls' play becoming more calm and boys' play becoming more active. Girls still prefer to play house, but boys more often play superhero or monster. Groups are often larger than before, as friendships expand and children learn how to get along with more than one or two peers.

Five-year-olds like to build big buildings and then play inside the structures. Imaginative play is at its height just before and during this period. After children enter first grade and games-with-rules become the norm, make-believe play begins to wane. It is not at all prevalent among children much after age seven.

By about age seven, a cognitive change that allows more abstract thinking has taken place within the child. What happens to pretending? We speculate that it does not disappear at all but becomes a part of the inner self to be tapped by adults in daydreaming as well as in generating creative ideas. Adults who experienced a rich fantasy life as children may be the fortunate possessors of the skill to play around with ideas in their heads, just as they did with props and toys as children in preschool.

As you observe the children in your classroom on the last of the checklist items, you may want to make a list of the themes the children are using in their play. What can you do to help them add more themes to this list? Put out more props? Read more stories? Help the children make more costumes? Take children on more field trips so they will have additional real experiences to draw from? All of these activities are good ideas. Try them, and see how your children respond.

If You Have Not Checked This Item: Some Helpful Ideas

■ Have Big Building Supplies

Four- and five-year-olds like to build big structures to play in. Have the youngsters use hollow wooden blocks if possible. Or bring in wooden packing crates you get from a wholesaler. Cardboard cartons, plastic milk carton carriers, scrap boards, and lumber can be used for building pretend huts, forts, houses, boats, race cars, and fire engines. Play houses also can be purchased commercially, or made out of pup tents, by covering a card table with a blanket, or by hanging sheets over lines strung in a corner of the room.

■ Read a Book

Children love to hear about *Owliver* by Robert Kraus (New York: Dutton, 1974), the little owl who likes to pretend. Owliver first pretends he is an orphan, but when his mother and father object, he pretends to be an actor. This time his father objects and gives him doctor and lawyer toys to encourage more serious interests. His mother, however, gives him acting lessons, including tap dancing. He fools them both, of course, by growing up to become . . . a fireman!

The Trek by Ann Jonas (New York: Mulberry Books, 1985) is the story of a little girl who is big enough to walk to school on her own. As she walks along, she pretends that jungle beasts are everywhere. The illustrations show them hidden in crocodile sidewalks, giraffe trees, zebra hedges, and camel walls.

OBSERVING, RECORDING, AND INTERPRETING IMAGINATION

Information from the running record on three-year-old Sherry can be transferred to the checklist in Figure 13–1.

The information from the running record that was transferred to the checklist shows Sherry as a mature player in this imaginative role. The only blank on her checklist ("Uses exciting, danger-packed themes") is more typically observed in a four-year-old, especially a boy. Table 13–1, which describes the ages and stages of pretend play can help you interpret your findings. Since imaginative play is an area of strength and confidence for Sherry, her teacher should consider using a dramatic play activity to help Sherry in a checklist area that needs strengthening. For example,

Child Skills Checklist

Name _____ Sherry _____   Observer _____ Carolyn _____

Program _____ Arnot Nursery _____   Dates _____ 2 / 17 _____

Directions:

Put a ✔ for items you see the child perform regularly. Put *N* for items where there is no opportunity to observe. Leave all other items blank.

Item	Evidence	Dates
11. Imagination		
_N_ Pretends an action without taking a role	She is beyond this level of play	2/17
✔ Assigns roles or takes assigned roles	Took role as daughter but later tried to assign this role to Ann	2/17
✔ Takes on characteristics & actions of role	Got groceries off shelf, put them in bag, went to cashier, took them home	2/17
✔ Needs particular props to do pretend play	Uses props such as real boxes & bags in grocery play	2/17
✔ Can pretend with imaginary objects	I have seen her pretend this way	2/17
✔ Uses language for creating & sustaining plot	Talked constantly during grocery store plot	2/17
___ Uses exciting, danger-packed themes	No	2/17
✔ Uses elaborate themes, ideas, details	Carried out detailed actions in grocery store plot	2/17

Figure 13–1   Imagination observations for Sherry

Sherry has shown little development in the area of written language. Perhaps she could make a sign for the grocery store or pretend to write out a grocery list of things to buy in mock writing. All children's development is interrelated. We should remember to use strengths from other areas of a child's development when we design an individual plan to strengthen a child's particular needs.

Table 13–1   Development of imagination

Age	Child's Pretend Play Behavior
1–2	Goes through pretend routines of eating or other brief actions, in some cases
2–3	Replays fragments of everyday experience (e.g., putting baby to bed) Repeats routine over and over in ritualistic manner Uses realistic props (if uses props at all)
3–4	Insists often on particular props in order to play May have imaginary playmate at home Uses family, doll play, hospital, cars, trains, planes, and firefighting themes Assigns roles or takes assigned roles May switch roles without warning
4–5	Uses exciting, danger-packed themes (e.g., superheroes, shooting, and running) Is more flexible about taking assigned roles during play Uses more rigid gender roles (e.g., girls as mother, waitress, or teacher; boys as father, doctor, or policeman)
5–6	Plays more with doll house, block structure Includes many more details, much dialogue Carries play over from one day to next sometimes Plays more in groups of same gender

REFERENCES

Beaty, J. J. (1997). *Building bridges with multicultural picture books: For children 3 to 5.* Upper Saddle River, NJ: Merrill/Prentice Hall.

Berk, L. E. (1994). Vygotsky's theory. The importance of make-believe play. *Young Children, 50*(1), 30–39.

Bronson, M. B. (1995). *The right stuff for children birth to 8.* Washington, DC: NAEYC.

Caplan, T., & Caplan, F. (1983). *The early childhood years: The 2 to 6 year old.* New York: Putnam.

Davidson, J. (1996). *Emergent literacy and dramatic play in early education.* Albany, NY: Delmar.

Gowen, J. W. (1995). The early development of symbolic play. *Young Children, 50*(3), 75–84.

Hughes, F. P. (1991). *Children, play, and development.* Boston: Allyn and Bacon.

Johnston, J. M. (1987). Harnessing the power of superheroes: An alternative view. *Day Care and Early Education, 15*(1), 15–17.

Kiefer, B. Z. (1995). *The potential of picturebooks: From visual literacy to aesthetic understanding.* Upper Saddle River, NJ: Merrill/Prentice Hall.

Pena, S., French, J., & Holmes, R. (1987). A look at superheroes: Some issues and guidelines. *Day Care and Early Education, 15*(1), 10–14.

Segal, M., & Adcock, D. (1981). *Just pretending: Ways to help children grow through imaginative play.* Upper Saddle River, NJ: Merrill/Prentice Hall.

Singer, D. G., & Singer, J. L. (1990). *The house of make-believe.* Cambridge, MA: Harvard.

Singer, D. G., & Singer, J. L. (1977). *Partners in play: A step-by-step guide to imaginative play in children.* New York: Harper.

Singer, J. L. (1973). *The child's world of make-believe: Experimental studies of imaginative play.* New York: Academic Press.

Smilanski, S. (1968). *The effects of sociodramatic play on disadvantaged preschool children.* New York: John Wiley & Sons.

SUGGESTED READINGS

Beaty, J. J. (1996). *Skills for preschool teachers*. Upper Saddle River, NJ: Merrill/Prentice Hall.

Bergen, D. (Ed.) (1988). *Play as a medium for learning and development*. Portsmouth, NH: Heinemann.

Isenberg, J. P., & Jalongo, M. R. (1993). *Creative expression and play in early childhood education*. Upper Saddle River, NJ: Merrill/Prentice Hall.

Levin, D. E., & Carlsson-Paige, N. (1995). The Mighty Morphin Power Rangers: Teachers voice concern. *Young Children, 50*(6), 67–72.

Nourot, P. M., & Van Hoorn, J. L. (1991). Symbolic play in preschool and primary settings. *Young Children, 46*(6), 40–50.

Paley, V. G. (1984). *Boys and girls: Superheroes in the doll corner*. Chicago: University of Chicago Press.

VIDEOTAPES

Basche, K., *Respecting how children learn through play*. Child Development Media, Inc., 5632 Van Nuys Blvd., Van Nuys, CA 91401.

Magna Systems, Inc. (1993). *Play*. Magna Systems, Inc., 95 West County Line Rd., Barrington, IL 60010.

LEARNING ACTIVITIES

1. Use the imagination section of the Child Skills Checklist as a screening tool to observe all the children in your classroom. Compare the checkmarks for children who score well in the sequence of imagination development with their checks in social play and language development. Can you draw any conclusions from this comparison?

2. Choose a child with high-level skills in imagination and make a running record of him or her on three different days. What new details did you learn about the child's pretending?

3. Look over the activities suggested, and choose one for use with one of the children whom you have determined needs help in this area. Carry out the activity you have prescribed for the child. Record the results.

4. Take a field trip with your children to a site of interest where they can see and meet people at work in a special field. Put out appropriate props in your dramatic play and/or block areas after you return, and record the kinds of pretend play that take place. Is the play any different from what went on previously? If so, how do you account for this?

5. Carry out one of the book activities from this chapter with one child or a small group, and see if it stimulates any pretending. How could you extend this pretending?

CHAPTER 14

Sharing Observational Data with Parents

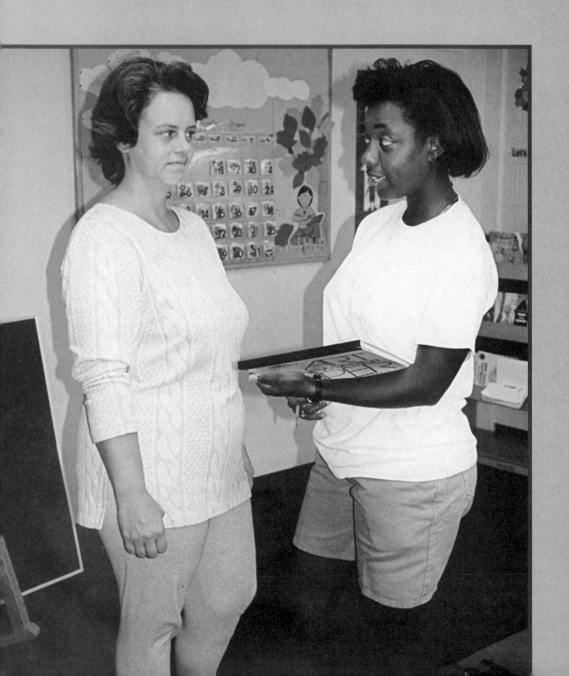

INVOLVING PARENTS IN THEIR CHILDREN'S PROGRAMS

Early childhood programs have recognized the importance of involving parents in their children's education and development. Many preschools, Head Starts, nursery schools, child care centers, prekindergartens, and kindergartens have done everything in their power to bring parents closer to their children's programs. They schedule parent visits, parent conferences, parent newsletters, parent volunteer opportunities, and parenting workshops. Such programs are aware of the overwhelming research that shows:

> The closer the parent is to the education of the child, the greater the impact on child development and educational achievement. (Fullan, 1982, p. 139)

There is no doubt about it. When parents are closely involved with their children's preschool programs, children tend to bloom. Youngsters seem to understand that if Mom and Dad know the teacher and the teacher knows Mom and Dad, then whatever happens in school is all right. All of these significant people will be talking about the child, making sure she is on the right track, and helping her along whenever she needs help.

Nevertheless, it is not always easy or even possible to involve all parents in their children's education. Most parents work these days and find it difficult to participate or even visit their children's programs. Some parents find it uncomfortable to visit schools where they may feel out of their element. Others think it is the teaching staff's responsibility to care for their children during the school day, while they take responsibility for their children at home. Is there some way all parents can be convinced to become involved?

Focusing on the Child

A most effective approach that many preschools have adopted is to focus on the child, not on the program. Both parents and teachers want the child to succeed in school and develop to his greatest ability. Thus it is the child who should concern the parents and program: What is he like? What are his interests at home and at school? What is his favorite activity? How does he get along with others? What would his parents like to see him accomplish this year?

As teachers begin to develop a closer rapport with family members, they can communicate their own strong interest in this child as an individual, and their commitment to helping him grow and develop in preschool. They can describe to the parents how they start by determining where each child in their class stands in his development. Then they are able to plan activities to meet each child's needs.

They can talk about finding out how the child handles herself in a strange, new environment; how she deals with stressful situations; whether she plays with others; whether she can share and take turns. They can discuss what they want to know about the child's physical development; whether she can climb, draw with crayons, cut with scissors, build with blocks, sort things that are alike, ask questions; whether she ever tries to write or if she likes to paint; and what kind of pretending she does. At the same time, they will be asking the parents what kinds of things they would like to know about their child in school.

371

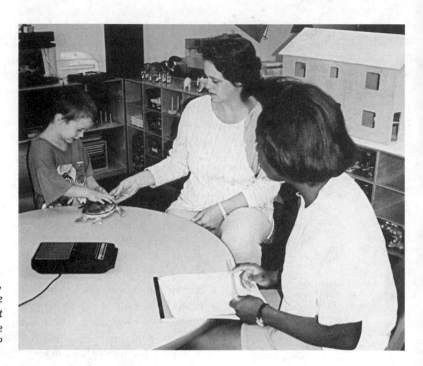

When sharing data with parents, teachers need to focus on the child, not the program. What would the parent like to see the child accomplish this year?

Such discussions need to be completely informal and not overwhelming to the parents. There is no need to pursue a long list of questions or child developmental needs. Play it by ear. The idea is for the parents to understand your personal concern for their child, as well as the specific activities the children will be involved with. Stipek, Rosenblatt, and DiRocco (1994) found that

> the more specific she was about what children gained from the activities, the more parents appreciated the activities' value; thus, for example, she pointed out that playing with Legos and pinching and pulling clay help children develop the coordination necessary to hold a pencil and form letters. (p. 8)

Such conversations with parents should also let them know that the teaching staff spends time looking at their child individually to determine where she stands developmentally, and that the staff has found that the best way to determine where the child stands is to observe her by using an observation checklist to guide them.

Using the Child Skills Checklist

When the time is right, give the parents a blank copy of the Child Skills Checklist, telling them that this is what you and the teaching staff use as a guide to look at where their child stands developmentally. Have them flip through the Checklist with you, looking at the main topics. Together you might go through the items under self-identity. Since their child has already been in school for a week or so, you can tell them what you have been able to check off so far in this area.

Are they surprised? Did they realize how well their child was able to adjust? If this is not the case, you may have to ease their concern that their child isn't "seeking other children to play with" yet, but that he no longer clings either to the parent or the teacher as he did during the first week of school.

Make sure that the parents understand the purpose of the Child Skills Checklist: that it is not a test, but an observational guide to child development; that it helps you look for the areas of strength that each child possesses and note the areas needing strengthening. No two children develop the same, nor should we expect them to. Such a checklist helps you note where each child stands and how to help each one progress in specific areas of his development.

Then take the next important step in involving parents in their child's program: Ask them if they would like to try observing their child at home in this same way. Tell them you would like to give them a blank copy of the Checklist for them to put somewhere handy in their house—maybe on the refrigerator door—where they can check off items they see their children performing. Point out that this can be very helpful to them as they note the different items their children accomplish. It can also help you, if they care to share any of their observations. But make sure they understand that you are not asking them to do this observing for you, but rather for them to learn more about their child in the same way you do in the classroom.

This is a big step for parents to take, and a completely different type of activity than most are used to. Be sure you have established some sort of rapport with the parents before you present this idea. Make sure they understand that looking at their child by using a checklist should be interesting and fun for them, not a chore, and that it can be "for their eyes only." They do not need to share it with you or anyone else unless they feel like it. Tell them that there is no "right" or "wrong" involved. Whatever they see they can check off. If they feel like writing down what the child did under "evidence," so much the better.

If parents buy into the idea and begin to observe and record their children's behavior at home, they will want to share what they find with you because: (1) they will want to know what certain items mean, and (2) they will want you to know how their children are doing. Point out that they may not be able to check off some of the items because the Checklist is designed to look at classroom activities rather than those in the home, and because children cannot be expected to accomplish every item all at once. Development occurs over time with maturity and practice.

What you are doing by giving parents the Child Skills Checklist is much more important than merely involving them in observing their child more closely. You are making them a part of the teaching team. You are helping to make them professionals.

MAKING PARENTS PROFESSIONALS

One of the reasons most parents often feel so ill at ease with teachers is because they occupy such a different role. Teachers are the professionals and they are not. In fact, most parent involvement programs focus on "helping parents learn more effective ways of working with their children" (Kasting, 1994, p. 150). There is nothing wrong with this focus. It does, however, imply a superior position for the teacher, and therefore an inferior role for the parent. The teacher has information to impart that the parent needs to learn. As Kasting (1994) notes:

> Rarely do parents and teachers collaborate on the basis of mutual respect and shared responsibilities. (p. 159)

Parents who accept the role of observing their child just like the teacher does can begin to change the balance of this relationship. They can, in fact, begin to become child care professionals in their own right. After all, they know more about their child than anyone else. Their influence on their child is more powerful than anyone else's. But they need to be aware of the significance of child behavior. By observing their child using the Child Skills Checklist just as the teacher does, they learn what is important to look for. As they discuss this information with the teacher, they learn what these findings mean.

Parents who have become child observers get really excited about what they are discovering. After all, their child is of great importance to them. Now they are beginning to unlock the "secrets" of child development that teachers seem to know, but

Parents who observe their children at home and share their findings with the teacher can become true partners with the teacher in child care and development.

they did not. As they share their findings with the teacher and the teacher responds by sharing her observations with the parent, their relationship changes dramatically. They become true partners in child care.

Arlene Kasting, Coordinator of the Child Study Centre of the University of British Columbia in Vancouver, Canada, reports on the model parent involvement program using shared observations that her center has developed: Addressing the Needs of Children Through Observation and Response (ANCHOR). In this project, parents and educators observe together children's activities in the preschool classroom either on closed-circuit television or in videotaped sequences. She notes:

> The shared observation experience brings parents and educators together in a common educational task. Parent and educator relationships are defined as partnerships. This view of parenting and teaching as complementary processes is integral to the project. (1994, p. 146)

Although this was a group observation of a classroom of children containing the parents' own children, and not a home observation of a single child as discussed here, the resulting relationships of parents and educators changed for the better. Parents were not treated as persons needing instruction by educators, but as full partners in the observation process. Their input about their child's behavior was valued as a key to understanding the child. Parents felt most respected when teachers listened attentively to their remarks and asked them to give even more details. Suddenly they, not the teachers, had become the source of information. Kasting (1994) records the remarks of one parent:

> I have better observation skills . . . When you look at kids, you tend to look more closely at their interaction; how they are doing it and also why they are doing it . . . And there are differences in people. We all come out to the same end, but there are so many different ways of reaching it. And you somehow have more confidence in yourself as a parent. You're more secure about the decisions that you make. (pp. 147–148)

Although the parent does not mention it, there is another important outcome for parents who do shared observations. They develop a trust in the program because the program has entrusted them enough to give them a professional's checklist and believe they are capable of using it. And, of course, they are. They may need your help in explaining what some of the items mean and your suggestions for looking at one section of the Checklist at a time, but you should be just as happy as they are about their new role.

As they look at the Checklist items and realize that the teaching staff is also using these same items to observe their child, it brings parents much closer to the teaching team because they feel a part of it. They may feel shy at first about showing you their filled out Checklist, but most parents will at least tell you what they observed for specific items. This information should be extremely helpful to you when you discover how the child behaves in his home setting—which is often quite different from school behavior.

Conversing about Checklist results makes parent involvement a real joy for all parties concerned. You and the parents will develop reciprocal trust, and you will look forward to hearing from parents about their children. Still, you may wonder how you will have the time to keep up such a running commentary with many parents.

SHARING OBSERVATION RESULTS

Communication Methods

Programs that have tried using the Checklist as described report a wide number of program/parent communication methods:

1. exchanging information when parents bring children or pick them up
2. phone conversations
3. faxes or e-mail
4. planned parent conferences or home visits
5. informal breakfast meetings before work
6. information sent home and returned via the child

This last method seems the most popular. Teachers run off many copies of the Checklist and send out one sheet at a time to share with parents what they have checked off on a particular day. Parents are free to write on the same sheet what they have observed and return it with the child the next day. Teachers are the ones who need to initiate the use of the Checklist, but once parents become involved, they often reply without prompting.

All of the written communications are kept in a child's folder or portfolio (see section later in this chapter) along with a record of phone or e-mail messages and a summary of conference results. Once a Checklist has been completed by a parent or teacher, the program can invite the parent to help interpret the results and discuss how they can be used in the program or at home.

Interpreting Checklist Results

When the teacher of one preschool class, Laura S., had finished observing four-year-old Andy on three different days for about half an hour each time (see Figure 14–1), she had a much better idea of Andy's strengths as well as areas needing strengthening. Her observation confirmed for her that Andy did not usually play with other children, but seemed to prefer doing things on his own. He seemed independent, making choices on his own, defending his rights, being enthusiastic about the things he chose to do, and smiling much of the time. She chuckled about his characteristic tuneless humming as he busily engaged himself in block-building or racing little cars. She always could tell where Andy was by his humming.

Being happy and smiling were especially important clues to Laura about the overall status of any child in her class. Andy demonstrated few inappropriate behaviors, in fact, except for his quick temper when other children tried to interfere with his activities. Laura had tried to get him to express his feelings in words, but without success. Now she noted that he really did not speak all that much. Somehow she had missed that important aspect of his behavior because he seemed content, and possibly because he did vocalize . . . if only to hum.

Now she noted that although she could understand him if she listened closely, his speaking skills were not at the level of the other four-year-olds. She began to wonder if this might be the reason he did not get involved in playing with the others. Because dialogue is so much a part of make-believe play, a child without verbal skills might feel out of place, she reasoned. She couldn't wait to hear from Andy's mother to see what she had observed on the same items.

Laura had a strong hunch that Andy was highly creative. Watching him build elaborate roads for his race car and talk to himself as he played alone or parallel to the others, he seemed to invent all kinds of situations for the miniature people he played with. She noted that creativity certainly did not show up in his arts skills, but she reasoned that his difficulty with small motor skills may have caused him to avoid painting, drawing, and cutting.

In looking for areas of strength, Laura picked out his enthusiasm and good self-concept, his large motor skills, his cognitive skills, and his imaginative play. His special interests seemed to be block building, water play, and all kinds of outdoor play. She thought he was a bright boy who used his cognitive ability in playing by himself, rather than joining others. Areas needing strengthening included language; small motor skills; using writing, drawing, and painting tools; controlling his temper; and especially playing with the other children.

Sharing Checklist Results with Staff

To confirm her interpretation of the Child Skills Checklist observation, Laura shared the results with the two other classroom workers. They were also surprised about how little Andy verbalized, and that they too hadn't picked up this fact previously. What had they missed about the other children, they wondered? One of them decided to observe Andy on her own, using the Checklist to see how her results compared with Laura's. The teacher assistants were fascinated by the details Laura had gleaned in a very short time and by the way she had interpreted Andy's inability to join in group play.

Sharing Checklist Results with Parents

Laura contacted Andy's mother and found that she, too, had completed her copy of the Checklist. Since she worked all day, she wondered if Laura could meet her at a nearby restaurant for coffee after work in the late afternoon. Andy's grandmother would pick up Andy and take him home. When they met for this first conference, both teacher and parent were full of enthusiasm for what they had discovered. Laura confided to the mother that she always looked for a child's areas of strength first because that gave her the best picture of the youngster. Also she used the child's areas of strength to help him improve in areas where he might need strengthening. The two decided to exchange Checklists to see what each had observed.

This was the first time that the teacher, Laura, had exchanged Checklists with a parent. Usually she was the one who had done the observing and the parent was on the other side of the fence waiting for her pronouncement. This way was so much better, she decided. First of all, she did not have to explain the observation method to

Child Skills Checklist

Name _Andy_   **Observer** _Laura S._

Program _Riverside Head Start_   **Dates** _$^{10}/_5$, $^{10}/_7$, $^{10}/_8$_

Directions:

Put a ✔ for items you see the child perform regularly. Put *N* for items where there is no opportunity to observe. Leave all other items blank.

Item	Evidence	Dates
1. Self-Identity		
___ Separates from parents without difficulty	upset when mother leaves	1/5
✔ Does not cling to classroom staff excessively	Plays by himself	$^{10}/_5$
✔ Makes eye contact with adults	Looks teacher in eye when she talks to him	$^{10}/_5$
✔ Makes activity choices without teacher's help	Goes directly to activity area of his choice	$^{10}/_5$
___ Seeks other children to play with	Plays by himself	$^{10}/_5$
___ Plays roles confidently in dramatic play	Does not do this play	$^{10}/_5$
✔ Stands up for own rights	Will not let others take his toys; pushes, grabs, hits	$^{10}/_7$
✔ Displays enthusiasm about doing things for self	Hums a tune while he plays	$^{10}/_5$
2. Emotional Development		
✔ Allows self to be comforted during stressful time	Lets teacher hold him	$^{10}/_5$
✔ Eats, sleeps, toilets without fuss away from home	Yes	$^{10}/_5$, $^{10}/_7$, $^{10}/_8$
N Handles sudden changes/ startling situations with control		$^{10}/_5$, $^{10}/_8$

Figure 14–1   Child Skills Checklist for Andy

Item	Evidence	Dates
___ Can express anger in words rather than actions	Sometimes hits or pushes when angry; No words	10/5
✔ Allows aggressive behavior to be redirected	Follows teacher's suggestions	10/5
___ Does not withdraw from others excessively	Does not play much with others	10/5
✔ Shows interest/attention in classroom activities	Likes blocks, cars, water play especially	10/5, 10/8
✔ Smiles, seems happy much of the time	Always smiles and hums	10/5, 10/8
3. Social Play		
N Spends time watching others play	Is beyond this level	10/5
✔ Plays by self with own toys/materials	Pretends with small cars, people	10/5
✔ Plays parallel to others with similar toys/materials	Pretends with small cars, people, next to other boys	10/8
___ Plays with others in cooperative play	Not often	10/8
___ Makes friends with other children	Has no close friends	10/5
___ Gains access to play in a positive manner	Does not try to gain access	10/8
___ Maintains role in ongoing play in a positive manner	Does not play much with others	10/8
___ Resolves play conflicts in a positive manner	Sometimes hits or pushes	10/5
4. Prosocial Behavior		
✔ Shows concern for someone in distress	Comes over to child who is crying	10/5

Item	Evidence	Dates
___ Can tell how another feels during conflict	*Does not respond when asked about this*	$^{10}/_{5}$
___ Shares something with another	*Does not seem to know how to share toys. Hits.*	$^{10}/_{5}$
___ Gives something to another	*Does not do this*	$^{10}/_{5}$
___ Takes turns without a fuss	*Has trouble with favorite toys*	$^{10}/_{5}$
✔ Complies with requests without a fuss	*Does what teacher asks*	$^{10}/_{8}$
✔ Helps another to do a task	*Helps Nat with building*	$^{10}/_{7}$
N Helps (cares for) another in need		$^{10}/_{5}$, $^{10}/_{7}$, $^{10}/_{8}$
5. Large Motor Development ✔ Walks down steps alternating feet	*Yes*	$^{10}/_{5}$
✔ Runs with control over speed and direction	*Does a lot of running*	$^{10}/_{5}$
✔ Jumps up and lands on two feet	*Jumps on playground*	$^{10}/_{5}$
N Hops on one foot		$^{10}/_{5}$
✔ Throws, catches and kicks balls	*on playground*	$^{10}/_{5}$
✔ Climbs up and down climbing equipment with ease	*On playground; good control*	$^{10}/_{5}$
N Moves legs and feet in rhythm to beat		$^{10}/_{5}$

Figure 14–1 *continued*

Item	Evidence	Dates
_N_ Moves arms and hands in rhythm to beat		$10/5$
6. Small Motor Development		
✔ Shows hand preference (which is "_right_")	Eats, picks up things with right hand	$10/5$
✔ Turns with hand easily knobs, lids, eggbeaters	Uses egg beater in water play easily	$10/7$
✔ Pours liquid into glass without spilling	Fills plastic glasses and bottles at water table	$10/7$
___ Unfastens/fastens zippers, buttons, Velcro tabs	Needs help taking off and putting on jacket	$10/5$
✔ Picks up and inserts objects with ease	Puzzles	$10/5$
___ Uses drawing/writing tools with control	Does not draw, write	$10/5$
___ Uses scissors with control	Does not use scissors	$10/5$
_N_ Pounds in nails with control	Not available	$10/5$
7. Cognitive Development: Classification, Number, Time and Space		
_N_ Identifies objects by shape		$10/5$
✔ Identifies objects by color	Tells colors of clothes	$10/8$
✔ Identifies objects by size	Tells sizes of cars	$10/5$
✔ Sorts objects by likenesses	Plays sorting games	$10/8$

Item	Evidence	Dates
✔ Puts events in a sequence; objects in a series	Knows daily schedule in sequence	10/8
___ Counts how many are present	Can count to 10, but not things	10/8
✔ Knows what happens today	Knows daily schedule	10/8
✔ Can build a block enclosure	Uses blocks with ease	10/8
8. Spoken Language		
N/ Listens but does not speak	Beyond this level	10/5
✔ Gives single word answers	Sometimes. Does not speak much	10/5
✔ Gives short-phrase responses	Sometimes. Speaks softly	10/5
___ Does chanting and singing	Not usually	10/5
___ Takes part in conversations	Not usually	10/5
✔ Speaks in expanded sentences	Sometimes	10/5
✔ Asks questions	Asks "When Mama will come?"	10/5
N/ Can tell a story		10/5
9. Prewriting and Prereading Skills		
___ Pretends to write with pictures and scribbles	Does not use writing tools	10/5

Figure 14–1 *continued*

Item	Evidence	Dates
___ Makes horizontal lines of writing scribbles	same as above	10/5
___ Includes letter-like forms in writing	same	10/5
___ Makes some letters, prints name or initial	same	10/5
✔ Holds book right-side up; turns pages left to right		10/8
✔ Pretends to read using pictures to tell story	Likes hearing stories, sometimes tells them	10/8
N Retells stories from books with increasing accuracy	His speaking is limited	10/8
N Shows awareness that print in books tells the story	same as above	10/8
10. Art Skills		
✔ Makes random marks on paper	Not often; likes finger painting	10/7
___ Makes controlled scribbles	Does not use art tools	10/7
___ Makes basic shapes	same as above	10/7
___ Combines circles/squares with crossed lines	same	10/7
___ Makes "suns"	same	10/7
___ Draws person as sun-face with arms and legs	same	10/7
___ Draws animals, trees, flowers	same	10/7

Item	Evidence	Dates
___ Draws objects together in a picture	*same*	10/7
11. Imagination		
_N_ Pretends an action without taking a role	*Is beyond this level*	10/5
___ Assigns roles or takes assigned roles	*Does not play much with others*	10/5
✔ Takes on characteristics and actions of role	*Motorcycle driver*	10/5
✔ Needs particular props to do pretend play	*cars, people*	10/5
___ Can pretend with imaginary objects	*No*	10/5
✔ Uses language for creating and sustaining plot	*Talks to himself while pretending*	10/5
✔ Uses exciting, danger-packed themes	*In solitary play with cars, people*	10/5
✔ Uses elaborate themes, ideas, details	*In solitary play*	10/5

Figure 14–1   *continued*

the mother. Also, she found herself waiting with anticipation to examine the mother's Checklist to see how it compared with her own, and whether it would shed any more light on Andy's development.

The mother was a bit hesitant to exchange Checklists at first because she didn't know if she had done it right. But Laura assured her that everyone felt that way at first, even the classroom staff. She said all of the items on the list were positive, so you couldn't really go wrong. If you saw the behavior, you checked the item. If you didn't see the behavior, you left the item blank. If there was no opportunity to observe, then you wrote in an N.

Laura noted that Andy's mother put Ns for some of the items related to classroom activities. Sometimes she crossed off a word or two and changed the item to something similar from the home. For example, she changed "dramatic play" to "car and truck" play. She seemed to have written many Ns where toys and materials were concerned. But the main difference between the two Checklists seemed to be Andy's play with others. At home he sometimes played with his brothers, shared and took turns, and did not express aggression. The mother had written in brief explanations under the evidence section, just as Laura had done.

Andy's mother was very interested in Laura's observations. She told Laura that Andy was the youngest of three brothers, and did not seem to have the language skills at age four that his older brothers had shown. She also noted that Andy preferred to play alone, but she had never considered that his speaking skills might be the cause.

She told how all three boys invented their own games because they had few toys at home. As a single working parent she had all she could do to provide for their food and clothing needs. When Laura suggested that Andy might like to continue water play at home in the sink with empty containers, his mother thought this was a fine idea and also a way that he might help her with the dishes! She was especially pleased that Laura thought Andy was bright on the basis of his water play games and block building in the center. She asked Laura for other ideas for making up games with household throwaway items. Laura offered to lend her a booklet full of ideas. When Laura also mentioned that the center liked to send home picture books for parents to read to their children, Andy's mother said she thought Andy would like this a lot.

Planning for the Child Based on Checklist Results

Laura was delighted with the outcome of the meeting. She had never had a parent conference go so well. Andy's mother wanted to continue observing, so Laura gave her another Checklist to use. Then she took out a learning prescription form for Andy and showed the parent how she and the staff used it to plan for a child based on Checklist results. This time she and the parent filled it in with areas of strength and confidence that they had detected from their two Checklist observations (see Figure 14–2). Then they discussed three areas needing strengthening for Andy, and recorded them on the form as well. (See Chapter 2 for a reproducible copy of this form.)

Next they considered ways to use Andy's strengths to help him improve in learning to play with others, developing better speaking skills, and improving his small motor coordination. Laura of course had a better idea of what activities were available in the classroom, but she listened closely to the mother's suggestions. She told Laura that Andy did know how to play with others just like he did with his brothers, so they both agreed to list as the first activity "Ask Andy to help new boy learn to use climber." This might help him make a friend he could play with. Laura said she thought he might like to help Russ learn to use the outside climber because Andy was so good at it. Talking and helping one other child should not be so difficult for Andy in the beginning as playing with a larger group.

Laura told the mother about the book *Louie* by Ezra Jack Keats (New York: Scholastic, 1975), with its title character who was never heard to speak until he first saw puppets speaking. She thought he would enjoy the story, and that maybe she could make a paper cone puppet with him. Laura said they both could read the *Louie* book because children enjoy hearing the same story repeated. She would send home

---

Learning Prescription

Name ___Andy___   Age ___4___ Date ___10/ 12___

Areas of Strength and Confidence

1. ___Good self-concept, happy, helpful___
2. ___Creative in block building, water play___
3. ___Good large motor skills on outside equipment___

Areas Needing Strengthening

1. ___Learn to play with others___
2. ___Develop better speaking skills___
3. ___Improve small motor coordination___

Activities to Help

1. ___Ask Andy to help new boy learn to use climber___

2. ___Read Louie and give him puppet to play with___

3. ___Do medicine dropper, water & food colors in muffin tins___

Figure 14–2   Learning prescription for Andy

a paperback copy of the book. Meanwhile, she would read the classroom copy to Andy and a small group of children and then have them each make a simple paper cone puppet like the ones in the book. Laura then would use her own puppet to engage the children in talking through their puppets. Once they got the idea, she would extract herself from the pretending and let them play on their own.

Laura said she planned to do this during the activity period every day with small groups of children, always trying to include Andy. She hoped Andy and the others would like the activity enough to make other puppets on their own. This would also involve Andy with small motor and art skills. She also decided to work on Andy's problem of learning to control his temper through the puppet play . . .

by having her own puppet get angry and hit her, and asking the others to help her puppet express anger differently.

In case Andy did not get involved in making his own puppet, she thought the medicine dropper activity with colored water in a muffin tin should interest him because of his fascination with water play. The staff decided to try these activities for a week and then discuss the results at their planning session the following week. They had already planned to do similar observations for each of the children as time permitted and to involve their parents in observing at home.

Ongoing Observations by Parents and Staff

Parents had been introduced to the idea of observing at home when they enrolled their children for preschool at the beginning of the year. They were told it was voluntary on their part, but that many parents found it to be an interesting way to learn more about their child. Not all the parents in Andy's class agreed to observe at first. But during the first parent meeting when they heard other parents talking about how much they liked the activity, several more agreed to try it. They were impressed with how the teachers were asking them to find out important things about their child by doing the same thing the teachers did. Only parents who had trouble speaking English were still unsure of

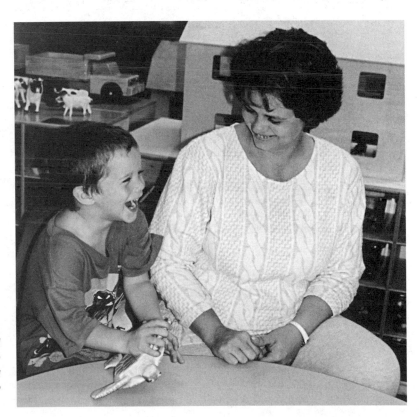

Parents are often so pleased with what they learn about their child through observation that they want to continue this observing when the child moves on to kindergarten.

what to do. Laura suggested maybe one of their neighbors with children in the program could help them, and maybe their older children could translate the Checklist for them.

When home observing really caught on among most of the parents, Laura kept several copies of *Observing Development of the Young Child* on hand for the parents to borrow so they could read about the items they were observing. The classroom staff of three adults took turns observing each child at three different times during a week, and soon had completed a Checklist for all 18 of the children.

Laura finally invited parents one by one to observe in the classroom using their own copy of the Checklist. Although those who worked all day felt they could not participate, Andy's mother got so caught up with observing her child that she arranged for time off to visit the classroom and observe once a month.

Laura decided that shared observations like this gave her the most successful parent involvement program she had ever known. The parents were so pleased with what they learned about their children and the program that they wanted to continue it next year when their children attended a public school kindergarten. Laura agreed to meet with a group of the parents and school personnel to make the arrangements.

DEVELOPING COLLABORATIVE PORTFOLIOS

Teachers who have initiated shared observing with parents sometimes carry this sharing one step further. They ask parents to participate in helping create a portfolio for their children. Many early childhood educators have adopted the portfolio as one of the best methods for assessing ongoing development of each child. A portfolio is an individual systematic collection of documents that reflects what a child does in a classroom. It is usually assembled by both teachers and children, and emphasizes both process and product in the documents collected (Tierney, Carter, & Desai, 1991).

Teachers of preschool children have long participated in collecting youngsters' artwork and writing scribbles. So have parents. Bringing together such a collection allows all involved to provide a more in-depth assessment of children's development.

The teacher must provide the framework for collecting items; otherwise, the results may become a meaningless hodgepodge. Criteria for choosing items might be the following:

1. products representing each area of child development
2. products related to learning objectives of teachers and parents
3. products showing ongoing development over time
4. a variety of products including teachers' records, parents' records, photos, artwork, writing scribbles, lists of favorite books, completed Checklists, anecdotal records, communications from parents, tapes of child's speech
5. products that can be used for meaningful communication with parents and other professionals
6. products that can be used for making curricular decisions

Once the collecting has started, teachers must date each piece of evidence and include who chose it and what it represents. For example, a sheet of art scribbles may represent emergent drawing or it may be emergent writing, depending on how it is done and what the child has to say about it. Where will you keep these products for each child? Puckett and Black (1994) suggest:

> There is no one way to assemble, store, and retrieve portfolio contents. Methods will depend upon the types of portfolio products chosen. . . . File folders, expandable folders, hanging files, pocket folders, oversized sheets of construction paper folded in half and stapled, stacking baskets, corrugated cubbyhole units, wall filing units, and uniform sized boxes are just a few of the possibilities. (p. 199)

Programs that use the Child Skills Checklist as a basis for observing and recording child development often collect portfolio evidence for each of the 11 Checklist areas of development for every child. In addition to pages from the Checklist itself contributed by teachers and parents, sample items could include:

Self-identity
    photos of child showing classroom accomplishments
    anecdotal records about child from classroom meetings
    parents' communications about child at home

Emotional development
    teacher's records of how child handles stress, anger, joy
    names of books child likes to hear when under stress
    finger painting child made to relieve stress

Social play
    photos of child playing with others
    list of dramatic play themes child participates in
    parent communication about child playing in neighborhood

Prosocial behavior
    teacher's records of how child shares, takes turns, helps
    parent communication of child's helping at home
    name of helping storybook child likes to hear

Large motor development
    photo of child on outside climber
    photo of large hollow block building child helped build
    parent communication on child climbing stairs up and down

Small motor development
    sample of cut-and-paste art work
    anecdotal record of child zipping jacket, tying shoes
    photo of child pounding nails into wood

Cognitive development
    pictures with colors child identified
    photo of block enclosure child built
    computer printout of child's number game

Spoken language
    tape of story child tells
    list of songs child sings
    funny words child likes to say

Prewriting and prereading
    page of scribbles child makes
    list of books child likes to hear
    sign-up sheet with name child prints

Art skills
    sample of easel painting
    sample of art work from home
    photo of playdough creation

Imagination
    hand puppet child made for pretending
    videotape of child in dramatic play role
    running record of child pretending with small figures

As the school year progresses, teachers need to add to each child's portfolio regularly. This can happen if portfolios are actually used in an appropriate fashion, and not just as storage containers for children's products. They should be the focus for classroom planning sessions and team meetings with parents. Whether or not parents contribute, they will want to view and discuss the contents of their child's portfolio from time to time. Many educators are beginning to realize the value of a portfolio's use with parents:

> One promising use of portfolio is a parent-education piece. That is, you review the portfolio with parents. Besides seeing child progress, parents learn about developmentally appropriate practice in a practical, specific way. Examples of organizational categories for portfolios include products from a theme on personal growth, favorite stories, special science projects, or other materials chosen by child and teacher to show to parent. (Mindes, Ireton, Mardell-Czudnowski, 1996, p. 234)

During team meetings and parent sessions, the focus should be on what you have observed the child accomplishing and thus what you have interpreted her present needs to be. Activities for helping the child to accomplish these needs can be discussed and planned as the child's products and observational data are shared. Both parents and staff can contribute to such discussions in a meaningful way as they learn how children develop through the observations they have done.

Observing the development of young children is thus a teaching as well as a learning technique that should benefit all of its participants—teachers, college students, children, and parents—because it outlines each aspect of child development carefully, objectively, and positively. Promoting development in young children works best when it focuses on assessing their strengths. When you know the strengths of each child in every aspect of development, you will be able to design your program to meet an individual's needs as the children in your classroom work and play together creating their own unique selves.

REFERENCES

Kasting, A. (1994). *Respect, responsibility and reciprocity*: The 3 Rs of parent involvement. *Childhood Education, 70*(3), 146–150.

Mindes, G., Ireton, H., & Mardell-Czudnowski, C. (1996). *Assessing young children*. Albany, NY: Delmar.

Puckett, M. B., & Black, J. K. (1994). *Authentic assessment of the young child*. Upper Saddle River, NJ: Merrill/Prentice Hall.

Tierney, R. J., Carter, M. A., & Desai, L. E. (1991). *Portfolio assessment in the reading-writing classroom*. Norwood, MA: Christopher-Gordon.

VIDEOTAPES

National Association for the Education of Young Children. *Partnerships with parents*. NAEYC, 1509 16th St. NW, Washington, DC, 20036-1426.

LEARNING ACTIVITIES

1. Discuss with members of the classroom team how parents have been involved in your program in past years, and whether this method has been successful. Record in some detail what the role of the different team members has been and what they have to say about it.

2. Make a list of ideas of how team members can focus on the child when meeting with parents. Include what materials they will need to take to parent meetings, and how they will discuss these materials with the parents. Also note how the team members will elicit information about the child from the parents. (Sit in on a parent meeting if possible.)

3. Discuss with team members the possibility of using the Child Skills Checklist with the parents for home observation of their child. Record their comments about this idea, both negative and positive. Make a list of what you believe that parents could learn from such observations and the sharing of results with the teaching team.

4. Discuss with team members the idea of making parents professionals. Why would they want to do it? How can they do it? What would be accomplished if this happened?

5. Put together a portfolio for one of the children. Involve other team members, the child, and parents if possible. What did you include? Why? How did you organize the portfolio? How will you use it?

Index of Children's Books

Index